ADVANCED
TAROT

AN IN-DEPTH GUIDE TO
PRACTICAL AND INTUITIVE TAROT READING

PAUL FENTON-SMITH

BLUE ANGEL®
PUBLISHING

ADVANCED TAROT
An In-Depth Guide To Practical And Intuitive Tarot Reading

This printing 2022

© 2021 Paul Fenton-Smith

Published in 2021 by Blue Angel Publishing®
80 Glen Tower Drive, Glen Waverley
Victoria, Australia 3150

Email: info@blueangelonline.com
Website: www.blueangelonline.com

Edited by Jamie Morris & Leela J. Williams

Rider-Waite Tarot Deck®, known also as the Rider Tarot and the Waite Tarot, reproduced by permission of U.S. Games Systems, Inc., Stamford, CT 06902 USA. Copyright ©1971 by U.S. Games Systems, Inc. Further reproduction prohibited. The Rider-Waite Tarot Deck®is a registered trademark of U.S. Games Systems, Inc.

Blue Angel is a registered trademark of Blue Angel Gallery Pty. Ltd.

ISBN: 978-0-648746-82-9

Dedicated to Alexander,
with gratitude.

With thanks to my wife, Melinda, for her patience
and to Cathy Jonas, for her editing skills.

THE MAJOR ARCANA

0. The Fool

1. The Magician

2. The High Priestess

3. The Empress

4. The Emperor

5. The Hierophant

6. The Lovers

7. The Chariot

8. Strength

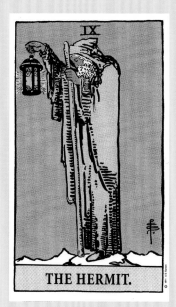

9. The Hermit

10. Wheel of Fortune

11. Justice

THE HANGED MAN.

12. The Hanged Man

DEATH.

13. Death

TEMPERANCE.

14. Temperance

THE DEVIL.

15. The Devil

THE TOWER.

16. The Tower

THE STAR.

17. The Star

18. The Moon

19. The Sun

20. Judgement

21. The World

THE MINOR ARCANA - WANDS

Ace of Wands

Two of Wands

Three of Wands

Four of Wands

Five of Wands

Six of Wands

Seven of Wands

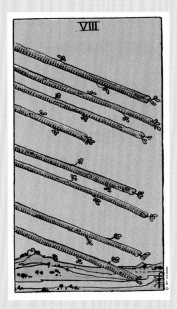

Eight of Wands

Nine of Wands

Ten of Wands

Page of Wands

Knight of Wands

Queen of Wands

King of Wands

THE MINOR ARCANA - CUPS

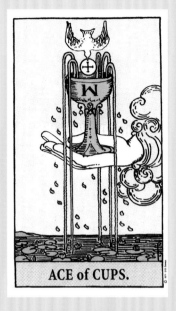

Ace of Cups

Two of Cups

Three of Cups

Four of Cups

Five of Cups

Six of Cups

Seven of Cups

Eight of Cups

Nine of Cups

Ten of Cups

Page of Cups

Knight of Cups

Queen of Cups

King of Cups

THE MINOR ARCANA - SWORDS

Ace of Swords

Two of Swords

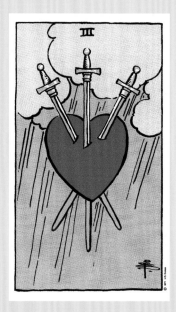

Three of Swords

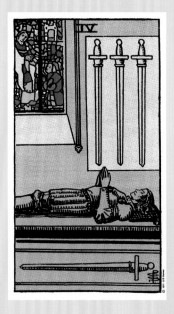

Four of Swords

Five of Swords

Six of Swords

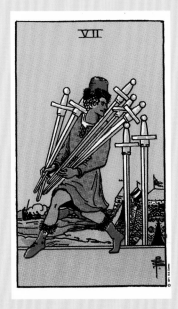

Seven of Swords

Eight of Swords

Nine of Swords

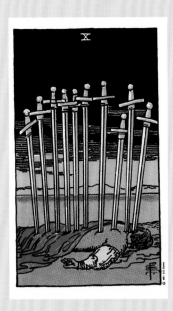

Ten of Swords

Page of Swords

Knight of Swords

Queen of Swords

King of Swords

THE MINOR ARCANA - PENTACLES

Ace of Pentacles

Two of Pentacles

Three of Pentacles

Four of Pentacles

Five of Pentacles

Six of Pentacles

Seven of Pentacles

Eight of Pentacles

Nine of Pentacles

Ten of Pentacles

Page of Pentacles

Knight of Pentacles

QUEEN of PENTACLES.

Queen of Pentacles

KING of PENTACLES.

King of Pentacles

CONTENTS

Card Meanings

A Telescope Aimed at the Future

"I've read for you before, haven't I?" Her face, piercing blue eyes and silvery blonde hair seemed familiar. I was completely unprepared for her reaction.

"Yes," she muttered reluctantly, glancing away at the white damask tablecloth, deliberately avoiding my gaze. She sat on the edge of her chair while I searched my memory.

"I'm sorry," she murmured. "Last time I was here, I was very critical. You mentioned that you could see me working in a shop. I had never worked in my life and when you said this, I thought you were guessing. Afterwards, I said I didn't want your recording. I felt like you were wasting my time."

As she said this, I remembered her name — Sabine. She had left that session with a cold, dismissive stare, before setting a brisk pace towards the front gate. As she powerwalked up the steep driveway, I thought to myself, "That went well." I never expected to see her again.

I had clairvoyantly glimpsed an image of her standing beside a shop counter on a quiet day, staring out at the sunny street through the window. When I described the scene, Sabine had looked at me as though I was crazy. She had sighed with disappointment and it was apparent that she felt she had wasted her time travelling across town in pursuit of an accurate prediction.

Sabine had immediately corrected me, by saying she'd never been employed. Her wealthy husband provided a very comfortable life. Sabine's daily routine involved regular lunches with her girlfriends, gym visits plus shopping and beauty treatments. Her live-in housekeeper took care of daily domestic chores while day staff cooked and maintained the well-manicured gardens. In between trips to Paris and New York to attend fashion events and Monaco to catch up with friends, she also shopped with her sons, nineteen-year-old Marco and fifteen-year-old Lucas.

Feeling pressured by her abrupt, adverse reaction, I intuitively re-scanned ahead into her life and saw the same scene. Usually, when this occurs, I know that the foreseen circumstances are likely to be significant in that person's life. However, Sabine clearly wasn't interested in exploring why she might be working in a shop, so I politely suggested that we move on to her more immediate questions.

Afterwards, I wondered if I should have taken more notice of her classic sky-blue leather handbag. The gold fasteners looked expensive, even to a man's eye. I wondered if I'd misinterpreted what I had seen or simply got it wrong. Sometimes when clairvoyants are stressed or uncentred, accuracy suffers. Perhaps I wasn't grounded enough when I sat down to read for Sabine.

After berating myself momentarily, I realised I had correctly described some of her friends and family members. She had taken offence at my description of her longer-term future, one far removed from her current reality. As she left, I reminded her that if she knew with certainty what the future held, she wouldn't need to consult me. She ignored my comment and strode back to her car and her comfortable life.

Today, Sabine seemed different. Her eyes were less judgemental and reflected deep sadness. She didn't know where to begin. While shuffling the deck, she told me why she had returned. Two years after her previous reading with me, her husband died suddenly from a heart attack. Her son Marco took over the company without any business experience. Within three years, the firm was bankrupt. While she desperately juggled creditors and tried to find viable solutions, the bank seized the family home to cover outstanding debts. It was a dismal time for her.

Soon they were renting a shabby two-bedroom apartment with their lavish silk curtains spilling down to the cluttered floor as a reminder of better times. At forty-eight years of age, Sabine had to find her first job. She wasn't qualified for a professional position, but after several exhausting months, she found part-time work in a clothing store.

"It was difficult," she sighed. "I lost all of my friends. I couldn't afford to lunch with them. There was no money for shopping. After using up my frequent flyer points, I couldn't travel overseas. I was unable to service my Jaguar, so that was sold. Even my parent's furniture that was in storage for the boys had to be liquidated." She faltered momentarily, exhaling deeply and then continued.

"I lost everything. At least Lucas had finished school. I couldn't have maintained the school fees. One afternoon, I was working alone in the boutique. It was a quiet spring day. I stood staring out into the bright sunshine at a couple of well-dressed women who were shopping, having fun like I once did. They looked tanned, relaxed and carefree. They laughed while packing designer shopping bags into a shiny, black SUV. I imagined them sipping champagne with a lavish lunch, followed by more retail therapy, while I stood in the shadows, enviously glimpsing fragments of my old life. I felt so disconnected from their lifestyle. While they had credit cards for each day of the week, most of my wage was spent before I received them."

> "Then I remembered what you'd told me. You said you saw me working in a shop. I thought you were a fool back then. I didn't listen to the rest of your reading. I just wanted to pay your fee and stop wasting my time. I didn't want the recording, but I remembered bits of it."

"It was hard. I had never scrambled to pay a bill before. When Steve died, I couldn't even get out of bed for several weeks and didn't open my mail or email for a month. Suddenly everyone was demanding money. I was drowning in debt and couldn't pay anybody. So, I closed the blinds, turned off my phone and retreated to bed. My son eventually summoned a doctor who told me that I had two options. I could voluntarily check myself into the psychiatric ward of a hospital or take antidepressants and work my way back into life. It was a different existence: smaller, harder, without a safety net. It was bleak, gruelling and relentless, but one of the hardest parts is that it has taken me eighteen months to save the money to have another session with you. Well, I'm ready to listen now," she said softly.

I sat motionless, holding my breath. I wanted to give Sabine a very clear reading after what she had endured. This weight of responsibility is what many tarot readers experience when reading for others — to clarify a client's available choices without pushing any particular agenda. Sometimes it's complicated, knowing what to look for, how much to say and what to rephrase or edit because the client might not be ready to hear it.

Fortunately, Sabine's harsh personal winter was over, according to the cards she selected. I could see a new love relationship and some study, plus a different career leading to financial independence. She was unlikely to ever return to her long lunches and daily shopping jaunts. Instead, I glimpsed her travelling through Europe with her new partner.

Bleak times are often followed by memorable summers. Had we explored the shop scene in her initial reading, Sabine could have been alerted to her approaching personal hardship. She might have had time to lay the groundwork for changing circumstances. Instead, expectations narrowed her focus and she sailed into uncharted waters, completely unprepared.

Several years after her second reading, I met Sabine again. She remained behind after my talk in a bookshop to tell me that she had met a new man and they had moved in together. She was happy to have a home with a garden again and was considering courses that might improve her career prospects.

"Is that an engagement ring?" I asked.

"Yes, it is," she replied beaming. "When I saw you listed as the speaker tonight, I had a shock. It brought all that hardship back to me. It seems so long ago now. Those were dark days, but you told me that the sun would reappear and it has." I felt happy for her.

Consulting the tarot for guidance about a wise course of action can mean the difference between being successful or living with regrets. The death of her husband would still have occurred but Sabine, having been forewarned, could have been much better prepared. The intervening years might have provided a chance to study for a career or learn business management or even take a job for work experience in preparation for the devastating changes. Depending on the cards on the table and what I saw clairvoyantly, it is likely I would have told Sabine that sudden change was approaching and that her lifestyle was likely to change drastically as a result. I'd have effectively told her that summer was ending and a long, cold winter was approaching. Knowing in advance gives the client time to prepare.

> Secure in the belief that her husband would always be there to support her meant Sabine had little motivation to labour for a living. Most people work because they need to, not because they want to. Knowing ahead of time that a storm is approaching can be shocking, but after the panic subsides, practical options can be explored. Instead, Sabine unexpectedly had the multiple demands of burying her husband, dealing with grief, supporting her sons and staving off bankruptcy. Forewarned is forearmed.

Sometimes, a tarot practitioner has to decide how much information to relay to a client to avoid overwhelming them. Occasionally, a reader might not glimpse any major changes ahead. This can occur when clients want to focus on immediate issues, such as a possible retrenchment, the ill-health of a parent or a floundering relationship. More skilled practitioners allow clients to set the focus of questions but as intuitive abilities strengthen, readers can take a few minutes at the end of a session to psychically look ahead five or even ten years for major opportunities or obstacles. This book is about getting the tarot part of the process right while developing intuition.

Eventually, it's possible to combine personal memory of tarot card meanings with intuitive flashes of specific information. After describing the King of Wands to a client from memory, intuition can offer a more detailed description of the individual such as his favourite hobbies, how he loves to walk his Doberman down by the river after work or that he yearns to buy and renovate an abandoned house in the country.

Intuition can enhance a tarot reading and confirm some of the unique or quirky qualities of the person being described. However, cementing a fundamental knowledge of individual card meanings is essential for those times when personal intuition takes a holiday. Having studied astrology, I sometimes describe the qualities of a swords person in astrological terms. These individuals have air sign qualities (Gemini, Libra and Aquarius) so they are usually sociable, quick-minded, talkative and curious about people and life. If intuition doesn't flow easily during a reading, despite the reader having clear knowledge of card meanings and other studies (astrology, palmistry etc.), it's possible to flesh out details of a person without seeing the individual in the mind's eye.

Intuitive and Logical Readings

A recent client wanted to know about the future of a possible relationship and became irritated when I asked him about the small boy and the older girl I could see in the cards. His current wife and children didn't feature in his plans for this relationship, but he was not prepared to leave them. I described the people who would be hurt by his pursuit of an affair, but he was completely influenced by his own desires.

He didn't want to know about any fallout, only about the conquest itself. To remind him of his current responsibilities, I mentioned that the new partner might come and go from his life but his children will always be his children. With his narrow focus, he'd lost awareness that decisions and actions usually have consequences. The ramifications of his choice to live a secret life while deceiving his wife and children might last his lifetime. The effect on his children's self-esteem could resonate for decades and even further, down through the generations.

Some clients come with tales of woe about their 'beastly' partners. This can include how they were driven into the arms of another because of the cold-hearted nature of a spouse. My policy here is to silently ask myself, "Do I buy this?" If the answer is *yes*, I treat them accordingly. If the answer is *no*, I bring this into my relationship with the client. That is, I mention how it's difficult to believe they have told me the whole story. Sometimes, it's necessary to be subtle. However, when a client is stubbornly self-righteous, a more straightforward approach can be required. I felt one client was using me to help him convince himself of something, so I said, "Look, I'm having difficulty with this."

"With what?"

"With what you're saying."

"Why?"

"I don't buy it."

"What?"

"This excuse about how you only cheat on your partner and keep it secret to avoid hurting her."

His denial of any responsibility for the issues in the present relationship and his ability to justify his pursuit of someone else left me wondering if his wife might eventually be glad if he left her for another woman.

If I still don't believe what I'm hearing, I continue to protest. The second objection is usually more direct. If I believe I'm being fed a line of deception, I lean forward, establish close eye contact and say, "You're telling me all this but I'm not convinced. Others might accept what you're saying but I don't. You're not attempting to deceive a psychic, are you?"

When a reader colludes with clients, allowing them to justify poor behaviour or deceive themselves, they risk losing respect. Clients are likely to feel the person was not very observant. Also, when a reader turns a blind eye to one matter, there is a risk of overlooking other, perhaps significant, issues. It is better to work on the understanding that people consult tarot practitioners to be told what the cards reveal. I believe I'm not doing my job effectively if I consciously overlook some situations.

When giving a reading, a tarot reader might speak fluently and confidently without pausing to glance at the cards on the table or needing confirmation. This fluidity usually happens when the reader is working intuitively. When intuition (inner knowing) flows, a reader might describe a person's car, dog, children's school uniforms or where a partner hides additional income. However, do be careful. Readers need to know the limits of what to divulge. For example, when clients want to know about the current relationships of former partners, readers need to set boundaries. It is not good practice to trespass into the lives of people who are not present for readings and therefore unable to give consent about the information revealed. This is so even when it involves a client's son or daughter. A general question about a family member is okay. When a reader senses the line of questioning is moving from concern to intrusiveness, it's time to set a boundary.

Intuitive readings occur when a clairvoyant establishes a clear but invisible psychic cord of energy to the client. Through this cord, it is possible to retrieve almost all information required from within that person's energy field. (For more information on psychic cords, see my book *A Secret Door to the Universe*.)

Reading intuitively occurs only occasionally in the first hundred sessions. The subconscious mind gradually begins to search for intuitive information about the client while a reader is consciously interpreting the cards. Intuitive readings happen more frequently as a reader becomes comfortable and confident with intuitive techniques. The process becomes natural when a cord is established between the reader and the client.

A reader's nature determines how information is received. A person might receive dates, names, times, images and sometimes pictures that are metaphors for the client's situation. For example, when examining a layout for someone who feels trapped by job responsibilities, the reader might see an image of a prisoner watching a clock, while impatiently awaiting release. It's the task of the tarot practitioner to sort out the symbology and the scenes from real life.

Occasionally, the reader's intuition is in complete contrast to the cards on the table. When this occurs, there is a process that can improve accuracy. Take a few moments to examine yourself and how you are feeling. Do you have anything invested in the outcome of the question or layout? Is what you are presently hearing, seeing or feeling related to a previous reading or your own life? If personal intuition conflicts with the cards on the table, mention it to the client. For example:

"I am slightly confused here. The cards suggest your business is successful and will remain so, but I feel within myself that there is a basic problem you need to deal with before you can achieve your goals. Does this make sense to you?"

Opening a conversation with the client allows both of you to reach an understanding of what is happening. When your intuition enhances what you see in the cards, read the layout and include the intuitive information. Often, the patron agrees with both the cards and your intuition and provides background details that clarify the reading. Sometimes, this additional information suggests the reading is addressing more than one question.

When Harry asked if it was wise to work for a specific organisation, the layout was confusing. It transpired that Harry had the option of either full-time employment or working flexible hours as an independent contractor. To clarify the possibilities, I suggested he separate the options into questions, each requiring a different layout. Consequently, it seemed Harry would have more flexibility and a better income by working on contract for that particular company.

> There are practical steps for improving personal intuition and they all involve using it regularly. The more an individual uses intuition, the more it develops. In one exercise I do with advanced tarot students, I ask a volunteer to pose a question and select cards for a seven-card layout.

I place each card in position but leave them face down on the table. I then give the volunteer the reading without turning any of the cards over. Unable to see the faces of the cards, I'm forced to rely on intuition. I am effectively reading the backs of seven cards while answering the volunteer's question. After the reading, I place the cards back into the pack without looking at any of them. This drives some students crazy with curiosity.

While a client selects cards and asks a question, the reader's intuition is already fathoming the answer. Subconsciously, the reader knows the answer to the client's question before a card is drawn. Reading the cards face down, helps practitioners connect with the concealed inner parts of themselves that already have that knowledge.

When there is a clear question to answer, it's possible to interpret a spread using specific card meanings. However, there is potential to increase the detail of a tarot reading by training personal intuition to complement the card meanings. If a client asks whether she will purchase a new home in the next twelve months and the answer is yes, it might be helpful for the practitioner to describe the property. This description could include a glimpse of the view, an ornate staircase or a black-and-white cat perched on a wall at the back of the garden. It all helps to narrow the search.

Sometimes, readers can become engrossed in the logical meaning of the cards, the combinations and the number of reversed cards and overlook the big picture. As a simple exercise, before describing the first layout in a reading, I make the following statement to myself, "The client's issue today is ___ ." When feeling confident, it's possible to extend this to, "The client's life pattern is ___ and the current spiritual lesson for this person is ___ ." I then allow my intuition to fill in the gaps.

Intuitive training is as significant as learning the card meanings. Using clairvoyance (clear seeing) is not always exciting and it's not easy at first. With practice, it can blend seamlessly with your knowledge of the card meanings. A simple way to improve psychic ability is to devote the final five minutes of each reading to what you sense.

When I started reading tarot, I'd say to clients, "I'm picking up a bit more but I'm not sure about it." Clients invariably invited me to say what else I was sensing. To cover myself for possible inaccuracies, I'd say, "This part might be wrong, so feel free to discount its significance." I'd then speak freely about what I sensed. Over the years, five minutes at the end of each reading eventually became ten minutes and finally intuitive reading combined naturally with a logical interpretation of the cards on the table.

However, intuition can be unreliable. Being skilled at logical interpretation means you will be able to provide accurate readings, with or without intuition. With a straightforward question and a familiar layout, it is possible to give a good tarot reading without using intuition.

Looking into the hearts of people occasionally involves glimpsing great pain and sorrow. Sometimes, when I see what people have survived, I am awed by the courage it takes for them to get out of bed and approach another day. In noticing the emotional scars some clients carry with them, I feel my own worries diminish. Despite tortured childhoods and horrendous events that would cause most of us to give up or surrender to madness or substance abuse in an attempt to forget, some people find the unwavering strength to carry on and even to love and support others again.

As a tarot reader, it is necessary to tread carefully and compassionately and present information as diplomatically as possible. A reader needs to know the limits of what to divulge, regardless of what the client insists on hearing. Sometimes, a person is not ready to hear what the reader says.

Many years ago, as a young man, I read for a woman who wanted to know about her two daughters, one married and one single. She pressed me for more and more information and without thinking, I continued speaking. I told her that her son-in-law was having an affair and that when his wife (her daughter) discovered it, their marriage would end. She was shocked and I realised by her extreme reaction that I had divulged too much information.

The woman telephoned me the following day to say I shouldn't have told her. I knew she was right. It was my responsibility to know when to deny her the information she sought by sensing her limits. As a reader, it's not possible to retract information. She had to live with it. Whereas, if I had retained information, she might have left only feeling I was holding back some details.

She has since consulted me again to say the events unfolded as predicted. In hindsight, she felt she was better prepared to listen and offer support when her daughter phoned to declare her marriage was over. I was relieved that this situation resolved itself but have since become much more discreet in what I reveal in readings. Sometimes, tarot readers discover boundaries through trial and error. To give a stranger a tarot reading is to be invited into that person's life — but it's important to remember you're a guest and to respect this privileged position.

People sometimes search for answers to questions without thinking of ways to cope with the knowledge provided. It reminds me of an old saying: "When the gods want to punish us, they answer our prayers." Individuals may not have considered the consequences of hearing an answer to an important question when they insist on being told everything. The more someone sees (clairvoyantly), the more influence this person has. With power comes responsibility. When using this authority tactlessly or irresponsibly, there are likely to be unpleasant consequences for such thoughtless actions.

Sometimes the consequences are immediate. Reversed wands clients are likely to lash out at a practitioner if a reading shatters their personal view of the world. From shouting to storming out and penning stinging reviews online, they can vent loud and long. It doesn't help if the reader's predictions prove to be correct in time because bad reviews have a long shelf life in the digital world.

More information is not always better because some events are best left to unfold at the appropriate time. Clients might be better prepared for change when it arrives than they are years in advance. In a recent pure clairvoyance reading, I was reading for a woman in her twenties who had been married for three years. She asked if she'd outlive her husband and I immediately saw she would outlive all three of her husbands. Telling her she was likely to marry three times probably wouldn't have been helpful at that point, so I confirmed she would survive him, but that's all.

It's best to avoid questions that don't help the client. If someone asks where he or she will meet a new partner, there is generally nothing that can be done to meet that person a month or a year sooner. The individual might not be ready for a relationship. In one reading, I explained that the man wasn't available earlier because he was the primary carer for his ageing mother. He felt it was his duty to help his mother die peacefully in her own bed. Even after she died, he needed eighteen to twenty-four months to grieve her loss, dispose of her possessions and sell the house before being emotionally ready for a long-term relationship. If my client had met him earlier, the relationship might have fizzled out, due to his intense sadness.

During a reading about forthcoming opportunities, a client asked, "Where will I meet him?"

I explained I never answer this question because if I told her they'd meet at a bus stop, she might hang around bus stops for the next two years and still not meet him a day earlier than predicted.

Then I asked myself this question: "Is it possible to zoom in on the physical circumstances of their first meeting?"

I did this and glimpsed Tracy standing in a cloakroom at a yoga studio. She held a pair of shoes in one hand as she looked at a wall of cubicles. Each cubicle held a pair of shoes and some also contained handbags.

A man arrived and simply said, "Excuse me, please," as he stepped around her and placed his shoes into an empty cubicle. The moment she heard his voice, a tingle ran through her body and she immediately thought to herself, "This man will be my husband." He didn't even glance at her. Instead, he quickly left to find a mat and a space in the large, crowded room before the session commenced.

They didn't speak during or after the session, but she noticed him at subsequent classes. There were a few short conversations afterwards, during the next few months but no exchange of numbers or serious interest shown by him. As summer faded, Tracy decided she must have imagined the intense, unexpected feeling she experienced when she first saw him.

With the onset of winter, fewer students lingered after classes, preferring instead to head home and stay warm. During a downpour one evening, Tracy stood beneath a small porch outside the studio waiting for a chance to dash to the train station, when a car appeared at the kerb. The window opened and her yoga colleague Theo asked if she'd like a ride. She nodded and dashed for the door.

During the reading, I glimpsed the following events from Theo's perspective. He felt calm during the drive but was unable to resist asking Tracy if she was hungry. He explained he hadn't eaten since lunch and usually grabbed a bite to eat nearby on his way home after class. This wasn't strictly true, but Theo didn't want the ride to end. He needed more time to understand why he was acting out of character by inviting a stranger for dinner. He carefully chose a brightly lit café so it didn't seem like an intimate dinner and as they began to talk, Theo felt more at ease with Tracy than he expected.

During dinner, Tracy noticed he listened attentively to everything she said, as one does when exploring someone or something new. He insisted on driving her home to continue his journey of discovery but remained in the car when she alighted. When driving away, Theo became aware of an internal conflict. He wondered if they might develop a significant relationship over the coming months but thought that if it didn't work out, he'd probably need a new yoga class. He spent the rest of the journey home reflecting on their conversation over dinner and through previous interactions to glean anything he could about Tracy.

Tracy barely slept that night, waiting for a text, a phone call or any sign that Theo felt the same way about the possibilities. Glancing ahead ten years, I saw their two children. The younger boy had Theo's unruly, dark curly hair, while her extraverted daughter was the family performer, enjoying any chance to dance or be seen.

I asked Tracy if she attended yoga classes. She explained that she had left a class because it was too far away and was currently searching for a new one. I told her about the meeting of a potential partner through a yoga school but didn't elaborate on details about Theo. After all, surprise and free will are parts of the joy of the human experience. It was enough to reassure her that she'd meet a long-term partner and have a family.

Understanding the Reading Process

Mischa looked disappointed when the cards said *no* to her dream home. I understood the many hours she'd spent researching her potential purchase, planning how she could improve the property and the house-warming party. After such a clear *no* from the tarot, she didn't know where to go from there.

One difference between an accomplished tarot reader and a novice is how the person guides the client through the reading process. An experienced reader understands that simply answering a client's question doesn't end there. The client can ask another question on the same subject, broadening or narrowing the focus as required.

If Misha receives a *no* answer to her question about purchasing the property at 17

Gardenia Street at auction on Saturday, the reader might offer her a range of follow-up questions, such as:

- Is there another suitable home I can purchase in that neighbourhood in the next six weeks?

- Can I find another perfect home if I broaden my search area?

- Is it wise for me to increase my budget to purchase a home in this neighbourhood?

- Is it best to wait for the real estate market to change direction?

- Is this a suitable suburb for purchasing a home in the coming months?

- Will I purchase that property? (She might buy it a week after the auction, outside of the scope of her original question.)

While Mischa is asking her question, filled with hopes and expectations about the life she'll soon be living in that home, the state government might be completing plans to build an overpass behind that house. The 1200 cars and trucks that will eventually pass over the property every hour when the project is completed could exacerbate her young son's asthma. These vehicles might also deposit black soot on her windowsills and her outdoor furniture.

Neither the reader nor the client knows why it's not wise to purchase that property that day but experience has taught me that when the cards offer a definite, unequivocal no, there will probably be a story about why it was unwise in the coming years.

This occurred to me in 2011, when my wife and I found a beautiful 130-year-old home after viewing eighty or more properties. The cards were consulted and clearly indicated that it was unwise to purchase the property. I visited the location one afternoon in peak hour to see if the busy road might be an issue because my home office would have been close to the street.

I sat in my car on a side street and counted each vehicle for a few minutes. I knew traffic was an issue when I'd counted 153 vehicles passing the house in 120 seconds. This continued relentlessly for two hours. I realised my elderly clients would probably only visit me once at this address, as they'd be traumatised by the endless traffic streaming off the nearby freeway. Some might not even make it home after a reading.

If a person asks about a new business venture and the answer is no, it's usually wise to explore other possible business avenues or ask if a steady job might be a better option. Readings aren't always about encouraging clients to pursue their dreams. Sometimes, their goals are flawed. They might require a lot of money to launch successfully or maybe a huge corporation is about to enter that market and dominate it entirely.

In the depths of the global financial crisis of 2007 to 2008, I had a range of clients asking about the viability of existing businesses and new options. It was overwhelming to hear their tales of hardship. After reading for around ten people, I estimated they had collectively lost $23,800,000 in the previous two years. These weren't only new ventures. Some of those businesses were more than 25 years old and had operated successfully for decades.

When a client looks shattered at hearing the pursuit of a dream business venture won't build wealth, it is sometimes necessary to point out that deciding not to proceed might save a fortune, plus several years of sheer hard work. In these readings, remind your clients that they are not asking for reassurance but to have an important question answered. A persistent client might follow with a question like: "What can I do to ensure the success of this venture?" This could be followed with a range of questions including:

- Have I picked the best location for this enterprise?

- Are the current partners suitable for this business project?

- Do I need a better product, service or approach to the market?

- Do I have sufficient funds to bring this business idea to its intended market?

- Will I have a better business plan or idea within twelve months?

- Am I attempting to begin a new venture at the wrong time in the wider economic cycle? (There's no point launching a great business two weeks before a catastrophic recession.)

- Do I need to do more research and refine my business plan before proceeding?

Beyond interpreting cards on a table and clarifying clients' questions, tarot readers often need to ask questions to help refine current issues. Sometimes, it is necessary to break subjects down to clarify the steps ahead for a client.

In a reading for Emma, who at forty-three years of age had not married nor had a long-term love relationship, it was necessary to clairvoyantly look ahead fifteen years, well beyond the scope of a traditional tarot reading. I did this because when she asked about future relationships, there were no possible partners appearing in the cards on the table (a two-year window).

I scanned ahead for partners but also for relationship patterns. Emma was unhappy. Growing up, she expected to meet someone special, marry and have a family, just like most of the people in her street. Instead, Emma had a few brief liaisons and lived alone with only a cat for company. I noticed she subconsciously expected a man to arrive and make her happy, to effectively lift her out of her entrenched misery. When men did approach her, she still felt lonely and unfulfilled. As a result, she let opportunities for love fade away. She'd forget to return phone calls, allow conversations to wilt and effectively starve her potential partner's passion.

> I saw two serious opportunities ahead for her but unless she transformed herself, she'd let them both go and end her life living alone. Her actions in the future were likely to ensure that she remained single unless she realised that she had the power to change her life direction.

My aim when reading for someone is to answer this question: "How can I inspire hope within this person today?" In Emma's reading, it was proving difficult. I wanted her to clearly understand the limited opportunities ahead for her and the work required to make one of those prospects a successful marriage.

I began with a question. "What are you prepared to do to make yourself ready for the love of your life?"

Her reply was instant. "I am ready. I've been ready for years," she insisted.

I anticipated the ball coming over the net and returned the serve immediately. "Really? Do you want a relationship to add to your happiness or to make you happy without any effort?" I probed.

She pursed her lips and eyed me directly. I continued. "Is it possible for you to perceive a solid relationship as the icing on the cake and not the cake itself?"

"What do you mean?"

"I mean that you need to be happy before Mr Right arrives. As it stands, your disappointment in potential partners surfaces early on in proceedings and they move on. Are you prepared to do some serious preparation for your long-term happiness?"

"What would that involve?" she asked, rising to the challenge.

"Firstly, it would mean making a list of what you contribute to relationships, not what you want from them. This would be a carefully considered list of your strengths, personal attributes and innate talents. Secondly, it would require ongoing counselling. I'm not describing several one-hour sessions but a few years of weekly sessions to resolve some emotional baggage."

"And would this bring the right man along?"

"No, yet it might ensure you don't discard the two remaining major opportunities you have left in this lifetime. Looking ahead, I saw two significant possibilities for you. Unless you change, you are likely to repeat your current pattern and retreat from both of them."

One path ahead for Emma included regular counselling sessions. This therapist understood how to motivate stubborn, stuck individuals so that they felt safe enough to embrace change. With the help of her counsellor, Emma is likely to pursue her possibilities when each of the two men arrives. If she chose to continue therapy, there were many other additional benefits for Emma aside from a new partner.

The second path was essentially the past five years on repeat. It was likely to result in a lonely old age, accompanied by several cats and a range of books. Tarot readers generally glimpse a limited portion of a client's life and can only initiate small changes in a single tarot reading. Real change usually requires time, mental flexibility and emotional persistence.

The answer to my question about how I might inspire hope within my client that day was clear: my task was to help Emma realise that change was possible and her past was not necessarily a reliable guide to her future. Clients cannot evolve until they believe change is possible. I reminded Emma that those who insist that meaningful personal transformation is not possible are simply people who have become stuck and not yet grown.

"It's so hard to change," she murmured.

"Yes, you're right. That's why you'll have that supportive counsellor next to you, helping you throughout the process. When you marry one of those men, be sure to invite your counsellor. She will have earned her place at the banquet."

Fundamental Questions for the Cards

Many clients want a tarot reading because they need answers to life's fundamental questions. These might include personal relationships, career, finances, family and health. It is a reader's task to clarify each question so that it is not ambiguous or two questions in one. If a client asks, "Is it wise to pursue a relationship with Toby or Lars?" she is effectively asking two separate questions.

It is reasonable to assert that, no matter how it is asked, every query is fundamentally about happiness. Enquiries about a new job might hold the possibility of increased income or more responsibilities. However, the unspoken issue of happiness or fulfilment is inherent. Questions about how to pay off huge credit card debts might appear as pursuing emotional stillness or inner peace but this serenity eventually leads to happiness. The daily dread of how to shift the burden of mounting debt can affect sleep and reduce concentration and optimism.

> Generally, when people focus their allotted time around one issue, such as a potential or former relationship, the completion of a course or regaining health, it is necessary to be patient with them. They are revealing how they believe the path ahead will lead to happiness.

Notice the words they emphasise and the phrases they rush across. When people feel uncertain about a subject, they tend to scurry through the parts of a sentence related to it. If they feel what they are saying is impossible or have been ridiculed for wanting a specific goal, they'll often momentarily close their eyes while talking about that subject. Sometimes they close their eyes to avoid glimpsing a possible scornful expression on the reader's face. However, by closing their eyes, they do not notice the reader's compassion.

This occurred in a recent reading when I asked Clara what vocation she wanted to pursue. When she told me her dream, she lowered her voice to almost a whisper, blinked slowly (possibly to prevent seeing an adverse reaction) and rushed through the keywords.

"I'd like to *improve my intuition* and become a *professional medium*, working from home," she said. For a short time after saying this, she was unable to look me in the eye.

"That's a good goal," I said. "What are the next steps for achieving your objective of working from home as a professional medium?"

She sighed, relieved I wasn't telling her it wasn't possible. Clara explained that she had read a range of books, completed some courses and practised regularly but wasn't sure about the next steps. We explored the possibilities of advanced classes, private lessons, as well as finding a suitable mentor to guide her towards her objective.

Her lack of eye contact and hushed tones indicated that Clara wasn't yet confident of her ability to achieve her goal. I sensed this was a pivotal moment and that any practical words of encouragement were likely to be remembered when doubts surfaced. I reminded her that achieving her goals required tenacity and that courage isn't an absence of doubt but an inner determination to forge ahead despite fears or reservations. I also highlighted that she'd taken some steps towards her goal by completing courses, reading books and strengthening her skills through practice. These all provided a solid skill base for her future work.

If I had sensed that Clara was being unrealistic about her desires, I'd have asked her a few questions. These would have been designed to help her realise she was unprepared for the journey ahead. This might have allowed her to determine for herself if she was ready to climb the mountain to reach her goal.

There are fundamental parts of life that, when balanced, improve stability and personal fulfilment. When upheaval occurs in any of these areas, people sometimes go in search of a tarot deck. Life issues can usually be resolved by examining options and making choices. Identifying alternatives in any presented issue is what skilful tarot readers do well.

To help refine important issues into clear questions, a range of categories are listed below. Suitable possible queries are also listed within each category. These are by no means the only alternatives but they are a useful reference.

An Essential Questions Menu

Take a moment to decide if any of the questions below clearly address your current issues.

Personal relationships

1. What does the future hold for me in personal relationships, generally?

2. What does the future hold for my current relationship?

3. What can I do to improve our relationship?

4. Is it wise for me to pursue this relationship?

5. Is it wise for me to pursue a relationship with ____?

6. Is _____ interested in pursuing a love relationship with me?

7. What is the underlying lesson for me in this relationship?

8. What do I bring to this relationship?

9. What is the gift or fundamental lesson for me in this relationship?

Finances

1. What does the future hold for me financially?

2. What can I do to ensure financial success for myself?

3. What am I currently doing to prevent myself from becoming financially secure?

4. Is it wise for me to sell my shares in (x number of) months?

5. Is it wise for me to invest in _____?

6. What behaviour patterns do I need to change to ensure financial stability for myself?

Career

1. What does the future hold for me in my career, generally?

2. What does the future hold for me in my current career?

3. Is it wise for me to continue in this current occupation?

4. Will I still be in this job in (x number of) months?

5. Am I suited to a career in (alternative occupation)?

6. What is the underlying lesson for me in my current position?

7. Is it time for me to undergo training for a new vocation?

Family

1. What does the future hold for my mother (or father)?

2. What does the future hold for my brother (or sister) in their business?

3. Is it wise for my mother (or father) to purchase the house at (address)?

4. What does the future hold for my mother's (or father's) health?

5. What can I learn from my family this year?

Happiness

1. Will pursuing my current path lead me to long-term happiness?

2. What can I do to increase my happiness?

3. What do I need to resolve to enjoy a deeper sense of fulfilment?

4. What can I give back to others in a meaningful way?

5. What strengths do I have that I can utilise to increase personal fulfilment?

Self-development

1.   What do I currently need to focus on in my self-development?

2.   Which element is it wise to focus on during the next two years (fire, water, air or earth, i.e., wands, cups, swords or pentacles)?

3.   What do I bring to my friendships and relationships?

4.   What area of personal development have I ignored to my detriment?

5.   Will pursuing _____ be worthwhile for me at this time?

Health

1.   What does the future hold for my health?

2.   What does my physical health currently reveal about my attitudes to life?

3.   What do I need to resolve to enjoy a fundamental sense of happiness?

4.   Will physiotherapy (osteopathy, chiropractic, massage, yoga, Pilates or meditation, etc.) alleviate my current spinal problems?

5.   How can I best maintain and improve my physical health?

6.   What is the underlying spiritual cause of my current physical health issues?

Note: If you are not a trained medical or health practitioner, don't diagnose. Instead, recommend clients seek confirmation by qualified medical or alternative health practitioners regarding any health information given during a reading.

Spirituality

1. What is my present spiritual lesson?

2. What are my current spiritual strengths?

3. What do I need to learn to fulfil my life purpose?

4. What do I need to resolve from my past to pursue my life purpose?

5. How can I confirm that I am on my correct path, spiritually?

6. How can I contact and communicate with my higher or spiritually evolved self?

7. What does the future hold for my relationship with God, Buddha, Mohammed, etc.?

Children

1. What does the future hold for (the child's name)?

2. Is it wise to encourage my child in the study of _____?

3. What is the underlying cause of my child's nail-biting (nightmares, etc.)?

4. What do I need to concentrate on to help my child develop?

5. What can I do to help my child feel fulfilled?

6. What is my child here to teach me spiritually?

7. What is my child's underlying spiritual lesson?

Travel

1. What does the future hold for me regarding travel?

2. Will I travel overseas in the next 24 months?

3. Is it wise and/or safe for me to travel to _____ this year?

4. Will I have enough money to travel to _____ this year?

5. Will I be able to earn an income as I travel?

6. What will I learn from this trip?

7. What is my underlying lesson in my forthcoming travel to _____?

Specific projects

1. Is it wise to pursue this goal?

2. Can I achieve this goal within two years?

3. Is _____ a suitable person to partner with for this project?

4. Will this product (or service) succeed in its current format?

5. Have I identified the right market for this product or service?

6. What obstacles can I expect to face in this process?

7. What personal strengths or talents can I apply to this process to reach my objective?

Relationship patterns

1. What is the underlying issue contributing to my current relationship patterns?

2. What do I need to change within myself to enjoy more rewarding love relationships?

3. Do I need to resolve problems from a past partnership to be ready for new love opportunities?

4. What positive qualities do I bring to relationships?

5. What do I need to do to be ready for new love?

The Importance of Yes/No Questions

Wording a question so it can be answered *yes* or *no* is useful when wanting to quickly eliminate several alternatives so you can focus on the most suitable path. For example, the question may be about financial investment and have five possible alternatives. Choices might include:

1. Investing in shares.
2. Purchasing an investment property.
3. Starting a business.
4. Buying a share in a business.
5. Placing money in a cash management fund.

Unless the intention is to invest in all five options, eliminate some of them by asking yes/no questions. The questions might be worded this way:

- Is it wise for me to invest this money in _____ shares?
- Will an investment in _____ be worthwhile?

Determining answers accurately takes a skill that develops with practice. Hopefully, a reader has developed this ability before someone approaches asking about an 'opportunity of a lifetime' that requires the proceeds of years of careful saving. For a clear *yes* answer, both the answer card (the fourth card in a seven-card spread) and the outcome card (the seventh card in a seven-card spread) need to be upright and in accord with each other (see the layout section for details). A sample layout follows.

Question One

Please note that this is only one interpretation of the cards shown. Another reader might glean additional information from this layout and still be right. Adding personal intuition to the logical meanings also increases the amount of information provided.

Question: Is it wise for me to invest in _____ shares?

CARD 1: The past
The Six of Wands suggests there has been financial success in the past. Perhaps the person has invested in a venture (possibly shares) previously and this investment has been rewarded.

CARD 2: The present
The Ten of Pentacles describes a situation in which the client is cashed up, possibly with solid investment opportunities available.

CARD 3: The near future
The Death card indicates that change is approaching, if not in the share market, then in the company whose shares you plan to purchase. It can also suggest a personal transformation in the next few months, resulting in different needs or goals.

CARD 1: THE PAST
Six of Wands

QUESTION
ONE
SPREAD

CARD 7: THE OUTCOME
Ten of Cups Reversed

CARD 2: THE PRESENT
Ten of Pentacles

CARD 6: ATTITUDE
Four of Pentacles

CARD 3: THE NEAR FUTURE
Death

CARD 4: THE ANSWER
The Hierophant

CARD 5: SURROUNDING ENERGIES
Knight of Wands

CARD 4

It's too early to consider this card yet because it's best to answer each question after examining all the cards in a layout. Each card has significance and overlooking the influence of the unexamined cards can reduce accuracy. If this was a general reading, it would signify the client. As it is a question, it represents the answer to the question. It is read last because clients sometimes stop listening after they have heard the answer to their question and might miss valuable information contained in the fifth, sixth and seventh cards.

CARD 5: **The energy surrounding the question**

The Knight of Wands describes an almost cavalier attitude to investment, at this point — plus impatience to move ahead with financial plans. The individual feels confident in the share market at this time and enthusiastic about wanting a stake in it. This card can also describe an exuberant friend or associate who is urging immediate speculation.

CARD 6: **Personal attitude to investment in the share market**

The Four of Pentacles suggests being keen to hold on to money while considering a more conservative, less risky investment. This card highlights a person's desire to acquire shares in blue-chip companies with sound business management and solid track records.

CARD 7: **The outcome**

The Ten of Cups reversed suggests that investing in shares now might leave this person feeling excluded from groups of people who are important. This could refer to fellow investors or peers. Reversed, this card suggests it is unwise to invest in shares at this time. By returning to the previous upright card in the suit, the Nine of Cups, this person needs to value what has been achieved through hard work and financial discipline. In valuing the effort required to save for an investment, the individual is less likely to be reckless when investing it.

CARD 4: **The answer**

The Hierophant card indicates a need to invest where others are investing or a desire to conform to what is expected. A five, The Hierophant suggests this approach is not the only viable option. There may be other more suitable investment possibilities that need investigation. The fives in tarot are cards for change and when upright, they usually indicate narrow-mindedness. Both the Four of Pentacles and the Hierophant are cards for the astrological sign of Taurus, indicating a Taurean person influencing the situation or a Taurean attitude to finances. Taureans tend to be conservative investors and diligent at saving. However, there are always exceptions to the rule.

Question Two

Before moving on to the second investment question, fold the previously selected cards back into the pack and re-shuffle the deck. Then select seven more cards. It is necessary to think clearly about the specific question while selecting each card.

Question: Is it wise for me to purchase an investment property?

This is a basic interpretation, before adding any additional cards.

CARD 1: The past

The Two of Cups suggests there may have been a house purchased with another person in the past. This arrangement worked well, as they were equal partners and both were happy with the arrangement.

CARD 2: The present

The Emperor in the present position, plus the King of Swords in the surrounding energy position (below), suggests people from the legal profession giving advice. Perhaps these advisers are counselling on current financial affairs. It might signify a lawyer or an accountant clarifying tax deductions and hidden ongoing costs related to owning a property. The Emperor indicates a disciplined man who is an advisor. His advice is practical. It sometimes describes the personal discipline and realism required to save money plus a pragmatic, unemotional approach towards an intended investment. This common-sense approach is likely to prevent rash decisions. It also points to the acceptance of the time required to secure quotes on repairs or improvements as part of the total amount to be invested.

CARD 3: The near future

The Two of Pentacles suggests that there are two or more viable options in the next three months. This might indicate two potential properties or types of properties (such as houses vs apartments). The client is carefully weighing different alternatives, deciding what choice is most suitable.

CARD 5: **Surrounding energies**

The King of Swords describes a legal or professional person currently giving advice. It can also highlight the need for clarity when weighing up options for purchasing an investment property. This card shows a desire to be clear-minded when making a final decision to avoid living with the consequences of a mistake for years to come. It might also suggest the presence of an astute friend or advisor assisting during this process.

CARD 6: **Attitude**

With the Queen of Swords reversed, fears are stronger than hopes at this time, making the person more cautious. There could be vivid memories of previous difficulties connected to owning property or the fear of making a monumental mistake. It can also suggest a woman who is pointing out all the pitfalls in property investment. She is a natural critic. During home inspections, she'll find every carpet stain, cracked window pane and creaky floorboard in the premises. This might help when negotiating a better price but it might also undermine personal confidence in potential investments.

CARD 7: **The outcome**

The Page of Swords reversed suggests a child is involved. If so, they are a talkative, mentally curious young person. If the card represents a personal aspect of the client, it can highlight hesitation. It can also suggest ungrounded confidence that better options might be forthcoming. This reversed Page also emphasises unrealistic plans, such as viewing properties that are unaffordable or considering an abandoned, dilapidated dwelling without previous renovation experience. The reversed Page of Swords occasionally describes waiting on delayed news, such as a surveyor's property report or a decision regarding acceptance of a low offer. Sometimes, this card indicates scattered thinking, perhaps from the information overload of viewing too many properties in short succession.

CARD 4: **The answer**

The Five of Cups describes grief and loss. When related to the question, it can mean the loss of a relationship that probably resulted in the division of assets that provided the money to invest in property. Sometimes it indicates feeling alone in the investment process. This isolation might be caused by restricted finances or having to move far away from a previous residence. The river in this card, which separates the person from the castle, gives the impression that the person wants to live in an unaffordable area.

CARD 1: THE PAST
Two of Cups

QUESTION
TWO
SPREAD

CARD 7: THE OUTCOME
The Page of Swords reversed

CARD 2: THE PRESENT
The Emperor

CARD 6: ATTITUDE
Queen of Swords reversed

CARD 3: THE NEAR FUTURE
Two of Pentacles

CARD 4: THE ANSWER
The Five of Cups

CARD 5: SURROUNDING ENERGIES
The King of Swords

Altogether, the answer is no, it is not wise to invest in property this year. This seven-card layout can be repeated for each of the five investment alternatives. Although this may take up a whole reading and clients might find this time consuming, the information gleaned will help them make stronger financial decisions.

Wording Questions for Accuracy

Most tarot readers strive for accuracy but sometimes it's difficult to speak with certainty, especially when both the reader and client are surprised by the direction ahead. Clara was astonished when told that her comfortable life was about to change suddenly. As a reader, I was equally taken aback because she had enjoyed a stable home and work life in the decade since we'd met.

"I love my home, my husband and our dogs. We have a fantastic life and I wouldn't swap it for the world," she stated. "What could possibly alter this?" I wasn't sure about the trigger for change but the cards suggested she'd have a new home and partner within two years. It was perplexing for both of us, so I reassured her that she has free will in all predictions.

In Clara's next reading, she explained that she had awoken one day and decided it was time for a new direction. She began by leaving her job and changing industry, where she met Tom. Months later, she had separated from her husband and was living with Tom, far away from her old life and her previous home.

"There was no big upheaval. I simply woke up one morning and realised that chapter was over. There was nothing to do but move forward. When I met Tom, I instantly knew that we were going to be together for a long time. I couldn't pass up the opportunity."

Accuracy is important in predictive readings but knowing what question to ask can be even more significant. Questions vary from extremely broad to deliberately narrow and both are necessary.

The broadest question I encourage clients to ask is, "What do I most need to know right now?" This fundamental query helps clarify what is essential to the present. It is in the present that we have the power to change direction, make choices or renew existing commitments. However, most people have specific enquiries relating to immediate issues. Well-prepared questions can focus a session, allowing the reader to provide more specific details about relevant topics. Often, an important concern requires several carefully phrased queries to clarify available options.

When a client asks about a current relationship and it appears to be ending, it is the reader's task to explain that the partnership is likely to dissolve, perhaps extinguishing fading hopes the client has to reconcile differences. It's also the practitioner's responsibility to provide a way to look beyond current circumstances. This might include encouraging the person to ask, "What does the future hold for me in love relationships, generally?"

If this does not yield satisfactory results, there are other options, including:

- What can I do to prepare myself for my next long-term love relationship?

- What do I need to resolve within to be ready for a long-term love partner?

- How can I best nourish myself emotionally before and during my next relationship?

- What do I need to know right now that will help me towards a loving partnership?

- What do I bring to love relationships?

- What do I offer a potential partner?

It's important that the reader identifies underlying issues and tactfully presents these to the client. During a recent reading, forty-six-year-old Alma asked about her marriage to Joe. I explained that she seemed unhappy and that there was another man in the background. Alma then explained that she had been separated from her husband for almost two years, during which time she began another relationship. Joe promised to change, so she ended her new union. They were reunited. However, she felt trapped and unhappy several months later when she realised that Joe was not going to change. She enquired about the other man but the cards indicated that this opportunity had passed. Alma then asked when she'd meet her next life partner. It was a reasonable question but I clairvoyantly glimpsed two contradictory needs within Alma. Although she was a practical, conservative woman (Queen of Pentacles), she was attracted to passionate, exciting men. Her husband appeared in the layout as The Emperor reversed and the other man was represented as the reversed King of Wands. Both men were risk-takers, reckless and adventurous and these characteristics worried her.

"How can you fulfil your need for adventure without feeling nervous about impending chaos?" I asked. She explained that her husband was currently risking his established business by investing in day trading and cryptocurrencies and his losses for the previous four months totalled almost $60,000. The other man had been declared bankrupt twice and was also financially reckless.

It was important for Alma to realise that these opposing needs restricted her ability to settle into a long-term relationship without feeling uneasy about her financial future. One option was for her to take responsibility for her economic well-being and ensure that her investments were protected from her partner's risky behaviour. Another choice involved finding a more stable partner and balancing this with adrenalin-charged activities such as sky-diving, surfing, camping trips, public speaking or tango lessons.

Sometimes, however, the question isn't as obvious, especially when enquiring for yourself. I know it's not possible to be objective when reading for oneself but many readers do this. I recently cut the cards when our twenty-one-month-old 4K television stopped working. It was well past its one-year warranty, yet still too new to be written off, so I searched online for local repairers. If it was unfixable, it would have cost us $160 per month to own for its brief working life.

I asked the cards if it was wise to take the TV for repair at one, then another, then a third service centre and the cards signalled a clear no. After hunting down the warranty card, I confirmed that it was my responsibility to repair it but I wasn't ready to give up. I asked if it was wise to purchase a new TV but the cards indicated that wouldn't lead to a positive outcome.

I pondered this for a while, then remembered that my wife has the persistence to find solutions to almost any problem. I then asked this question: "If I hand this issue over to my wife, will she find a better solution to fixing the TV?" The answer was a resounding yes. I retrieved the old TV from the garage and we temporarily lived like campers without a smart TV and no access to Netflix or apps on the TV.

A few days later, my wife searched online for the manufacturer's website. I instantly wanted to tell her I'd already done this but quickly remembered that I had asked about handing the issue over to her and allowing her to find the best solution. When she selected the same three local service centres I had picked, I quietly left the room to quell my urge to tell her she was retracing my footsteps. Thirty minutes later I took her a cup of tea and discovered she had already found the best solution.

While I was steadfastly looking away, she was scrolling down the manufacturer's web page to read about product recalls and acknowledged issues with some models of televisions. She discovered our model was on a list of products the company would fix without charge.

The next day, I phoned the manufacturer and they emailed a form that I filled out immediately. Five days later, a technician arrived and quickly replaced some components in the TV. I didn't have to drag a heavy TV to a service centre and it didn't cost me any money. I was delighted. I had to do nothing more than know what question to ask the cards and then hand the issue over to someone better than me at finding solutions. I thanked my wife for her diligence and myself for finally taking my own advice and keeping my mouth firmly shut when it mattered.

Some of the clearest, most beneficial tarot readings result from knowing the appropriate questions to ask at the time. It can be a complex process when a reader has to zoom in on specific issues while trying to understand how these relate to the client's whole life. Maintaining a balance between the macro and micro viewpoints can be a juggling act but it often improves reading outcomes.

Like any professional, an adept tarot reader makes complex processes look easy. It simply appears as if two people are having a comfortable conversation. However, outward appearances can conceal how the reader guides the session towards questions that clarify a client's issues. It's a purposeful conversation and with repetition, tarot readers become adept at leading the dance. This is why experienced readers often charge more per session. Clients are not simply paying for the reader's time and attention; they are reimbursing the practitioner for the years spent studying, practising and refining tarot knowledge and reading skills.

When training tarot readers, it's evident that previous, seemingly unrelated careers can contribute to individual style. Former schoolteachers tend to coach clients, whereas ex-project managers encourage people to map out clear paths to their life goals. At the end of introductory tarot courses, I usually ask participants this question: "What particular skills, talents and experience do you bring to your readings that make your services unique?" Responses have included previous careers in finance, natural therapies and raising a family as a single mum. One student said that being married to a gambler who routinely hid his winnings around the house, taught her how to intuitively find his stash when the family needed groceries. She has since helped friends find their partner's hideouts.

Limitations of the Tarot

The tarot, like any tool, has its limitations, especially when considering human error and confusing layouts. Other difficulties arise from an intense desire for a particular outcome or wanting to give clients encouraging news during difficult times. Paranoia, denial of reality and poorly worded questions can also affect the clarity of readings.

It is important for a tarot reader to resist the temptation to override the free will of a client. Professional readers predict the future, detail the past and illuminate the underlying causes of events but they don't dictate what a person should do. Everyone has free will in choosing a preferred destiny. Readers might observe warning signs or highlight significant opportunities ahead but the ultimate decision to accept or resist an option lays with the client.

Occasionally, I wrestle with an urge to shout when clients cannot hear me because I'm contradicting what they want to hear. This occurred when Mai asked about her job. She had been in the accounts department of a mid-sized company for almost three years and she wanted a promotion to a supervisor's position.

She asked the cards, "Will I be offered a promotion with this company within six months?" It was a clear, concise question and Mai seemed astute and capable and she had the relevant qualifications for a higher position. I explained that her current company was about to be absorbed into a larger organisation and that in around three months, most of her department would be retrenched. Many positions would be duplicated and the new owners were planning to slash jobs in her department. It was time for her to look for a new job elsewhere.

"So, are you saying I won't be offered a promotion?" she asked.

"I'm saying you are unlikely to be working for this organisation in three months. You can begin searching for a new position ahead of your co-workers or wait to be retrenched. If you delay, you'll be in direct competition with your co-workers for any available jobs. What would you prefer to do?"

"But I'm good enough to be promoted and someone is leaving a supervisor's position on the fourth floor next month," she insisted.

"Are you aware of the negotiations regarding the sale of your company?" I asked.

"No. No-one has said anything about retrenchments. There are no retrenchments."

"This doesn't surprise me. Have you ever worked in a company where they announce sweeping retrenchments in the middle of sale negotiations? It's guaranteed to send share prices plummeting."

"If I'm not offered the position on the fourth floor, can I ask if another position will be available in this company in the next six months? I don't mind if it's in another department."

"What company? In a year from now, there will be a new name and sign on your building and the letterheads will have a different logo. I'm giving you a tsunami warning and you're still trying to find the best position on the beach for your towel. Do you have a snorkel and flippers?" I enquired.

I then suggested Mai ask the cards about new positions at other companies and the results were very optimistic. I could understand her frustration. She had worked diligently towards the role she desired but wanting something is not enough to secure it. Mai returned twelve months later to say that when the workplace changes arrived, she had already accepted a position in a larger company. When she played back her recording, the reality of what I said sank in and she immediately became proactive in her search for a better job. She thanked me for forewarning her.

Sometimes, extreme desire can cause inaccurate tarot readings. When a person comes for a reading with an excessive yearning for an outcome, this highly charged energy affects the cards selected. Occasionally, this can create confusion between what is seen in the cards on the table and the reader's instincts.

Whenever I feel this contradiction, I immediately say, "I'm confused here. The cards tell me this relationship looks fabulous but I can't shake the feeling there are deep-seated problems that are not being addressed." I usually then tell the client what I see in the cards and what I sense myself. This typically leads to a conversation that clarifies the issue for both of us.

This occurred with Craig. He arrived a few minutes late for his reading and I guessed he'd slept on a park bench the previous night. He explained he had barely dozed off at all in three nights. His dishevelled appearance, bristly face and harrowed look portrayed a man who was profoundly troubled.

Before I could explain the shuffling procedure, he began sobbing and I noticed he was shaking. He said, "She just walked out. We were happily in love and ... living together and ... and ... one day she just walked out the door." I offered him some tissues and time to compose himself. The shaking subsided but he looked lost. It was as though he didn't know how he had come to be sitting across from me, holding a pack of cards.

Craig had an all-consuming desire that influenced every card in every layout in the reading. After a chaotic general reading, he asked his first question, which was, "What does the future hold for our relationship?" After positioning the cards as they were selected, I became suspicious of the perfect spread in front of me. It was incongruous. The layout detailed the happiness, commitment and peaceful stability of a relationship between two compatible people with common goals. However, Craig had just explained that Sonia had decided she did not love him and had left without any explanation. He was distraught but beneath his pain, I sensed suppressed anger.

The cards and the reality were conflicting because of Craig's acute longing for Sonia to return. Reading for someone in such a state rarely results in an accurate forecast. It is wise to arrange an appointment a week away to give the person time to rebalance. (I missed the opportunity to do this with Craig as he had spoken with my receptionist and was given a last-minute cancellation.) When someone is in a heightened state of desire, the cards usually reflect their yearnings rather than the true situation.

Another mental state that can affect the accuracy of a tarot reading is paranoia. I have a friend who loves to open my tarot pack with emotionally loaded questions such as, "Is my girlfriend faithful to me?" He has even gone one step further by asking, "Will she always remain faithful to me?"

I asked him, "Have you always remained faithful to yourself, to your own principles?"

He continued with similar questions that I steadfastly refused to answer.

"Why won't you respond to my questions?" he asked.

I replied, "If you want to pick a fight with Camellia, then do it honestly. Don't use your stupidity and insecurity to ruin a healthy relationship."

I had visions of him sitting complacently about the house, treating Camellia badly, safe in the knowledge she would always remain faithful to him. The tarot was designed for more profound insight than this.

Self-denial can also derail a reading and cause a client to misunderstand what is being said. Travis was unshaven, unkempt and seemed like a man existing entirely on strong coffee and sugary drinks. He had been day trading in shares for almost a year when he consulted me for a reading. He was convinced a tranche of shares was about to significantly leap in price. After investing $20,000 in the stock, it dropped in value. Still convinced of the eventual price increase, he borrowed another $40,000 and purchased more stock.

His $60,000 investment was currently worth $47,600 and he was still searching for ways to borrow more money for what seemed like a reckless venture. From my perspective, it appeared he wanted me to collude with him and confirm his expectations of a big windfall in the coming months.

Instead, his first layout included the Six of Pentacles, Ten of Pentacles and Ace of Pentacles cards, all reversed. The answer to his question about the outcome of his investing was the Ten of Swords. The bleak cards were at odds with his fervent belief that he had glimpsed a rising trend in the market that no-one else had noticed. It's sometimes challenging not to side with clients when they're adamant but it's unethical and not good for business long term.

It was a delicate dance of getting him to accept reality while inspiring him towards his original goal of building wealth. I began by asking him how much sleep he had on an average night in the previous month.

"Five hours. Sometimes six," he replied.

"How many coffees do you have on an average day?"

"Four or five."

"Black or white coffee?"

"Double espressos."

"That's probably more than the average barista, who's making 250 coffees a shift." He shrugged at this and I asked him what his original goal was in pursuing day trading. He explained it was to build wealth.

"How much have you earned or lost since you began?"

"Six or seven," he mumbled.

"Earned or lost?"

"I'm down six thousand."

"What about the $12,400 you're down on that individual stock."

"That doesn't count because I haven't cashed out yet."

"Yes, but as soon as you sell, the paper loss becomes a real loss. Remember that you still owe the bank $40,000. Let's round your losses up to $20,000, which they will be if you hold that stock much longer."

He sighed and fell back into the chair. Hearing the total amount aloud amplified his dilemma and made it suddenly seem real. He'd been earning an income through casual work but his last contract had expired a month before. Travis was living on credit cards while borrowing to invest. He didn't need a tarot reading to tell him it was risky behaviour but it was important to be honest with him about what the cards on the table indicated. I asked him what he would have earned on an IT contract for the previous month and he told me around $10,000. It was time to clarify his situation.

"Let me see if I've understood this," I said. "You've been without a contract for a month while focusing on day trading at home, which has cost you around $20,000. That's $30,000 less than if you'd worked on contract and enjoyed a full night's sleep almost every night. How exactly is this building wealth?"

He stared at me in silence. Had I gone too far? Had I shattered his dreams and forced him to confront his escalating losses? He wrestled with his metallic watch band for a minute, while mentally processing this news.

"F**k. It's been a waste of time. A complete waste of time!"

"Not necessarily. If anything, it might have taught you that you have a preference for lower-risk investments that allow you to sleep at night."

"Like what?

"Perhaps blue-chip stocks or real estate."

"Or investing in start-ups?" he suggested hopefully.

Clients sometimes have a tremendous emotional investment in a set outcome, and consequently, only hear selective fragments of their readings. They ignore all information contradicting what they believe. Everyone does this occasionally. (If you are convinced you see things exactly as they are, ask a child to describe what he or she sees and you might be surprised.) The children's story *The Emperor's New Clothes* is a classic illustration of this point.

Poorly worded questions can also cause confusion. The simple question "Will my business be successful?" can be broken down for the client into several questions to achieve the most accurate reply:

- Will my business be financially successful?

- Will my commercial venture achieve a turnover of $ ___ per year within two years?

- Will I achieve my financial goals within a year?

- Will I consider my business to be a success in two years?

- Is it wise for me to pursue this project as a commercial venture?

- Is my current business plan the most appropriate one at this time?

- What can I do to improve this endeavour?

- What do I most need to change within myself to improve my business?

- How can I increase my personal fulfilment within my planned career strategy?

- What is the most important lesson this enterprise can teach me?

- Where is my business leading me?

I was surprised the first time a client arrived with a written list of questions. I felt disheartened that spiritual issues were ignored, along with the desire to know and learn the lessons behind trials and triumphs. I was being idealistic. However, it was soon apparent that this particular client was more focused than most. She sought a reading with carefully identified goals in mind and afterwards she knew her needs had been met.

I now recommend all clients bring a list of questions to avoid the frustration of remembering queries after the session has concluded. Sometimes, the information contained in a reading is overwhelming to the client and they are too emotionally distracted to contemplate important issues. The most significant question has to be asked first, as a less important matter is often influenced by a more urgent one.

Chelsea asked about the possibility of resuming a recently finished relationship. She was overwhelmed at the recent loss and not ready to release her hopes of a revival. When I told her that this was unlikely to happen, she immediately moved on to a question about her job. However, the career layout only included cards relevant to a relationship, indicating that she was still preoccupied with her romance. I asked Chelsea if she wanted to know more about relationships, perhaps in a general sense and she confirmed that she did. After she selected different cards with a relationship query in mind and we explored why her recent partner departed without explanation, we returned to career issues. I was then able to provide clarity about career direction, as Chelsea's more important matters had been addressed and were no longer preoccupying her.

Sometimes, several cards found in a previous relationship spread appear in the next layout. This can happen if clients' relationship questions have not been fully answered to their satisfaction or if other aspects of their issues need to be highlighted. Liam's general reading was centred on his love relationship, with the reversed Queen of Cups as the fifth card in a seven-card layout. The reversed Cups Queen also appeared in several of his questions concerning further relationship issues. In the general reading, I explained to Liam that his partner was leaving because he repeatedly abandoned her for his career and his friends.

In answer to his first question, I revealed that his partner was unhappy and why. In reply to the second, I pointed out that Liam was also unfulfilled, as he attempted to decide what was more important in his life: friends, work or the relationship. In answer to the third question, I highlighted Liam's behaviour patterns within relationships and how he was repeating his father's patterns.

After his fourth question, I quizzed him about his hopes for a love relationship and outlined what I perceived to be his partner's expectations; I then compared the two so he could see the fundamental differences between them. In reply to his fifth question, I explained what Liam was likely to gain from pursuing the relationship and what he'd have to sacrifice to continue it.

After these five questions, his final one was, "What does the future hold for me in relationships?" This last reading went beyond his current partner and allowed a glimpse at other possible relationships. The layout detailed another woman (the Queen of Pentacles), who was likely to understand his need to work hard and who might support him in his pursuit of financial independence. Liam did not seem to hear the answer to this question but I felt it might benefit him when he later replayed the recording of his reading.

It is important to remember that a tarot reader does not have the right to tell the client what to do because this interferes with a person's opportunities to learn from current circumstances. A reader's task is simply to illuminate what is apparent, rather than persuade clients to specific viewpoints. If the reader is a low-risk investor and a client thrives on chancy, volatile investments, it's not the reader's role to insist the client modify his behaviour. Only when a person is taking wild chances but not coping with the consequences is it time to help that individual assess the options.

Amber wanted me to tell her to leave her job because it did not satisfy her. However, I realised her dissatisfaction with her workplace was merely a symptom of an unacknowledged problem. She hoped I would take responsibility for her life and felt that paying me a fee somehow enabled this. I tried several times to point out that she was free to change her job but that the underlying causes would not be resolved simply by a different workplace. Amber did not seem to hear me and I realised she was asking the wrong question. The real issue was to find out what type of career might best suit her and what qualities she needed to develop to make the most of this new occupation.

I described her as one-part accountant and one-part adventurer. The accountant portion wanted a safe, precise sort of job, whereas the adventurer needed outdoor involvement that might challenge her and offer new frontiers every day. Amber's very different internal aspects contributed to her fundamental job dissatisfaction. Every time she had a secure, comfortable job, she was bored to distraction within weeks. However, whenever she was in a less predictable position, she became insecure and longed for the stability offered in more conventional careers.

As a reader, my challenge was to find a way to show her that her opposing desires were making her alternately restless and then insecure. Then, it was necessary to examine ways for her to fulfil both needs. As I described the opposing parts, she laughed with recognition.

"What about working in a secure position and saving up to travel overseas for your adventures each year or two? That way you might have the benefits of both worlds," I suggested.

"Where would I go?" asked the conservative part of her.

"The wilds of Africa, no less," I said, as we both laughed.

"But ..."

"Yes, yourself and three complete strangers in a Jeep without a roof. You'll be out there on the plains, day and night, in search of wildlife. This is not a comfort cruise, but a real safari with tents and all provisions carried on board."

She pondered this for a minute and realised that it was possible to thoroughly meet her diverse needs. As an afterthought, I added that this was only one way but she seemed content to pursue the possibilities I had outlined.

The Tarot as a Window into Others' Lives

Generally, people's basic needs are very similar. The pursuit of rewarding work, positive friendships and significant relationships is universal. Creating a life that is rich with meaning can be complex and difficult for some while seemingly easy for others. Some individuals come for a reading seeking enlightenment and the opportunity to probe the inscrutable parts of their psyche. But with only forty-five minutes for lunch, they are often confined to a tarot reading of twenty minutes while devouring a sandwich.

A thorough reading usually takes about an hour and only five or six issues are examined in that time. Sometimes, clients want answers to questions they are not ready to deal with. The reader needs to confine them to subjects that will benefit them in the short-term. Instead of answering questions about the viability of long-term world peace or the ultimate pursuit of happiness, clients are likely to receive more precise answers to specific short-term questions about health, career, love relationships, career choices and travel options.

Sometimes, a reader glimpses something during a reading that makes them laugh. You've no doubt heard of art designed to shock or provoke a visceral response but what about art to trigger spontaneous laughter? During a recent reading, I saw that Amy's friend Tracy was determined to have one last trip, despite her medication regime, before she was too ill to travel. She would ask Amy to accompany her and the pair would venture to Europe.

I intuitively saw the following: five days into the trip, Tracy was weary and overwhelmed. She decided to stay in bed, so my client Amy went for a walk around the small Italian town. In a quiet lane, she came across a shop selling gifts, local arts and crafts. Amy stood before a small, unevenly framed painting that was plainly terrible. It belonged in the *Bad Art Gallery*. It was so awful it made her laugh, so she bought it for Tracy to cheer her up. When she unwrapped the gift, Tracy burst into laughter and stated firmly "You shouldn't have. No, really!" She shook her head as she smiled and said flatly, "I'll treasure it." Once home, Tracy was going to display it proudly on the mantel in her living room before working on a long and uninteresting backstory to tell guests. Every time she was to glimpse the uneven frame and the lack of detail on the canvas, it would bring a smile to her face.

A study of the tarot highlights the human condition. I believe we are all searching, even those who appear to be stuck, resistant or resting. Giving a reading is sometimes an opportunity to illuminate the way to a suitable path so that clients can fulfil their unique life purposes. The underlying life themes or spiritual lessons are revealed through the major arcana cards (covered later in this book). These cards are often sprinkled throughout tarot layouts and can reveal the spiritual lessons clients are embracing or wrestling with.

When I have painful news to deliver to a client, I always ask myself, "How would I like to receive this?" I try to tell the person the way I'd like to hear it. Compassionate delivery of information that may cause offence or pain can help a client feel supported. Sometimes, it's necessary to suggest some possible questions that might help the person determine the best options in their changing personal landscape.

Occasionally, it is inappropriate to say anything. In a recent psychic development course, I was demonstrating how easy it is to penetrate the psychic protection of a student to illustrate that some psychic protection techniques are ineffective. I retrieved some simple information from the student that she couldn't immediately relate to. I felt it was necessary to mention a few clear, concise facts that would confirm to her and to the class that I had penetrated her auric energy field and had access to information about her.

What came up was that she was unhappy with her present partner, a man who was aloof and self-absorbed. I then realised she was looking for love in the wrong place; she was due to have a love relationship with a woman, where she'd find fulfilment. Sensing she was unaware of her sexuality, it was inappropriate for me to state my findings in front of the class. I told her I couldn't retrieve anything more and asked for another volunteer to demonstrate the exercise.

However, it is rare that a reader is unable to share what lies ahead due to exposing information to others, as readings are generally private matters. If a client appears to be uncomfortable with what is being said, it might be necessary to pause the recording and offer to continue without recording that section. Sometimes, a client points silently towards the microphone on the table as a signal that they don't want a question and its answer to be recorded. Why clients request privacy is not important. That clients receive privacy when required is paramount.

Even repeat clients can be surprising. Tristan consults me regularly about business issues. He usually arrives with twelve questions, despite repeatedly being told that I can answer up to five in a one-hour reading. He frequently asks questions within questions. It's like giving three full readings in one hour. I finally decided not to read for him again but when he phoned for another appointment, I booked him before realising who he was.

When he sat down, I decided to find out his underlying need and meet it, reasoning that if I did so, Tristan might not feel the urge to ask so many questions. I explained the general reading carefully and we talked for a few minutes. His fundamental need became clear to me. Tristan was under enormous pressure with his business and he wanted someone to understand what he was going through. Although his business was thriving, Tristan felt no-one around him understood what sacrifices he regularly made to keep the business afloat. The more affluent he became, the more those around him took for granted that he didn't need to be comforted and nurtured. After all, he was successful. He was showing me that all of us, even prosperous people, still have a basic human need to be heard, loved and nurtured.

I listened attentively and he felt heard by me. Then a strange thing happened. This normally aggressive, controlling and exacting man suddenly became like a small child, sobbing into some tissues. I had stumbled on his fundamental requirement: to be allowed to be vulnerable for even five minutes within the demanding life he had made for himself.

He apologised for "losing control like that" but I was probably more helpful to him in the preceding five minutes than in all his previous readings. In essence, I had done nothing but allow Tristan to express what he had stored up within. Having addressed Tristan's concealed needs, we concluded our session five minutes early and he looked completely satisfied. That was the first time in five readings that he left without the desire to ask an extra question.

Another example of finding a client's unspoken requirements occurred with my homoeopath, Maeve. During consultations, she carefully questions me about what I think I need. Maeve then ignores me, combining what I've told her with what she feels is right for me.

At first, I felt upset that she didn't listen to what I was saying but I eventually realised that Maeve was listening between the words to my fundamental requirements. Now when I consult Maeve and she asks me what I think I need, I tell her I don't know. She then asks me to tell her how the past months have been. While I launch into my life story, Maeve usually reaches for her bottles and begins mixing a tincture.

To keep readings simple, it's essential to discover a person's underlying need. However, if a reader is heavily influenced by a client's perception or personal desires, it's possible to become confused and exhausted. A client's deeper requirements are often concealed, even from themselves. It is the reader's task to unearth them.

Discovering the client's unacknowledged need comes with practice and requires intuitive development. The simplest way to foster this instinct is to state silently to yourself, while the person is shuffling the cards, "The client's need today is ___ ." Most requirements are simple. The individual might be desperate to be loved, to be heard, to be reminded they have strayed from their path, to be praised for their actions, to be shown compassion or, occasionally, to be questioned about the motivation behind their words and actions.

Everyone has conscious requirements and underlying needs. Meeting these veiled, often unaddressed desires can sometimes help surface wishes to subside. Tarot is a useful tool for discovering underlying spiritual requirements and can also highlight steps to finding profound spiritual nourishment.

The tarot provides a glimpse of the hidden, otherworldly side of life. It is a window through which it is possible to glean personalised spiritual direction. Fulfilling a profound purpose can lead to lasting happiness and fulfilment. A reader can help others discover their underlying reason for living and encourage them to access lasting nourishment and significant accomplishment.

When More Clarity is Required

If the outcome of a reading is not clear, it's likely the right question is not being asked. Determining the best question or series of questions to clarify a direction can take time but it's usually worthwhile.

When 27-year-old Maria asked about the future for love relationships, her layout contained no obvious opportunities for a partner in the next two years. Instead of proceeding with the next question on a different topic, I suggested she ask one of several possible questions to clarify her path. These included:

- Do I need to release someone from my past to be ready for a new love relationship?

- What can I do to prepare for my next long-term love relationship?

- Have I already met someone who will make a suitable spouse if I choose to pursue a relationship?

- Is my next long-term partner currently in a relationship?

The final question can encourage the client to have patience should a potential partner not be ready for romance. There's no point meeting Mr Right while he is focused on saving a failing relationship. Pursuing a new relationship before the existing one has resolved could cause his current partner to blame you for their breakup. The emotional aftermath could make yours a transitional liaison rather than a lasting one.

Skilful readers often have a short conversation with a client to narrow the focus of a question. Karen was nearing retirement age and had recently purchased a country cottage. She planned to retire to her garden home, with views of rolling hills and walking paths nearby.

She awoke one morning in a state of panic, unsure she was doing the right thing. Karen booked a reading to ask if it was wise to move to the country. A few different questions could cover this issue, including:

- Is this a suitable time for me to move to the country?

- Is my new cottage ideal for the next stage of my life?

- Is it prudent to remain in my current job for the next two years to save additional money to fund my retirement?

- Is it wise to retire to my cottage this year?

- Is it worthwhile to rent out the cottage until I'm ready to move into it?

- Is the new cottage the most suitable location for me to live in retirement?

Karen opted to ask if it was prudent to remain in her current job for the next two years. The cards suggested it was not the best choice for her. We rephrased the question for a period of one year and the cards indicated that this was wise. Karen was nervous about her life transition and with good reason. If she changed her mind, it would not be possible to return to her current job or get a new career at age sixty-one.

This answer ruled out the question, "Is it wise to move into the cottage this year?" Karen then asked if her new cottage was suitable for the next stage of her life.

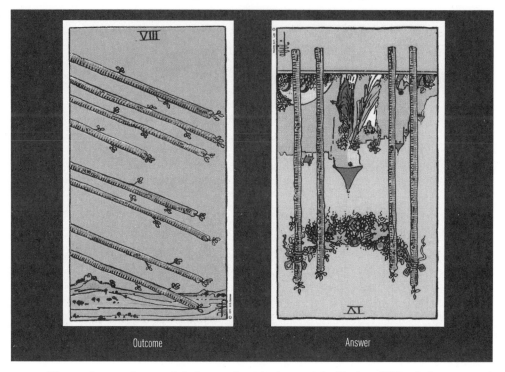

Outcome   Answer

The cards were less straightforward, with the upright Eight of Wands (success and ease of movement towards goals) as the outcome and the reversed Four of Wands (being unsettled in home environment or living in temporary accommodation) as the answer. I interpreted this to mean that the move was fine but within two years she might move again. The reversed Four of Wands doesn't indicate settling into an environment. Instead, it indicates a temporary home or not feeling anchored in the neighbourhood. Living in a location soon reveals how suitable it is for personal needs.

Karen was upset at this prediction and hesitant about moving from the city if her next move wasn't permanent. To alleviate her fears and clarify the move, I intuitively scanned ahead to see images of her new life in three years. I picked this time frame because it allowed for her to leave her job, move into the cottage and then move again.

The intuitive images revealed Karen would be living in a grand old home surrounded by beautiful established gardens. This was not a cottage but it did have a small cottage in the grounds. She was supervising renovations and preparing a website for paying guests. Karen was creating a guesthouse close to a tourist town after the previous owner had sold it to move into aged care. To afford this property, Karen had to sell her cottage. If my glimpsed images were any guide, she had no regrets.

To be certain this path would be fruitful, I scanned ahead five years, beyond the renovations. Karen was running a successful business with the assistance of a small staff of locals. She had converted a large dining room with expansive views from a wide veranda into a café that drew in customers all day. The cafe also promoted the accommodation. Clearly, her retirement would have to wait.

I could have added another card to the upright Eight of Wands (the outcome card) to clarify the answer without having to use intuition. The Eight indicated Karen would be happy with her life in two years despite no longer being in her retirement cottage.

I thought Karen might have to wait two years to realise the prediction was correct. During this period, she was likely to move again because her needs were changing. By scanning ahead, it was possible to clarify that although Karen was primed to leave the city for a new life, she was not yet ready for retirement. Working in her current job for another year might also allow her to accumulate more savings towards the purchase of a grander property in two years.

Karen had made the best plan possible she could for her future but it seemed life had prepared an even better plan. Having glimpsed her future, my only hope is that I'm offered a substantial discount and a room with a view when I visit.

Reading Under Pressure

There is always a level of pressure when giving a tarot reading, even after decades in practice. It's a delicate balancing act that aims for clarity, detail and accuracy while speaking with compassion. Sometimes, it's not immediately apparent that a client is experiencing searing pain or loss around a personal issue. I've learned to repeatedly ask every person if what I've said makes sense and then rephrase or clarify anything that is unclear.

I appreciate precision in tarot readings, so I designed a question menu to help clients ask the clearest questions possible for their circumstances. Often, this list is a guide for what is possible and after viewing it, people can word their queries more carefully. Occasionally, an individual is completely prepared and has itemised and edited a list of questions before phoning to book a session.

Sasha's email request for a distance reading was clear and succinct. After receiving some worrying news about her health, she became increasingly anxious. She wanted a telephone reading to examine her options and to clarify her current health condition. She was about to have a live tooth removed under general anaesthetic to access a lesion that would then be tested for cancer. Sasha explained that several years earlier, an elderly relative had the exact same type of lesion above a tooth that had revealed cancer. Given the family history, it was prudent to be vigilant with symptoms.

We agreed on a time for the reading and the next day she sent me her list of questions. Glancing down her list, I realised she had won the award for the most prepared client I'd seen in forty years of practice. Not only were the questions grouped but once we had a *yes* or *no* answer there were follow up questions ready.

As I looked more closely at the details of each question, my throat tightened. This was going to be very difficult. The outcome could be life or death. The decisions Sasha was about to make centred on blood tests, full-body scans and surgery, with more decisions and interventions to follow. If I made a mistake and guided her in the wrong direction or overlooked anything, it's possible my actions might shorten her life expectancy.

She was listening intently to everything I said and I needed to be very clear before speaking. I knew if I paused too long to collect myself, she'd fear the worst. I asked her for a bit more time to clarify what I saw. While I was aware of the mother, wife and human on the other end of the phone, I was suddenly sharing her dread. The only option was to zoom in on each question and briefly ignore the consequences of what I had to say.

Sasha's list included the following:

- There is a strong history of cancer in my family. Is there cancer anywhere in my body that is being missed?

- Is this an undiagnosed autoimmune condition such as Lupus or Antiphospholipid Syndrome?

- Is this lesion a primary cancer of some kind?

- Is this a secondary cancer of some kind?

- If secondary, will the surgery and reconstruction go smoothly to plan with no disfiguration or complications?

- If secondary, where is the primary cancer?

After reading her list, I wrote to Sasha immediately to explain that I could not diagnose cancer during a reading because I'm not medically qualified. There are proven scientific tests she could take for this type of finding. Sasha is also a tarot reader, so she understood this. She simply wanted to know what tests were needed to address her ongoing health issues.

I also pointed out that a thirty-minute reading only covered up to four specific questions and her list ran to twenty-two possible queries. She explained that she had seen me use a single card for each option in a Five Alternatives Layout but the enormity of the questions made a single card for each option impossible. I explained that we'd get through what we could in the allotted time. It's a delicate balance between speed and accuracy. There is a risk of sacrificing one for the other in readings.

Before Sasha's reading, I studied her questions carefully, identifying what was reasonable to ask during her telephone session. She began with this: "Will the surgery and reconstruction go smoothly and end successfully?"

The two key cards (out of seven) in this yes/no question were the answer card and the outcome card. Both had to be upright, constructive cards for this to be a clear yes. The answer card was The World reversed and the outcome card was the upright Empress. The World is optimistic both upright and reversed. Upright, it indicates lasting success whereas when it appears reversed, success is temporary. When reversed, it is as though the person climbs a tall mountain (successfully achieves a goal) and at the summit, discovers an even taller peak to be climbed.

The Empress upright highlighted a comfortable home environment that might be a supportive place for Sasha to recuperate after her surgery. As a number three card, it suggested constructive progress and a return to normal life but the reversed World indicated this surgery was unlikely to be the end of her health issues. We discussed the possibility of gaining more information and making informed decisions.

Intuitively, I was shown a mental image of Sasha standing in her kitchen, drinking a deep green liquid every day. I asked her what it was. She explained that she used to drink a green liquid for internal body cleansing but hadn't done so for a few months. I suggested she resume this for two or three months to see how she felt at the end of the period. It had obviously had a positive impact on her health previously.

At the end of our telephone session, Sasha was happy with the information she had received. She wrote the following day to say that she was going ahead with the surgery after asking her surgeon a few more questions.

Sasha didn't put unreasonable demands on me during her reading but I felt the burden she experienced regarding her health issues as the reading unfolded. I usually explain to students in advanced tarot courses that the pressure a reader experiences during a reading never subsides completely if the reader is aware of personal duty and responsibilities.

The tarot has limitations and specific layouts have additional restrictions. Tarot reading is not designed for long-range questions (past the three or four-year mark) and one-card cuts are not suitable for anything more than questions about finding a car park, buying a coffee or taking a jacket out with you for a day trip. They simply lack accuracy.

Added to this, many inexperienced tarot students use one-card cuts repeatedly, often cutting the deck again if they don't like the card they have drawn. In the 1980s, I watched in horror as my co-tenant David cut my tarot deck thirty-six times with random questions. He was like a boy with a new toy, slurping coffee with one hand while turning over cards with the other. He didn't even pause to write down his findings. At first, he took out the book and searched for the page with the card's meaning on it but soon he just cut the deck and studied each card for a few seconds before returning it to the pack.

Later, David followed me into my home office asking questions and I suggested he ask the cards whether he was asking too many questions. He cut to the upright Ace of Swords.

"What does the Ace of Swords mean?"

"It means *yes*," I replied. "You don't need the cards to tell you that. I'm going to confiscate them until you display more maturity," I said, swiping the cards from him before he could ask another question.

Setting Boundaries in Readings

Accurate and successful readers are usually in demand by the public, which is great. However, it's beneficial to have a life aside from readings to remain nourished and to replenish energy reserves. Setting and maintaining boundaries around work and play is useful and usually requires self-control.

This discipline can involve setting limits with clients who want to see you when it suits them but not you. Busy modern lifestyles can limit time for consulting a reader but telephone and Skype readings make this easier.

Novice readers usually need to read for friends to build their tarot skills. These are some of the most difficult readings to give because friends are not used to the beginner in the role of the tarot reader. As a result, friends are likely to challenge the reader, answer their phone just when the reading is gathering momentum or text a friend from the reading table to relay the news as it is being given. Professional readers rarely have to endure such treatment. Partly because of the higher cost of a session, clients are more likely to listen carefully and not be distracted.

Another boundary is determining when you will be available to read for people. Many years ago, I was in meditation when my guides clearly instructed me to take Thursdays off to write. They explained that I needed one whole day each week for writing to ensure the books didn't take too long to be completed. I moved my client days around to accommodate the new writing days and in the first month, five potential clients wanted only Thursday appointments. These individuals were not interested in any other days or evenings but I reluctantly honoured the commitment I had made to write on Thursdays.

Many tarot readers and clairvoyants don't establish strong personal boundaries between themselves and their clients. This is understandable, considering that clairvoyants penetrate the emotional and psychic boundaries of others for a living. Some clients also have weak personal boundaries, sometimes requiring gentle but clear reminders of the agreements or commitments made towards the reading process.

I sometimes refuse to read for a client if that person is having too many readings. One caller explained that she didn't like what the last five tarot readers had recently told her and wanted another opinion. I politely explained I didn't want to be part of her survey.

It's reasonable to refuse to read for someone who is intoxicated. It is also best not to read for others when you have consumed alcohol, as it diminishes sound judgement. If a client seems to be behaving irrationally or is aggressive, it's best to terminate a reading or not read for this person.

Proficient readers usually refuse a client who asks them to do something illegal, immoral or downright seedy. This includes requests for manipulative magic spells or curses to be placed on people as well as advice on how to evade the law or track down a partner who does not want to be found.

In one reading, a man in his late forties wanted to ask about a planned love affair. His question was, "If I have an affair, will my wife find out?" When the answer was yes, he wanted to ask what month she'd discover his affair, so he might end it the previous month. His justification was that he "didn't want her to take him to the cleaners for a bit of fun."

"Like your first wife did?" I asked pointedly.

"How did you know about my first wife?" he said with surprise.

"You've asked me to look into your life. I'm looking. If I can look ahead, I can also look at your history."

> I've known female tarot practitioners who only consult with women and it's a person's right to refuse to read for any individual for whom they cannot give an unbiased reading. If a reader has a destructive or traumatic history with one gender, this is likely to reduce clarity, as it's difficult to read for people when you're uncomfortable in their presence.

Mostly, boundaries are about time. In the first conversation, it is best practice to tell clients how long the session will last. If readings last one hour, then tell the client when the final question has arrived, so the person can ask the most significant remaining question. One client, who despite being told that I cover a general reading and up to five specific questions in a one-hour reading, arrived with thirty-six questions. I saw her list and repeated my question limit before we began.

She attempted to ask five questions in one when enquiring about potential husbands for her single daughter. I asked her if she wanted speed or accuracy. "Both," she replied.

"I can offer you one or the other. If you want the best combination, that will include up to five questions in this reading. If I have to explain this to you repeatedly, it will include only four questions because my sessions last one hour."

A year later, she returned for another reading and produced her yellow notepad again. A single question was written at the top of the page. When I had answered her question, she turned over the page to reveal one more question at the top of the next page. I asked to examine her pad and counted 25 questions on 25 separate pages. I looked at her in silence as she realised that she was attempting to dissolve the boundaries I had set to structure the reading effectively.

A skilful tarot reader usually looks beyond a client's press release to see what is occurring. A person who is committed to pretending that life is fine may be unintentionally secretive or misleading. Although patrons want tarot readers to be accurate, they are sometimes afraid of what might be revealed. They want the reader to tell them everything — but to ignore any inconsistencies between their beliefs and habits.

A client who had a serious illness consulted me about its emotional and spiritual causes. I saw clairvoyantly that his lifestyle was in direct conflict with his desire to be well. Inwardly, a significant part of him was tired of life and wanted to die. He sought help from medical practitioners and natural therapists and both made a difference to his state of being but the underlying issues persisted.

During this process, he consulted me four times to check whether his desire for well-being was in harmony with his life. Each time, I noticed the subtle incongruence (namely, that he was depressed by thoughts of the life ahead of him). To his credit, he began the painstaking process of adjusting his thinking. With the aid of doctors and natural therapists, plus an occasional visit to a clairvoyant to monitor his attitude, he reversed his 'terminal' condition. I was glad I didn't collude with him by turning a blind eye to what he didn't want to see. Otherwise, I'd have been unable to assist him in his quest for good health.

The change occurred when he accepted that his choices could shape his direction. A good friend gave him various books at the rate of one a week. These ranged from biographies of great artists to gardening books. They offered potential interests he could pursue when his health was restored and he gradually became motivated to live longer. I saw that having someone in his life who wanted him to survive and to thrive, along with a few new creative pursuits, were sufficient to inspire healing.

Giving Distance Readings

Sometimes students run out of friends, work colleagues and neighbours to read for when building tarot skills. Occasionally, former students from introductory courses return to repeat a course just to meet a new group of like-minded people. To widen the circle of available people to practise readings on, consider distance readings. These include readings by phone, Skype, Facetime, Slack, Zoom, WeChat and other apps.

While some prefer being seated face to face with a tarot reader for the encounter, the surroundings and the privacy, others enjoy the convenience of distance readings. A distance reading can save hours fighting traffic, car parking fees and road tolls. Instead, it's possible to sip tea or coffee by the fire in the living room at home, knowing a recording of the session will arrive via email within a day.

Some of my clients close the office door for a 'telephone meeting' during a busy working day. Sometimes, I have to pause while a colleague interrupts the reading with an urgent question for the client. One client who is on the road most of the day parks his car on the side of a highway or in a shopping centre car park at the appointment time. Early one evening, a busy executive took her appointment in the back seat of a hire car, as she headed for the airport for an international flight.

The drawbacks of distance readings include demanding toddlers who want parental attention. I suggest parents make appointments after bedtime or on days when someone can look after the young ones.

One of the benefits of distance readings is made clear when people need a series of sessions over a short period. When Brett and Celia were looking to buy a house, the market was hot and sometimes properties didn't make it to the open house on weekends. Celia's first phone reading was to narrow down their preferred neighbourhoods. Two weeks later, she had a Skype reading to see if they might be successful at two forthcoming auctions. Her next reading was to restart their search after becoming disheartened. Her final reading was in person, where I was able to describe some of the rooms and the layout of the home they'd eventually purchase. She found that home in a neighbouring suburb three weeks later and they settled in a few months afterwards.

Visual people prefer to see the reader during the session. Traditionally they have avoided telephone readings but Skype and similar apps have provided a platform for distance sessions for them. A couple of years ago, a client was excited to see my office again during a distance reading. She had visited from Europe for a session the previous year and was happy to see on Skype that it was just as she had remembered. At her request, I swivelled my iPad to show her the laden lemon tree in the back garden outside my office window.

"Many more than last year," she said approvingly. After the reading concluded, I asked her to show me where she lived and she took her device outside and down to the end of the street to reveal the sandy shores of the Greek island. I was tempted to arrange a two-week house swap, as it was summertime in Greece.

Cleansing Between Clients

Friends and clients usually want tarot readings when they have significant issues or decisions to make. They are frequently tense or emotionally confused when they arrive and during the reading process, they can unconsciously release pent-up emotions into the environment. Therefore, it is wise to cleanse the workplace of these residual energies after clients have left. Otherwise, the reading space might develop a cold, uninviting energy which is repelling to clients and reader alike.

Just as a tradesperson maintains a clean personal workplace, tools and reputation, so too must a tarot reader. Forming positive habits early on helps support your energy reserves and a welcoming environment for guests. Maintaining fresh energy in the workspace requires a few simple steps.

Maintaining a Clean Personal Workspace

1. Keep a lighted candle burning during tarot readings. Fire helps to break up unwanted psychic and emotional energy. An open fire in a fireplace usually restores the energy balance to a room very quickly. Make sure the flame is safe.

2. Open the windows at every opportunity between readings to allow fresh air to pass through the room. Fresh air sweeps away undesirable energy. Obviously, if the outside temperature is -10°, this technique is inadvisable.

3. Once a month, put a bowl of water in the room to absorb negative energy and replace the water daily for five days. You can disguise the water by placing it in a vase with flowers.

4. Having restored the workplace, it's also vital to cleanse yourself. This can be done by sitting beside an open fire, swimming in the sea or a pool. Even sitting beside the sea (sea breeze), having a bath, taking a long walk or gardening can have a purifying effect. These methods include the four elements (as shown by the four suits of the minor arcana), so one of them is likely to appeal to you.

5. Regular meditation helps restore internal balance and centre you. Remaining centred is mandatory when helping clients resolve their personal issues.

6. It is advisable to use some form of spiritual protection before commencing a reading, as you don't always know what you are dealing with in terms of energy. Some readers surround themselves with white light, ensuring it covers the top of their head and goes under the soles of their feet. Others mentally ask for protection before they begin.

7. Burning incense or smudge sticks can also break up adverse energy in a workplace. Smudge sticks are dried herbs, such as lavender, sage or rosemary, bound together with cotton; they are set alight and the smoke from them penetrates the room. An average smudge stick is about fifteen cm long and you burn it for ten minutes then immerse the glowing tip in water to extinguish it. You might cough and splutter when using a smudge stick but they are very effective.

8. Some tarot readers prefer to use an oil burner in their workplace. Pure essential oils such as rosemary, lavender or sage can be used to cleanse the room without the side effects of smoke, which needs to be dispersed. Oil burners can be a problem if you spill or overpour the oil as you are about to sit down to a reading. I use orange oil. When I slip and pour ten drops instead of three into the burner, it's like giving a reading in an orange grove.

When tarot readers don't cleanse their workplaces, they risk problems with their physical health. Absorbing detrimental psychic and emotional energy can eventually weaken them, although the physical health difficulties vary from reader to reader, according to predisposed weaknesses. Some readers suffer from increased asthma or poor sleeping patterns, while others unexpectedly crave sugar, chocolate, coffee or worse.

Accuracy and Confidentiality

For accuracy in the reading process, avoid shortcuts when reading for friends or strangers, including:

- hastily using one-card cuts for substantial questions.

- reading over a glass of wine at dinner with friends.

- attempting to impress strangers with your abilities when out socialising.

- reading for someone when another person is within earshot.

Do avoid passing comment on other readers. Unless you were present for a session given by another reader, it's not possible to accurately judge the reader or the methods employed. This is also true for card layouts. If you are not present when someone gives a reading, your perspective of the process is limited to textbook card meanings. In the moment, it's possible to find a unique and accurate meaning for a set of cards in a layout that are not obvious from a distance.

The process of building confidence and improving one's working knowledge of the tarot comes with practice, so try to give readings to friends, acquaintances, work colleagues and strangers at every opportunity, to build skills. The act of doing this can assist with learning if time is taken to reflect on each reading afterwards. Theory is fundamental, whereas applied concepts build a whole range of practical skills, including how to tell someone their desired goal is unlikely to be achieved or that life has different plans from their current goals. Students who have learned from books, with limited practical skills, often don't fare well during tarot assessments. They lack the underlying confidence that comes from giving dozens of readings to friends and strangers.

Sometimes, life has more rewarding plans for a person than current hopes, dreams and wishes. Being focused on goals is key to achieving them but being open to better opportunities can sometimes lead to surprising outcomes. In a recent reading, a client explained how five years previously she had asked about a love interest, only to be told about another potential partner. She left that reading feeling dejected. But when the predicted man arrived, she was ready to explore this new opportunity.

"The previous man left after three months, as you told me he would. I didn't give any thought to the other man you described until recently when he arrived on my doorstep wearing the felt hat you described in your reading. We've been seeing each other for a few months but when I saw that hat, I dug out your recording. You described his nature, a few of his interests and even his dog. I'd like to ask about us in the future and this time I want good news."

A reader can't engineer results. Fortunately, the news was encouraging.

If a reader looks far enough ahead, peering past the person's present winter, it's possible to glimpse another unique summer ahead. Without disregarding current struggles, it's vital to be able to describe some positive opportunities ahead for a person. This can help an individual recognise an opening when it is presented. Summers eventually follow winters. Knowing what the next summer will look like can reignite courage and hope for the future, with confidence that effort now will bear fruit later.

Clients need to know that what is said during a reading remains confidential. To this end, the names and details about any person included in the examples in this book have been changed to protect their identities. I sometimes change the gender and other details when using a real-life example to illustrate a card meaning.

Confidentiality means not talking about clients' issues to close friends, family members or in online posts. The exception might be discussing a reading with a supervisor without naming or identifying the person you're talking about. Sometimes a supervisor can help a less experienced reader to deal with issues that arise from clues gleaned during a tarot reading.

Information that provokes an emotional reaction in a reader might include details about domestic violence, broken relationships due to drug addiction or betrayal, homelessness, shared parenting after a divorce or criminal activities. It's essential to unpack these triggering incidents with a counsellor or a more experienced reader, to better understand personal reactions and how these responses might affect clarity during a reading. If a reader doesn't process emotionally provocative incidents, there is a risk of reducing sensitivity, resulting in reduced intuitive awareness.

Being a tarot reader involves being sensitive to the needs of others and this sensitivity can make readers vulnerable to emotional overload from time to time. This is one reason that psychic cleansing is an essential ritual for practising readers.

When Denton arrived for a reading, he seemed panicked. A soft-natured man in his twenties, he spoke with an urgency that made me wonder if something had recently triggered him. His story unfolded to reveal he'd had the month from hell after a profoundly challenging year.

Denton worked in a psychiatric wing in a major hospital, mostly in a locked ward.

Patients often arrived accompanied by police officers, usually after lashing out at strangers in public places. These individuals need drug tests and clinical assessments. Sometimes they could not be assessed immediately and remained on the ward for several days. Denton had been physically attacked four times in twelve months and one of his co-workers had been stabbed to death two weeks before he arrived for his reading.

"I don't feel safe anymore. We've asked management what they plan to do about our security and they have no plans to change anything. It's unbelievable. The people making decisions about our safety work in comfortable offices far away from the ward. I'm furious that they don't care. I don't want to go to work. I need to find a new job."

"Have staff been offered counselling to deal with the loss of their co-worker?" I asked.

"No."

"So let me be clear here. You work in mental health and the person in charge of mental health in the whole state, hasn't thought to offer you support for working in a violent workplace?"

"That's right."

"How can I support you today?" I asked, and he burst into tears. Part of me wanted to suggest that he find a lawyer and commence a class action suit against the upper management but that would have to wait. Denton needed support to unpack the emotional trauma of a violent workplace and the recent murder of a co-worker. After that reading, I needed a deep cleanse, as I had spent an hour steeped in Denton's fear, grief and anger at the injustice at work. He had every right to feel angry and upset. It was my job to witness those feelings with sensitivity. To ensure objectivity, I re-set myself before welcoming my next client.

Improving Clarity by Reading Reversed Cards

To allow for life's shades of grey, it is vital to include reversed cards in readings. Using only upright cards limits the subtleties of insightful interpretations. Having no reversed cards in a deck can also lead to inaccuracy when answering yes/no questions. Some practitioners suggest life is difficult enough without adding reversed cards but this is based on the assumption that all reversed cards are more detrimental than upright cards.

Some cards that are more positive reversed than upright include:

- all the fives, including The Hierophant
- the Eight, Nine and Ten of Swords
- The Devil

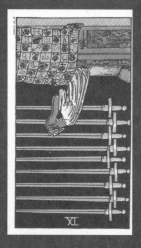

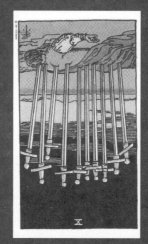

Cards that are more positive reversed than upright

Cards that are still encouraging, even when reversed include:

- The High Priestess
- The Star
- The Sun
- The World

Cards that are still encouraging, even when reversed

The Tower is an exception in that it is sometimes less serious in its effects when reversed than upright. This is a card for sudden, unexpected change that can be shocking. Often the chaos found in the reversed card is happening to someone else when this card appears reversed. A retrenchment thinning out office colleagues but not directly affecting your job is an example. Although you'll lose some sleep and tiptoe around at work for a few weeks, you're still employed. While former colleagues are searching for new jobs, you're left grieving their loss and wondering how many more jobs might be at risk in the coming months.

The argument that readings are more helpful when all the cards are all upright overlooks their use for reflecting how circumstances have been in clients' lives, how they are presently and how the future looks. If an individual is entering a long personal winter, being told ahead of time allows that person to prepare. This is even more significant when a country is entering a financial winter. During the global financial crisis, I read for many small business owners who desperately wanted to be told that business would pick up in a few months. However, it simply wasn't true.

Had I suggested this, they might have left feeling unrealistically assured. This confidence might have led them to splurge their last available funds, or even borrowing money to invest in advertising that wasn't going to work. Depleting reserves of cash can be detrimental to any business, especially when the immediate future is not bright.

When the buying public is fearful about recession, retrenchments and not being able to pay their bills, they usually close their wallets tight until the fear subsides. A business owner who anticipates a period of slow sales can trim stock levels, keep overheads low and postpone expansion plans until spring arrives. Telling clients everything will be fine to make them temporarily feel better is irresponsible in these circumstances.

If a financial winter is approaching, it is essential to warn the client about what to expect. It is equally vital to look ahead and see what is likely to happen beyond the restricted period. Describing the personal spring ahead can provide reassurance for the individual to do what is necessary to keep business afloat until the next upswing.

The secret to knowing the reversed meanings for each card is this: a reversed card suggests the client is struggling to master the card's lesson. To avoid feeling frustrated or overwhelmed, it usually benefits the person to return to the previous upright card (in the same suit, for minor arcana) to master the particular challenge it contains.

Toby's level of enjoyment drops when he struggles with a new and unfamiliar sequence of chords and notes during a piano lesson. He begins to lose confidence and becomes impatient with himself. If the teacher pushes him through the process, he might feel overwhelmed. If he's a swords student, it's likely he'll begin to inwardly criticise himself, his lack of practice or his fingering technique.

Before he abandons his piano lessons, the teacher asks him to stop for a moment and return to playing a piece she knows he can play with ease. As he plays a favourite piece of music, his confidence bounces back and his fingers begin to regain their dexterity. When she feels that he is ready, Toby's teacher encourages him to attempt the difficult piece again.

This is how it is with the tarot, too. If a person is struggling to master the lesson of the Seven of Wands, he or she needs to return to the Six of Wands to rebuild confidence and familiarity with the wands process before returning to the Seven.

Continuing with the piano analogy, learning each tarot card meaning is like learning the notes on a piano keyboard. When you need to find one or every D note on a keyboard, you know where to look for them. In tarot terms, you learn to recognise cards and distinguish between the Ace of Swords and the Ace of Cups.

Next in piano study, we learn scales. The notes in a scale are like the cards (ace to king) of a tarot suit. So, when playing in the key of G, it's possible to know which notes fit harmonically into the song. Then we learn chords. Chords are groups of notes that blend together to form a rich, full sound. Chords are card layouts. A reader might use a three-card layout or a seven-card spread to answer a question.

More experienced piano students learn to read music so they can play songs or scores from sight. In tarot terms, this is like reading a layout and interpreting the significance of each card in combination with the other cards in the spread. Just as a piece of music has a mood, a tempo and a theme, so too does each tarot layout.

Eventually, Toby learns to play a complete piece of music, a whole song or several songs. In tarot terms, this is like giving a complete tarot reading. Each card has a specific meaning in a particular layout and several layouts make up a reading. A full tarot reading is like a whole concert event. Like a live music experience, clients usually want to listen to it again. That's why recordings are essential. Using the manuscript as a guide, the musician can act on inspiration or intuition for a unique interpretation of the song. An experienced tarot reader can smooth out the highs and lows in a reading to offer consistency and ensure a warm, positive experience for each client. When you see a more experienced reader, you're paying for skills developed over years of readings.

Learning basic card meanings is essential but these definitions are not always helpful during a reading. It's necessary to step back and see the whole layout to decide how each card fits with the others to form one complete picture.

In the 1980s, I visited an art gallery in London to see an exhibition of Claude Monet paintings. Enormous canvases were positioned around the room and unwittingly, I stood too close to each painting to see it clearly. I was so close that all I could see was dots and brush strokes. Disappointed, I decided to leave. As I reached the exit, I turned to glimpse the room one last time and was stunned by the beauty of the huge paintings. At that distance, I was surrounded by the subtle hues of glorious gardens captured in soft sunlight. I stood transfixed; by stepping back, it suddenly made sense.

People consult tarot readers and clairvoyants to have someone who is objective peer into their lives. Readers are hopefully at a distance where they can see what has happened, events that are currently unfolding and what is likely to occur in the future. Reading upright and reversed cards helps clarify the picture the reader presents to clients. Hopefully, this image includes the blacks, the whites and all the shades of grey.

The Temperance card reversed, for instance, suggests an individual is unable to see the big picture at the moment. The path ahead is obscured. If the person returns to the upright Death card (although it's not necessarily on the table during the reading) the lesson of the Death card is to surrender to change and release what is no longer relevant for progress. This yielding process allows life to clear the path ahead so the Temperance lesson can be more readily mastered. By gracefully allowing change (the Death card), it's possible to glimpse life's bigger picture (Temperance). When seeing the rewarding consequences of decisions, it's easier to accept change in the present.

The lesson of each card is supported by the knowledge and understanding of all the preceding cards in that suit. If it's a major arcana card, it's reinforced by all previous major arcana cards. To use a construction analogy, the walls of a house rely on a solid foundation. When these walls are fully braced, they can support the roof.

Reading with reversed cards is necessary to provide accurate answers to yes/no questions. Reversed cards in the answer position or the outcome position usually give a *no* answer. Remember that the following cards are more positive when reversed.

- Five of Wands, Five of Cups, Five of Swords and Five of Pentacles.

- The Devil.

- Eight or Nine of Swords.

There can be considerable pressure for a reading to be right.

- "Is it wise to purchase this house?"

- "Will my son be sentenced to jail time at the end of his trial?"

- "If I stay on at work, will the company be able to afford to pay my superannuation when I retire in four years?"

- "Is it better to leave work now, while the company can still afford to pay me my entitlements?"

These are important questions that deserve full, accurate answers.

Students sometimes complain that remembering reversed card meanings is difficult. However, this method only requires that readers recall the upright meanings of each card. Just be aware that the client has to return to the previous card to build confidence and refocus before attempting to learn the lesson of the current reversed card. It helps to know what every card looks like so it's easier to picture, for example, the upright Eight of Cups when the reversed Nine of Cups appears in a layout.

If reversed Seven of Wands is the answer to a question about starting a new business, it means the person can benefit from returning to the Six of Wands to enjoy a period of stability by clearly focusing on personal goals before tackling any other challenges. The Seven of Wands reversed shows a person struggling with overwhelming obstacles. To avoid being crushed by oppressive demands and burdens, it is necessary to return to the Six of Wands, rest a moment and enjoy some stability before pursuing additional challenges. This is sometimes difficult for fiery individuals, who are easily bored and find routines stifling rather than reassuring. In any piece of music, there are rest periods between the notes to give the music context. If the notes follow each other without rests, it taxes the listener's mind to make sense of the cacophony.

If the Hermit reversed is the answer to a relationship question, it suggests the person is unable to muster sufficient strength to reflect on present relationship circumstances. It is beneficial to return to the upright Strength card and rediscover personal courage to face relationship issues. It's useful to think about one's actions, reactions and desires for the relationship. This reflection allows time to explore different choices and move forward with increased awareness.

Reversed Aces return to the upright ten cards of the same suit. For example, an Ace of Wands reversed indicates being unable to start new projects because of too many oppressive burdens. These might include not having enough energy, money or foresight to pursue one's goals. In returning to the Ten of Wands, it's possible to recognise the need to delegate some responsibilities before beginning a new project.

An Ace of Swords reversed implies confused thinking that delays planning. This sometimes suggests gaps in logic, memory lapses or inability to clearly see the significant details of a project. The Ace of Swords reversed suggests benefiting from returning to the mental restrictions of the Ten of Swords. It's easy to see how so many swords (or alternatives) can lead to confusion. Choices don't always simplify situations. Sometimes, they increase problems.

The Fool reversed indicates hasty or foolish action. It can also highlight a lack of trust within or relying too much on others for advice. Although it can be beneficial to take counsel from valued friends, ultimately, it's vital to find time to reflect on the long-term consequences of personal decisions and actions.

The Fool reversed indicates a need to return to the upright World card. This allows an individual to remember their personal place in the world. Seeing oneself in the context of a much bigger picture can clarify what choices and actions are appropriate. A different perspective can highlight opportunities and reduce self-centredness.

Kings reversed can signify the shadow side of that king or a need to return to the maturity of the upright knight of the same suit, whereas the queens reversed can return to the upright page of their suit. This means a reversed Queen of Wands can highlight the undesirable qualities of her suit or suggest a return to the immaturity of the Page of Wands. Often, reversed court cards reflect a person's unfavourable qualities (for example, immaturity) being uppermost. The reversed pages suggest very young children physically or emotionally immature adults.

A reversed knight can regress to the qualities of the page of the same suit but reversed pages don't revert to a previous card. Sometimes children act younger than their age when tired, overwhelmed or under prolonged pressure. In these instances, a 14-year-old reversed page might throw a tantrum, hurl a broken toy out a window or burst into tears and run off to another room.

Sometimes, a tarot reader has an unrealistic desire to provide good news to clients, wanting to be an optimistic mystic. Life isn't always that simple. Sometimes, explaining to clients that current plans won't work, helps them adapt their approach and pursue more realistic outcomes. Ignoring threats or stumbling blocks is one step short of removing any cards that might make clients feel uncomfortable. These might include Death, The Tower, The Devil, the Three, Four, Five, Eight, Nine and Ten of Swords or other challenging cards, such as the Five of Cups and the Five, Seven and Nine of Wands. And that's only one step away from reading with playing cards, leaving all the spiritual lessons of the major arcana out of the equation. A balanced reading includes both the supportive paths ahead and the temptations and distractions from those routes.

It might be necessary for people to undergo discomfort, pain and sorrow because it helps them to grow. In London many years ago, I had to give a client some bad news about a raft of investments he held. It was well into a recession that had begun the previous year and it was crucial for him to understand that the worst of the financial winter was still to come. After the reading, he hugged me for being the first reader of five to clearly outline what he could expect. If he was swimming in a cold ocean and I had assured him that the shore was only 100 metres away, he'd give one final burst of effort to reach the sanctuary of the sand. However, if the shore was actually 760 metres away, that final push might have worn him out before he reached safety.

When confused about the meaning of a reversed card, adding another to the card in question sometimes clarifies the situation. Occasionally, it is necessary to engage the client in conversation to establish what is going on in order to apply the correct meaning to the reversed card. This is not fishing for information but a chance to give the individual a personally tailored description. For example, when describing the reversed King of Swords during a recent general reading, I asked the client if the man represented by the card might be in her work or home environment. I described him as a person who is full of ideas and plans but not practical in making his intentions real.

Her response was this: "The only flaky man I know would have to be my husband, Geoff, God bless him."

It's a gross oversimplification to suggest that all reversed cards have adverse meanings. Aside from The Devil and all the fives, which are more positive inverted, most reversed cards, as discussed, simply mean that to master the challenge of the current card (present situation) it is necessary to return to the previous card and focus on that lesson before proceeding.

The Sun card, however, is optimistic upright and reversed. The only difference is that the person might be more aware of the pressure to perform when the card appears reversed. The reversed World indicates success but not a lasting situation. It's likely to be followed by a great challenge and its equivalent success. The High Priestess reversed indicates a reconnection with friends or a widening of a person's social circle after a period of reflection.

It is a reader's job to suggest what is necessary to master the current challenge. A metaphor for the reversed cards and the opportunities contained within them is that it is like repeating a year at school. If a person does not successfully complete grade five, there is an opportunity to repeat the year to master the course content instead of being thrust prematurely forward while struggling to catch up.

The reversed cards take this process one step further. If a person is not coping with grade five, there is an opportunity to return to grade four and revisit previous challenges successfully completed where the work is easier. This provides confidence to approach grade five afresh to master its specific lessons.

While court cards can represent people, a reversed court card does not necessarily describe a reversed life. It can indicate a passing set of circumstances. An upright king or queen might become temporarily reversed after a serious setback, such as an emotional, financial or career disappointment. It's possible that the reversal is reflecting current circumstances and, in time, the same court card will appear upright in a subsequent reading.

A King of Cups who has produced dozens of paintings and held a range of exhibitions at art galleries might become depressed for a period and sink into becoming a reversed king. When his malaise lifts and he is inspired to be creative again, he'll usually appear as an upright king in his readings. A reversed Queen of Swords I met at a party some years ago seemed anxious, agitated and slightly chaotic but when I met her a year later, she was talkative, enthusiastic and focused. It turned out her mother had died two months before the original meeting and she was in the middle of dividing assets between warring siblings. She was stressed and grieving her loss, so she wasn't at her best in the first meeting.

On a lighter note, I telephoned a Queen of Wands friend recently and asked how she was feeling. "Reversed. That's how I'm feeling. Bloody reversed," she answered, as we both laughed. I guess we all have 'reversed' days.

As these examples suggest, sometimes, people are simply temporarily reversed due to immediate circumstances. However, if there has been significant trauma or chaos earlier in life, a person might become reversed for years or even decades at a time. The next chapter offers some tips to turn a reversed life upright again.

Tips for Turning a Reversed Life Upright

Some people endure such difficulties early in life that many of the desirable characteristics of their personality type are frustrated or twisted. The process of resolving past issues and turning undesirable habits around requires courage, time, effort and persistence. Worthwhile goals are rarely easy but often provide steady rewards for the effort required.

If a wands person exhibits only unfavourable traits, the result might be loneliness as this individual is likely to have fought with friends and family members who eventually retreat to safety. This person could also suffer the debilitating results of sports injuries or reckless behaviour, such as a car accident resulting from driving too fast.

A pessimistic cups individual is likely to feel stuck, creatively frustrated and might eventually turn to alcohol or medications to take the edge off life's sharp corners. These people often quietly blame others for their predicaments while hiding from opportunities that could lead them back into authentic, creative and meaningful lives.

Emotionally damaged swords people tend to struggle with anxiety and mental chaos, sometimes preferring to gossip than participate. These individuals are usually surrounded by half-completed projects because they are better at talking about their plans than acting on them. Sometimes swords people overthink situations, perceive too many possible obstacles, eventually becoming overwhelmed and giving up.

Discouraged pentacles people tend to be stingy, even in retirement. They form rigid habits and feel resentful when these are interrupted. Sometimes, they use their wealth to control others, including the annual cheque to family members given after they have attended a family Christmas or a Thanksgiving lunch. Some cynical pentacles individuals leave their entire estates to one child to punish other siblings.

A reversed life for a wands person:

- Constant arguments, aggression and fights.

- Road rage.

- Impatience at having to wait in line.

- Intolerance for crowds and having to share with others.

- A constant sense of competitiveness with friends, colleagues and family members.

- Furious temper tantrums or doing or saying things that are later regretted.

- Friends, family or colleagues, fearing sudden outbursts and lacking trust, tend to walk on eggshells around these individuals.

- A range of short friendships that don't lead anywhere.

- Alienation from friends and family.

Creating an upright wands life:

- Exercise to release pent-up frustration.

- Chop wood, walk, pump iron, mow the lawn or clean the house to relieve stress or reduce frustration.

- Set achievable personal goals, plus reasonable rewards for when each task has been completed.

- Step outside and breathe deeply, while resisting the urge to punch someone.

- Lead the fight for a worthy cause. This might include organising demonstrations, generating publicity or coaching a sports team.

- For long-term benefits, grow a garden to remember that everything has its season.

- Learn to negotiate. Bullying others into submission doesn't usually inspire support and commitment.

- Get away to the country regularly. A weekend in nature, bushwalking, fishing trips or camping can restore patience and balance.

- Let go of unwinnable battles and fight those that offer a chance of victory.

A reversed life for a cups person:

- Difficulty forgiving and releasing the past.

- Bygone hurts linger like a persistent, damp fog.

- Feeling stuck while daydreaming or fantasising about escaping to a glorious new life.

- An overwhelming sense of longing for someone or something from the past, when life held more promise of happiness. If former potential was not achieved at that time, it's probably best to let it go.

- Feeling depressed and unmotivated by current opportunities.

- Feeling alone and not fully understood by anyone.

Creating an upright cups life:

- Consciously restrict habitual reminiscing or regretting past events to ten minutes per day. Cancel all other attempts to live in the past beyond that indulgent ten-minute period. Be deliberately mindful of this habit.

- Train the mind away from obsessive feelings and towards constructive thinking.

- Analysis can help make sense of feelings.

- Become deliberately and consciously aware of escaping from the drudgery of daily life into dreams and fantasy. A dream is not a plan; it's a pastime.

- To make changes, devise simple, manageable steps. Write them down and tick them off one by one as each step is completed.

- Take up creative pursuits that provide emotional nourishment. These might include writing, painting, gardening, learning a musical instrument, photography, fishing, surfing, sailing or a language, etc.

- Join a book club, a painting class or any group with a creative purpose.

- Make room each day for beauty, creativity and love.

- Get a puppy to siphon off the need to nurture others.

- Volunteer for a charity to help disadvantaged people.

A reversed life for a swords person:

- Surrounded by people who continually gossip.

- Feeling scattered and lacking real focus in life.

- Short-term jobs, friendships and relationships resulting from a low boredom threshold.

- Commencing courses, careers or even books but then rapidly moving on without completion, while gradually noticing that friends and colleagues are buying homes, new cars and taking expanded holidays because they have finished studies and secured well-paid jobs.

- Being easily swayed by interesting conversation and grandiose empty promises. Abandoning a long-term job, relationship or stable home on a whim because someone painted a picture of a fabulous life in another place, with nothing more than vivid, descriptive words.

- Being unable to sleep at night, trying to understand why someone has said what they have said. Allowing ideas or conversations to swirl restlessly around in the brain, unchecked.

- Once the enthusiasm has gone, plans becomes burdensome and less likely to eventuate.

Creating an upright swords life:

- Stop overthinking everything.

- Remember that words do not make deeds. Talking endlessly about a project is not the same as physically doing it.

- By constantly talking about a new idea, the energy and passion for the project are likely to dissipate. When excited by an inspiration, get in and do it.

- Learn to meditate. Stilling the mind is an escape from incessant, debilitating thinking.

- Remember that life doesn't always make sense. People aren't always logical.

- Learn something new. Complete a course in design, the history of architecture, website design, creative writing, political science or career-related studies. Learning new skills and subjects can distract the mind from aimless wandering or worse — the harmful thinking of self-criticism.

- Pick a subject and investigate it thoroughly.

A reversed life for a pentacles person:

- It feels like life is all work and no play.

- Past promises to leave an unrewarding job or lifestyle have gone unheeded, due to fear of change.

- Being a source of stability and financial abundance to family but feeling stifled by this restrictive obligation. There is more to life than getting and spending.

- Duties and responsibilities loom large every week, as personal dreams of a simpler life slip away unattended.

- Believing all that is needed for a happy life is 20 per cent more income, despite the fact that current income is much more than it once was. There is a dread of pedalling vigorously to achieve, while financially standing still.

- The risk of finally retiring from work and realising personal interests beyond work are non-existent. Retirement looms like a huge chasm, instead of appreciating the gift of time to explore hobbies and interests.

Creating an upright pentacles life:

- Take time every day to shift focus from money, stability and responsibilities and deliberately concentrate on playing and having some fun.

- Explore new ideas, concepts, conversations and ideas through books, attending talks and meetups, especially with people who have different values.

- Challenge resistance to fresh ideas, habits, people and experiences. New friends and behaviours might become old friends and familiar routines, eventually.

- Remember that the most valuable currency in life is time. It's impossible to renew this resource, so spend it wisely and appreciatively.

- Read books on investing, handling money and making money work for you.

- Establish constructive money habits to thrive, instead of constantly striving to meet financial goals.

- Join an investors' support group to explore investment trends, new markets and different ways to conduct business.

- Learning about different approaches to business can foster greater success.

- Mentor someone about the importance of making realistic plans, writing a budget and saving to invest in the long-term future.

- Be grateful daily. Gratitude has a beneficial effect on a person's mindset. Instead of a constant focus on what is lacking, concentrating on current opportunities and support can be liberating.

- Join a business association that raises money to help the local community to thrive.

- Add a few new constructive personal habits every year.

- Review individual possessions and let go of those no longer needed. Recycle belongings regularly.

A Range of Tarot Layouts

There are numerous layouts used to determine the past, the present and the future. Below are several easy spreads. Complicated layouts are unnecessary. The reader's task is to clarify the most likely outcome of unfolding events. Simple, straightforward layouts can assist with this process.

The One-Card Cut

A one-card cut is the simplest method for gleaning information quickly from the cards. It's a method preferred by tarot students when reading for themselves. Ordinarily, reading the cards for yourself is not recommended. However, this advice is rarely heeded, so simple one-card cuts are popular. In advanced tarot courses, I ask for a show of hands to get a sense of who agrees that it's unwise to read for yourself because you cannot be truly objective. All of the hands in the room are raised. I then ask who has read for themselves in the past thirty days and again, all of the hands are raised.

Simple, practical yes/no questions are suitable for one-card cuts. This is not the most accurate of readings, as only one card is used to give the whole answer. It is not recommended as a reading method for complicated or significant questions. Therefore, simple questions such as "Should I arrange an appointment with my hairdresser for next Wednesday?" are suitable, whereas "Will we be at war with _____ (name of country) in the next three months?" is too momentous a question to assess with a single-card cut.

The steps are as follows:

1. Briefly shuffle the pack, reversing the cards several times during the process using a twisting motion, like removing the lid from a jar.

2. Place the pack face down on the table and close your eyes.

3. While thinking of the question, cut the pack with your non-writing hand, turning the cards over to reveal the face of the card cut. Remember to turn cut cards over as a single unit, sideways, to ensure the card remains as it was (upright or reversed) when it was cut.

4. Study the card and relate it to the question you asked.

5. If this card doesn't make sense to you, slide it onto the table to reveal the card immediately beneath it. These two cards combine to answer your question. (Resist the temptation to slide fifteen cards from the top of the cut pack, one by one, until you arrive at a card perfectly suitable for your desired outcome.)

Avoid the urge to cut the cards for every minor decision you have throughout the day:

- Should I book a cab ahead of time?

- Should I ring Marianne before dinner tonight?

- Is it wise to cancel the newspaper?

- Am I asking a ridiculous number of pointless questions of the tarot today?

Two cuts for a decision between cereal or toast for breakfast is bordering upon addiction. It begs the final question: "Is it wise for me to stop asking trivial questions?"

However, there are times when a series of one-card cuts are worthwhile, as when Emily was about to set up practice as a professional reader, having given 120 readings and successfully completing her written and practical examinations. She wanted to know where best to advertise her services to maximise her returns. (There is an old saying in advertising that states: "Half of all advertising money is wasted but which half?")

Emily spent a week looking through printed and online magazines and websites before preparing a list of possible places to advertise. When she sat down to cut the cards her list contained six potential advertising sites. She cleared her mind and asked, "Is it wise for me to publicise my services in _____ this month?" for each of the six options.

The cards gave a clear *yes* to two of the six areas but indicated *no* to a free local newspaper that she felt sure was a worthwhile place to advertise. Emily advertised in the two places the cards had signalled *yes* and kept an eye on the newspaper that received a clear *no* to see why the cards declined it. At the end of the month, she was satisfied the cards had been accurate because it had rained heavily on three of the four delivery days for her weekly newspaper that month. As wet newspapers usually don't get read, Emily knew that advertising in it would have been a waste of money.

Emily's question to the cards was precise, focusing the marketing period to one month, as her budget was limited. She laid the groundwork, researching the advertising possibilities before sitting down to cut the cards. This is an example of the powerful combination of logic, intuition and practical application. Logic and intuition are beneficial partners.

Prepare the question carefully to avoid an ambiguous conclusion. The clearest questions receive the most straightforward answers. If Emily had asked generally if it was wise to advertise in the local weekly newspaper, she might have wasted three out of the first four weeks of advertising money.

A substantial question deserves a full reading, not a one-card cut. It warrants an independent reader with a full layout. Sometimes, that can be challenging. The moment you find a suitable reader, she has booked a removalist for the next weekend because she's moving a thousand km away without any intention of returning.

I recently found myself urgently cutting the cards when I was due to give a pure clairvoyance reading. I always meditate before these readings and meet the client in meditation. This person can ask two questions via email before the session and I ask the client's higher self these questions during the meditation. I record the answers before the person arrives. I prefer to do this when the individual isn't present, so I'm not feeling pressured to speak while gleaning information. I can take my time and explore the nuances of each question, if necessary.

Several years ago, I gave two of these readings on one day and both clients had the same first name: Karen. As I often work with only first names, I mistakenly met the second Karen in meditation prior to the first Karen's reading. Basically, I asked the second client's higher self the first client's questions. To remedy this, I now request a head-and-shoulders photo of each client who books a pure clairvoyance reading.

Recently, two clients, a mother and daughter, booked pure clairvoyance readings and sent me a single photo with both of them. Twenty minutes before the first reading, I sat down to meditate and realised I didn't know which person in the photo was my first client. I phoned them but the call went unanswered. I didn't want to begin my meditation after the client arrived, as it would set me back twenty minutes and my day was fully booked. I felt anxious and frustrated that such an oversight might derail my day.

I shuffled my tarot deck and using a one-card cut, asked if the person on the left in the photo was Lesley. The cards indicated this was correct. To test it, I then asked if the person on the right in the image was Lesley and the cards indicated no. I then asked if Lesley was going to arrive for the first reading and the cards again indicated yes.

It was a stressful start to my meditation, so reaching a calm, centred stillness took longer than usual. I was still in a meditative state, when a voice called out from the waiting room, "Hello!"

I closed my energy-field down and opened my office door to see the woman who appeared on the left-hand side of the photo standing in the doorway.

"Welcome. Come in. Which one are you?" I asked and was relieved when she confirmed that she was Lesley. I returned to my meditation and retrieved the information to answer her questions before we began the main part of the reading. Although the day had begun with a wobble, the one-card cuts ensured I didn't run late all day.

The Seven–Card Layout

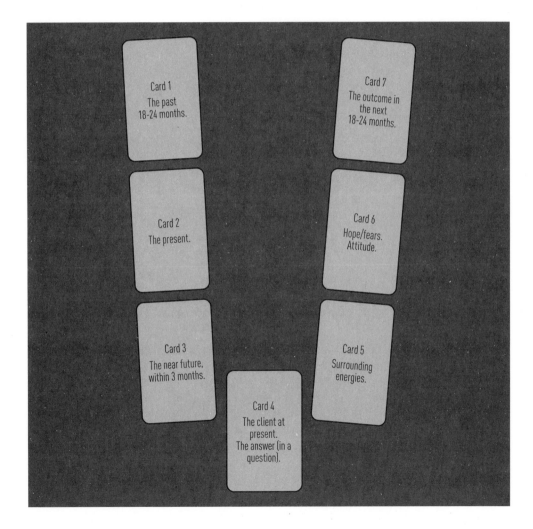

This simple layout can be used for general readings or for specific questions.

The client shuffles the pack, inverting (reversing) the cards occasionally.

The reader instructs the client to place the cards, one at a time, into three piles on the table in a left to right motion. The reader demonstrates this process for the client while giving instructions. The purpose for this is for clients to touch every card in the deck and to give the pack a thorough shuffle. When the client has done this, the reader combines the three piles into a single pack again.

The reader slides the cards out into a line across the table, from which the client selects seven random cards. When selecting cards, the person's eyes are shut and he or she uses their non-writing hand. If it is a general reading, the client does not have to think of anything specific when selecting cards. The reader counts each card aloud after it has been selected so clients know when to stop.

If it is a question layout, the client concentrates upon an agreed topic while selecting the cards. It is important for the reader to know the clear question being asked before the client selects cards. This helps to avoid ambiguous queries or several questions bundled together as one. The client might want to ask about a pending promotion, being offered another position in the company or if it's wise to leave the organisation and pursue a career elsewhere. This is too much for one clear question and is best broken down into three separate enquiries. Combining questions or topics usually decreases accuracy.

An example of separating one issue into several questions occurred when Luca asked about buying a home. House prices had been out of her range for several years, yet she managed to save a substantial deposit. With the local real estate entering a dip, she wasn't sure whether to buy immediately or wait, in the hope of affording a better home in six months' time. I separated her possible questions into the following:

- Is it wise to purchase a home in the next three months?

- It is better to wait six months or longer before buying a property?

- Is it wise to wait for a year or more before committing to a property purchase?

- If I wait, will I be able to afford a home in my desired area?

Place the cards on the table in the order they are selected.

CARD 1. **The past:** Represents events within the last two years.

CARD 2. **The present:** Four weeks either side of today

CARD 3. **The near future:** Usually up to three months into the future.

CARD 4. **The client** or the **answer to a question:** In a general reading, this represents the client at present and events currently occurring. In a question layout, this card signifies the answer to the question. Consequently, it is read last, despite being the fourth card.

CARD 5. **Surrounding energies:** This shows the people or circumstances around the client or relevant to the question at present.

CARD 6. **Attitude:** The client's hopes and fears are shown in this position. In a question layout, the hopes and fears are directly related to the question.

CARD 7. **Outcome:** The results of current circumstances up to twenty-four months from the present moment. In a specific question layout, this card represents the end result of the question.

The Action and Consequences Layout

This layout is designed for people who want to know what has caused or contributed to their present circumstances and what they can do to influence a likely outcome. Five cards are selected while thinking of a statement such as, "my current job" or "my relationship with Karl."

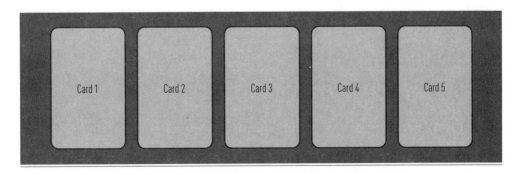

CARD 1. **The cause of current circumstances:** This card can represent an issue linked to beliefs that have contributed to circumstances.

CARD 2. **The present circumstances:** This card relates to the job or relationship under consideration.

CARD 3. **The outcome of current circumstances:** This card suggests a possible outcome if no deliberate actions are taken to alter the existing direction.

CARD 4. **Action needed for an alternate desired result:** If a person wants a different objective, new choices and actions may be required.

CARD 5. **New outcome:** The outcome resulting from the action taken in card number four. Using a different approach to solve a problem occasionally results in a changed outcome. This is not to imply that we have complete control over all events in our lives but that continuously doing the same thing while expecting different results is unreasonable.

This layout is designed to emphasise there is some control over personal destiny by highlighting the consequences of individual actions before decisions are made or steps taken. Examining some of the causes of current circumstances puts the situation into perspective before deciding upon a course of action. Being forewarned of an unwanted outcome while there is still time to avert it provides an opportunity to carefully revise plans.

Remember that some situations are completely beyond one's control. Sometimes, people are confronted by immense personal suffering. This layout does not address those intense situations but is more suitable for everyday issues, such as travel, job changes, study or relocation.

The Horoscope Layout

After shuffling the cards thoroughly, the person selects twelve cards, eyes closed, using the non-writing hand. It's best for the reader to count each card aloud so the client doesn't become confused.

Selected cards are placed, with the first card at the 1 position on the dial (see image below for card positions). Each subsequent card is placed into position as it is selected.

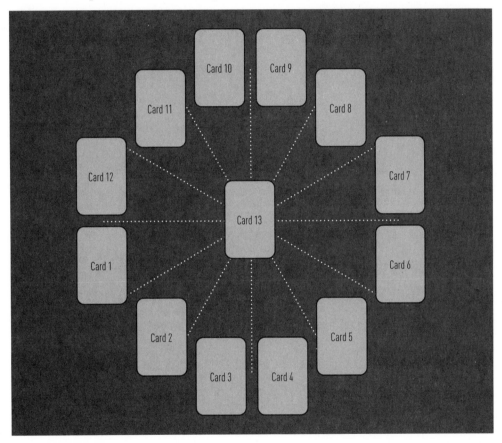

CARD 1. **Persona:** How the person presents him or herself to the world, as well as how others view this individual.

CARD 2. **Values:** Inner values as well as material attachments are shown here. This represents personal values, including self-worth.

CARD 3. **Communication:** This card shows the individual's ability to communicate with people in the home environment including neighbours, siblings and relatives. It also highlights communication with colleagues at work. Short trips might be indicated by certain cards here, including the Ace, Three or Eight of Wands, The Page of Swords, Temperance or The Chariot.

CARD 4. **Home environment:** The person's home or home feeling is accentuated here. It often relates to impressions of home from childhood. Mother and mother issues can also be represented here.

CARD 5. **Creativity:** The card in this position indicates creative energies available, as well as opportunities for self-expression and financial speculation. Children are also indicated here.

CARD 6. **Health, work and service:** This is not about career but highlights the person's day-to-day working environment. Physical and mental health and well-being are also shown here.

CARD 7. **Relationships:** This location accentuates what it is possible to learn from close friends regarding partnerships and relationships.

CARD 8. **Transformation:** Legacies, taxes, inner growth or metamorphosis and regeneration are all shown here. This area also highlights any potential for extreme change.

CARD 9. **Higher learning:** The focus here is on philosophy, longer journeys and adult learning and education.

CARD 10. **Career:** The individual's position in the world through career or public recognition and worldly achievements.

CARD 11. **Friends:** This card highlights the types of associations preferred as well as hopes and wishes. It also includes knowledge that strangers bring to this individual through meetings, books or digital media.

CARD 12. **Secrets:** This location deals with hidden fears and worries, along with sacrifices made for spiritual advancement.

CARD 13. **The year ahead:** This card is placed in the centre of the circle and represents the year ahead, in general terms.

The Three Generations Layout

The Three Generations Layout is useful when someone wants to glimpse the bigger picture, to see what patterns of behaviour and beliefs have been passed down through three generations of their family.

The reader needs to ask how many children the client has, prior to selecting two cards for each person involved in this layout. The card positions represent:

INDIVIDUAL	NEGATIVE TRAITS	POSITIVE TRAITS
Father	Card 1	Card 2
Mother	Card 3	Card 4
Client	Card 5	Card 6
Child one	Card 7	Card 8
Child two	Card 9	Card 10

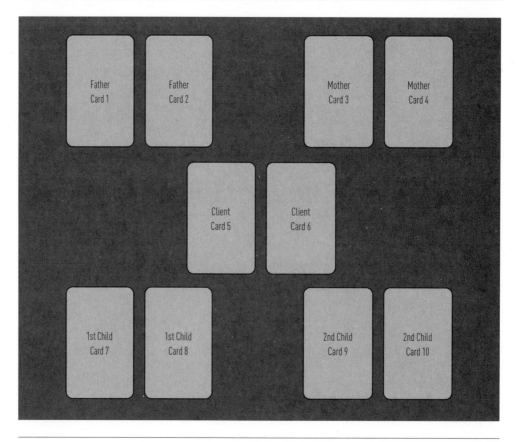

Two cards are selected for each individual. Please remember the positive and negative habits for each child are learned traits and not necessarily inherited characteristics. An additional card can be added to each of the children to see what might balance or assist any learned adverse habits.

Achieving a Goal Spread

Occasionally, a person is focused on a specific major goal and wants to clarify how to achieve that objective. It's possible to ask a range of questions using seven-card layouts but this takes a lot of time. Some clients are happy to invest an hour if they walk away with clarity about the path ahead. Others, however, have additional questions, such as:

- Do I need an outside investor to reach the next stage of my process?
- Is Ted a suitable person to partner with for this goal?
- It is possible to achieve my plans within two years?
- If so, which of the three options is best for me?
- Where is the strongest market for this product or service?

Using seven-card layouts, a reader usually needs two hours to answer questions about the path to the goal, plus the additional questions listed above. Long-term objectives that entail enormous investments of time and money often require a few sessions, especially when decisions made after a tarot reading can save time and costly mistakes. To shorten this process, I've designed a tarot layout that covers some fundamental aspects when pursuing major goals.

The client focuses on a specific target that he or she wants to achieve while choosing seven cards with eyes closed and using the non-writing hand. These cards are placed in a V-shape as they are selected.

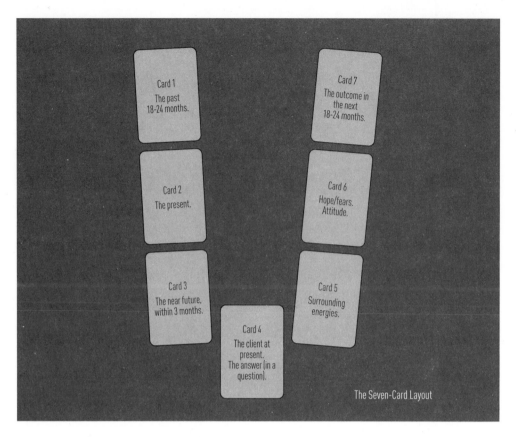

The Seven-Card Layout

CARD 1. Where the individual is in life presently.

CARD 2. The strengths the person has within for self-support in this quest.

CARD 3. Opportunities and people who are likely to provide assistance towards this objective (the reader can request up to three additional cards for this position, as more than one person might provide support for the client's endeavour).

CARD 4. What the person can achieve if he or she pushes ahead towards the goal.

CARD 5. People likely to resist the person's endeavours or circumstances that might provide opposition.

CARD 6. Inner obstacles to overcome in the process of achieving the desired goal.

CARD 7. How the person is likely to feel at the end of this process.

Designing Your Own Layouts

Designing a layout to suit personal needs is a relatively simple process. After identifying the information needed from a layout, it's possible to determine how many cards are necessary. Creating a layout to suit one's needs can be practical and rewarding.

An example of this might be the following. James is planning to travel to England to speak at a convention and sign copies of his latest book. He might ask four or five questions about the proposed trip using the seven-card layout or using a layout expressly designed for the issues involved.

These are some of the obvious questions James might ask about the planned trip:

- Will it be financially successful?

- Is it wise to visit England at the time currently planned?

- Will I feel content with the outcome upon my return home?

- What obstacles await me in the pursuit of my plans?

- What is the underlying spiritual lesson for me in attending this convention?

Instead of asking five individual questions, it's a simple process to design a layout to answer them all. James shuffles the pack and selects five cards. Their positions are as follows:

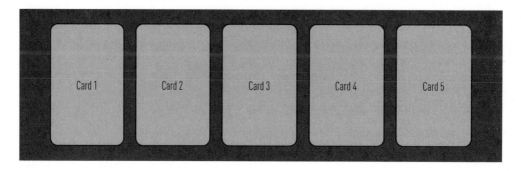

CARD 1. The financial aspects of the planned trip.

CARD 2. Whether it is wise to visit at the currently intended time.

CARD 3. How James will feel about the trip and the talk upon his return home.

CARD 4. The obstacles (if any) James can expect in this trip.

CARD 5. The underlying spiritual lesson in visiting England to deliver a talk at the convention.

It is practical that the reader decides how many cards need to be selected and what each position means before the client chooses any cards. It's hardly an effective reading if one decides after the cards have been selected that the best ones are about the client's relationship, while the challenging cards are focused on career.

The Three Issues Layout

One reader I know works in a shop where she gives fifteen-minute readings, which have to be clear and concise. She has designed a layout that answers the three basic concerns her clients have: relationship, career and financial matters. With these three issues in mind, a specifically designed layout might look like this:

The client shuffles the cards, cutting the pack and inverting the cards three or four times.

The reader then fans the cards across the table in a line, allowing the client to select six cards with their non-writing hand and eyes closed. When the client has selected six cards, the reader then asks for another three cards to be chosen, placing them in the order shown below.

The positions are as follows:

CARD 1. Current relationship circumstances.

CARD 2. Future relationship circumstances.

CARD 7. The underlying lesson for the client in relationships at present.

CARD 3. Current career circumstances.

CARD 4. Future career circumstances.

CARD 8. The underlying lesson for the client in their career at present.

CARD 5. Current financial circumstances.

CARD 6. Future financial circumstances.

CARD 9. The underlying lesson for the client regarding present finances.

This layout is designed for readings limited by time constraints. In a full one-hour reading, this kind of layout is unnecessary, as each area can be explored in greater depth through seven-card layouts.

The Seven-Year Cycle Layout

For people searching for a glimpse of the bigger picture, the seven-year cycle layout is useful for a partial or even a whole life reading. It is most useful when the client needs to know what period of their life is adversely affecting them presently. This layout can also be used with specific questions in mind, such as: "Which period of my life has most affected my attitudes to money?" or "What stage of my life has caused the most unresolved issues?" or "What time in my life does my fear of horses stem from?"

A word of caution: this reading is best done when the client is feeling optimistic. If a person is vulnerable or likely to take interpretations literally, the reading might mentally linger for years to come. It is worthwhile phrasing long-term predictions positively and to remind clients they have free will to shape outcomes. Every cloud has a silver lining and sometimes it's the reader's job to find it.

The client selects one card for each seven-year period of their life. That means one card for each seven-year period up to their present age and for, at most, seven years ahead. So, if Bradley sits down for a reading at thirty-six years of age, he will select six cards, taking him up to forty-two years of age.

Resist the temptation to read the remainder of the person's life, as the tarot is best suited to short-term readings. There are too many possibilities for change through the use of free will over longer periods.

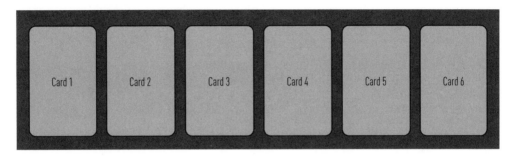

CARD 1. 0-7 years of age.

CARD 2. 7-14 years.

CARD 3. 14-21 years.

CARD 4. 21-28 years.

CARD 5. 28-35 years.

CARD 6. 35-42 years.

Essentially, Bradley wants to know which period of his life is affecting him most at present. The cards selected are listed below. Bradley accidentally selected two cards for the second position, thinking he had only one card in his hand. I usually include such an extra card for the sake of clarity. If a person repeatedly selects two cards at once, however, I repeat the instruction to select one card at a time.

Interpretation

CARD 1. 0-7 years: Temperance reversed

This period was chaotic and Bradley was unable to glimpse where he was heading as he grew to adulthood. Perhaps his home life contained a great deal of upheaval or he moved houses often in that first seven years. Temperance indicated that he had no clear vision of life ahead or direction before the age of seven.

CARD 2. 7-14 years: Knight of Wands and The Hermit reversed.

Filled with enthusiasm, Bradley was very active but unable to reflect upon his past actions in order to learn from them. The influence of a Sagittarian person is possible, as both Temperance and the Knight of Wands are cards for the sign of Sagittarius. Sagittarian's enjoy learning, travel, freedom, teaching and exploring the great outdoors. These people thrive on challenges and often possess natural leadership abilities.

The Hermit reversed suggests he probably avoided reflecting on his actions by keeping busy. As a result, he may have struggled with schoolwork, preferring sports and physical activities, instead.

CARD 3. 14-21 years: The Emperor reversed

Bradley exhibited poor discipline and might also have lacked helpful adult male role models. It's likely he was active, reckless and unable to pace himself to complete important tasks by their deadlines.

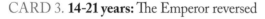

CARD 4. **21-28 years:** The Hanged Man reversed

This was a difficult period for Bradley, as he needed to stop and consider his past actions and decisions about life but he probably railed against this. The Hanged Man reversed suggests Bradley was restless but powerless to change his life. It was crucial for him to realise the need to clear away some of his emotional baggage and discover where he fit in and perhaps his true purpose.

CARD 5. **28-35 years:** Seven of Swords

Through this period, Bradley was hiding from life while attempting to control his destiny by using his mental strength. He was adaptable but did not reveal himself emotionally to people close to him.

CARD 6. **35-42 years:** King of Cups

Bradley is maturing into the King of Cups and he is emotionally available, self-disciplined and more likely to choose a creative, emotionally rewarding career. The chaos from his early years is behind him now and ahead there are opportunities that will emotionally satisfy him.

Before completing the reading, I suggested to Bradley the possible influence of people of three different astrological signs. These were Sagittarius (Temperance and the Knight of Wands), Virgo (The Hermit) and Aries (The Emperor). He confirmed that he has a sister who is a Sagittarian and his parents were a Virgo and an Aries.

Sample Tarot Readings with Interpretations

When a tarot reader presents information or news that is unexpected, it's often necessary to help clients understand what is being said using additional information. This involves requesting extra cards to help clarify parts of the reading or suggesting follow-up questions that might be helpful.

Claire sat down with a specific career question, expecting to have her hopes confirmed. She asked if she'd be offered an interstate job by a company where she had been interviewed the previous day. The question was, "Will I be offered this position?" The cards she selected are listed below.

CARD 1: THE PAST
Seven of Pentacles

WILL I BE OFFERED THIS POSITION?

CARD 7: THE OUTCOME
The Chariot reversed

CARD 2: THE PRESENT
Two of Pentacles

CARD 6: ATTITUDE
King of Cups

CARD 3: THE NEAR FUTURE
Eight of Swords

CARD 4: THE ANSWER
Page of Pentacles reversed

CARD 5: SURROUNDING ENERGIES
Eight of Pentacles reversed
Additional: Six of Pentacles reversed

Claire's first question: Will I be offered this position?

CARD 1. **Past:** Seven of Pentacles

"It appears you have become satisfied with your career efforts and have been thinking about improving personal skills to improve your job prospects."

CARD 2. **Present:** Two of Pentacles

"There are possibly two or more choices of career path, so it's necessary to examine these options carefully. You're also weighing up the costs involved in relocating for this job."

CARD 3. **Near future:** Eight of Swords

"You might feel restricted if you wait for this position and even if you accept it, you could still feel limited in what you can achieve in the job."

CARD 4. **Answer.**

This card is considered last (after card seven) to ensure clients hear all relevant information before being given the answer.

CARD 5. **Surrounding energies:** Eight of Pentacles reversed

"The reversed Eight of Pentacles suggests you are no longer committed to your current job or that the company who has interviewed you is not sure about hiring you." (At this point, the reader can request another card to clarify the card meaning. I did this to determine which of the above meanings applied to the Eight of Pentacles.)

ADDITIONAL CARD 5. Six of Pentacles reversed

"You are likely to be leaving your job soon (within four weeks), so keep your eyes open for other opportunities."

CARD 6. **Attitude (hopes and fears):** King of Cups

"Is there a man interstate that you're interested in?"

"Yes. My ex-partner moved there seven months ago and we've been in touch on the phone a bit lately. I'm not sure how things will go with Ferdi. Does it say what the future holds there?"

"Only that you've been thinking of him. That's another question, which we'll come to after this."

(It's critical for the reader not to be distracted from the current spread by another question until the layout interpretation has concluded.)

CARD 7. **Outcome:** The Chariot reversed

"The reversed Chariot card suggests it's unlikely you'll be offered this position as expected."

CARD 4. **Answer:** Page of Pentacles reversed

"The reversed Page suggests you won't be working in the position and with the reversed Chariot as the outcome, it may take some time before you give up hope of being offered it." (The Chariot is a reversed number seven, suggesting do not hold on for too long.)

WHEEL of FORTUNE.

"Basically, you are unlikely to be offered this position. Now, please select two more cards to clarify the present time." (These additional cards are placed either side of the Two of Pentacles in the present position to highlight two current alternatives.)

ADDITIONAL CARD 1: Ten of Pentacles

"This suggests an offer from a large company or organisation. Is the company in question a large organisation?"

"No, it's only about fifteen people, I guess."

ADDITIONAL CARD 2: Wheel of Fortune

"The upright Wheel of Fortune suggests improvements in career circumstances and viable opportunities. Although you're unlikely to be offered the job you interviewed for yesterday, there is another worthwhile prospect around you within the next four weeks. This is confirmed by the reversed Six of Pentacles, which can represent leaving a job."

The reader's task is to help maintain Claire's focus on the other possible job opportunities, as well as on the man who appeared in her first question.

"Would you like to ask about Ferdi, about your career generally, about another specific job or career direction or about something else entirely?"

"I'd like to look at the future with Ferdi, especially if I'm not going to be offered this position interstate."

"There are several possible questions to clarify your choice. These might include:

1.   What does the future hold for our relationship?

2.   Is it wise to pursue a love relationship with Ferdi?

3.   What does the future hold for me in love relationships generally?

"This last question is a general one and not limited to Ferdi. Do any of these questions appeal to you or do you have a more suitable question?"

"Oh, I want to ask them all."

"You can — asking them one at a time. Which question is most significant for you?"

"What does the future hold for us and is it wise to pursue a relationship with him?"

"That's actually two questions in one. Let's take each question one by one." (It is advisable to understand the question your client is asking to avoid ambiguity. It also helps the reader to deliver a clearer explanation.)

She paused for a moment to decide which question to ask and then spoke. "What does the future hold for Ferdi and me?"

"Sure. As you think of that question, I'd like you to select another seven cards with your non-writing hand and with your eyes closed." I shuffled the cards briefly (without reversing any cards), having placed those from the previous question back into the pack.

Claire's second question: What does the future hold for Ferdi and me in a love relationship?

CARD 1. **Past:** Ace of Wands

"There was a passionate and enthusiastic start to this relationship or to a new stage of the relationship in the past. You may have journeyed together or travelled to spend time with each other, as the Ace of Wands describes physical movement and action."

CARD 2. **Present:** Eight of Cups

"Presently, you're considering walking away from this possibility, as you feel you've outgrown it. This isn't a disaster but a realisation that you have other opportunities that might help you to grow more than this relationship presently does."

CARD 3. **Near future:** Page of Wands reversed

"There are likely to be delays in starting a new stage of this partnership or in resuming your partnership with Ferdi. It's possible you feel that Ferdi is childlike in his approach to relationships, self-focused and unable to compromise."

CARD 5. **Surrounding energies:** Ten of Wands reversed

"The reversed Ten suggests one of you is weighed down with work responsibilities and may be consumed by career obligations. This may hinder attempts to pursue the relationship. Did Ferdi move interstate for a job?"

"Yes, for a promotion."

CARD 6. **Attitude (hopes and fears):** Five of Cups

"In this position, the Five of Cups indicates a fear of loss. You seem to be more concerned about this partnership not working than confident that it will work successfully. It might be time to address your fears."

CARD 1: THE PAST
Ace of Wands

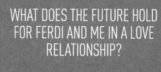

WHAT DOES THE FUTURE HOLD
FOR FERDI AND ME IN A LOVE
RELATIONSHIP?

CARD 7: THE OUTCOME
Hierophant reversed

CARD 2: THE PRESENT
Eight of Cups

CARD 6: ATTITUDE
Five of Cups

CARD 3: THE NEAR FUTURE
Page of Wands reversed

CARD 4: THE ANSWER
Eight of Pentacles reversed

CARD 5: SURROUNDING ENERGIES
Ten of Wands reversed

CARD 7. **Outcome:** Hierophant reversed

"The reversed Hierophant represents a need to be open to opportunities, as it is a reversed five. This might mean you can pursue an unusual type of partnership with Ferdi (such as a distance relationship) or that life will provide you with suitable romantic opportunities if you remain open-minded."

CARD 4. **Answer:** Eight of Pentacles reversed

"Your commitment to this relationship might wane over the next two years and it's unlikely you'll remain as interested in Ferdi as you are at present. The result is that you'll be open to pursuing different directions. Does this make sense to you?"
    "Yes. But if it's not Ferdi, then who is for me?"
    "Well, you can ask a general relationship question to explore broader opportunities."
    "Okay, let's do that."

Claire's third question: What does the future hold for me in relationships?

CARD 1. **Past:** Judgement reversed

"There has been a period of emptiness surrounding love relationships. You may have felt others could not reach you emotionally or that they did not offer you something worth pursuing. Perhaps you felt discontented."

CARD 2. **Present:** The World

"Opportunities for a successful love relationship are around you presently, so stay alert to the possibilities. This could include someone significant who was born overseas."

CARD 3. **Near future:** Knight of Cups

"In the next three months, there is likely to be a soft-hearted, romantic man around you who is offering a relationship."
    "Can you tell me more about that?"
    "Yes, select one more card with your eyes closed."

ADDITIONAL CARD: Three of Pentacles

"Are you currently studying or planning to attend a course in the next three months?"

"Yes, I have a course booked for next month. It's just two weekends, though."

"Well, I see that this man is linked with study or learning in some way. This Three also suggests you are able to learn from the opportunity presented and build a solid platform for that or subsequent love relationships. It shows you doing the groundwork necessary for a stable long-term relationship."

CARD 5. **Surrounding energies:** Three of Cups

"The Three of Cups confirms there are several opportunities around you presently. In a relationship layout, this card is a bit like standing at a bus stop: there's not a bus for a long time and then suddenly two or three arrive in five minutes. Can you add a card to that one?"

"Sure."

ADDITIONAL CARD: Eight of Cups

"The Eight confirms that these new opportunities may help you release your past and present partners, as you realise, they cannot provide what you need emotionally."

CARD 6. **Attitude:** Knight of Swords reversed

"Is there a man around you who is quick-thinking, impatient and sometimes unpredictable?"

"From the past or the present?"

"Either. It's just that your attitude seems to focus on a man who is impatient and unpredictable. He's probably talkative, sociable and a skilful networker. Perhaps you're hoping for an exciting man but fear such a person might be unreliable. If it is a specific man you have in mind, he might be an air sign: Gemini, Libran or Aquarian."

"It's just a hope. There's no-one else right now," she explained.

CARD 1: THE PAST
Judgement reversed

WHAT DOES THE FUTURE HOLD FOR
ME IN RELATIONSHIPS?

CARD 7: THE OUTCOME
Queen of Pentacles

CARD 6: ATTITUDE
Knight of Swords reversed

CARD 2: THE PRESENT
The World

CARD 3: THE NEAR FUTURE
Knight of Cups
Additional: Three of Pentacles

CARD 5: SURROUNDING ENERGIES
Three of Cups
Additional: Eight of Cups

CARD 4: THE ANSWER
Justice
Additional: King of Swords

CARD 7. **Outcome:** Queen of Pentacles

"In the next eighteen to twenty-four months, you become more settled, focused on your career, content and fulfilled in your life. You seem to be quietly confident due to your stable home and work life. At that stage, relationships are likely to become a smaller part of your life while you pursue a career and other goals."

CARD 4. **Answer:** Justice

"The Justice card suggests you are taking responsibility for your relationships and your life generally and that you are likely to be pleased with the results of your decisions and actions. This is a card for the sign of Libra, along with the Queen of Pentacles and the Knight of Swords. Is there a Libran man around you presently?"

"Not that I know of."

"Could you add another card to the answer, please?"

ADDITIONAL CARD: King of Swords

"This King is clear-minded, likely a professional man and someone who enjoys interesting conversation. He could be a Gemini, Libran or Aquarian but his nature is more clearly shown than his astrological sign. However, there are now four possible cards on the table signifying a Libran, so keep an eye out for a Libran man.

"To summarise, it appears there are two men coming into your life. The first is romantic and he's likely to arrive within three months. The second man is more emotionally mature than the first and probably older.

"You have free will in all things predicted, so you can take either, both or neither of the men I've described. It's interesting that Ferdi, who appeared as the King of Cups in your first question, has not appeared in this layout. Does this make sense to you?"

"Yes, it does."

"Now, shall we return to your career questions?"

"Yes. If I'm not moving interstate for that job, what's coming up?"

"As you select seven cards, focus on this question: What does the future hold for me in my career?"

Claire's fourth question: What does the future hold for me in my career?

CARD 1. **Past:** Three of Swords

"There was a strong disappointment in the past with career. What happened?"

"I was retrenched from my job after six years, without notice. It was such a shock."

CARD 2. **Present:** King of Swords

"I see a professional man around you in your work. He is intellectual, organised and clear-minded. Can you relate to this description?"

"My boss. He's a project manager and he heads up teams of twenty to thirty people. He's pretty organised. Why's he coming up?"

"It's likely he's an encouraging influence in your work environment at present."

"Yes, that sounds about right."

CARD 3. **Near future:** Nine of Cups

"There's a strong sense of personal fulfilment related to career in the next three months. You're able to derive great joy and a sense of accomplishment from your work in the immediate future."

CARD 5. **Surrounding energies:** Nine of Pentacles

"This suggests you have a successful career, resulting from careful planning and long-term commitment. It describes a comfortable lifestyle but you want to share it with a close partner. Basically, your work life is fine at the moment, allowing you to focus on other interests."

CARD 6. **Attitude:** Death

"You hope to change jobs and perhaps career direction. This card suggests you expect to conclude a chapter in your working life and move on to other challenges in your career. I see it as hoping for the end of your current career or type of career because the card is upright."

CARD 7. **Outcome:** Three of Wands

"You're likely to move forward with career plans, perhaps travelling with your work. Career opportunities might take you to new cities, as this card can include travel."

CARD 4. **Answer:** Nine of Wands reversed

"It appears that you're afraid of committing yourself to one career long term. When you review your past career, your focus is on the frustrations. Perhaps you're ignoring the achievements? Try to keep a balanced perspective when reviewing the past and if you've been working too hard for too long, it might be time for an extended overseas holiday.

"The reversed Nine reverts back to the Eight of Wands, which suggests you need one of those glorious, memorable summers of fun, friends, love and travel before considering long-term career commitments."

"To summarise, the three nines indicate that you're finishing a chapter in your career; the Death card suggests you're happy to let the old chapter go in favour of new opportunities. Does this make sense to you?"

"Yes."

"Would you like me to clarify any area for you?"

"Just the answer section please."

"Sure. Please close your eyes and select one more card for me." (This card is placed beside the answer card, the card in position number four.)

ADDITIONAL CARD: Four of Cups

"This highlights your need to go within to find what connects you to life. In doing so, you can discover what fulfils you, careerwise. It suggests that by finding inner sources of nourishment outside of work, you can remain balanced during periods when your career is stressful or demanding. Can you please add another card to qualify this further?"

ADDITIONAL CARD: Three of Cups

"After a period of reflection, career opportunities will increase. This card also suggests friendships will be forged with colleagues and that you'll have a supportive, fun workplace

CARD 1: THE PAST
Three of Swords

WHAT DOES THE FUTURE HOLD FOR
ME IN MY CAREER?

CARD 7: THE OUTCOME
Three of Wands

CARD 2: THE PRESENT
King of Swords

CARD 6: ATTITUDE
Death

CARD 3: THE NEAR FUTURE
Nine of Cups

CARD 5: SURROUNDING ENERGIES
Nine of Pentacles

CARD 4: THE ANSWER
Nine of Wands reversed
Additional: Four of Cups   Additional: Three of Cups

environment. Both the answer and the outcome are number three cards, suggesting growth in career.

"To summarise, there are three nines and three threes in this layout. When a number appears in a layout three or more times, it usually has greater significance. The nines refer to a career chapter concluding, whereas the threes describe growth and progress in career. With the Three of Swords in the past position, the hard part is behind you as far as your career is concerned."

Claire had consulted me with a list of questions but it was up to me, the reader, to provide the most appropriate order for them. As her former partner, Ferdi, appeared in a question regarding a career move, he was obviously a fundamental influence.

Before tackling a general career layout, I encouraged Claire to ask about a possible relationship with Ferdi. If things had looked encouraging regarding a relationship with Ferdi, I'd have suggested that Claire ask different questions, such as whether there would be a different job offer in Ferdi's city or whether Ferdi would return to be with her. As it was, a single question eliminated Ferdi from the equation and Claire chose to ask about relationships generally before returning to a career question.

If a client asks a specific question that results in a discouraging answer, you can follow it with a broader question. If they ask about purchasing a house they recently inspected and the answer is no, you can direct them to ask if they'll find another suitable house within three months. If the answer is still no, you can direct the client to ask another question, such as: "Is it wise to remain where I am currently living?" or "Is it wise for me to rent a place until I find what I'm seeking?"

Almost anyone can accept a *no* if they are shown other viable options. Sometimes, it is necessary to explain to people that they won't achieve their desired goal because they won't want it in two years. As individuals grow and develop, personal objectives change. The tarot usually predicts these changes.

Claire came for a reading to confirm that she was about to secure a new job interstate, but instead received information about two new men, a change in career direction and verification that she was not likely to have a solid future with Ferdi.

I met Claire again about four months later and she told me she had never heard back from the interstate company and Ferdi had found someone else. Standing beside her at the time was a Knight of Cups. The slender man with soft eyes, long eyelashes and a gentle handshake was introduced as Neville. He was a poet in his spare time. It appeared that exchanging Ferdi's phone calls for Neville's poetry had enhanced Claire's well-being; she looked positively radiant.

Helping clients formulate appropriate follow-on queries becomes easier with practice. A reader needs to remain objective enough to ask the questions a client might not because they are too emotionally involved. With practice, simplifying clients' issues, breaking them down into a clear, concise form, becomes natural. Vague questions often result in confusing answers. It is a reader's job to clarify issues and distil them into relevant enquiries.

It's necessary to keep it simple. If a client insists upon complicating each issue, take a moment to determine what their underlying query might be. Try to distil the issue to a single word and then examine the possible questions available.

If you identify the underlying issues and suggest questions the client can ask, their personal anxieties often dissipate. This strategic approach to tarot readings helps address clients' unspoken issues.

When Jenny's reading was becoming bogged down, I used this technique. The statement in my mind was: "The underlying issue today is not being valued." Soon afterwards, Jenny explained she had given all of herself to Sam but he still left her for someone new. On closer examination, it appeared to be a life pattern for Jenny, beginning with parents who didn't value her as a child. It's often difficult to appreciate oneself if early carers have not modelled this respect.

Ben consulted me about his relationship with Rebecca. He explained that she was keen to be married but he had been divorced previously and was a bit resistant to repeat the process.

Ben's first question: What does the future hold for my relationship with Rebecca?

CARD 1. **Past:** Three of Cups

"Did you meet Rebecca in a group situation, such as a party or a course of some sort?"

"Well, yes. We were both on a self-development course together a few months ago."

"I see it as an enjoyable event and you felt included in the group process."

CARD 1: THE PAST
Three of Cups

WHAT DOES THE FUTURE HOLD FOR
MY RELATIONSHIP WITH REBECCA?

CARD 7: THE OUTCOME
Two of Pentacles
Additional: Wheel of Fortune

CARD 2: THE PRESENT
Seven of Wands

CARD 6: ATTITUDE
Ace of Swords

CARD 3: THE NEAR FUTURE
Nine of Wands

CARD 5: SURROUNDING ENERGIES
Nine of Pentacles

CARD 4: THE ANSWER
Queen of Cups
Additional: The Tower   Additional: The Emperor reversed

CARD 2. **Present:** Seven of Wands

"There seem to be some obstacles to overcome if you want to pursue this relationship. Are you busy with work or with other commitments?"

"Yes, I'm flat-out at the moment. Does it look good for us?"

"I'm coming to that in a moment."

CARD 3. **Near future:** Nine of Wands

"In the next few months, I see you're hesitant to pursue this liaison more seriously. You are reviewing the past and recalling difficulties and pain. That's not to imply that this relationship will cause you any heartache but that you have memories of previous difficult partnerships."

CARD 5. **Surrounding energies:** Nine of Pentacles

"This Nine describes a comfortable life, financially. It suggests that you have taken care of your monetary needs and are now ready to extend yourself into a relationship. Basically, you are successful but now you need someone to share your success."

CARD 6. **Attitude:** Ace of Swords

"This position represents your attitude. It's not necessarily reality but how you currently perceive circumstances. It suggests that you have a clear vision of where this relationship will lead if you pursue it seriously. You seem confident that you can succeed if you take the next step in your relationship with Rebecca."

CARD 7. **Outcome:** Two of Pentacles

"I see financial decisions regarding your relationship. Perhaps you are planning to relocate or change jobs, which might affect your finances and your ongoing connection with Rebecca. This can signify the financial deliberation that precedes action. Please add another card to the Two of Pentacles."

ADDITIONAL CARD: Wheel of Fortune

"This suggests that if you pursue this commitment further, you'll be happy with the outcome. It describes a period of growth and development in your relationship with Rebecca, so the outcome is encouraging for you both."

CARD 4. **Answer:** Queen of Cups

"I see that Rebecca is sensitive, emotionally supportive and ready for an intense emotional connection with you. She has been thinking about it but it's not her nature to force the issue, so she's waiting for you to take the next step. In summary, it appears wise to pursue a deeper commitment with Rebecca. There is likely to be beneficial growth and development in your relationship if you do so. Does this make sense to you?"

"Yes."

"Would you like me to make anything clearer before we move on to your next question?"

"Yes, please. I'd like to know more about the next few months, if that's okay."

"Sure. Can you select another card for me, please?" The additional card Ben chose was The Tower.

"Can you give me another card, please?" The additional card was The Emperor reversed. I had requested another card to accompany The Tower, so I didn't tell Ben there was likely to be an unexpected upheaval in the next twelve weeks without explaining what he might expect. If the layout ended on The Tower, Ben might feel uneasy or become preoccupied with a possible shock ahead.

ADDITIONAL CARDS: The Tower, The Emperor reversed

"This seems unrelated to the earlier cards. The Tower suggests there could be sudden changes and, alongside the Emperor reversed, these changes could result from your own lack of discipline. Does this make sense to you?"

"Er, sort of."

"Well, to continue, the actions you are weighing up in the Nine of Wands might not just be about Rebecca but also to do with other things in your life that could cause sudden changes and problems in your relationship with her. Have you been considering some course of action that might disrupt your relationship with Rebecca?"

"No. Not that I can think of."

"Well, I'll ask you to reflect on this and we'll move on to your next question."

"Okay. Now I'd like to ask about another girl I'm interested in."

"Oh. Now it comes out. Can I ask you this? If you pursue this other girl, might that cause some upheaval in your relationship with Rebecca?"

"It might."

"So, what's your question?"

"What does the future hold for Jenny and me?"

"Okay. There are several ways you can ask this question. You can ask:

- What does the future hold for our relationship?

- Is it wise for me to pursue a relationship with Jenny?

- What does the future hold for me in love relationships, generally?

Ben's second question: What does the future hold for our relationship?

CARD 1. **Past:** The Star reversed

"Was there an Aquarian person around you in relationships in the recent past?"

"No, not that I remember."

"Had you lost faith in love relationships for a time, preferring your freedom instead?"

"Yes. I didn't have a relationship for four years. I just didn't want one."

CARD 2. **Present:** Ten of Cups reversed

"It seems you are keen not to repeat your family patterns in relationships and that Jenny is from a different social group. I don't think she mixes with your social set, presently."

"Yes, that's right. She's much younger than me and her friends are very different from mine."

CARD 3. **Near future:** Page of Cups reversed

"It seems you won't know where you stand with Jenny in the coming months."

"Yes. She's off overseas in a few weeks for a long holiday."

"Could you add another card to this for me, please?"

ADDITIONAL CARD: Nine of Cups reversed

"It's apparent that this holds no fulfilment for you in the next three months. Pursuing this relationship is unlikely to nourish your heart. The reversed Nine of Cups often describes addictive or compulsive behaviour. Is your attraction to Jenny compulsive in some way?"

"No, not really. She's just someone I met who I'm attracted to."

"And what do you think Jenny can offer you that Rebecca cannot?"

"I hadn't thought about it really. I haven't been in a relationship with Rebecca long enough to know what she's like."

"But you must have some inkling of her inner nature."

"She's fairly secretive, really."

"So that makes two of you, then."

"Oh, I'm not secretive."

"So, you've told Rebecca about Jenny, then?"

"Er, no."

CARD 5. **Surrounding energies:** Three of Cups

"Is Jenny already in a relationship or about to start one?"

"I don't know. We've only met a few times, so I don't know that much about her."

"Can you add another card for me, please?"

CARD 1: THE PAST
The Star reversed

CARD 7: THE OUTCOME
The Moon

WHAT DOES THE FUTURE HOLD FOR
OUR RELATIONSHIP?

CARD 2: THE PRESENT
Ten of Cups reversed

CARD 6: ATTITUDE
Page of Wands

CARD 3: THE NEAR FUTURE
Page of Cups reversed
Additional: Nine of Cups reversed

CARD 5: SURROUNDING ENERGIES
Three of Cups
Additional: Page of Swords

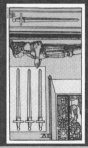  

CARD 4: THE ANSWER
Four of Swords reversed
Additional: Justice reversed   Additional: Seven of Wands

ADDITIONAL CARD: Page of Swords

"How old is Jenny?"

"I think she's twenty-one."

"And what astrological sign is she?"

"Pisces."

"Then this Page confirms there is someone else around her at present who is also interested in a relationship with her."

CARD 6. **Attitude:** Page of Wands

"You seem to be keen to pursue a love relationship with Jenny and you're confident it will give you what you want. You might have unrealistic expectations for a relationship with her and only time will tell if your hopes are realised."

A page in the attitude position can suggest wanting a child but this rarely appears in readings for men. It can also indicate that the person asking the question is emotionally immature, having the hopes of a page when, at age 29, he's traditionally almost a king.

The appearance of two pages in the layout could indicate that a child will feature significantly in the coming years, perhaps forcing a commitment to someone.

CARD 7. **Outcome:** The Moon

"The Moon suggests that if you pursue this relationship, it may have to be kept secret from others. Although this may increase the passion and excitement, it is also likely to restrict its development."

CARD 4. **Answer:** Four of Swords reversed

"This reversed Four suggests you are becoming restless with the possibilities in your present relationship and want to throw caution to the wind and pursue a relationship with Jenny, regardless of the consequences. Can I have another card, please?"

ADDITIONAL CARD: Justice reversed

"You might disregard the consequences now but you'll have to live with them later. The reversed Justice card suggests ongoing arguments and disputes, which are likely to be in your relationship with Rebecca after she discovers your relationship with Jenny."

"So, how can I stop Rebecca from finding out?"

"Don't bother. She appeared earlier as a Queen of Cups. This Queen is very intuitive, so my guess is that she knows already."

"But I haven't done anything yet."

"True, but your energy and your commitment have strayed from her and she instinctively knows it. It's really your choice what you do in your love life but I don't think you'll be hiding much from Rebecca. Can I have another card, please?"

I requested an additional card to glimpse the outcome of the ongoing disputes shown in the reversed Justice card.

ADDITIONAL CARD: Seven of Wands

"This tells me you'll have an uphill battle on your hands if you pursue a relationship with Jenny, which is likely to cause issues in your relationship with Rebecca. If you change your mind and decide to settle with Rebecca at a later date, she won't trust you again. Do so at your peril. So, what do you want to ask next?"

"I'd like to know if it's wise to pursue a relationship with Karen."

"What's the story? Exactly how many girls do you have back there?"

Ben's third question: Is it wise to pursue a relationship with Karen?

CARD 1. **Past:** Temperance.

"There seems to have been peace and stability around you emotionally in the past. Perhaps you were able to see where you were heading long term in love relationships or knew what sort of relationship suited you. There was also a period of travel in the past two years."

"Yes, I was overseas for a few months."

CARD 2. **Present:** The Magician reversed

"This is not a suitable time to pursue a love relationship with Karen. The reversed Magician suggests you might be using a position of power to exert an influence over her. Is this so?"

"Er, well, we met on a meditation course and I was paired with her to support her after the course finished. I'm more familiar with this meditation, so I guess she looks to me for guidance. In that way, maybe I have a position of power but it's not considerable."

"Perhaps not. Does Karen look to you for help when she gets stuck with her meditation practice?"

"Yes, I guess so."

"Then that puts you in a position of power. Be very mindful of the possibility of misusing it. With power comes responsibility."

CARD 3. **Near future:** The Emperor reversed

"The reversed Emperor in the near future suggests you need to be more disciplined where love relationships are concerned. More is not always better and in this case, more partners could translate into more demands. It's also possible that Karen has an erratic man around her who has poor impulse control. If he flies into a jealous rage, you might need the services of a first-rate surgeon."

The reversed Magician and the reversed Emperor in the same layout is a warning sign. As Ben didn't seem to exhibit the signs of aggression and impatience of the reversed Emperor, it was possible this card described a man already around Karen.

Ben did, however, exhibit signs of the reversed Magician such as reduced empathy and compassion and other narcissistic traits.

CARD 5. **Surrounding energies:** Page of Wands

"This Page suggests you are eager to pursue this relationship and that it could start in the next four weeks if you want it to. It can also suggest you're more interested in beginnings

CARD 1: THE PAST
Temperance

IS IT WISE TO PURSUE A
RELATIONSHIP WITH KAREN?

CARD 7: THE OUTCOME
Queen of Pentacles reversed

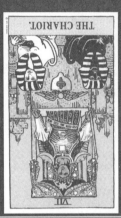

CARD 6: ATTITUDE
The Chariot reversed

CARD 2: THE PRESENT
The Magician reversed

CARD 3: THE NEAR FUTURE
The Emperor reversed

CARD 5: SURROUNDING ENERGIES
Page of Wands

CARD 4: THE ANSWER
King of Cups reversed

than in maintaining long-term relationships."

CARD 6. **Attitude:** The Chariot reversed

"The reversed Chariot suggests you are torn between your heart and your head regarding pursuing a love relationship with Karen. It also hints at you looking forward to a new relationship as a way to avoid past emotional issues regarding relationships. Is there a past relationship you still need to resolve emotionally, aside from the relationship with Rebecca?"

"No. Not that I can think of right now."

CARD 7. **Outcome:** Queen of Pentacles reversed

"The reversed Queen of Pentacles describes Karen as practical, realistic and currently lacking in confidence. She enjoys nature and money is fundamental to her but she may have had poor training around handling money growing up. Is she an independent woman?"

"Yes, I guess so."

CARD 4. **Answer:** King of Cups reversed

"This reversed King confirms to me that you have unresolved emotional matters from past relationships which are driving you forward to seek new opportunities. These issues might make it difficult for you to stay in one relationship when more commitment is necessary due to past betrayals. Does this make sense to you?"

"Not really."

"Okay, I'll break it down a bit more. How is your ability to trust in relationships?"

"Not very good, I guess."

"Is your lack of trust related to an incident in a past relationship?"

"Not that I can think of, no."

At this point, I tuned in clairvoyantly and was given the year 1988. "What was happening in relationships in 1988?"

"Let me see now. Oh, yes. My girlfriend at the time left and moved interstate."

"Why did she move?"

"I guess she was restless for something new."

"And did she ask you to go with her?"

"No."

"Did you want to go?"

"I never thought about it, really."

"Thinking about it now, would you have liked to have accompanied her interstate?"

"Not really. All my friends are around me and I like it here."

"Did you discuss her intended move?"

"No. She just decided one day and she was gone a few weeks later. It was all a bit of a surprise, really."

"And how have your love relationships been since then?"

"Well, I was married for three years and then she left and went overseas."

"This is starting to look like a pattern to me. Have any other partners moved away as they ended their relationships with you?"

"No, just those two."

"So, do you feel you've resolved the issues from the two relationships you've described to me?"

"Yes."

"Then you're not carrying any emotional baggage from the past and you're ready to commit yourself to a long-term relationship?"

"How do I answer that?"

"Honestly, I hope. The issue I'm hearing is one of commitment. For someone to leave and move away there might have been weak commitment or perhaps those women sensed you were not committed to them and so they moved on. The fact that you've asked about three different people for possible relationships suggests you don't yet have a firm commitment to Rebecca. Is this a reasonable assessment of the situation?"

"Yes."

"What would you need to make a serious commitment to build and maintain a lasting love relationship?" It was a probing question and I didn't expect an answer. I figured he'd still be answering that question six months after the reading.

As I observed him, Ben seemed to become weary and heavy. The self-assured young man who entered the room forty minutes ago was fading, being replaced by someone who appeared tortured and bruised by life. As the facade crumbled, we approached the real issue behind his consultation.

"The thing is ..." he said, pausing as he searched for the words. "Just when you think things are going well, they up and leave. I don't get it. I'm sick of being left by women, so I recently decided that if it was a choice between leaving or being left, I'd leave every time."

He sighed, having admitted to himself and to me, his real issues underlying the relationship questions.

"So, do you have these extra women like Karen and Jenny in case you have to leave suddenly?" I asked softly.

"I guess so," he muttered and nodded.

"So, let's return to what I said about your relationship with Rebecca. In that layout, she appeared to be loving and supportive and I couldn't see that she had any intention of leaving. By your own admission, she wants to get married. Doesn't that suggest she wants to be with you for a long time to come?"

"Yes, it does. But my first wife wanted to get married. She thought it would be for life, but where is she now?"

"Okay. The issue here seems to be one of trust. Can I suggest a question to ask the cards?"

"Sure."

"What do I need to do to rebuild my trust in love relationships?"

"Okay, that sounds fine."

It had taken several questions to arrive at Ben's underlying issue: trust in love relationships. As a reader, it is prudent to remain non-judgemental. It's difficult to do this, sometimes. When a person feels acknowledged and not judged, trust is possible. Ben's values are different from mine but we are two fellow beings colliding for a short time. During this brief meeting, I have the opportunity to ask Ben some questions that might help him understand why happiness currently eludes him.

When dealing with unacknowledged issues, a tarot reading is often only the start of a long journey of self-discovery. As a reader, it is best to have some business cards of a trustworthy counsellor or meaningful books you can recommend, so they can complete the inner work you have highlighted to them.

Ben's fourth question: What do I need to do to rebuild my trust in love relationships?

CARD 1. **Past:** The Tower

"There has been a sudden change in the past that swept a relationship away without warning. The resultant shock probably left a period of upheaval in your life. Can you relate to this?"

"Yes."

CARD 2. **Present:** Eight of Pentacles

"You seem to be more committed to making the most of your life currently — although the emphasis might be in favour of career or financial matters, instead of emotional fulfilment, with the three pentacles cards in the layout. Your focus is on those areas you can control."

CARD 3. **Near future:** Nine of Wands reversed

"When it comes time to review your emotional commitment in the coming months, you are likely to examine the past closely, ignoring anything that worked out well but focusing on situations that ended badly. It's helpful to keep a balanced view of your emotional past, so you can make unbiased decisions in the future.

"With this Nine reversed, there is an opportunity to return to the previous upright card, Eight of Wands, to find inner strength and focus before returning to the upright Nine again. At that point, you can reassess where you want to go next. The Eight of Wands is a time of uncomplicated fun, taking each day as it comes, enjoying relationship and life opportunities as they approach.

"I see the Eight of Wands as one of those halcyon summers you remember fondly over a glass of chilled white wine with friends. You are overdue for one of those summers, so don't take life too seriously at the moment. In playing and laughing, you are also growing."

CARD 5. **Surrounding energies:** Ace of Pentacles reversed

"You are currently more focused on career and financial issues than on emotional matters. The Ace also emphasises feeling unable to have a committed love relationship until you have sufficient money to support your lifestyle."

I paused to allow him to absorb what had been said and to collect himself. This probably wasn't what Ben imagined when he came for his reading but ignoring the unspoken issues would have done Ben a disservice. This question is designed to show Ben what he can do about his current relationship patterns if he is aiming for long-term fulfilment.

CARD 6. **Attitude:** Five of Wands reversed

"The reversed Five of Wands suggests you are hopeful of including a partner in your life and not leading two separate lives with diverging interests and goals. This is likely to involve discussions and negotiations, especially around hobbies and interests or weekend activities, as you discover each other and negotiate shared experiences. The reversed Five indicates the need to return to the previous card, the Four of Wands, which suggests a stable life together in a comfortable home."

CARD 7. **Outcome:** Temperance

"If you keep the bigger picture in mind, finding a suitable partner is easier, as this person is likely to share your spiritual path already. Being aware of personal purpose and emotional needs, you can receive some of the support you require. This may take the form of assistance and backing from people who share your life perspective or simply the knowledge that if your relationship ends your spiritual path continues."

CARD 4. **Answer:** Ten of Pentacles reversed

"This reversed Ten suggests a need to rely less upon material and financial structure for emotional fulfilment and more on people or spiritual nourishment."

"How do you mean?"

"Perhaps you can find some of the support you need through meditation to re-centre yourself. More nourishment might be found through friends and your partner,

CARD 1: THE PAST
The Tower

WHAT DO I NEED TO DO TO REBUILD
MY TRUST IN LOVE RELATIONSHIPS?

CARD 7: THE OUTCOME
Temperance

CARD 2: THE PRESENT
Eight of Pentacles

CARD 6: ATTITUDE
Five of Wands reversed

CARD 3: THE NEAR FUTURE
Nine of Wands reversed

CARD 5: SURROUNDING ENERGIES
Ace of Pentacles reversed

CARD 4: THE ANSWER
Ten of Pentacles reversed
Additional: Six of Wands

through nature or through growing a garden. The choices are endless when you look closely. Please select another card to go with the Ten of Pentacles."

ADDITIONAL CARD: Six of Wands

"You are likely to succeed in overcoming personal trust issues within the next two years while enjoying a supportive love relationship at that time. This upright Six is a card of triumph and it confirms that your energies are congruent. You are not scattered in your desires and if you have a close partner, it is likely you are both focused on the same goals. Does this make sense to you?"

"Yes, it does," he said with a sigh of relief.

Ben came with questions about several women and his current emotional opportunities. Beneath these questions lay the real issues. This reading provided an opportunity to address both his immediate questions and his profound issues but that does not always happen.

Sometimes, clients don't want to know about buried issues, preferring instead to have their fortune told. Difficulties arise when there is precious little ahead of them they consider to be worthwhile and they don't want to hear about personal contributions to their current circumstances.

A client may leave feeling disappointed with the reading. From an emotional point of view, I like to know I've given the best reading I can for that day; from a business point of view, I realise clients who are pleased with what they have been told usually spread the word about me to others. However, I still refuse to give false hope.

What is the point of making people feel optimistic for a few days or weeks when their confidence is built on fantasy? Sooner or later they'll realise the predictions were wrong and then they will have lost several months or years. The reader will have lost a potential long-term client.

Although not all the news was encouraging for Ben, he left with information about his relationship with Rebecca, details of possible relationships with Karen and Jenny and an understanding of why he was afraid of long-term commitment in love relationships. It's up to him what he does with that information. A tarot reader's task is to give clients the necessary information to help them make realistic decisions. People have free will; sometimes they need encouragement to use it.

The reader's part of the obligation is to put aside some time and focus carefully on each person's questions and the issues behind them. Clients think they are paying only for an hour of your time (if consultations are one hour) but in fact they are also paying for the months and years you have spent honing tarot-reading skills. They need all those effective habits developed along the way, such as not drinking when reading the following day, meditating regularly, attending courses to further personal knowledge and perhaps even training in counselling to enhance personal observations in readings.

As a professional reader, it is important to improve one's skills and knowledge continually. By becoming a better reader, clients receive clearer, more accurate information and are prepared to travel further or wait longer to have readings. They'll also refer friends and colleagues.

In many ways, the purpose of the tarot reader is similar to that of a storyteller. The tarot reader tells a story, which is a metaphor for the client's life or current circumstances. Through listening to these stories, clients can recognise current circumstances and glimpse where life is heading.

Tarot readers are well placed to help people review their steps and reassess their purpose. This can mean highlighting what they are doing that prevents them from achieving significant goals. Usually, this involves revealing what they already know on some level, what their friends have longed to tell them but could not, for friendships are often based on what we do not say to each other.

It is vital not to collude with clients when their hearts are set on an unrewarding outcome. At best, this leads to eventual disappointment when dreams are shattered and at worst, people might miss more beneficial opportunities because they remained in a dead-end job or a loveless marriage.

Collusion is more enticing when a reader has to tell a client a desired love relationship is not likely to eventuate and nothing else is immediately on the horizon. There is the temptation to let the person have someone to focus on until another opportunity emerges, whereas the client might benefit from being aware of a personal winter: a time of fewer possibilities.

This occurred with Francine, whose anxieties and phobias prevented her from having a job, socialising, being in noisy environments or being in any place where an escape route wasn't in direct line of sight. She was desperate to fall in love but her problems prevented even a first date. I explained that she might need to resolve some of these issues before a relationship was possible but she countered that the right man for her would love her just as she was. I felt I had to be more forthright.

"Okay, so let's imagine Tom asks you out on a first date. It's dinner at an Italian restaurant."

"I can't eat Italian because I'm dairy intolerant. No milk or cheese."

"Okay, it's a Thai restaurant. He calls for you and, as you close the car door, your anxiety kicks in. You can see your escape route but you can't take it at sixty kilometres per hour in traffic. So, I guess you drive your own car."

"I don't drive. I don't have a licence."

"Now, you arrive at the restaurant and are seated downstairs in the basement. It's down a long, dimly lit passage, past the kitchen and the storeroom. It's crowded with thirty-five people loudly celebrating a birthday party. How would you feel as you sat down, with the back of your chair pushed up against the sweaty back of a part-time wrestler at a nearby table? He's broken out into a sweat after eating the chilli crab dish."

"I'd have to leave. I don't like touching other people."

"Okay. But Tom is attracted to you, so this means he's probably interested in touching you, perhaps holding you at some stage. Maybe not today but eventually. He's desperately hoping that you find him attractive and that you might want to kiss him, too. You explain to Tom that the meal has to be dairy-free, the venue can't be too loud or crowded and that you need to sit close to the entrance, due to your anxieties. He nods and suggests a picnic."

"As long as it's not too hot, as I burn easily," she said hastily.

"So, the following Sunday, Tom calls for you at noon and you go on a picnic. That way you can bring your own food and carefully scrutinise Tom as he toys with the tofu salad and a gluten-free sandwich. Then a big dog approaches you rapidly, barking and running as fast as it can."

"Oh, I don't like dogs."

"It's a park on a Sunday. As you glance around you can see eleven dogs, two horses and a ferret."

"I'd have to leave immediately."

"Does Tom ask for another date?"

She held her breath for a while as she erased the scene of an approaching dog.

"No but I could meet someone who likes the same food as I do."

"Yes, of course, through the gluten-free classifieds, presumably on the noticeboard at the local health food store."

I imagined an ad that read, *Calm, easy-going man seeks complicated woman for dairy-free distant intimacy. I live within walking distance of an organic café, private yoga classes and a quiet local library. I have no pets; I speak softly and I respect and maintain personal boundaries at all times.*

Francine deserves to be loved but avoiding most social situations limits her chances of meeting Mr Right. I suggested an internet meeting via an online dating site but she shuddered and shook her head. We explored shared-interest groups, from sewing and pattern-making workshops to book clubs and church groups but one or more of her anxieties was triggered with almost every option.

I suggested she see the play *84 Charing Cross Road*, about a friendship that blossoms when a customer in America writes (on paper) to request a title in an antiquarian bookstore in London. I explained that Francine might update the mode of exchange by using email. The added benefit was that she'd only wait a day or two for a response, instead of a month.

Working on the theory that it's important to walk before running, I suggested Francine experiment with friendships before exploring love relationship opportunities. This process takes focus away from immediate possible relationships to what Francine might do to expand her world in small but meaningful steps. She might meet like-minded people by volunteering for bush regeneration projects at her local parks. These gatherings usually take place early on Sunday mornings in local parks or wilderness areas and involve a dozen people who weed and tidy the area to give local flora a chance to thrive. They often break for morning tea and conversation before disbanding until the following week. There would be less pressure than pursuing an intimate relationship and give Francine the freedom to express herself without commitment. It essentially offered short periods of social interaction, giving her time to become familiar and eventually comfortable with the process.

Interpreting a Tarot Layout

The card meanings given for the general reading below are not the only possible interpretations. They are simply a guide to how a reading might look when transcribed. A different reader might add subtle personal nuances based on their unique perspective and this is to be expected.

When students explain that the card interpretations I've put forward conflict with meanings given in books they have read or previous tarot courses, I ask them to put aside the previously gathered information and listen to what is being offered in the course. Afterwards, they can combine what they feel best fits each card from a range of sources. This is what makes each tarot reader unique. It's also why experienced readers usually charge more per reading than beginners. A tarot reader brings years of study, practice and life experience to a session and focuses it all on a person's current issues. The more books read, courses completed and direct reading experience to draw upon, the clearer the client's session.

This is a general reading.

CARD 1. **Past:** The Chariot

Meanings include:

- Remaining mentally focused on personal goals.

- A Cancerian.

- A person with leadership qualities who produces effective results through focus, discipline and persistence.

- In health terms, it can represent the stomach or the breasts. Sometimes it highlights digestive problems caused by stress. It can also indicate a slow lymphatic system.

- Balancing the inner world of dreams and hopes (the moons) with the needs of the outer world.

- In a travel question, it can signify travel by rail or car.

CARD 2. **Present:** Six of Pentacles reversed

Meanings include:

- Spending a large sum of money.

- Leaving or losing a job or a source of income.

- A period without financial stability, due to lack of income.

- An expensive purchase, such as a house or a car.

- Not earning personal worth, due to a lack of awareness of how to value individual skills and talents.

CARD 1: THE PAST
The Chariot

CARD 7: THE OUTCOME
Four of Wands   Additional: Six of Swords

CARD 2: THE PRESENT
Six of Pentacles reversed

THIS IS A GENERAL READING

CARD 6: ATTITUDE
The Emperor reversed

CARD 3: THE NEAR FUTURE
Queen of Swords reversed

CARD 4: THE ANSWER
Eight of Pentacles

CARD 5: SURROUNDING ENERGIES
Queen of Pentacles

- Spending money to feel better in ways that are not beneficial, such as gambling or squandering personal financial reserves. Allowing unique desires to become a burden, such as the need for a huge home or an extravagant lifestyle, which might reduce opportunities for travel, learning or new opportunities.

- It's time to examine attitudes to money and to update them. This Six reversed indicates benefitting from a return to the previous upright card in the suit, the Five of Pentacles. The five describes restricted circumstances, perhaps due to lack of preparation for a personal financial winter (i.e., no savings for a rainy day).

CARD 3. **Near future:** Queen of Swords reversed

Meanings include:

- Mental criticism.

- Doubting personal ability to do a task well, while insisting on perfection.

- Poorly considered plans.

- Clouded thinking.

- Previous strategies not working in current circumstances. A need to update attitudes or beliefs to ensure constructive progress.

- An anxious person who becomes easily stressed when tasks seem overwhelming.

- A critical female friend, associate or family member whose 'advice' may undermine the individual's confidence. Someone who instils doubt instead of confidence.

- Lack of success due to confused or illogical thinking and planning. The clouds are now above the person's head in this reversed card, strengthening doubts and increasing the focus on past failures. It's difficult to sort the unnecessary from the worthwhile when making plans.

CARD 4. **Client or answer to the question:** Eight of Pentacles

Meanings include:

- Study or learning and mastering new skills.
- Commitment to a job or monetary plans.
- Previous successful financial endeavours strengthen confidence in current plans.
- Faith and assurance that effort will produce desired results.
- An awareness that work can be spiritually fulfilling (the blue tunic) and physical effort (the red tights) can be profitably directed into meaningful pursuits.
- Focus and effort bring rewards.
- The process of adding new skills to existing abilities for self-improvement.
- Living within personal means (the upright pentacles) while working towards more meaningful goals.

CARD 5. **Surrounding energies:** Queen of Pentacles

Meanings include:

- A calm, practical woman who is responsible with money.
- The need to balance working hours with time spent in a natural environment. Nature is energising and adds perspective.
- Success through practical planning and a well-developed work ethic.
- Someone who understands the timing of life's seasons and knows when to move and when to wait with plans.

- A woman who understands that planning is only the first part of a successful project. Effort must follow design for clear-cut results.

- It highlights the kidneys, the digestive system, or alternatively, a practical woman supporting plans around health.

- Success due to a realistic approach to the effort required to achieve one's objectives.

CARD 6. **Attitude:** The Emperor reversed

Meanings include:

- An undisciplined person.

- Hoping to be rescued from a current dilemma.

- Expecting to cruise along and reap rewards without effort.

- Wishing that someone in charge, such as a father, boss, examiner or a judge, will be lenient.

- Hoping that a woman (the previous upright card, The Empress) might assist with goals.

- Someone who has not yet mastered self-discipline.

- By returning to the previous upright card, The Empress, it's possible to succeed with the assistance of an earthy, practical woman.

- In a health reading, it can signify headaches or lack of personal discipline with maintaining supportive health habits, such as walking, yoga, Pilates or regular gym visits.

CARD 7. **Outcome:** Four of Wands

Meanings include:

- Stability.

- Settling into a new home or work environment.

- Resting or adjusting after a period of change.

- A community celebration.

- Consolidating one's physical environment. This might describe a home renovation completed or a more sociable approach to life after a period of travel (the Three of Wands).

- Sometimes it suggests positive news about health after an illness. Following an 'all clear' from the doctor, it's time to move on with life.

- Balanced heath due to regular exercise and a stable home environment.

OUTCOME (ADDITIONAL CARD): Six of Swords

This additional card is meant to extend the outcome, per the client's request. It is effectively the upshot of the outcome.

Meanings include:

- A tranquil period after turmoil.

- Travel overseas.

- Making sense of past emotional struggles.

- Recognising the value of family and friends after a transition from difficult times to more harmonious days.

- A peaceful ending of a chapter.

- Surrender to change and acceptance after a period of upheaval.

- Looking forward to an emotionally calm period ahead.

- In health terms, it indicates tranquillity after a difficult period. A client selected this card after affirmative medical results following surgery to remove a breast lump. Twelve years later, she's still in sound health.

Card Meanings

The Minor Arcana

Events and Opportunities

The fifty-six cards of the minor arcana are divided into four suits, similar to playing cards. However, unlike playing cards, the minor arcana of the tarot has a fourth court card in each suit, the page or child, in the family. The knight in the tarot is equivalent to the jack in the playing cards.

The minor arcana deals with everyday events and actions and their consequences. If a client is travelling overseas, the minor arcana cards are likely to outline the preparations, the stress involved and the people around that individual. For thorough scrutiny of a person's underlying spiritual lessons, it is necessary to consider the twenty-two cards of the major arcana.

The suits of the minor arcana are the four elemental approaches to life. They are fire (action and enthusiasm), water (emotions and creativity), air (thought and communication) and earth (practical determination). The suits represent four paths to understanding.

Each path is equally important and despite appearances, no direction provides a shortcut to understanding. All provide opportunities as well as obstacles to be overcome while pursuing personal goals. Following an unusual trail can sometimes help an individual master issues because the person gains a different viewpoint or perspective during the process.

Although each suit offers a distinctive path to understanding and fulfilment, individuals take steps at their own pace on their unique personal journeys. History is filled with stories, books, films and plays about the challenges presented by different routes and how people have triumphed over obstacles to reach an enlightened understanding of life.

Unlike my introductory book, *The Tarot Revealed*, this book groups each of the minor arcana card numbers together to emphasise the similarities of the cards, while highlighting the different approaches of the four suits. Basically, all the threes in the tarot have a similar meaning: growth and progress. The approach to progress differs according to the suit. In a general reading, for example, the Three of Wands can indicate travel or physical progression with plans, whereas the Three of Cups describes a group celebration or a shared success. The wands approach is sometimes self-focused, often involving competition with others, whereas the cups path involves communal activities, with people supporting each other in a group process.

The Three of Swords indicates sadness, grief or loss. This card represents growth through the pain of an ending that results in a new understanding of life. Loss can help an individual make the most of people, circumstances and opportunities, while they are present. The Three of Pentacles describes financial growth or progress. Plans usually require funds to maintain momentum or financial investment to reach the desired objective.

The wands approach to life frequently entails competition, goals and achievement, whereas the cups style often involves relationships, family or shared objectives. The swords path tends to focus on theories, ideas and understanding concepts while the pentacles approach tends to value financial stability or abundance.

Worthwhile goals require each of the elements (fire, water, air and earth) to reach successful conclusions. People who balance and embrace all four aspects within themselves usually lead more harmonious lives. When individuals lack one of these elements, it's possible to find a partner, coach or other support person with those qualities who can assist towards a successful outcome.

If a person lacks fire, this individual is likely to display limited passion and enthusiasm for new opportunities. Fire (or wands energy) represents the ardent self-belief that it's possible to conquer the competition and achieve one's goals. It is a driving force to start a project and get it across the finish line before someone else does. Without fire, there is no urge to fight back when bullied or sidelined.

People who lack water (cups qualities) often have limited compassion or empathy for others. These individuals prefer working alone rather than with teams and they may struggle in careers or projects that provide social benefits, such as in social work, counselling, as carers or teaching small children.

A distinct lack of planning or strategy is often evident with people who lack air (swords qualities). Failure to plan towards an endpoint or to re-shape plans when required is a stumbling block to many great projects and ideas. These individuals are usually uncomfortable negotiating with others or networking to discover who can assist them with their goals.

When people give scant attention to funding a project, they usually lack the element of earth (pentacles qualities). These individuals fail to ask how they'll finance the process and who'll buy the product or service. The element of earth provides a realistic approach to plans. When adding an earthy or pentacles person to a project management team, the likelihood of a successful outcome is improved if advice is heeded.

The Tarot Suits

Four Unique Approaches to Life

There are four suits of the minor arcana: wands, cups, swords and pentacles. They describe four tribes or families of like-minded people. The following examples illustrate the fundamental differences between these four approaches to life.

Wands people tend to be impatient, enthusiastic, passionate and forthright. They are motivated by competition to achieve goals and they resent long meetings and protracted negotiations. These people are dynamic, passionate, impatient when opposed, energetic and assertive. They are usually self-motivated, optimistic, inspirational, risk-takers, high-spirited, egotistical, tactless and sometimes aggressive and prone to exaggerate. Despite being seventy-eight years of age, King of Wands David still climbs stairs two at a time, considering those he leaves in his wake to be listless and lazy.

Cups individuals are usually compassionate, patient, reflective and sentimental. These people prefer partnerships and cooperation to competition, enjoying the shared rewards of a team effort. They are usually delicate souls and sensitive to the needs and values of others. Cups individuals tend to be emotional, intuitive, caring, nurturing, protective and imaginative. When opposed, they can become secretive, sulky or passive-aggressive.

Swords people are usually talkative, curious, quick-minded and analytical. They are adept negotiators, appreciate ideas and concepts and enjoy networking in social situations. Swords individuals tend to be intellectual, observant, sharp-tongued, objective and inventive. When their shadow qualities emerge, they can become anxious, indecisive, overly talkative, hyperactive and mentally scattered and they thrive on gossip.

Pentacles individuals are often practical, conservative, hardworking and cautious. These people enjoy saving money and spending time in nature. They prefer what is familiar to new opportunities and derive a sense of security from comfortable routines. These people are usually realistic, grounded, materialistic, pragmatic and hard-working. When continually frustrated or opposed, they can become resistant to change, greedy, covetous and resist spending money.

Examples of tarot personality types are around us constantly. Even brief observations of people can confirm this. I witnessed the directness of a wands approach in 1986 when studying hypnosis. One of the teachers, a psychiatrist, arrived in a wheelchair and started the lesson. He was an enthusiastic speaker and we were in fits of laughter throughout the evening.

I mentioned to a wands friend who was also attending that it wouldn't surprise me if the teacher was perfectly healthy and able to walk but had decided to arrive in a wheelchair to teach us not to form opinions about our clients before knowing the whole story about them. My friend mentioned this to the teacher during a tea break in the third week and he roared with laughter.

Then he explained. "I can walk a bit, but I use the chair because I have multiple sclerosis. Some days are better than others. But it's a reasonable version of events."

I wanted the earth to open up and swallow me whole when I realised how tactless I had been to even suggest such a thing to my friend and I was angry with her for mentioning it to him. She didn't mean any harm; she simply displayed a lack of tact as wands people are prone to.

An example of wands and pentacles behaviour occurred while I was teaching a course several years ago. It was midwinter and we had an open fire going all day. During the lunch break, two students decided to head for a local cafe for a bite to eat.

"Is it cold out there?" asked the Queen of Pentacles.

"Not really," replied the Queen of Wands.

They left but the Queen of Pentacles returned a minute later, shivering.

"It's freezing out there," she muttered, collecting her coat. The Queen of Wands reasoned that if she was cold, she could walk faster and speed up her blood circulation, whereas the Queen of Pentacles wanted to be comfortable for the whole journey.

"Which court card am I?" is often asked during introductory tarot courses. As I describe the qualities of each court card, many students can relate to more than one. Most people exhibit the qualities of two different suits and sometimes even three. I have a friend who seems to combine the wands and swords suits perfectly. She has the swords qualities of being curious, talkative, sociable and is an excellent negotiator but when she's frustrated, she can suddenly become a Queen of Wands. She is immediately bossy, forthright, impatient and demanding.

In a recent course, a soft-spoken girl asked which court card she was. Her blue eyes and blonde hair suggested that she could be a Queen of Cups. I observed her during the course and later suggested she might be a Queen of Wands, instead, as she sometimes displayed a fiery temperament. She disagreed with me until another student reminded her of her actions at lunch in a local cafe. She had stood up and shouted for service, declaring she was "... bloody starving over here!" to the amusement of the other diners. We often share the qualities of two court cards but usually display more characteristics of one type.

From seeing a little Page of Wands throwing a tantrum in the supermarket, to observing the Knight of Swords sitting with a list of questions in the second row of a lecture theatre at a talk on politics or philosophy, it is easy to understand the meaning of a card when you see it in action. For aware tarot readers, the world is their classroom.

On a visit to my accountant many years ago, I sat in a chair outside his office observing the open-plan main office. A dozen people worked steadily but in noticeably different ways. One woman spoke softly to someone on a headset phone while typing rapidly onto her keyboard. It sounded like muffled rain on a tin roof as her hands flew across the keyboard. I guessed she was probably a Queen of Swords, adeptly multitasking.

Another woman glanced up and noticed me looking in her direction before quickly averting her gaze. Instead of the boldness of a Queen of Wands, she displayed the innate shyness of a Queen of Cups.

A man sat with his back to me. From the appearance of his desk, I guessed he might be a King of Pentacles. Two biscuits were visible through a small plastic container, saved for later. The container had a sticker with his name on it. It was an orderly solution to the fluctuating availability of office biscuits — save some aside in your own container early in the morning and consume them at 3 o'clock with your afternoon tea.

Presumably, his training in economics and basic observation had revealed a rapid increase in the demand for biscuits between 10 and 11:30 a.m. with the limited supplies often being exhausted before lunch. Perhaps he preferred fruit for morning tea and avoided disappointment by securing a personal ration for the afternoon break.

Another man leaned back in a chair while on the phone. He tossed a baseball into the air repeatedly as he spoke, putting it down on the desk only when he needed to write something in a pad. The loosened tie, dishevelled appearance and messy desk suggested he might be either a Knight or a King of Wands.

When I entered my accountant's personal office, the walls were lined with framed photos of cricketers, suggesting another King of Wands. It's possible that everyone in his office was an accountant or trained bookkeeper yet had different approaches to their daily tasks according to their types.

As a general rule, there are usually more wands people on construction sites because they enjoy the outdoors and don't mind a bit of noise and action. There are occasional visits from architects, engineers and other swords people, who turn up in suits and hard hats, carrying plans, clipboards and iPads with lists of measurements.

Wands people don't usually enjoy paperwork, so if they work for themselves, they need an assistant or a partner to send invoices and keep records. They thrive in sales and marketing and are often adept at promoting themselves.

In the 1980s, a cheeky young wands friend was applying for a position in an office. It wasn't a job he desired but he needed to pay his rent. Jason felt the interview went well and at the end, he asked the interviewer how many applicants she had interviewed for the job.

"You are number 41. I have one more after you."

"Then how will you remember me?" he asked bluntly.

"I probably won't," she replied. He knew he had around ninety seconds to say or do something to ensure he was remembered, so he began speaking as he formed his plan.

"I'm going to stand up now and take all my clothes off so you'll remember me," he said, as he rose from the chair.

"It's okay. I'll remember you," she said immediately. He had no plan to remove his clothing but simply to stand out in a crowd of interviewees. It worked. He was hired for the position. Of course, in this day and age, he'd probably be arrested and escorted from the building but this interview occurred in the 1980s.

Cups people enjoy group activities when everyone works in harmony. However, when there is strife or competition, they usually seek solitude. Careers such as creative writing, photography, painting, web design, improving the user experience with websites and counselling appeal to cups people. They usually thrive in jobs where they can make an emotional difference and in careers that are not filled with too many stressful deadlines and demands.

If you want to start a business but don't know how to go about it, a swords person is the best type to help you make clear, effective plans. These are the individuals who are not afraid to phone thirty strangers in a day to solve an issue, ask questions most people don't even consider asking and help create a network of helpful individuals along the way.

Swords people thrive where they can meet new customers, negotiate solutions that benefit everyone and exchange ideas. They are quick to release old habits when shown a better way to accomplish a goal and they make excellent trainers, project managers, lawyers, supervisors, teachers or business coaches. They excel in any career where communication is paramount.

Departments that require stable, predictable individuals who enjoy routine and repetitive work, usually thrive with plenty of pentacles people. In business, they fundamentally understand that the purpose of commerce is to create wealth or eventually sell the organisation to make a large sum of money, so they work diligently towards that long-term goal.

Pentacles individuals thrive in accounts departments, government planning and finance, banking and with a healthy dose of wands energy, in business finance and acquisitions. Add even more wands energy and they are attracted to the stock market. Extreme wands energy entices these people to casinos or horse tracks, hoping that one more wager will make up for a bad month of betting. They are risk-takers.

Within any business there is a combination of types. And even in an industry, such as accountancy, practitioners differ in approach according to their type. It's the same for sales. A wands (fire) salesperson wants to achieve the highest sales total of the whole team every month. Life is a competition for wands individuals, where the ultimate goal for any contest is to win.

Cups salespeople usually have a basic desire to make customers happy with their purchases. They are prepared to spend more time with each potential buyer to listen to their needs and sometimes to their life stories. They like to forge emotional connections with their clients and are usually helpful with after-sales service.

Swords salespeople are effective negotiators and often have a carefully rehearsed response to any quibbles or doubts customers may present. Pentacles salespeople, however, eventually realise that competing for sales in a crowded market is expensive, especially when advertising, marketing and staff budgets are considered. Instead, they believe it is more rewarding to sell wholesale, needing less staff to service a smaller number of clients who usually purchase on a larger scale.

While a wands salesperson is proud to have closed four sales in a day, the pentacles sales associate might take weeks to close one. However, that single sale might be for many units. As the wands person spends each week selling retail because he prefers associating with lots of customers, the pentacles individual cuts the sales force, the marketing budget and the advertising expenses, allowing for an immediate wholesale discount to buyers of multiple units.

These different types simply represent diverse perspectives. One approach is not necessarily better or worse than another. They all add their talents to a situation. If you're in a hurry to fill a 5,000 seat venue for a guest speaker at short notice, a wands or swords person is likely to be more effective than cups or pentacles individuals. Wands and swords people are quick to act. Wands people won't take *no* for an answer, while swords people usually have a ready-made network to assist with suppliers, etc.

When preparing an annual ballet or opera program, a cups person might design a beautiful booklet and orchestrate a memorable first-night event, while a pentacles individual could find the best corporate sponsorship to pay for the printing and the food and drinks at a gala performance. Everyone has a unique set of talents that are a blend of the four basic types.

Four Stages of Maturity

As children mature into adults, they pass through the four suits of the minor arcana as detailed below. When people struggle to master a stage of development, it is likely they'll exhibit some or all of the negative qualities of the suit. However, when individuals progress with their development, they no longer display those qualities.

Wands

This phase is about learning to discipline oneself. Before children learn to pace themselves, they might eat until they feel unwell or forget to eat because they are enjoying themselves.

Prior to teenagers learning temperance, they sometimes drink alcohol until they are ill or stay up half the night and pay the price the following day. The wands phase is an opportunity to gain self-discipline over temper, passion and enthusiasm. With a surplus of energy and a strong will, it's not always an easy task. It's a process of harnessing enthusiasm and passion towards a goal and sustaining the fire within to maintain momentum. Too much passion can cause arguments with others, while too little enthusiasm means momentum is lost at the first hurdle.

The shadow side of wands can be overly competitive and combative when they can't get their way. If they have missed the learning around planning and pacing themselves, they may tire early and fail to reach desired goals. They can be easily diverted by a new tangent that holds the promise of instant happiness. Negative wands people often end up living with the consequences of an intemperate or undisciplined lifestyle. This can include poor health or financial hardship in later years if personal energies or finances are squandered early on.

These individuals sometimes seek drama and conflict to feel more alive. If so, they may push friends and partners away in their quest for more excitement and risk loneliness in later life. They are gamblers and risk-takers, often taking huge chances without sufficient thought for the likely consequences. Too much spontaneity is not necessarily beneficial.

Cups

This phase involves learning how to share with others. It's an opportunity to discover how to relate to others and appreciate people with similar or different personal values. It is a process of discovering how central love, creativity and joy are in everyday life. The cups approach is usually nurturing, protective and secretive. Sometimes, cups people feel they are too emotionally sensitive and fragile for this world. This phase is one of learning how universal love can alleviate existential aloneness.

In the shadow side of cups, there is a tendency to become self-absorbed, melancholic, resentful and unwilling to forgive or forget. Old hurts can be restimulated by mentally replaying past events or clinging to past opportunities not pursued. These individuals cannot relate easily to others and want life on their own terms. Instead of asking or negotiating to have needs met, they expect others to instinctively know what they want and become resentful when unexpressed demands are not addressed.

Negative cups people tend to sulk or withdraw if unable to get their own way. These periods of silence can extend to weeks, months or even years, while they avoid discussions, negotiations or attempts at resolution. There is a risk of a lonely life, filled with regret. They can squander present opportunities while brooding over past hurts. Without creative avenues for personal nourishment, they can become depressed.

Swords

A swords phase is an opportunity to learn to socialise with other people and discover how to effectively negotiate to have personal needs met. It is about recognising the increased power of a team effort. People on this path tend to be intellectual, observant and inventive. They can be hyperactive and sometimes anxious when stressed. This perspective is about appreciating the benefit of strangers with different perceptions who offer new perspectives and solutions to life's challenges.

People who miss the lessons in a sword phase have a propensity for criticising themselves and others. They can lack social skills and become sarcastic, cynical or bossy. The shadow aspect of swords uses sharp words or interfering ideas to divide teams, friends or partners. This can be through gossip or as a result of insecurity about not being popular.

These individuals can become narrow-minded when faced with people of different beliefs. They also tend to be quick to find a weakness in a plan and plant seeds of doubt in the intentions and ideas of others. They habitually undermine their own goals and the plans of others by vacillating or being overly critical. Their indecision can sometimes descend into mental chaos. When this happens, resolutions prove impossible because they are afraid that a better alternative or path is just around the next corner. A postponed or avoided choice usually results in opportunities evaporating when circumstances change.

Pentacles

Pentacles people are learning to balance previous lessons of self-discipline, sharing with others and working in teams, as they realise the need to financially fund their existence. They are discovering how to harness groups for practical purposes. Through self-discipline (wands), noble motives (cups), careful planning and team effort (swords), pentacles people can direct their energies towards long-term stability. These people are learning about the power of persistence, patience and quiet determination. They are long-term planners who endure well after others have given up. This perspective involves the need to pace oneself for the long haul, ensuring a comfortable, routine and financially stable existence.

With negative pentacles, there is an insatiable desire for wealth or material possessions. These people sometimes display a constant physical hunger (masking underlying, spiritual emptiness). They can struggle with increasing debt levels. Although they recognise the importance of money in providing better life choices, they often have poor fiscal training. Personal goals and unconscious financial beliefs are at odds with each other. It's possible to retrain with better financial strategies to alter their trajectory but this requires time, commitment and prolonged effort.

These people are often unable to pace themselves for long-term fulfilment. They lack the patience and persistence of upright pentacles, preferring to live the good life immediately. They can be hedonistic. They cannot delay gratification, want everything instantly and often end up paying with interest. A $350 jacket purchased with a credit card can end up costing twice as much when someone isn't paying more than the minimum repayments for a while. The act of purchasing can temporarily alleviate the frustration of not having enough money to live comfortably. However, the long-term result can be external (financial) or internal (spiritual) poverty. Everyone can display the negative traits of fire, air, water and earth, especially when frustrated or stressed.

The Aces

The aces represent the beginning of new projects. Each ace shows a different approach to starting new ventures. Aces highlight a desire to forge ahead, to take charge and lead from the front.

Three or more aces in a layout indicate a fresh start or a change resulting in a new environment. Three or more reversed aces in a layout suggest opportunities are being blocked or delayed at the moment. The individual is unable to see or pursue new directions presently. It is a time of being overloaded by present commitments.

Each ace contains a hand extending from a cloud holding the object of the suit (a wand, cup, sword or pentacle). These hands reveal auric energy fields, indicating that the object is a spiritual gift or inspiration. The clouds behind each hand mask an unseen, etheric world. The aces show the initial idea or motivation to pursue each path to its conclusion. They are not guarantees of success but represent ideas that are worth pursuing.

The wands direction indicates fulfilment through action, achieving and conquering life's obstacles. It is a path of direct experience. This adventurous route requires the courage to learn from doing. It's the slowest way to learn but very effective because each mistake is ingrained. This is why wands people are impactful teachers; they have direct familiarity with what works and what doesn't.

The cups objective is inner peace, contentment through uniting with others while providing support and being sustained by creative pursuits. The message here involves remembering that we are spiritual beings in physical bodies and that both the soul and the physical body need nourishment. It's a path of shared encounters, through love, friendships and family or group activities.

The swords path offers the possibility of understanding why life is the way it is. It reveals the power of thinking to sort useful ideas from merely novel concepts. It hints at a successful life resulting from effective life strategies. Whereas wands people learn by doing, swords people learn by reading, talking, discussing, observing and combining ideas and possibilities. The swords perspective is more comfortable with theories than direct involvement. These are ideas that come when someone notices patterns in their surroundings.

The pentacles path suggests the rewards of commitment, peace and a comfortable environment in later years. It highlights earthly stability after prolonged effort. While cups people keep one foot in the spiritual world and the other in the physical, pentacles people accept that, although a spiritual force may have put them here on earth, it is up to each individual to embrace their environment and make the most of life. They effectively have both feet in the physical, practical world.

To make the most of their environment, pentacles people understand the value of persistence, steady effort, planning for the future and the power of compound interest. They instinctively understand that money or wealth equals choice. The more sources of income an individual has, the more options available to them. It is not necessarily a pursuit of happiness but a simple desire for comfort that drives this path. Earthy individuals realise wealth makes plans possible.

At the end of each route lies the objective of the journey. The wands direction presents a wealth of experience, while a cups path offers treasured memories. The swords approach contains an abundance of ideas, concepts and beliefs, whereas the pentacles path provides material wealth and comfort.

In combination, each path is a necessary pillar in a stable society. Wands people prefer adventure, excitement and direct involvement. Cups people need nurturing and creativity with compassion for individuals who are struggling. Swords people help us understand ourselves through theories and concepts while noticing patterns in behaviour, in society and the universe. Pentacles individuals provide financial stability that forms a more cohesive society. While cups people offer kindness and charity to the poor, a pentacles approach is to encourage the underprivileged to improve their skills and find stable sources of income for better lives.

Ace of Wands

This Ace represents urgent physical action. Wands people think that plans are for other people; they like to transform their ideas immediately into action before they lose the essence of the inspiration. 'From impulse to accomplishment through action' is a simple description of the Ace of Wands. When this card appears in a layout, there is usually sufficient energy and enthusiasm to begin new projects or initiate the first steps.

ACE of WANDS.

In this card, the hand extends from a cloud, indicating inspiration for action comes from a spiritual source. In a relationship layout, it can suggest a new partnership or a new stage of an existing one. It's the act of inviting someone to lunch or dinner, asking for a phone number or initiating a conversation.

In relationships, the wands approach is to step forward confidently and risk rejection by asking a person out on a first date, whereas this boldness is rare in a cups person. Wands people are not shy, retiring types. 'No risk; no gain' is the spirited attitude of most wands people. Occasionally, this card suggests meeting a new partner while roaming, as the Ace of Wands represents travel.

In a general reading, the Ace of Wands describes a call to action. It's a physical beginning — the act of taking a concrete step towards a goal. It can indicate travel, movement (to a new job or home) or simply pushing plans forward.

In a career layout, this card describes an occupation that involves travel or in which the person is outdoors or even on the road for part of each day. It can suggest the enthusiastic pursuit of a new job or the process of exploring different opportunities. The Ace of Wands can highlight the start of a new job or a different position within the client's current organisation. Sometimes, if the occupation involves project work, the Ace represents beginning a new assignment.

In a relationship question, the Ace of Wands indicates an individual who is motivated to pursue a new opportunity. Sometimes it occurs in a layout when a person is about to travel interstate or overseas in pursuit of love. It might be to cement an Internet romance, to follow someone who has already departed or to be introduced to a potential partner by a distant relative.

In a health query, the upright Ace of Wands indicates sound health and vitality. This individual has sufficient energy after a busy week to pursue sports, spend time at a gym or enjoy a long run. Wands cards indicate an interest in the outdoors and physical activities.

Ace of Wands Reversed

The reversed Ace of Wands suggests an inability to transform personal impulses or ideas into reality. This is often because of too many existing commitments. There isn't enough time or sufficient energy for another project at the moment. Sometimes, there is a period of hesitation or a lack of confidence preventing a person from taking the first steps on a journey.

Returning to the lesson of the previous card, the Ten of Wands, will help resolve issues. The Ten of Wands shows a person struggling under the burden of too many commitments or obligations. Removing some of those stresses might create the time and space to pursue a new project. Adding another goal to an already hectic workload often results in disappointment.

Wands people don't like delays because they are impatient. They favour honesty over tact, as it allows them to get to the heart of a matter quickly and efficiently. Wands people sometimes pace around, biting their fingernails or impatiently tapping their fingers on a desk when held up or frustrated about beginning new projects. Delaying gratification is not easy for them. They are action people, so wasting time aggravates them. They worry that if they don't act now, someone else might come along and take this opportunity and make it wildly successful. Being innately competitive, wands people usually regret abandoning an idea or a plan that someone else has eventually made successful.

Brian is a classic wands person. One day, he sat with me in a cafe awaiting an important phone call. He repeatedly checked his phone, fiddled with his empty coffee cup and asked me the time, despite the watch on his left wrist. His eyes darted around the room in search of something to occupy his attention while he fidgeted with the coffee cup.

Unable to contain himself, he started scrolling through the names and numbers saved in the phone memory until he came to a name he remembered. He made a brief call, throughout it fiddling continuously with a teaspoon, until he said goodbye. About thirty seconds after he'd hung up, his telephone rang. The call he'd been expecting had come through while he was on the other call and it had gone directly to his message bank. He became even more frustrated when he returned the call as the other person had already left for lunch.

"Arrrgh!" he growled aloud, drawing the attention of everyone in the cafe. Ignoring them, he glared at his telephone. I felt my enjoyment of lunch fading, so I confiscated his device until we'd finished eating (another wands action). He glared at me for my initiative and I pointed to his plate. "Eat. Then, you can call him again."

In a general reading, the reversed Ace of Wands indicates delays in acting on plans. It's time to return to the previous upright card in the suit, the Ten of Wands, to realise there is no room for any new commitments until completing or delegating some existing projects. Use this period wisely, so that when it's time to move forward, there is a clear path to personal goals. Resolving unfinished projects is necessary, so the path ahead contains fewer obstacles to new plans.

In a career layout, the reversed Ace of Wands can show delays in career progress. This person might be waiting for a new position that won't be available until funding is approved for a project. If the individual is self-employed, it can suggest that current frustrations are due to unfinished business.

In a relationship question, this card describes someone who is eager to push ahead with a relationship but might not have carefully considered the long-term implications of current plans. Delays at this time provide an opportunity for reflection on the different expectations of spouses, as well as each person's unspoken needs. Interruptions also provide time to resolve past relationships and prepare for a new partnership.

In a health query, the reversed Ace of Wands describes exhaustion resulting from pursuing too many projects or interests. A return to the previous upright card in the suit, the Ten of Wands, shows a person burdened by too many commitments. Each project or scheme seemed simple at the beginning but most of them have blossomed into complex, long-term challenges. Sometimes, this card describes a plan to increase one's daily physical exercise — an intention that involves the use of much of one's limited available time. Plans are delayed and many are eventually shelved because of obligations and limited time. This is not someone who has time to rest and smell the roses. This is a busy person who cannot even remember planting roses.

Ace of Cups

The Ace of Cups represents a time of feeling connected to life emotionally and spiritually. On the types of days represented by the Ace of Cups, I awaken with ideas for a story or a project I'm working on and am so excited about the creative possibilities of the day ahead I am unable to remain in bed a minute longer.

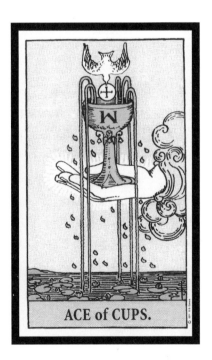

ACE of CUPS.

In this card, the hand extends from a cloud to hold a cup flowing over with emotional and spiritual fulfilment. The red water lilies emphasise the passion and physical energy required to make ideas real. There is a desire to translate creative inspiration into physical form. This might represent a piece of music, a joke, a banana cake, a painting, a series of photos of roses in bloom, writing a talk or preparing a presentation. Giving an idea physical structure allows it to be shared with others.

The white wafer held in the dove's mouth signifies the spiritual component of an idea or a creative endeavour. This can mean capturing the concept in a painting, a photographic image or written form to maintain its unique essence. If an idea is shared verbally before it is crystallised (photographed, painted or written down), there is a risk that the input of those who hear about it might dilute or change it from its original concept. What inspires the artist, writer or musician can be rendered into creative structures and shared with others.

In a general reading, the Ace of Cups represents a spiritual and emotional connection to life. This occurs when a person falls in love, begins a rewarding creative project or discovers new friends, hobbies and interests that provide spiritual and emotional nourishment. In answer to a question about pursuing a relationship, a job or a new direction, the upright Ace of Cups confirms fulfilment is likely to accompany this choice.

In a career layout, this Ace confirms a job that offers creative nourishment and emotional rewards. Ongoing personal satisfaction may come from making a difference to the lives of others, supporting a community or bringing a unique, creative approach to current tasks. When this card is in a career layout, the individual is motivated to pursue work goals and generally finds emotional satisfaction in day-to-day duties and responsibilities.

In a relationship question, this is a card of happiness, fulfilment and joy. In answer to a question about love, it confirms contentment, emotional connections and inner peace. The Ace of Cups can indicate a new relationship or a beneficial fresh stage in an existing one. It also indicates that a person has plenty to offer a partner, due to strong connections to spiritual and emotional nourishment. An individual who feels complete and fulfilled before commencing a new relationship is often secure enough to establish a stable partnership. When one is solidly connected to a spiritual source of energy, this person can sometimes help others to centre themselves. However, it is critical to be aware that long-term fulfilment comes from within, not from others. The only lasting sustenance in life is spiritual nourishment; everything else is fleeting. If a partner decides to leave, there are feelings of loss but a key, spiritual source of fulfilment is also available. Although this doesn't diminish the sadness, it can minimise feelings of isolation and devastation during the change.

In a health query, the upright Ace of Cups indicates balanced health. This individual can be emotionally and spiritually nourished and connected to life through friends, interests and pursuits.

Ace of Cups Reversed

The Ace of Cups reversed suggests a loss of spiritual connection. The person is relying too heavily on other people for fulfilment. This often leads to disappointment.

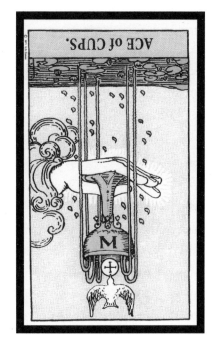

Sometimes, the reversed Ace can indicate a fluctuating time of momentary gains followed swiftly by a disconnection from spiritual and emotional fulfilment. If the individual's friends or partners leave, other sources of emotional and spiritual nourishment become scarce and the person's mood swings from high to low.

This is a time to consider the value of the previous card, the Ten of Cups. Returning to the Ten of Cups highlights a chance to be surrounded by friends and family who are inclusive and supportive. It is time to remember that love, recognition and backup come from many sources. The group shown in the Ten might be a sports team, a religious or spiritual community, a walking group, a meditation circle or a regular yoga class or book club. The Ten of Cups is the perfect antidote to the aloneness shown with the Ace reversed. Sometimes, in a busy life, it's easy to overlook friends, family and supportive people.

If being surrounded by friends or family is not possible, look within for fulfilment. Meditation or quiet, reflective thinking while fishing, walking or gardening can be beneficial. Consider what nurtures you, emotionally and spiritually. Some nourishing activities include listening to music, drawing, eating wholesome food or spending an afternoon in the garden or by the ocean. Getting in touch with nature is an easy way to forge spiritual connections.

In a general reading, the reversed Ace of Cups indicates disconnection from life and from emotional fulfilment. It's time to reconnect with existing sources of emotional sustenance or find new, satisfying activities. This reversed card can describe a person who seeks emotional nourishment through others, which only offers fleeting happiness. It's time to establish solid personal habits and interests that provide emotional and spiritual contentment.

In a career layout, this card suggests the person is unhappy with a current occupation. It describes a job that is routine, without challenge and maybe emotionally depleting. Instead of changing jobs, it might be time to find personal avenues for nourishment outside career. These might include yoga, meditation, personal-interest courses, or joining a book club, a cycling team or a spiritual development group, so career is not the sole source of fulfilment.

In a relationship question, the person might not feel connected to a partner or may not even be in a relationship. The reversed Ace indicates an inability to maintain a connection with avenues of personal nourishment, resulting in boredom or unhappiness. It's time to return to the previous upright card in this suit, the Ten of Cups, and spend time amongst your spiritual family. Being with like-minded people who value and understand you can strengthen the resolve to build and maintain genuine connections to joy.

In a health query, the reversed Ace of Cups describes health issues stemming from unhappiness or lack of immersion in life. It also indicates there is no real motivation to improve health without the prospect of joy. It's time to clarify how life will improve with healthy new habits. By returning to the previous upright card, the Ten of Cups, this individual can reconnect with like-minded people and feel more supported in personal pursuits. This might mean strengthening bonds with physical family or being amongst a spiritual family of like-minded people. Once strong bonds are established to sources of personal nourishment, health is likely to improve.

Ace of Swords

The Ace of Swords highlights an intellectual or thoughtful approach to beginning a new project or adventure. It represents an idea or concept with a practical, workable plan for completion. Swords people like to plan or at least to come up with ideas which can then be discussed with others. This exchange of views is not necessarily for the purpose of refining ideas but simply for the sake of talking about something, as swords people usually enjoy interesting conversation.

By discussing their plans, swords people often enlist the help and support of others. Sometimes, it is only through talking about their intentions that these ideas become real or possible. Occasionally, they tell so many people what they intend to do they feel obliged to do what they have said they'll do. Swords people can talk themselves in and out of situations.

In this card, the wreath and the crown represent the ability to make plans work in the physical world, for ideas alone are cheap. Everyone knows someone who is filled with creative schemes that they believe are going to make them wealthy beyond their wildest dreams. However, taking those concepts all the way to practical completion is another task entirely. Words are not deeds.

ACE of SWORDS.

The Ace of Swords represents a clear vision of the path ahead. Jade showed me her outline for a novel she was writing and it demonstrated that she had a vivid concept. On a large, white sheet of paper, she had pasted around sixty small bright-yellow sticky notes that contained each scene or part of the story. The beginning, middle and the end were laid out clearly and Jade was systematically working her way to the finale. She was actually writing sixty short stories, using the same characters throughout. It was so clearly laid out that the next step of physically writing the novel appeared deceptively simple.

"Almost anyone could write a story with this system!" I exclaimed.

She laughingly replied. "Yes, they could but don't tell them or I'll never find a publisher."

The double edges of the sword represent the awareness of what it takes to turn an idea into reality. Basically, this card represents clarity of thought. While the Ace of Wands illustrates the old saying that a journey of a thousand miles begins with a single step, the Ace of Swords suggests that a successful voyage usually begins with a well-considered plan.

The cloud symbolises Spirit, the birthplace of all effective ideas. The hand firmly holding the sword emphasises a secure grasp of a concept. It's possible to turn that thought around and play with it while considering new applications for existing ideas.

An example of playing with a perception occurred when my son was six years old. I was putting him to bed when he started his routine of extending his awake time.

"I'm hungry."

"No, you're not. You couldn't finish your dinner only an hour ago."

"Then I'm thirsty," he continued.

"Look. You've had enough to eat and to drink. In fact, you've had enough of everything, so just go to sleep," I said firmly.

As I closed the door, I heard him quip, "I haven't had enough of tomorrow."

In a general reading, the Ace of Swords is a card for beginning with a clear plan. It is the awareness that the moments spent thinking and organising now can save time and expense later. It represents success through clear thinking. Swords people understand that a carefully considered idea that is tweaked and adjusted through the implementation phase has a better chance of success. The upright Ace shows an awareness of different viewpoints. This might include understanding how an end-user might find the product or considering how some people might be inconvenienced by pursuing this plan.

In a career layout, this card describes having a focused idea and including everyone in the organisation in the design process so that many issues can be addressed before the proposal is actioned. During initial planning meetings, colleagues with different training and perspectives are likely to see flaws in an idea that can be addressed without having to undo any existing work.

In a relationship question, the Ace of Swords highlights an awareness of the similarities and differences between partners, plus their willingness to negotiate to find a win/win for each spouse. It can describe a relationship with a shared purpose. This might be to buy a home, start a family, get out of debt or move to another town to escape bossy relatives.

In a health query, the upright Ace of Swords can represent a forthcoming medical procedure. It also describes a clear plan to build or maintain sound health plus awareness of what to avoid and what constructive habits will increase health and vitality.

Ace of Swords Reversed

The Ace of Swords reversed indicates a loose grip on a concept. It can reveal a half-baked idea or poor planning that results in failure. It sometimes describes an attempt to apply old logic to a new problem. This reversed card suggests thinking is currently clouded or illogical.

Returning to the previous card in the suit, the Ten of Swords, we see a person weighed down by destructive thinking, fruitless ideas and debilitating beliefs about life. Before new plans can be made, it is necessary to grasp this sword firmly and cut away outdated beliefs or mindsets that restrict personal progress. Sometimes, old attitudes prevent a person from even contemplating an action that might offer a solution to current issues. It's not that the person has carefully considered and then discounted a possible answer. Instead, the resolution seems invisible to that individual.

During a reading for Erin, her whole focus was around career. She had lost her confidence after a difficult relationship and left her job as an office manager. After a prolonged period without work, she found a position packing boxes in a factory and worked there for almost five years.

She was exhausted by the long hours and freezing work environment in winter and wanted a new job with potential for promotion. It was a reasonable desire but when Erin tried to word specific questions around new directions, her mind went blank.

I offered her a few different possible questions, including:

- What do I need to do to prepare for a more rewarding job?
- Is it time to complete some short courses to upgrade my skills for a new job?
- Will I be offered a suitable new position within four months?
- Is it wise for me to apply for office jobs in the coming months?

It was as though she had decided that a factory job was what she deserved for the rest of her life. I decided to take a different approach.

"Do you like your work in the factory?"

"It's okay, I guess."

"Do you feel you fit in with your fellow workers?"

"No. I've always felt the odd one out there."

"When you worked as an office manager, did you feel that you fitted in with your fellow workers?"

"Yes. I loved it there. I was strict but fair as a boss and lots of people told me that at the end when I was leaving."

"Then why did you leave?"

"After Theo left me, I sort of went to pieces. I couldn't concentrate. I couldn't sleep and I wasn't eating. I guess I lost my focus."

"You lost your focus," I repeated. "It's been a while now. Have you regained your focus yet?"

"Yes, I think so."

"Then what would you need to do to be able to move towards a more rewarding job? This is not about accepting a new position but simply taking one step towards a new occupation."

By drawing her focus away from a new career and towards a smaller, more manageable step, Erin was able to examine a less demanding, more achievable move, such as updating her resume, taking some short courses or practising interview techniques.

In a general reading, the Ace of Swords reversed emphasises delays in the commencement of new projects. It is time to re-evaluate current plans. If new strategies or projects are rushed, this person is likely to feel dissatisfied with the results. The reversed Ace of Swords describes clouded thinking or hastily conceived plans. More time is required to clarify the end goal and consider possible obstacles before launching into a poorly prepared project.

In a career layout, the reversed Ace of Swords indicates uncertainty about a job or broader career direction. It might be time to reconsider the desired career path, to assess if it will meet personal needs. Then think about the steps required to pursue this objective successfully. This card suggests a clear career strategy is lacking. Pinpoint what you want and how you plan to achieve it, before rushing forward towards new opportunities.

In a relationship question, the reversed Ace of Swords indicates confusion concerning a relationship or what is required from a partnership. By identifying one's underlying needs, an individual can determine whether a potential partner or current spouse can meet those requirements. Returning to the previous upright card in the suit, the Ten of Swords, highlights unhelpful beliefs around partnerships, possibly from previous incidents. Old attitudes need to be carefully reconsidered, so a potential new relationship is not tainted by past events.

In a health query, the reversed Ace of Swords may indicate a medical procedure.

It sometimes suggests the person needs a clear plan regarding personal health and well-being. From organising a fitness routine to improved eating habits, this individual might benefit from considering how past decisions and actions have impacted their health.

Ace of Pentacles

The upright Ace of Pentacles represents a practical opportunity to start a new project. It symbolises investing personal resources, such as money, effort, time or energy into a plan and highlights the possibilities of that opportunity.

ACE of PENTACLES.

The card shows a cloud with a hand issuing from it, holding a single pentacle. The five-pointed star within the two circles points upwards as a reminder that purpose in life includes keeping one's mind above or in control of passions and desires.

The five points of the star represent a person's head (top), two outstretched hands and their feet. An individual's head is closer to the heavens. The garden beneath the hand shows flowers in bloom, symbolising the rewards of practical application and effort.

Pentacles people understand the value of hard work and usually do what is necessary to achieve their objectives in a practical way. The two lines encircling the star represent the need to contain personal energy and direct it towards a useful purpose. In answer to a question about starting a new project, the upright Ace suggests either that money is available to start it or that financial assistance is likely to be forthcoming.

Basically, pentacles are practical, believing it is pointless to be so 'heavenly' that you are of no earthly use. These people are unlikely to believe that money is only energy and we need to share it without thinking. They usually work tirelessly for a steady income and as a result, their attitudes towards money and practical issues are usually pragmatic. "What's in it for me?" is a typical pentacles question.

The following story is an example of the pentacles attitude to money. It took place in a crowded weekend workshop in the late 1980s. As more than a hundred people sat in a conference room, the workshop coordinator asked each of us to produce a banknote for an exercise.

Some people produced $5 notes, some $10 notes and soon one hero was waving around a crisp $100 bill. The exercise involved exchanging our notes for others' notes of any denomination continuously for a period of ten minutes. After ten minutes, the coordinator asked us to stop and pocket whatever we had in our hands and sit down. The energy in the room slowly changed from excitement to anger and in some people to rage. I looked at the man who had started with a $100 note and he was sitting staring at a crumpled $2 bill in his hands.

Ten minutes later, as we began another exercise, a man stood up with some banknotes in his outstretched hand and said, "I'm uncomfortable about this. You see, I started out with a $10 note and now I have two twenties and a five in my hands."

Before he could say another word, a man seated behind him stood up and snatched the notes from his hands, saying, "Problem solved."

I burst into laughter at the brilliant and immediate solution, while the man standing glared at me as everyone began talking at once, attempting to find the banknote they had originally held.

The teacher silenced us before he spoke. "So, money is only energy, eh? It seems to me you all have a lot of your own individual energy invested in something that is only energy."

While everyone had verbally agreed that money was only energy, few of us fundamentally believed this to be true. Pentacles people know money is fundamental and they usually want their share of it. It was a cups person who declared his discomfort and a quick-minded swords person who saw a chance and swiped the notes from him. Earlier, I noticed a showy wands person happily trading a crisp $100 note for a faded $10 bill. As we began the next exercise, he didn't look happy. This exercise was simply to provide a glimpse into participants' underlying attitudes to money and our financial habits. Eventually, harmony was restored and money was returned but I've never forgotten how quickly the process stripped away our rational attitudes to show us our fundamental beliefs about money.

In a general reading, the Ace of Pentacles describes a person who is living within her means. This is someone who can eliminate or minimise debt and live comfortably on a regular income. In a question about a planned investment, it indicates that the funds to proceed with plans are available. It can also describe a new job or financial offer.

In a career question, this card indicates a new job or a different position within the current company. In a general career question, it indicates a new job or a fresh source of income, such as a part-time evening or weekend business. If the question is about the success of an investment or a specific career project, the upright Ace usually indicates positive financial results.

In a relationship question, the upright Ace of Pentacles can indicate that a specific partnership might benefit the person financially. This describes a spouse who is economically stable or able to assist the individual build a more balanced financial future. In some layouts, this card can suggest the person meets a new partner through work. This sometimes occurs at a business conference, a meetup, a meeting with a supplier or even a colleague from another part of the same organisation.

In a health layout, this card indicates a practical approach to physical health. Pentacles people believe in preventative maintenance, so they usually eat well, exercise regularly, have regular massages and ensure they have enough sleep. They form moderate health routines to ensure they are fit and healthy in retirement.

Ace of Pentacles Reversed

The Ace of Pentacles reversed indicates a time when money is slipping through your fingers. This could involve poor financial discipline or spending beyond current earnings. This happens to everyone at certain times of the year, when annual or monthly bills arrive and must be paid. It also occurs when on holidays, so the card reversed does not always indicate a difficult financial time but basically that spending is accelerated.

If several reversed pentacles cards occur in a layout, it's more likely to be an ongoing financial issue, or perhaps poor childhood training around money. Either the individual doesn't feel deserving of financial stability or cannot hold on to it when money arrives.

Pentacles people understand that the wages of sin is debt. One description of sin is to 'avoid the mark' when aiming for a goal. For example, if Jake's goal is to save $400 per month towards an annual holiday and he only manages to save $200 most months, at the end of a year he'll have missed his mark. Jake is likely to have only $2,400 of the $4,800 required for the planned vacation. If he goes on holiday anyway, using credit cards to fund his expenses, he'll still be paying for it long after his suntan has faded. Pentacles people understand that to truly enjoy a break, it needs to be paid for with savings. The holiday is a reward for living within personal financial means.

Several pentacles clients have such ingrained money habits they don't use credit cards and won't take out loans. They buy new cars with savings and only borrow money for property mortgages on rental investments. One client explained that although she uses a credit card for convenience, she pays it off in full every month.

When the pentacle in this card is upright, the mind governs desires. Although an individual might want a new outfit in a store window, she won't purchase it unless she can afford it. When the pentacle is reversed, desires govern thinking. As a result, almost every desire is satisfied, regardless of cost or current financial circumstances. Eventually, new plans become strangled by the need to service existing debts.

The reversed Ace of Pentacles as an answer to a question about a project suggests that the plan is unlikely to be financially rewarding, possibly costing much more than anticipated. It can also indicate that there are insufficient funds to support the project. Poor cash flow is the bane of many businesses.

In a general reading, this Ace reversed indicates there are more expenses than income at this point. It describes a poor result from an intended investment or that the seed money for a new business is not available. It's time to return to the previous upright card of the suit, the Ten of Pentacles. This suggests that financial stability or initial investment funds could come through a larger organisation. This might be a bank or finance company or through taking a job with a large company and steadily saving towards the intended investment.

In a career layout, it can describe a job that provides poor rewards for the effort required. Here, the reversed Ace of Pentacles can suggest leaving a job or that the position is not well paid. Sometimes, it indicates that a person is under-employed or unemployed. Money is being spent but not fully replenished. In a question about the outcome of a job application, it usually indicates disappointment. It's time to keep searching for more beneficial options. In a layout about a small business, the reversed Ace of Pentacles suggests insufficient income to sustain the individual or grow the business.

In a relationship question, the reversed Ace of Pentacles indicates financial pressures affecting a relationship or restricting opportunities to meet a new partner. Perhaps one partner is trying to save towards a goal, while the other is spending with no thought for tomorrow. Long working hours with low wages is another example of this Ace reversed in a relationship layout. It can suggest meeting a new partner through a workplace or a previous job. In some readings, it highlights different approaches to finances increasing tension in a relationship. Occasionally, it suggests that one partner's job prevents a relationship from developing. In a recent reading, Clara explained she spent ten days onboard an oil rig in the North Sea and then four days off at home. Her partner complained about her absences and eventually left her for someone who worked locally.

In a health query, this Ace reversed indicates insufficient funds for properly maintaining health. The individual might not be able to afford a surgical procedure, dentistry, ongoing physiotherapy after an injury or to continue a gym membership to maintain fitness levels. Sometimes, it suggests the individual's job is harmful to health and well-being.

The Twos

With the exception of the Two of Cups, the twos generally represent decisions. The Two of Wands indicates a choice about action, such as moving home, changing jobs or taking a trip. It shows a quick conclusion about a course of action. The Two of Swords represents the process of weighing up two alternatives mentally, comparing their strengths, weaknesses, opportunities and any threats to a successful outcome. The Two of Pentacles suggests financial and practical decisions. This is a choice about what is affordable or financially wise.

The Two of Cups differs as it indicates a close relationship. This partnership involves shared decision-making. Therefore, the Two of Cups is still partly a card of choices. It's about considering how one's actions affect a significant other. It sometimes indicates deciding whether to trust someone, to let them into your heart and your life.

Three or more twos in a layout (including The High Priestess, the major arcana two) suggest a series of substantial choices. It is necessary to consider worthwhile alternatives and clarify the most suitable direction. This might occur when a person commences divorce proceedings. It might be necessary to choose a new home, different schools for children, modify financial arrangements, adjust to a reduced social circle and other less urgent but significant negotiations. Three or more twos sometimes occur in a layout at retirement when a person is faced with changes in daily routines, social circles and opportunities to pursue new hobbies and interests.

Two of Wands

The Two of Wands highlights a decision between staying in an environment that is familiar but no longer stimulating or making a change that holds promise but might not deliver anticipated rewards.

This card appears when a person is considering leaving home, a job or even a relationship that is restrictive. It's time to move on. Action is required and the Two describes the process of making decisions about the appropriate course to take. The individual on the card is wearing an orange tunic, which represents an enthusiastic approach to life. The red hat highlights a passion for adventure and for mastering the physical world.

The world in his hand suggests his internal landscape feels small and he is keen to pursue adventures and challenges elsewhere. The low walls that initially offered security, now stifle and curtail his need to have real contact with life. The person in the card makes decisions in his own time, leaving when he feels circumstances have little to offer. This is a typical wands approach to life: if it isn't stimulating, something is wrong. They thrive on tests and challenges. Wands people are at their best when they have achievable goals ahead. Goals give them immediate purpose.

The water in the distance symbolises emotional fulfilment but a true wands person usually tires of stability and eventually leaves a comfortable, stable environment for new opportunities. There is no real challenge in still waters, especially when exciting adventures beckon. Wands individuals generally don't fully appreciate stability and comfort but tend to feel compressed and rut-bound when life becomes routine.

As it's a wands card, this decision is likely to involve a physical environment. It generally suggests a choice about changing home or work circumstances. It's not about the effort of changing position but the decision preceding the action. When upright, it suggests this is a suitable time to proceed.

In a general reading, the Two of Wands indicates a physical decision. This is likely to centre on whether to stay or leave the home or workplace. There is no urgency while the individual weighs up the benefits and costs of each option. As an outcome card, it can suggest the time is right to move forward.

In a relationship question, the Two can indicate a choice about moving to live with a partner or relocating to accommodate a growing family. New possibilities beckon while there is no urgency to make an immediate change. This Two highlights reflection that precedes action.

In a career layout, it indicates a choice between remaining in a job or career and moving forward to new opportunities. Taking time to reflect on the risks is wise, as an increased income is not always sufficient reward to compensate for making the change. It might involve a significantly higher workload with more responsibilities but without equivalent financial rewards.

In a health query, the Two of Wands suggests a decision between two or more paths to resolve an ongoing health issue. This might involve considering a new location to improve health and well-being. This Two appeared in Lauren's general reading and reflected her increasing concerns about her son's asthma. Jacque's asthma attacks were increasingly stressing the eight-year-old and his family because they lived in a town that was in an enormous dust bowl.

In an investment layout, it can show the desire to stay in current circumstances while still moving forward. This might mean remaining in the current home while investing in a rental property elsewhere that allows financial growth and improvement without the upheaval of relocating.

Two of Wands Reversed

The Two reversed indicates a time when decisions to act are thwarted due to personal fears. There is a need to make new friends and pursue challenges in order to grow. However, this person might be avoiding opportunities because the challenges involved increase anxiety about possible disasters ahead. Too much time is spent weighing up the risks rather than the possible rewards.

Fear of making a poor decision paralyses action. This occurred with Bob's friend Logan. Friends since school, they have been jogging buddies for more than twenty years. During that time, Bob purchased a range of inexpensive homes in the local area, renting them out to build wealth for retirement. Their jogging route took them past two of these properties so that Bob (a King of Pentacles) could keep an eye on them every week.

Bob encouraged Logan to invest in a rental property also. Although he liked the idea, Logan felt nervous about making a poor decision.

"What if I have bad tenants who wreck the place?"

"Then you deal with them, just as I have over the last decade. It's not rocket science. We know this suburb like the back of our hands. I can show you a few places and help you to start your property portfolio."

Logan hesitated while Bob bought and sold more houses, moving away from simple, single-storey weatherboard cottages to expansive brick homes in more expensive suburbs. He regularly showed Logan pages from the local newspaper listing suitable properties and they inspected some. However, Logan was unable to make a decision.

Gradually some of the properties Logan had rejected returned to the market for sale at significantly higher prices. Bob decided to have another housing investment conversation with his friend. During a scorching hot afternoon, they paused beneath a tree to rest before tackling a steep incline. Bob took some old newspaper clippings from his back pocket and a small part of a more recent listing from the same newspaper.

"Look at these. Since you first asked me about buying a house thirteen to fourteen years ago, house prices have gone up significantly around here. You knocked back a few at $50,000 and then a couple of years later, some in the same streets at $70,000. In a few streets, almost every house has been demolished and replaced with several townhouses. These tiny townhouses are now selling at $250,000 each. Today those old knock-down homes are averaging $450,000 each. So, when are you going to act? If you had bought a pair of houses at $50,000 each back then, you'd be at least $700,000 ahead by now. Sometimes, it's a mistake not to take action."

Finally, his friend heeded the message and within a few months had acted decisively, purchasing an investment property in that suburb.

The Two reversed indicates it is time to return to the Ace to focus personal energy in one direction, to decide what single goal is enough to inspire necessary changes in current circumstances. The objective must be sufficiently rewarding and just out of reach enough for effort and pursuit to be necessary. By the time the goal has been achieved, the person has moved on from the previous home, job or other environment.

In a general reading, the reversed Two of Wands indicates hesitation when making a locational decision. The person might be delaying changing jobs, home environment or saving for retirement. It's time to return to the previous upright card, the Ace of Wands, and act decisively on plans. The person has become comfortable and usually fears change when the reversed Two of Wands card is found in a layout.

In a relationship question, the reversed Two of Wands can indicate a person is hesitant about entering a new phase of a relationship. This might involve moving in with a partner, marriage, purchasing a home together or divorcing a former spouse to become available for a new long-term relationship. When this card appeared reversed in Heng's question about possible future relationships, he explained that he didn't want to divorce his partner while his parents were still alive. By the time they had both died, Heng was sixty-three and felt he had left it too long to find a new life partner. I suggested he return to the upright Ace of Wands and travel before giving up on love. Three years later, Heng's new wife arrived for a tarot reading. They met in his childhood province when he visited China during his travels.

In a career layout, this card describes hesitation when attempting to pursue a new job or career direction. The person is tempted to remain in a current job despite obvious viable opportunities and benefits for taking the next step. The individual might be choosing between a new job in the same field or taking a bigger risk with a complete change of career direction.

In a health query, the Two of Wands reversed suggests additional stress is being experienced through being confined by obligations and responsibilities and fearful of making changes that might upset friends or family. It often indicates hesitation when making a decision about health options.

Two of Cups

The Two of Cups signifies a productive union between two people. Whether it is a business, a person or even a musical partnership, the Two of Cups upright shows it is a beneficial alliance. Basically, it's an equal relationship.

In similar positioning to The Lovers card, a man stands to the right and a woman stands to the left, as they face each other. This also echoes the major arcana number two card, the High Priestess. The two pillars in that card symbolise the masculine (right) and the feminine (left) or the rational and the intuitive/creative energies. The partnership of these two qualities results in creative ideas becoming tangible in the form of physical goals.

The union between the man and woman is symbolised by the winged lion above the two snakes around the rod or the caduceus. This represents the strength that is a result of their friendship or relationship. The snakes cross four times in this image, indicating the partnership nourishes them on four levels: physically, emotionally, mentally and spiritually.

In many relationships or interactions between people, one partner takes a more active role, while the other occupies a passive role. In this Two of Cups, the man takes the active role, reaching for the cup while taking one step forward, whereas the woman assumes a more passive role. In some relationships, roles are reversed and the woman takes an active role while the man is more passive.

The Two of Cups shows the harmony between active and passive personalities. If both partners are keen to take an active role, there are likely to be more arguments about direction as two independent people struggle for control. If both people prefer passive roles, there might be limited motivation to move forward, with no urgency to reach goals. It is not always a love relationship. This partnership might be a creative union, with one person writing the music while the other composes the lyrics. It could be a viable arrangement where one individual paints canvases while the other promotes the product and arranges exhibition openings.

This card sometimes indicates two business partners in harmony with each other or simply a close friendship. It some instances, it shows two colleagues working well together on a project. In a love relationship layout, it indicates a compatible couple enjoying a devoted alliance.

In a general reading, the Two of Cups describes a nourishing association. Together, they can achieve more because each person brings something unique to the partnership. They work well together, each valuing the other person's contribution.

In a career layout, this card indicates a shared goal or two people working effectively together to complete a project successfully. It can describe a couple in business together. This partnership is successful because each person is aware of the other and they realise that both individuals have a right to be happy.

In a relationship question, the Two of Cups describes a couple who are close, equal and in harmony with each other. The winged lion indicates that this union produces intense passion, creativity and strength. It's a very beneficial card for a partnership.

In a health query, the Two of Cups indicates a close friend or partner providing support and care to encourage strong health. It can also suggest a close relationship is improving the individual's physical health. Sometimes, this involves a sympathetic medical specialist who is supportive during a health challenge. Generally, it indicates sound health.

Two of Cups Reversed

The Two of Cups reversed represents an imbalance that occurs when spiritual fulfilment is lost or obscured. When this link is disrupted, relying too heavily on other people can be debilitating. To ensure a continuous supply of replenishment or support, these individuals might attempt to control friends, family or colleagues for fear of being alone or unable to satisfy personal emotional and spiritual needs.

The reversed Two can describe a relationship or a partnership where both parties are emotionally unfulfilled; it is a union where each person believes they are not whole without the other. The Two of Cups reversed indicates an affiliation or union that is complicated but can be sorted out with sufficient will and courage to address the issues.

The Two of Cups reversed can indicate two people struggling to find a source of love that does not exist between them. There is always the option of returning to the previous card, the upright Ace of Cups, to reconnect with inner fulfilment. These spiritual attachments can occur through meditation, yoga, walking to enjoy some time alone, reconnecting with creative pursuits or simply remembering what they bring to relationships and what that's worth. When inner sources of nourishment have been re-established, it's time to return to the upright Two of Cups and enjoy equal friendships and relationships.

When reversed, the partnership becomes a struggle, as one companion relies on the other for personal happiness. This occurred with Ethan, who selected the Two reversed in a relationship layout. In the five years he'd been with Anke, their relationship had been rosy but gradually Ethan was worried they were losing their spark. Both Anke and Ethan had gradually relinquished their friends and family as they spent more and more time together. As they increasingly depended on each other for personal nourishment, they gradually spiralled down into a sense of emptiness.

It wasn't a difficult relationship. It simply lacked a wide range of nourishment sources. I encouraged Ethan to reconnect with his friends, his fitness regimen and the outside pursuits that had replenished him before meeting Anke and suggested that she do the same.

Nourishing yourself emotionally and spiritually is difficult enough in modern life without also having to be the single source of nourishment for a partner. The reversed Two of Cups symbolises someone who is relying too much on another person for replenishment at a cost to relationship harmony.

When Nicola selected the Two of Cups reversed, it described her home environment. At thirty-six years of age, she lived with her frail seventy-eight-year-old mother and feared she might never meet a man or have a family of her own. In the ten years since her father died, Nicola's mother, Alessandra, had withdrawn from her social circle. She left the house only when her daughter was present to assist her. This meant one shopping outing and one church visit each week.

Nicola rushed home every night to make dinner instead of catching up with friends or meeting a life partner. The layout suggested that without changing her life patterns, Nicola was likely to remain single for years to come. In a bid to help her mother to reconnect with friends and relatives she gave her an iPad. Over the next few months, she trained her mother to use the device. Alessandra didn't like emailing or texting but was excited when she discovered Skype and Facetime.

"I can see them. It's like they are right here in this room," she exclaimed. Gradually, Alessandra relied on Nicola less because her friends and relatives were more accessible. A few months later, Alessandra accepted an invitation to dinner at her cousin's home and asked Nicola to take her. Instead, Nicola downloaded an app onto her iPad and booked a ride with a private taxi company. When dinner concluded, Alessandra's nineteen-year-old nephew booked her ride home using the same device. Over the next two years, Alessandra widened her social circle and Nicola was free to reconnect with her friends and go on dates. When I read for her several years later, Nicola was engaged to be married and seemed much happier with her life.

In a general reading, the reversed Two of Cups represents a partnership that is a roller coaster ride. A harmonious morning can be followed by a tense afternoon and an argument before dinner, before sulking throughout dessert. There may be an element of jealousy or possessiveness in this partnership if one person relies on the other as a sole source of happiness.

In a career layout, this card suggests a close working relationship between two people with very different ideas of how to complete tasks. One person usually feels stifled or controlled by the other. There are benefits to returning to the previous upright card, the Ace, to find some other individual projects outside of that partnership that offer fulfilment.

In a relationship question, the reversed Two of Cups describes an underlying power struggle in a partnership. When people wrestle for control, there is usually minimal intimacy. This can trigger fears of abandonment as well as increase the other partner's desire for dominance. Basically, the reversed Two of Cups describes a changeable relationship that can become emotionally draining for both participants. It's time to return to the previous upright card, the Ace, to find emotional nourishment that limits reliance on a partner.

In a health query, the reversed Two can indicate a partnership or a relationship might be draining the person. This association is costing the individual physical and emotional energy that might be better spent in other areas of life. It's time to step back and find other viable sources of emotional sustenance.

Two of Swords

The Two of Swords represents decisions. It indicates brief periods when people retreat to decide where they fit in the world. It's a short time of reflecting on personal beliefs about life.

The person in the card sits on a stone seat, clutching two swords defensively, for protection, despite the blindfold. To see the real threats (if any) in this environment, it is necessary to remove the blindfold. Almost everyone has blind spots. To disconnect from unresolved fears and past hurts buried within, it is vital to perceive life as it really is, instead of peering through a dusty lens of past experiences. Sometimes, previous detrimental encounters leave people with distorted perceptions of life.

Some clients are so frightened about what they might hear in a tarot reading they select cards with shaking hands. Confidence in optimistic news has been replaced by the dread of a desperate and inescapable future, despite nothing undesirable in the reading. When this occurs, I accept that personal distortions are clouding perceptions, perhaps preventing them from being present for what is often an exciting opportunity.

When the Two of Swords occurs in a layout, it is time to peel away the blindfold of personal prejudice, opinion and partial fact and see life clearly, without distortions or judgments. This requires courage, effort and deliberate purpose.

The yellow shoes symbolise the examination of life through thoughts (yellow represents clarity of thought) while attempting to make sense of all those swirling emotions indicated by the water. The Hanged Man also has yellow shoes, suggesting use of thought to escape the confines of current circumstances.

In the Two of Swords, the person feels restricted by emotions and feelings. The moon above confirms an unsettling sense of dread, increasing with the onset of night. The moon in this card can also represent unresolved issues that can be accessed through dreams at night. This card has a similar meaning to the moon shown in the major arcana number two, the High Priestess. In the High Priestess card, the moon is at her feet, suggesting that encouraging and creative solutions to problems sometimes come from within, through dreams at night.

Occasionally when this card surfaces in a reading, I add two cards to it, one each side, to clarify the two alternatives available in that situation. For example, in one general reading, the Two of Swords appeared as the third card (representing the next three months) and I added the Ace of Pentacles and the Page of Swords each side of it, to consider the alternatives. The client agreed she was undecided about whether to save to take a brief holiday overseas soon (Page of Swords) or to continue to save her money (Ace of Pentacles) in order to have a longer holiday later.

Basically, this Two describes examining alternatives before making a decision. The person in this card might have reached for a blindfold to prevent distractions during this selection process. This can be done by retreating from social situations, meditating on possibilities or taking a walk alone to consider the viable options before deciding on a course of action.

In a general reading, the Two of Swords describes weighing up two alternatives before a decision is made. It sometimes signifies a brief retreat from daily life to reflect on immediate issues. This can be an effective way to clarify the next steps.

In a career layout, this card occurs when a person has to decide between two career alternatives. This might be two job offers, staying in a current position or accepting a promotion or two courses of study that lead in different career directions. The blindfold worn is useful in that it prevents immediate distractions from influencing this decision. It helps to still the mind to make a clear choice.

In a relationship question, this Two describes a retreat from life to reflect on a past or current love relationship. It can also indicate a period of reflection on love partnership patterns before commencing a new one.

In a health query, the upright Two of Swords shows a person choosing between two approaches to health. This individual is assessing choices, such as traditional medicine or an alternative approach and has retreated to consider these options carefully. It sometimes clarifies the situation when an additional card is added to each side of this card on the table to explore other possibilities. Each additional card represents one sword or choice. The client selects each extra card while thinking about each option.

Two of Swords Reversed

The Two of Swords reversed highlights mental confusion. It suggests too much thinking with scant direct experience. It describes a period when reasoning is chaotic and sometimes circular. Basically, it means that clear plans with specific conclusions are difficult to make and unlikely to be achieved during this period. It's time to make sense of personal feelings and decide how to re-enter life emotionally.

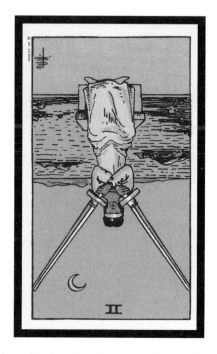

Perhaps after an unsettling event, the person is struggling to make sense of circumstances. He or she might feel overwhelmed or concerned about stability going forward. If, for example, workplace tensions unexpectedly spilled over into a raucous argument, staff might consider leaving or worry about possible ill-treatment in the future. This card could describe the mental struggle between hoping it was a one-off incident and actively finding a new job.

Sometimes this card suggests an attempt to make sense of several emotional issues simultaneously. The person needs to focus on one problem at a time. By tackling too much at once, it's likely that nothing will be resolved satisfactorily.

There are benefits in returning to the previous card in the suit, the upright Ace of Swords, to select a single direction with one set of beliefs about life. Tackling one concern at a time is a meaning for the upright Ace of Swords. By adding two extra cards (one each side), it's possible to highlight the issues that are confusing.

When reversed, the image shows the water above the person's head, suggesting that emotions are clouding logical thinking right now. Perhaps there are too many choices or several options appear indistinguishable from each other.

Returning to the previous card, the upright Ace of Swords, involves the process of eliminating choices by assessing the likely consequence of each path. With the water above the head of the person in this card, it's likely that relinquishing options will be an emotionally difficult process. It is also possible that the person is being sentimental about opportunities not pursued. This individual believes a different path would have produced a better outcome. It is not necessarily so. When the Two of Swords is reversed, it highlights fuzzy thinking.

Making sound choices involves discarding some options, possibilities, people and possessions. When a person plans to climb a steep mountain, it's necessary to pack accordingly. Luggage is unlikely to consist of a bookcase, a comfortable chair and a dining table. Instead, warm clothing is essential, despite the relentless heat at the base of the mountain on the day of packing. Ask yourself what attitudes, ideas or obligations are holding you back from pursuing your goal.

In a general reading, the reversed Two of Swords describes a drawn-out decision-making process. The person might be confused or unhappy with available options. Now the water (emotions) in this image is above the person's head (the intellect), suggesting that emotions are influencing thinking. When the Two of Swords is reversed, it is key to focus on the desired outcome rather than the past. By looking ahead, it is easier to notice and avoid obstacles. Emotions about previous actions and their consequences can obscure this process if allowed free rein. Remaining aware of fundamental long-term needs can lead to more productive decisions. By identifying goals and eliminating unfavourable choices, one strong path gradually emerges.

In a career layout, the reversed Two indicates a need to return to the previous upright card, the Ace of Swords, to remember the purpose of a planned career path with clarity. Perhaps the individual is lost or has been side-tracked by a demanding position that offers few prospects for advancement. It's time to clarify underlying needs before reassessing available paths to prosperous personal career goals.

In a relationship question, this reversed card indicates a person wrestling with how to walk back into life after an emotional setback. In attempting to make sense of past circumstances, this individual has retreated and cannot step forward until fathoming why events occurred. It can also show the process of making sense of recent events. Sometimes, it represents a decision to re-engage emotionally after a difficult relationship breakup or following grief over the loss of a loved one. This requires courage to refocus on long-term underlying needs (happiness and renewed participation in life) rather than concentrating on what has been lost or left behind.

In a health query, the reversed Two of Swords suggests the person is likely to be considering two alternatives to improving personal health. It describes a period of confusion where the individual might benefit from time alone to reflect on past choices and their consequences. When Natasha asked about knee surgery, she had been trying a range of exercises designed to help avoid medical intervention but without success. After 24 months, she was still enduring daily pain. The reversed Two of Swords described her reluctance to relinquish an option that wasn't working effectively for her. Her return to the upright Ace of Swords involved acceptance that surgery might be the best choice for her circumstances.

Two of Pentacles

The Two of Pentacles indicates it's time to put some money aside to be able to pay bills when income is low. (Pentacles people generally think ahead to ensure stability for the future and peace of mind for the present.) Basically, this card suggests financial decisions are being made.

The person in the card juggles two pentacles, dividing time, energy and money between several projects simultaneously. Most people juggle money, deciding what accounts to pay now and which can be paid later — or how much to save now and how much to spend. The individual in the card is dressed almost entirely in red (passion) and orange (enthusiasm), suggesting a strong desire and commitment to earning and managing personal finances.

The infinity symbol extending around and linking the two pentacles is a reminder that giving money away creates a temporary vacuum. This void might not be replenished with more money but there are likely to be opportunities, possessions or other forms of energy exchange.

The blue skies overhead indicate that finances are stable at this time. However, there is an awareness of the ebb and flow of financial tides (the boats in the background sail on heavy seas, suggesting that money comes and goes like the tides). This may be an opportune time to prepare for the future. Because both pentacles in this card are upright, it's likely that the person has discipline over expenses. With the stars in each pentacle pointing upwards, the individual's mind is likely to plan and control money, instead of impulsively spending.

If a person is deciding between two income sources, such as two job offers or different investments, adding two additional cards, one each side (one for each pentacle), usually clarifies the more favourable financial alternative.

In a general reading, the Two of Pentacles represents a time to make monetary decisions. This might involve choosing between two alternatives or deciding on the order of significant purchases. Financial circumstances are okay at this time, due to careful attention to income and expenses.

In a career layout, this card can signify a person who has two possible career directions or is trying to juggle a career with a small business or a personal investment. Perhaps a recent venture with a rental property is temporarily draining resources while the building is being renovated before first tenants move in. Sometimes, the Two of Pentacles indicates two sources of income. This may be a full-time and a part-time job or an occupation plus an investment. In Casey's reading, one income source was a job, while the other was a housemate whose room rental payments assisted with her mortgage.

In a relationship question, this card can show someone deciding on two relationship opportunities from a monetary perspective. It also suggests debating whether to share personal finances with a spouse. This decision might benefit both partners but can be fraught with danger, especially if one partner is reckless with spending while the other is more restrained.

In a health query, the Two of Pentacles can show the process of setting funds aside for building or maintaining personal fitness. This might include health insurance, yoga classes, gym membership, a personal trainer or regular vitamins and supplements. It can also indicate a decision about how a job affects physical fitness and energy reserves. Sometimes, this upright Two shows a person saving towards a medical procedure that might improve health and well-being.

Two of Pentacles Reversed

The Two of Pentacles reversed can suggest being overwhelmed by financial demands. Decisions are crowding in, making it difficult to choose which bill to pay first. It is likely that expenses are greater than income at this time. When the pentacles are reversed, the stars within each point downwards. Now, desires overrule thinking and planning. Despite every intention to live within personal means, impulse buying or unplanned purchases deplete financial reserves.

To rebalance the monetary situation, it is necessary to return to the upright Ace of Pentacles and make realistic plans. The Two reversed suggests there is no clear long-term financial plan. This can be due to the pressures of short-term demands. The water is above the pentacles when the card is reversed, suggesting that emotions are influencing or clouding monetary issues. This can indicate worry about current spending, feeling overwhelmed by the pressure of mounting expenses and unpaid invoices or simply dreaming that a lottery win will fix current ongoing issues.

For example, Miranda was trying to study and work part-time while raising her three-year-old daughter, Amelia. Miranda felt guilty about her job keeping her apart from Amelia part of each day but she saw no alternative. She had to work to feed and clothe them both, as her former husband did not provide any financial support. As a reader, it is wise to help Miranda examine her financial options without making decisions for her.

I suggested she defer her studies until Amelia was at school while taking another part-time position she had been offered that paid more than the job she currently held. Perhaps Miranda could resume her studies when Amelia attended school, in preparation for full-time, well-paid work later on.

When the Two of Pentacles is reversed, it's possible to add two cards, one either side, to clarify what financial pressures are significant now. When a person is clear about income and expenses, realistic decisions can be made.

The reversed Two of Pentacles in a layout suggests that the person may benefit from returning to the upright Ace, to determine their real income or the finite budget for a project. "Cut your cloth according to your means" is the saying that applies here. It's crucial to live within one's financial means.

In a general reading, the reversed Two of Pentacles indicates there is pressure to make financial decisions. This is a time when funds are limited and demands for payment are many. "What must I pay first?" is asked repeatedly. It might be time to return to the previous upright card, the Ace of Pentacles, to gauge if the answer to current issues is to increase income or decrease expenses. This card appears reversed during personal financial winters. Careful planning beforehand can help a person navigate turbulent monetary waters.

In a career layout, this card can describe an individual who has two jobs and is deciding if it's time to let one go. It might be time to relinquish both positions and find a suitable occupation that pays more. Because both pentacles are reversed, it indicates that this individual's desires might exceed their income. Spending is greater than earnings and pressure is mounting. It's time to remember the pentacles person's mantra, "The wages of sin is debt." Returning to the previous upright card, the Ace of Pentacles, allows the person to reassess income and reduce expenses accordingly.

In a relationship question, the reversed Two indicates a decision needs to be made based on financial circumstances. It might be that the person's partner lives interstate or overseas and this is a decision to book a flight to visit the spouse.

It can occur in a layout when a person is asking if current job demands are restricting a relationship or the opportunity to meet a new partner. Long hours or a demanding work environment may have left the person exhausted and isolated. Sometimes the Two of Pentacles appears reversed in a layout when one partner's spending habits is restricting both spouses' lifestyles.

In a health query, the reversed Two of Pentacles suggests that health-related expenses have previously been cut and personal health has suffered as a consequence. It's time to reassess how a job might be affecting health and vitality and how to better build and maintain health and well-being. This card is often also present when an individual is about to spend a large sum of money on a surgical procedure, such as dental work or back surgery. Sometimes the reversed Two of Pentacles highlights when a person cannot work due to poor health and confronts mounting bills with a limited income.

The Threes

The threes in the tarot describe progress with personal plans. The wands approach is through action, travel and physical conquests, whereas the cups path involves strengthening trust and exploring potential between creative partners, friends or lovers.

For swords people, progress might be found through an increased understanding of personal motives, goals and purpose, while for pentacles, advancement often means maturing financial investments, career development or simply growing a garden. For example, a pentacles friend took me outside one afternoon to show me the ripening apricots on the trees in his garden. He beamed with the pride of a man who is about to become a father.

Three or more threes in a layout can suggest that plans are progressing towards fruition. This is a sign of growth in whatever the layout question directly relates to. It's the progress from winter towards summer in the person's life. Opportunities are increasing now. The individual may be expanding social circles, improving career options, starting a family or saving towards a new home. Progress takes many forms and it often instils feelings of confidence and purpose.

Three of Wands

The Three of Wands indicates a time when a person's plans are progressing steadily. It is a card of travel, as Wands people enjoy roaming. Journeying, for wands individuals, represents adventure, freedom and excitement. At the very least, it's a chance to escape the stifling routines and responsibilities of everyday life.

The person in this card stands on a ridge overlooking the sea, with three wands firmly planted in the ground. He steadies himself with his hand on a wand and in doing so, becomes more connected with the earth. The fact that we view

the individual from behind suggests that he has moved forward from an initial planning phase (shown in the Two of Wands) to put plans into practice. This is an action card.

Its travel significance is indicated by the way the person stands, planning which boat to take for the next part of the journey. Every major voyage can be broken down into its smaller journeys or parts. He has completed a trek by foot and now contemplates a passage over water. His red cloak highlights the passion he feels while he plans the next steps on his journey.

This card also represents a progression beyond physical challenges towards emotional opportunities for growth and development. The person is moving away from the expedition on land (the physical world) and towards a sea journey (the ocean water represents emotions). On an ocean, this journey proceeds at a more leisurely pace, allowing for periods of reflection, both on past events and hopes for the future.

In a general reading, the Three of Wands indicates a time of growth, travel and progress with personal plans. In answer to a question, it usually suggests success and the fulfilment of plans. This card represents a time of growth, movement and few obstacles. Sunny skies suggest hope and confidence with current plans. This person is patiently waiting as the boats approach. It's time to consider the next phase.

When the Eight of Wands, the Ace of Wands, the Temperance or The World cards also occur in the same layout, it usually confirms travel. If the Two of Cups appears, it might signify progress with a love relationship, such as an engagement, a marriage or the purchase of property together.

In a career layout, the Three of Wands suggests a career involving regular travel, dealing with foreign countries (shown by the boats bringing goods to the shore) or an occupation that has the potential for great rewards if the individual remains focused on personal goals.

In a relationship question, the Three of Wands suggests a connection between two people is deepening and developing. It sometimes indicates travelling to spend time with a partner or travelling together for a holiday. This Three is a card for growth and progress in love, with few burdens or complications. Sunny skies confirm a time of confidence, anticipation of the shared journey ahead and advancement with plans moving forward.

In a health query, the Three of Wands signifies strong health and ongoing well-being. The person in this card stands on a cliff, watching as boats arrive and depart while planning the next steps. This individual is confident of success, based on past achievements.

Anticipating personal goals is a wands person's dream. If unwell, the prospect of plans progressing is sufficient motivation to get well soon. In a health layout, it sometimes indicates current robust health, a return to health or travelling for health reasons.

Three of Wands Reversed

The Three of Wands reversed represents delays in plans, plus a lack of growth. It is generally beneficial to return to the previous card, the upright Two of Wands, to decide which path or approach to goals is the most appropriate. Calmly considering all options and then choosing one inspires the individual to act to achieve desired objectives.

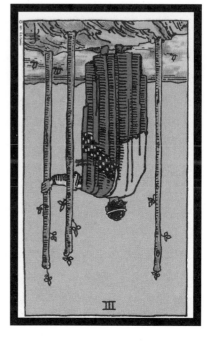

When the card is reversed, the water is above the person, suggesting that emotional issues need to be resolved before real growth can occur. Sometimes, it means that unresolved emotional issues are urging the person onwards, when rest is needed to reflect and decide what action, if any, is required. It's as though the person is impatient to push ahead with plans before the boats have arrived with necessary supplies. A return to the upright Two of Wands provides an opportunity to reflect on the best path to take in pursuit of desired goals.

As the answer to a question, the reversed Three suggests delays are likely to interrupt plans. If this card arises as an answer to the question "Will I be offered the new position in my company?" it suggests it is unlikely. This might be due to delays in organising the new job or because the person has not yet done enough to ensure he or she is the right fit for the work requirements. It is advantageous to return to the upright Two of Wands to reassess career direction if that job is offered to someone else.

This person is unlikely to be offered a desired position in the current organisation. Therefore, an appropriate follow-up question might be: "Is it worthwhile for me to remain with this company for the next two years?" This question might indicate whether another promotion is forthcoming or if better opportunities exist elsewhere.

Reversed wands often indicate delays due to distractions in the form of too many competing projects or opportunities. When reversed, wands cards highlight a tendency to begin new projects without any real idea of how and when they will be completed. Passionate wands people are easily diverted from the task and what is expected to take a few weeks might end up taking months.

A personal example of this was my book *12 Paths to Fulfilment*. I told my editor it would comprise thirty pages of text and be completed in thirty days. She laughed drily, with a raised eyebrow. She'd seen it all before. When it was finally printed, it had taken eleven-and-a-half years and ran to 187 pages. During this time, I wrote two other titles, another distraction. Wands individuals often begin new projects with great gusto and enthusiasm that gradually wanes when boredom sets in.

In a general reading, the reversed Three of Wands indicates delays with plans. It's time to return to the previous upright card, the Two of Wands, to decide on one specific direction and ignore distractions in the pursuit of that particular plan. Sometimes, this reversed Three indicates delays due to lack of focus on one precise goal or direction. Wands people sometimes begin several projects, knowing they'll narrow down choices as obstacles arise. Although having additional choices reduces disappointment when one path ends abruptly, there is a risk that worthwhile options are discarded because of lack of focus. More is not always better. Doing one job well is sometimes preferable to completing several tasks poorly.

In a career layout, the reversed Three of Wands can show impatience with current career progress. It's possible that the person needs to return to the Two of Wands to examine other potential career options or consider the possibility that current expectations are unrealistic. Determination and focusing on small, progressive steps are necessary right now. Wands people are not noted for their patience and delays in plans can fuel outbursts of anger.

In a relationship question, the reversed Three of Wands indicates slow progress with relationship plans or in meeting someone new. Patience is required now. If the individual is restless, there are advantages to reconsidering the previous upright card in the suit, the Two of Wands, to decide on a course of action.

In a health query, the Three of Wands reversed requires returning to the upright Two of Wands to find a new path towards health and well-being. It's time to consider where reserves of energy are presently being directed. Then, it is necessary to restrict the outflow of energy to people or circumstances that are draining personal vitality without reward. Occasionally, in the greater scheme, it's necessary to trim dead wood to avoid being bogged down. This card sometimes indicates delays with a return to stable health, possibly due to an overdue requirement for change in lifestyle. When forty-nine-year-old Ginny complained she was constantly exhausted, it was apparent she needed to give up partying five nights a week. Her resistance to 'becoming old' softened when I suggested she didn't need to give up wine completely but perhaps drink less but better-quality wines.

Three of Cups

The Three of Cups is a card of celebration, such as weddings, reunions, birthdays and Christmas or New Year's gatherings. It's time to commemorate shared success. The three people in this card are dancing together, celebrating a fruitful harvest. Blue skies above them hint at continuing growth and halcyon days ahead. The colours in their clothing represent their different motivations for participation.

The white robe suggests pure, altruistic motives, the red robe reveals a more passionate, enthusiastic approach, while the earthy tones of the third robe indicate a need to be grounded to receive basic rewards for physical efforts. There are only women in this card, representing generous community support, in good times and bad.

The Three of Cups highlights the people who have helped with one's goals and who are also present to celebrate achievements. It sometimes signifies a group effort, where all the participants benefit from the success of the project. It is actually a team effort, resulting in group success and shared celebration. The people who worked tirelessly together now enjoy the fruits of their labours.

The Three of Cups can suggest being surrounded by like-minded people, feeling loved and supported. Having people to enthusiastically share in personal success is as important as having friends who are supportive in difficult times.

In a general reading, this upright Three can indicate a wealth of opportunities.

After applying for dozens of jobs over several months without success, suddenly several positions are offered simultaneously. It also signifies supportive friends or colleagues and social gatherings such as a birthday party, a wedding, Christmas or Thanksgiving dinner or New Year's celebrations.

In a career layout, this Three indicates a harmonious workplace atmosphere, where people rely on teamwork to complete goals. Individuals are valued and appreciated for their unique skills and talents and success is shared. Sometimes, this card reflects several beneficial career opportunities arriving simultaneously. It's not unusual, after applying for a range of new positions, that a person improves interview skills to the point of being offered more than one suitable job in a short period.

In a relationship question, the Three of Cups indicates several suitable relationship partners arriving in a short period or a third person sharing the relationship, such as a child. It also shows a celebration, such as an engagement or a marriage or a birthday party. This card often occurs in layouts as a new year approaches and people enjoy festivities together. It's a card for emotional growth and progress in relationship and shows a person supported by friends and family.

In a health query, the upright Three shows that the person has a team of supportive people to help maintain good health. This might include supportive friends for emotional harmony, a personal trainer for physical health, a book club or a discussion group for an intellectual workout or a yoga instructor for spiritual well-being. Basically, it's a card for sound health and support from friends and family.

Three of Cups Reversed

The Three of Cups reversed reveals a lack of support from the community. The person is being ignored or other people are simply too busy with their own goals and problems to notice there is a need for more assistance.

The Three of Cups reversed is the other kind of Christmas celebration, where the family gathers together to finish last year's ongoing argument. After a few alcoholic beverages, opinions are stated candidly and fuelled by a few more drinks. The entire festivity resembles a wild pub at closing time. It's time to return to the previous card, the upright Two of Cups and to find a person who shares similar views to enjoy some time with this individual while staying out of the line of fire

Regarding family situations, the Three of Cups reversed can suggest a person causing tension through harsh words or actions. Sometimes, it indicates a relative living with a newly married couple. This could be a child from a previous relationship or a parent who resents the current situation.

In love relationship layouts, it can suggest a third person is involved. This could mean one party is having an affair or that a relative or close friend is unduly influencing the thoughts and actions of one partner. If there is a love triangle, the reversed Three of Cups suggests a need to return to the upright Two of Cups and decide what is critical, while rebuilding trust and intimacy.

In a general reading, the reversed Three of Cups suggests being among people with different interests and values. By returning to the upright Two of Cups, the person can find one close friend or partner with similar views, before expanding the circle of friends. For example, Grace felt out of place in her workplace. One afternoon, she recognised a woman from another department in the café downstairs during her lunch break. She was reading a self-development paperback Grace had just finished reading. They began talking about the book and discovered a range of common interests and talents. When Grace eventually moved to a new company, they were firm friends, sharing a bond that outlasted the job.

This card also describes a dysfunctional family attempting to celebrate while applying alcohol in large quantities. When things get out of hand, they might expect a whole team of uninvited guests — a SWAT team.

In a career layout, this card signifies a group of people that cannot cooperate together, due to ingrained competition — each person battles for rewards, recognition or promotion at the expense of the others. There is minimal respect for each other and a lack of team spirit. The Three reversed describes some annual office parties, where politics and hidden agendas are rife. It's time for this individual to return to the upright Two of Cups and find one supportive person while reducing expectations of the remaining colleagues. It can also describe stiff competition for available job vacancies, where the individual needs to be focused and adaptable to secure a new position.

In a relationship question, the Three of Wands reversed indicates the influence of a third person in a relationship. This might be a parent with strong opinions, a child from a previous marriage or even a secret affair. The Seven of Swords (secrecy), The Moon (hidden agendas) and the reversed Lovers cards in the same layout usually confirms a love triangle. More often, it's a family member whose influence limits the relationship in some way. In some readings, the reversed Three describes a whole group of friends who object to a partnership. This opposition might be based on religious or cultural differences, so the group is united in their opposition to this union.

In a health query, the Three of Wands reversed sometimes indicates low reserves of physical and emotional energy from being emotionally drained by surrounding people. Sometimes, workplace undertones or office politics are depleting the person, or home life is chaotic, resulting in poor health. If the individual is intuitively sensitive to others, it's vital to practice psychic cleansing exercises to restore energy balance. Occasionally, it requires a change to a more suitable environment.

Jennifer complained that workplace politics left her feeling exhausted at the end of each day. She was effectively an emotional sponge for the unexpressed hostility and her weekends were spent resting to be ready for another week of undercurrents, manoeuvring and office competition. It was apparent that she needed to change jobs but before that occurred, Jennifer had to learn how to cleanse herself of the negative energy she was collecting each day.

This involved taking a swim in her backyard salt-water pool every afternoon in summer (to wash away residual energy) or having a regular salt bath or practising yoga after work on winter evenings. These processes effectively reset her energy for family life and improved her sleeping patterns. Jennifer's new habits allowed her to build resilience and focus on finding a new job. Without regular cleansing, she didn't have the focus or the reserves of energy to seek different employment.

Three of Swords

The Three of Swords represents grief, emotional pain and loss. If into every life a little rain must fall, when the Three of Swords occurs in a layout, the person is being buffeted by turbulent storms. Some people shudder at the appearance of this card but anguish and sadness are necessary parts of life. This card shows rain clouds with three swords plunged into a heart. The implications of this vivid picture are immediately evident. It represents misery, sorrow or suffering.

This card may draw attention to the heart or indicate unresolved grief and loss is impacting physical health. Sometimes, people are unable to process searing emotional trauma because physical or financial survival depends on remaining focused on practical goals. Overwhelmed, they shrink from life to the safety of predictable routines.

When Marion's daughter, Heather, died in a car accident at 24, Marion was overwhelmed with pain and despair. While friends and family offered her kindness, support and patiently waited for her grief to subside, Marion faded away. She died seventeen months later from heart failure. Her doctor explained it to her husband by saying, "Technically, it was heart failure and that's what the death certificate states but you and I both know it was grief. Some of us can get past huge setbacks, while others simply can't. Hopefully, she is with your daughter now."

The Three of Swords indicates it is time to finally accept loss or sadness and allow it to pass. When grief is accepted, the pain can subside. For some people, it is not the ending itself that is the source of the greatest sorrow but the powerlessness to do anything about it. However, being vulnerable in life and surrendering to difficult circumstances is part of the human condition.

When the Three of Swords occurs in a layout, it indicates distress but this pain will eventually pass. Most adults have endured the Three of Swords, many times already. Losing a school friend who has moved away or not being picked for a sports team can result in grief and loss. Having to give up university studies to care for an ill parent or being abandoned by a partner without reason are also traumatic events.

In a layout with the Nine of Swords, it can describe self-torture with memories of past disappointments. Sometimes, it indicates powerful dreams at night as the subconscious mind attempts to unscramble past or present upheavals.

In the attitude position (hopes and fears) in a layout, the Three indicates serious apprehension about the outcome of the issue. If the person has asked about an upcoming situation and the surrounding cards are positive, the appearance of the Three in the attitude position can indicate an irrational sense of foreboding is overwhelming the individual.

In a general reading, the Three of Swords indicates sadness, loss and emotional pain. This might occur in a person's layout after a robbery or if a significant friendship has recently dissolved. It can also show the distress at being overlooked for promotion, missing out on a much-desired home at auction or the death of a pet.

In a career layout, the Three of Swords suggests a significant disappointment. In a question about investing in a business, it indicates that the person might regret the investment. In the past position, it highlights previous career setbacks. If the accompanying cards for the present are encouraging, it suggests a past pain has been healed. Sometimes, it confirms the sudden shock of losing a long-term job, the end of a business partnership or not being offered a promotion after strenuous effort.

In a relationship question, it can signify a separation or the grief that accompanies a relationship upheaval, such as the discovery of infidelity. It's more likely to result from a specific issue than a slow realisation that a relationship will never reach expectations.

In a health query, the upright Three of Swords describes concern with the heart. If the individual has asked if it's wise to undergo a surgical or other medical procedure and this card is placed in the answer or the outcome position, it indicates a disappointing conclusion. In a recent reading, Jayne had nursed her husband until his death and was now considering hip surgery for herself. The Three of Swords was located in the near future position and I interpreted it to mean Jayne might heal more rapidly if she waited. Her overwhelming grief at the loss of her spouse and her low reserves of physical energy after nursing him at home were likely to prolong her convalescence. I asked her to select one more card while asking, "Is it wise for me to postpone this procedure until next year?" The card she selected was the Six of Wands. This suggested she'd return to stable health if she postponed the procedure until her body was ready to absorb another shock.

Three of Swords Reversed

The Three of Swords reversed indicates an inability to accept or deal with pain or loss. It can represent a past sadness that is being suppressed or current circumstances that do not allow room for grieving.

An example of the kind of situation represented by the Three reversed was Holly, who was left to raise three young children alone, when her husband died suddenly, aged thirty-eight. She wanted to grieve but she had to feed and house the children. Her time for her own personal grief was almost non-existent, until fifteen years later when she collapsed into despair.

Before her children were old enough to look after themselves, she felt unable to remove her focus from simple survival. Suppressed grief rarely goes away of its own accord and as more pain is accumulated and unprocessed, stronger techniques are required to avoid facing it. Her children searched for recent causes for her depression, not realising her adult life had been an endurance marathon. With the assistance of a counsellor, Holly healed the past and learned how to take care of herself, without the added demands of her children.

When the Three of Swords reversed appears in a layout, the pain is often historical rather than current. Sometimes, it's necessary for a reader to ask probing questions to discover the underlying cause of current depression or emotional disconnection from life. Returning to the lesson of the previous card, the upright Two of Swords, encourages taking time aside for personal reflection. This can help to determine what is necessary and what can be released from current circumstances. It's time to make sense of events before stepping forward towards new opportunities.

Greg used his business as his way of avoiding a tragic past. Eventually, working hard couldn't distract him from his feelings, so he became involved in gambling and alcohol. After he lost his business, he had plenty of time to examine himself and how he felt. At first, he was angry, blaming everyone he believed was responsible for his bankruptcy. A proud man, he resisted help in any form for almost two years, until he hit a wall. At that point, he sought counselling for alcohol abuse and after he had been sober for several years, he regularly visited a counsellor to help him turn his life around. It was a slow and sometimes gruelling process, which resulted in Greg becoming calmer and more content with his achievements.

The reversed Three of Swords describes suppressed, unconscious grief from the past, which affects every personal choice and action. The stagnant pain needs to be felt and expressed properly, so it doesn't become an enduring burden. Suppressed emotions require plenty of energy to keep them buried, leaving limited vitality for new opportunities and for life in general. It is worthwhile discovering what has caused these feelings of despair and loss and for the individual to confront and acknowledge them, to move forward without unnecessary burdens. It is time to return to the previous card, the upright Two of Swords, to examine options and make some constructive choices.

In a general reading, the reversed Three of Swords can indicate that past unacknowledged grief is subtly influencing present decisions and actions. An example of this occurred with Damon, who was cut out of his late father's estate by his two brothers. Embittered at this unfairness, Damon became mean-spirited with his sons, refusing to help them financially as teenagers. By the time he realised the cause of his actions, his sons had grown up and moved away. He had plenty of time to reflect on how his relationship with his father had soured his connections with his own sons.

In a career layout, the reversed Three of Swords describes pain or bitterness at opportunities lost or feelings of not being acknowledged and promoted for work efforts. Instead of accepting that career dreams might never be fulfilled, it's time to return to the previous upright card, the Two of Swords, to decide on a different course of action. This might include retraining for a new job, updating a resume and applying for various positions in other organisations or mapping out a path to starting a business. In Cindy's situation, she had already completed her training but was not promoted to a level that matched her qualifications. It was apparent that, because her boss hired her to fill a simple bookkeeping position, he had no need for a trained accountant. It was time for Cindy to move on to another organisation that might better utilise her skills and reward her accordingly.

In a relationship question, this card describes emotional pain preventing a relationship from reaching its potential. This suffering might be related to a present partnership or result from a previous situation. The reversed Three of Swords highlights suppressing and moving on from pain without sufficiently processing the loss or upheaval. In relationship terms, it describes replacing a partner instead of grieving a loss. It's time to return to the previous upright card, the Two of Swords, to assess how best to re-enter life after an ending or a disappointment. It's not easy but it's also not impossible to trust again after a loss. By mentally unpacking past sorrows, it's possible to better understand events and gain an insightful sense of acceptance around painful circumstances. If past events are not mentally and emotionally processed, they can become emotional baggage that weighs heavily on the path ahead in life.

In a health query, the reversed Three of Swords can suggest current physical symptoms have underlying emotional origins. From ongoing stress to disappointments and personal setbacks, unaddressed issues can severely affect physical health. Shock, a sudden upheaval or periods of intense stress can filter down to physical health if not completely processed and released. This card can also describe concern around the heart that might require medication or medical intervention. A return to the previous upright card, the Two of Swords, allows the person to decide how best to resolve past sorrows and return to health and physical well-being.

Three of Pentacles

The Three of Pentacles represents the growth that is possible with solid foundations. A tall tree with shallow roots is likely to blow over in the first strong wind and this is obvious to pentacles people. This card shows the four elements (fire, water, air and earth) combining to build something enduring.

The three represents study and learning, either through a course or by acquiring new skills in the workplace. It signifies stable growth resulting from careful planning. It combines passion (wands energy) and imagination (cups energy) plus planning and strategy (swords energy) with patience and determination (pentacles energy) to produce successful results.

The card shows a scene involving an architect and a member of the clergy examining the plans for a church as a tradesperson sets to work on the structure. They are building a monument to God as a reminder of purpose in this world. The three pentacles in the arch above them remind us that all success, material or otherwise, comes from God or Spirit (the source of energy and life). To enjoy the fruits of the earth, it is necessary to remain connected to both the earth (the pillar supporting the arch stands firmly in the earth) and to Spirit.

Two smaller arches stand within one large arch, representing the Holy Trinity, the Father (God, the source) the Son (Jesus, Buddha, etc.) and the Holy Spirit, which is the invisible life force and depicted in all the aces in the form of the clouds. This multiplicity of three appears in many schools of thought, including the Kahuna teachings of Hawaii. They teach that everyone has a physical self, a mental self and a spiritual or higher self to whom prayers can be directed.

The clergy represents the element of water (cups), in the form of the person who meditates on hidden facets of life. The architect symbolises the element of air (swords), with plans, drawings and concepts. The skilled worker represents fire (wands), being the person who physically constructs the structure. The building itself embodies earth (pentacles) and is an enduring monument to what is necessary in life.

In a general reading, the Three of Pentacles describes establishing solid foundations for long-term stability. The threes are cards for growth and progress and the Three of Pentacles represents enough money to support plans at this stage. Most goals in life require money to make them possible. This is also a card for progress with study or learning new skills to cement a more rewarding career.

In a career reading, the upright Three of Pentacles indicates study or learning, either in a course for certification or by gaining practical skills through a supervised placement in an organisation. Many university courses require students to log a set number of hours of practical training in the field under the supervision of a more knowledgeable practitioner before a student can gain final qualifications. Basically, the Three of Pentacles indicates a solid foundation for career success. The three people working together in the card show the increased power and effectiveness of teamwork. This might refer to collaborative efforts within an organisation or to hiring a group of professionals to complete a project.

In a relationship layout, this card shows the process of establishing solid routines that support a long-term relationship. This might be a shared bank account devoted to saving a deposit for a home or living together and deciding the division of household responsibilities. Because it's a pentacles card, it is likely to emphasise a practical or financial approach to plans. It describes a relationship that thrives within a stable structure.

In a health query, this card emphasises supportive habits and routines that help maintain robust health. These might include regular walking, daily exercise, yoga, sport or ensuring a balanced diet. The typical pentacles person's approach to health is that regular daily effort now can prevent serious health consequences later. It's also a card for health study or completing health-based courses. These might range from healthy cooking programs to undergoing training in anatomy and physiology or personal stress management techniques. Basically, the Three of Pentacles indicates strong health.

Three of Pentacles Reversed

The Three of Pentacles reversed indicates a lack of growth resulting from insufficient planning or poor foundations for a project. It shows reluctance to learn from events. The person may repeat current patterns until lessons are learned.

This card suggests a repetitive pattern of behaviour that prevents a partnership from reaching its full potential. The four elements in the card are not combined harmoniously. Growth is inhibited until balance is restored.

The reversed Three can also indicate mediocre work or lacklustre living, due to insufficient planning or destructive personal habits, such as inconsistent income or erratic spending. There is no real foundation upon which to build a stable life.

It can also suggest abandoning study or a job that offers practical training. Sometimes, it describes leaving a course at its conclusion or undertaking brief training, such as a one-day workshop.

In a general reading, the reversed Three of Pentacles describes a repetitive life without progress towards goals. "It's the same thing every single day," is how one client described it. The frustration and boredom that often accompany this period can fuel ambition to undertake a course or work hard towards a better life. Pentacles people understand that training in the right field results in qualifications that can lead to a more stable income in the future.

While the upright Three highlights that effort made now can lead to future long-term rewards, this reversed Three indicates a lack of awareness around what is required to improve life circumstances. In Cody's reading, the reversed Three of Pentacles revealed a pattern of unfavourable associations around study. Poor grades at school, plus a failed attempt at completing a university course in engineering, left him overwhelmed. After changing career direction, he felt disheartened when contemplating improving his carpentry career through study.

Before attempting another course, Cody needed to reduce his anxiety around learning. As a Knight of Wands, he learns more easily through doing something, instead of theory, so I suggested he break his study into two separate parts. If he learned carpentry skills under the guidance of a skilful craftsman and then completed some courses to gain the theory and required certificates, it might be less stressful.

Every time he felt overwhelmed by the theory, he could ask his mentor to explain it using practical examples. To ensure Cody remained focused on his goal, he agreed that every time he felt like giving up, he'd ask himself if he'd be happy doing the same job in ten years' time.

The reversed Three of Pentacles requires a return to the previous pentacles card, the upright Two, and the financial decisions that card contains. In Cody's situation, the upright Two might involve making a monthly budget based on a smaller income than he would have if he was fully qualified.

A return to the upright Two allows a person to decide the best path to take for long-term rewards. Many successful people are victorious after several persistent attempts.

In a general reading, the reversed Three of Pentacles indicates a situation repeating itself. The individual needs to learn something before progress is possible. It sometimes suggests that insufficient financial resources prevent plans from being enacted. A lack of money is holding this person back from succeeding.

In a career layout, the reversed Three of Pentacles describes repetition in the workplace. Perhaps this is the third job where the boss plays golf most days, while staff have to manage in his absence. It might be time to find a different position or gain new skills and accreditation to move up the career ladder. It sometimes indicates that training for a better-paid position has been abandoned, resulting in the person feeling stuck in a career pattern. If this individual moves on to a different occupation without additional training, the new job is likely to resemble the old one, eventually. To break out of the rut, it might be necessary to do something different.

In a relationship question, the reversed Three of Pentacles sometimes suggests a pattern from previous relationships is resurfacing in this partnership. It might be that the individual needs to examine attitudes and behaviours in relationships or that the new partner has similar patterns to a previous spouse. It can be difficult to identify unconscious motivations for one's actions in a relationship and easier to blame a spouse when things go wrong. If a love relationship is like a dance, both partners need to know the steps to dance together. When an individual becomes weary of the current dance, it is necessary to learn some new steps. A counsellor might assist with the necessary retraining for a more rewarding love relationship. Past patterns learned from inadequate mentors can be burdensome. It's often more rewarding to change the steps in the dance by releasing old destructive beliefs and habits.

In a health query, the reversed Three of Pentacles highlights a recurrent health issue that is being treated but not cured. It might describe using a puffer for asthma attacks or creams for skin rashes without examining underlying causes. This allows current health issues to grow or to continue to exert influence on a person's life.

Dylan selected the Three of Pentacles reversed in a health reading and it described his need to use ointments for his recurring psoriasis. He outwardly seemed like a relaxed person but after a few questions, it was obvious Dylan was inwardly anxious most of the time. It was time for him to return to the previous upright card, the Two of Pentacles, to decide how he might invest some money into learning new ways to manage his anxiety and calm his inner stress. After some research, Dylan settled on three methods: hypnosis, meditation and swimming. Several hypnosis sessions helped him set stronger boundaries with others, while meditation allowed him to switch off at night before sleep. Swimming was effective in soothing the daily stress from his busy job and burning off some excess energy. This combination reduced his reliance on creams for managing his psoriasis. The reversed Three can also indicate it's time for the person to learn how to manage personal health to avoid long-term health conditions in old age.

The Fours

The fours in the tarot describe consolidation, the act of making concepts and plans real in the physical world. They show ideas as career choices, lifestyle options or the solid effort of creating a home. This process includes the enthusiastic wands' need to settle down in a suitable home or work environment, which they often resist due to a powerful desire for freedom. Cups people need emotional stability, so their efforts are usually directed towards building lasting love relationships.

The swords approach to consolidation is to take some time to make sense of circumstances through reflection. An idea or a concept applied in the real world to save energy, reduce the annual costs of a business or improve health is often the result of analysing a need or a problem. The earthy pentacles approach is to reinforce stability by saving money to ensure solid financial foundations for future plans. During the long days of summer, they remember winter will follow. Consequently, they prepare to ensure safety and comfort in difficult times.

Three or more upright fours in a layout suggest a period of stability resulting from sensible past efforts. They indicate the process of making solid, real progress. The fours represent tangible results that follow the ideas of the aces, the decisions of the twos and the efforts and growth of the threes. This is when an investment pays dividends to free up finances for other projects. This measurable progress occurs when a home renovation has been completed or a work project is progressing steadily due to sound strategies, persistence and focus. It's also when a person has saved sufficient money to buy a car, take a trip or invest in a business idea.

Basically, the fours represent practical efforts towards realistic goals. The wands four requires discipline over personal passion to ensure the individual doesn't leave before completing a project. The cups four typifies the recognition that happiness lies within and need not be affected by surrounding circumstances. The swords four is the understanding that ideas are worthless until they are realistically applied with measurable results. The pentacles four highlights acceptance that every idea usually requires money, effort and persistence to bring it from concept to design and finally to a product or a service.

Four of Wands

The Four of Wands represents moving to a new home or workplace. Wands are physical people, so this involves a physical move. Wands people enjoy fresh opportunities and encounters and, when deciding to change something, they usually do so rapidly. Passion triumphs over planning, so it's more important to achieve a goal immediately than smoothly. Only in maturity do wands people like to glimpse the consequences of their actions before taking physical steps towards an objective.

The Four of Wands indicates that the community benefits from the prosperous times. In this card, a welcoming wreath is tied to four upright wands, which stand firmly in the ground. Two people wave flowers, while another group stands in the background, outside the safety of the castle walls, indicating that they feel secure. The walls of the structure originally protected inhabitants from marauders, wild animals and other threats. Although many of these dangers have diminished in modern times, when tragedy strikes, most individuals still want to go home to feel safe.

Sometimes, the Four of Wands occurs in a layout when a home or work change is unlikely to take place. Then this card describes the refurbishment of present surroundings. The Four represents adjusting to a new environment or re-settling into the present one. This card highlights a stable home or work environment. The number four symbolises consolidation or practical application of the element of wands (or fire).

It shows enthusiasm and effort directed towards a practical purpose. This might mean building or extending a home, making a home more fit for the occupants before a new baby arrives or even taking a permanent job after years of contracting. Effort leads to stability with this card.

Wands people can be self-absorbed and when competing with others, they need to remain focused on the fundamental steps necessary to win. This means that individuals around them are often enlisted to help achieve their goals. A collaborative approach works if the other people share the person's vision or they feel inspired to participate in the process. However, it can become problematic if all the individual's goals are personal ones and don't include benefits for other participants. People are generally much more interested in pursuing goals that can serve the community rather than those that benefit only one individual.

In a general reading, the Four of Wands indicates adjusting to a new home or work environment. The fours emphasise stability, usually physical permanency. It's the process of becoming comfortable in living or work surroundings. If the person hasn't recently moved, he or she might have repainted or refurbished an existing home. As an answer to a question about a project, it indicates a solid, successful outcome.

In a career layout, this Four indicates a new position or a different job. As a consolidation card, it sometimes describes permanent employment after a period contracting or acting in a role temporarily. It can highlight the process of settling after a move to a new work location or feeling anchored in a role in an organisation. This card suggests support from co-workers in a stable work environment.

In a relationship question, this card describes settling into comfortable habits and routines and feeling supported. The couple might have jointly purchased a home or if the person is single, he or she is likely to be ready to meet someone new to establish a long-term partnership.

In a health query, the Four of Wands suggests stable health. A secure home or work environment, plus rainy-day money helps eliminate stress. Strategic planning and beneficial habits reduce the likelihood of becoming exhausted by surprise upheavals. The red and blue worn by the people in this card indicate that the person is being nourished physically (red) and spiritually (blue).

Four of Wands Reversed

The Four of Wands reversed suggests a lack of stability. It shows the inability to make plans solid in the physical world. Without discipline, passion and enthusiasm can be a waste of energy. Self-control and focus are more likely to keep projects on track than spontaneous bursts of unplanned effort.

This card can still represent an optimistic time but when reversed, the buoyancy is usually transient. The person may be working on a project that brings together compatible people with harmonious ideas but it's likely they'll each go their own separate ways when the assignment has concluded.

The temporary stability could be the result of the hard work of others and this person is simply passing through that environment. For example, when travelling, an individual might only spend a few days or weeks in a location before moving on. The permanent community is responsible for the maintenance of parks and gardens that the traveller temporarily enjoys while visiting.

When reversed, the castle is above the sky, suggesting a desire for freedom from the constraints of home and community. A return to the upright Three suggests it's time to cast off routines and responsibilities, to travel, explore new horizons and feel free. Eventually, the shine wears off of continual travel and stability beckons again.

In a general reading, the reversed Four of Wands describes a temporary situation. The person might be couch surfing or house sitting, moving from one location to another when each homeowner returns from travels. It signals a time to live in the moment, without detailed plans tomorrow.

In a career layout, this card describes contract or temporary work. Although enjoyable, there is a lack of permanence about the job. Sometimes this suits the individual, especially when travelling or planning on relocating. A client wanted a secure career but could not bring herself to play the corporate game, so she trained as an accountant and has worked on short-term contracts for over twenty years. Karin enjoys the variety of appointments, locations and workplace environments but manages to avoid most of the office politics. Over the years, in several career layouts, she has selected the Four of Wands reversed.

It sometimes suggests an opportunity to shop around before making a long-term job commitment or it signals that the person is presently unable to find permanent work. Occasionally, the reversed Four describes a job that involves continual movement. In Tracy's reading, the reversed card described her job perfectly. In the previous eighteen months, Tracy had travelled to forty-seven of the fifty U.S. states to talk about and demonstrate her company's products. She usually spent less than six days each month at home. She enjoyed meeting new people and discovering different cities.

In a relationship question, the Four reversed suggests being in a short-lived relationship before returning to the upright Three of Wands and deciding where to move to next. This person is experiencing a time of growth and joy but like all festivities, it will be over soon, so it's advisable to make the most of it.

Sometimes, it describes a holiday romance or partners who are moving regularly. This card is seen reversed when a couple travels together on an extended journey. It might show a partner who does not live in the home or works away from home. This occurred in Adrian's reading and he explained that he worked ten days in a row interstate and then spent four days at home, due to his job as an engineer in the mining industry.

In a health query, the reversed Four of Wands can describe an inconsistent approach to building and maintaining health. This sometimes indicates someone with faddish food tastes, or it might involve behaviour such as undergoing a strict no-sugar diet prior to undergoing a blood test for possible diabetes but resuming a sugar-laden diet directly after the test.

It sometimes suggests that impermanence in the person's home or work environment is currently reducing energy and vitality. If an individual is living out of a hotel or in a car, it's unlikely the current diet consists of home-cooked, well-prepared food. Shortcuts are being taken with diet and fitness routines that might influence long-term health.

Four of Cups

The Four of Cups represents an opportunity to reflect on current plans and present circumstances. It's a time to remember past sources of emotional and spiritual sustenance to ensure an emotionally rewarding connection to life. It is a chance to remember the Ace of Cups and the joy it offered through connection to spiritual purpose.

In this card, the person contemplating is aware of external possibilities but realises that inner fulfilment is paramount. The cup in the hand extending from a cloud is the key to enjoying the favourable moments suggested by the three cups on the ground. The individual is aware that commitment, effort and planning are required to pursue the opportunities represented by those cups.

Most outer sources of fulfilment are fleeting. This person realises the need for a reliable source of inner peace and happiness to provide nourishment between external accomplishments. The Four of Cups indicates consolidating this connection to inner peace (the cup from the cloud), as well as opportunities for outer fulfilment (the three cups on the ground).

Sometimes, it's necessary to take a step back from external events to nourish oneself internally. The person in this card is meditating or in reflection, with eyes closed. Meditation is one reliable way to access spiritual support and to rebalance physically, emotionally, mentally and spiritually. Other constructive habits for emotional nourishment include yoga, walking in nature, prayer, reading uplifting books, charity work, creative pursuits and play.

When life is a struggle or emotionally unfulfilling, there is a tendency to look back to earlier times, when a connection to life seemed more rewarding. In the Four of Cups, a person is seen looking back to the Ace of Cups, (being held by a hand extending from a cloud as it is in the Ace card) remembering the fulfilment once experienced. Sometimes, it's possible to re-establish former habits that offered an emotional connection. When this is unlikely, it's necessary to search for new connections. The blue sky suggests this is a hopeful time and that the individual is confident that profound personal fulfilment is possible.

In a general reading, the Four of Cups indicates examining ways to stabilise sources of spiritual and emotional nourishment. The Fours represent consolidation or making plans solid. In this instance, it points to an awareness of the importance of emotional and spiritual fulfilment. This individual is contemplating how to strengthen current sources of sustenance. It describes a person asking if they are happy and if not, why not. It is vital to think about happiness and gratitude because knowing that you're comfortable while in a buoyant surge allows that wealth of opportunities to nourish and sustain you when the moment passes.

In a career layout, the Four of Cups shows someone examining current options while conscious of an inner source of happiness. Even a difficult or demanding job is more acceptable when a person is already happy. This card indicates an awareness that fulfilling work is an essential part of a balanced, meaningful life. Because more than a third of life is spent at work, having a job that aligns with personal values can be central to overall satisfaction. If not, it is vital that there are alternative sources of spiritual and emotional nourishment outside the workplace.

In a relationship question, the Four of Cups indicates emotional consolidation. This describes someone taking responsibility for personal actions and how they affect emotional fulfilment. In this card, a person sits still, contemplating. Perhaps this individual is remembering the emotional and spiritual connection they felt when they last experienced the Ace of Cups. It's also possible that, while contemplating, this person is drawing down some of the spiritual light present in the Ace (the cloud in this card represents spiritual connection). By finding spiritual nourishment within, an individual becomes less reliant on others for happiness. This calming process also ensures the person has more to offer a relationship partner.

In a health query, the Four of Cups shows an individual taking responsibility for their spiritual and emotional fulfilment. Before a health issue results in physical symptoms, there can be imbalances in the person's emotional, mental or spiritual energies. By taking time to ensure spiritual and emotional balance, this person is improving physical health. The process might involve prayer, meditation, spending time alone in nature or staring up at a starry sky while realising personal troubles are minimal in a universal context.

Four of Cups Reversed

The Four of Cups reversed suggests disconnection from a source of inner fulfilment. Every cup reversed indicates current external opportunities are unrewarding right now. It is necessary to return to the upright Three of Cups and associate with people who know a path to inner peace or to new opportunities.

For example, Ellie had spent fourteen months struggling to write a book. During this time, she had declined all social invitations to focus on the task. At the end of this period she was exhausted and dissatisfied with the results of her work. I suggested she ring her friends and arrange to meet them for coffee or lunch, to reconnect. Within a month, she was increasingly socially engaged and feeling more optimistic about her progress. At a friend's house-warming party, she was given the name of an editor and mentor who works passionately with emerging writers. Several months later, she had redrafted her book with the help of her new editor and was delighted with the results.

In returning to the upright Three of Cups and re-integrating socially, Ellie was able to access the help she needed to move forward with her writing project. Going back to the Three allowed her to embrace the lesson of the upright Four on her way to completing her creative project. The upright Four is about solidifying connections to emotional and spiritual sources of nourishment. By feeling less isolated, she was able to allow more sunlight and opportunities into her life. Ellie was exhausted at the end of her first draft because she was giving everything to her book without replenishing herself. It was as though she was breathing out without breathing in again.

Sometimes, revisiting the upright Three of Cups provides a chance to pursue another direction entirely. This opportunity often comes through friends, social gatherings or workplace groups. The Three of Cups is a card of celebration, acknowledging significant milestones and gathering with your tribe to laugh, play and to catch up.

In a general reading, the reversed Four of Cups shows dissatisfaction with current circumstances. This person is disconnected from Spirit (the cloud in the Ace of Cups, shown in this image) and also from social opportunities. It's time to return to the previous upright card, the Three of Cups, to spend time with like-minded people in meaningful pursuits. It may require persistent effort to find the right people, as the three reversed cups in a row indicate a lack of emotional connection with people in the immediate environment.

In a career layout, the reversed Four of Cups suggests boredom or disconnection from existing job or career opportunities. In a question about finances, it can describe spending money to compensate for feeling emotionally or spiritually empty. Career rarely replenishes spiritual and emotional reserves of energy as effectively as meditation, prayer, yoga, singing or other spiritual practices, unless it involves great acts of kindness and charity. A meaningful vocation can offer spiritual sustenance but other paths to joy are also necessary for a balanced life.

In a relationship layout, this reversed Four can describe feeling unhappy or yearning for a past love (the cup held by the hand) that was unrequited or is long gone. It's possible that this yearning has exhausted the patience of current prospective partners, so it's time to return to the upright Three of Cups to explore new opportunities. If the person burdened by unrequited love is unable to release a former partner, it might be time to invite that person to lunch and discover how the previous companion has moved on with life. In the cold light of day, a short lunch with a former lover sometimes crystallises the futility of yearning, especially while ignoring more suitable opportunities for happiness by feeding sentimental fantasies.

In a health query, the reversed Four of Cups indicates that current health issues are connected to depleted emotional and spiritual energies. This card might appear reversed in a layout when a person has ended a love relationship and given up interests and pastimes that used to provide personal nourishment. A possible solution might be to reconnect with friends or like-minded people while pursuing activities that are emotionally and spiritually sustaining. These pastimes could include joining a book or film club, a debating group or meditation group or taking yoga, dance or art lessons. There are many different ways to nourish your soul.

Four of Swords

The Fours are cards of consolidation. The Four of Swords focuses on reasoning and contemplation, leading to intellectual clarity. It represents an opportunity to think about past conversations and actions and their consequences. It's an ideal moment to clarify plans and direction, to make sense of life. Reviewing past actions can save time and effort in the future, especially when we realise which ideas work, as well as those that don't.

The leadlight window in this card contains a scene of a devotee receiving a blessing from someone more senior. The person in the foreground is receiving this same support internally while meditating. His yellow body suggests his mind is active while he is physically resting.

Some people meditate, while others go to

psychotherapy. However, reflection is required as part of counselling to examine issues that surfaced during a session. Quiet time spent in contemplation is especially helpful in the swords suit, where thoughts and ideas about the future can overly excite a person, scattering energy or causing anxiety and pain. Thinking about and then planning a project before taking steps to complete it is often a winning combination.

In a general reading, the Four of Swords represents a time of reflection. This might occur between jobs, when away on holiday or during a period of ill-health. Some individuals ponder naturally, while others only deliberate when they are too tired to do anything else. It's time to reassess beliefs and discard outdated views and attitudes that clash with current life directions.

Learning involves two basic stages: action and reflection. If a person acts without sufficient analysis of efforts and consequences, past mistakes are likely to be repeated. If a person only ponders without action, life is merely a theory, never tested. The Four of Swords is a time to think about past actions in the pursuit of wisdom. Wisdom involves knowing what actions are likely to be fruitless and why. Contemplation also allows for unconscious motives to surface and be addressed. If an individual has an unacknowledged desire that is at odds with a major goal, it can create obstacles along the path to the objective.

The Four of Swords can also suggest a period of low physical stamina. The person might be unwell or exhausted after an extended period of stress or overwhelming deadlines.

In a career layout, the upright Four shows a person thinking about long-term strategy. It's time to map out the steps towards a successful career or review the current plan. Sometimes, it describes an individual who is blending into a work environment to avoid becoming a target for demanding management. This card featured in Chan's reading when the department manager's 'whipping boy' left for another job. Lying low became an effective way for Chan to avoid being the next target of workplace harassment.

In a relationship question, this card represents a time of withdrawal to contemplate past actions and circumstances. It might be an opportunity to discover why a past relationship collapsed or what type of spouse is most compatible for future partnerships. Before pursuing a new opportunity, it's beneficial to understand one's previous motivations. This can help avoid the repetition of past mistakes.

Marianne took a break between relationships to understand why she repeatedly partnered with creative, shy men. Although she had previously enjoyed sensitive, supportive partners, she realised she wanted a man she admired for his confidence and an ability to act on his plans. Marianne eventually accepted that an active, focused partner might be less sensitive to her needs and that this was an acceptable price to pay to be with someone she admired. The period of reflection was not wasted, as it resulted in a more rewarding long-term partnership.

In a health query, the upright Four of Swords indicates low reserves of physical energy. It sometimes appears in a reading soon after a client has undergone surgery or overcome a prolonged illness. Time spent in bed recuperating is an opportunity for reflection. It can turn up in a layout after a client has completed an arduous course while working part-time or at the end of a bitter divorce or a protracted legal dispute. Basically, the person is exhausted.

This Four represents an attempt to clarify strategy through thinking. Longstanding issues or attitudes may require days or weeks of reflection to map out viable solutions. When a person is ill or not facing daily demands, it's possible to devote more time to logical analysis and reviewing what has worked and what past efforts were wasted. Sometimes illness provides an opportunity for reflection on habits and life goals.

Four of Swords Reversed

The Four of Swords reversed indicates contemplation or self-scrutiny are overlooked, usually resulting in pain. At this point, the individual often has an active schedule. There is no opportunity to make careful plans, even though they could save time and energy in the long run. Although the mind is active, there is a lack of focus. Thoughts are jumbled and scattered.

Returning to the previous card in the suit, the upright Three of Swords, allows one to feel the pain of separation from life. When the grief phase eventually subsides, the person returns to the upright Four to make sense of events through reflection. At that point, the mind is less burdened by emotions.

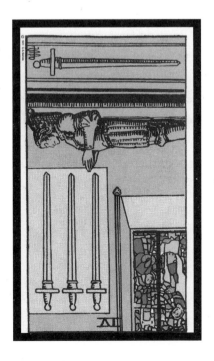

For example, Robert's mother died when he was six years old. Robert unconsciously concluded that all women leave sooner or later. Consequently, he chose to avoid romantic relationships as an adult to minimise the pain of loss. After some encouragement, he allowed the sorrow of his mother's death to sweep through him, reducing him to emotional rubble for nearly a year. When the suffering eventually subsided, he was more prepared to trust again.

The appearance of the Four reversed suggests a person who is rushing around, too busy to reflect on past efforts or events. By not thoroughly considering previous actions, there is a huge risk of repeating mistakes until behaviour patterns are finally addressed. It's time to stop, reflect and make plans for the future. Eventually, when thoroughly exhausted from overexertion, there is time to consider the past. Scattered thinking and scant regard for the consequences of thoughts or words are represented by this Four reversed.

Sometimes the reversed Four of Swords indicates a person who is unprepared to examine the cause of past upheavals. The pain of recent consequences is too raw to deal with alone, without assistance. An understanding counsellor or tarot reader can gently encourage the person to review past decisions, actions and consequences without blame or recrimination.

After his small business collapsed, Jonathan vowed he'd never work for himself again. Two years later, he was restless in a steady job and frustrated that he couldn't shape his own vocation. In his career layout, the reversed Four of Swords suggested that although he'd taken care of his income needs by securing a new job, he hadn't yet mentally unpacked and examined his recent business disappointment. He hadn't discovered why it ended badly. By asking several questions about his former business, it was apparent that Jonathan had picked an unreliable business partner. His associate, Todd, spent all available funds while leaving Jonathan to bring in new business and do the required work. Jonathan left the session with a clearer understanding of the effect that partnership had on his time and his business concept. About a year later, he returned to ask about a new business idea, one that he could manage alone.

In a general layout, the Four of Swords reversed indicates hasty action, a busy lifestyle resulting from poor planning or someone who is living on coffee, sugar and takeaway food to maintain a frenetic pace. It can describe a person who is frightened of returning to the pain of the previous upright card, the Three of Swords. Hyperactivity is this individual's way of avoiding loneliness or grief.

Sometimes, the reversed Four of Swords indicates low reserves of physical energy, possibly due to unresolved sadness. Returning to the previous upright card, the Three of Swords, involves re-experiencing the pain, allowing it to sweep through the body and mind and surrendering to the sadness. This allows the anguish to subside naturally, at its own pace. Otherwise, unaddressed issues can become burdens that influence current and future decisions.

In a career layout, this card describes the moment a person decides to resign or search for a new job in another company. This could be a reaction to disappointment, such as being passed over for promotion, ignored, treated poorly or worse. In Bianca's reading, it was because every idea she had was claimed by her boss if it worked and blamed on her if it didn't. Bianca was so angry she spontaneously left her job and started her own business. Despite a rocky start, her sheer perseverance eventually helped her thrive. She is now a proud, small-business owner who values her independence.

In a relationship question, the reversed Four of Swords may describe the moment a person has left a relationship and is exhausted but relieved. It's time to accept heartache and contemplate the future. Occasionally, this card indicates bold steps taken after a period of frustration in a relationship. An individual might be actively searching for a new partner without taking responsibility for how they have contributed to partnership issues. If a romance is stale, this person is ready to shake things up.

This card indicates an urge for action without thinking about possible adverse consequences. When Theo became bored with his marriage, he looked online for a mistress. After meeting Carla, they began an affair. Eventually, Theo suggested to his wife Pam that they have an open relationship. Pam reluctantly agreed but when she met Carla, the two women discovered they had more in common with each other than with Theo. After six months, they left him and moved into an apartment together. How does one explain to the boss at the annual Christmas party that his wife left to live with his girlfriend? Just because a person doesn't anticipate any detrimental consequences to impulsive decisions doesn't necessarily mean there aren't any.

In a health query, the reversed Four of Swords indicates low levels of physical stamina. It's time to take it easy while thinking about current circumstances and opportunities. It might also be a suitable time to address some grief by consciously returning to the previous upright card, the Three of Swords. Unacknowledged grief can add to one's baggage, and unless you have a personal Sherpa, excess baggage might prevent you from reaching your desired summit.

Four of Pentacles

The Four of Pentacles indicates being able to afford to put plans into action. The money is available to build a house, take a holiday or finance a project. This card indicates someone saving money or living within their means.

The person on this card is cloaked in red and black, with a thin line of pale blue. This suggests the individual is grounded in the material world. This is confirmed by the handheld pentacle. There are also more pentacles beneath the feet and on the head. The pentacles beneath represent money or material possessions that separate this person from the earth. The pentacle above disconnects the individual from the heavens because it covers the crown chakra.

The pentacle blocking the heart can leave someone feeling that possessions are more meaningful than people. It is judicious to guard against allowing material possessions to disconnect an individual from life. If that happens, the individual moves forward to the emptiness shown in the next card, the Five of Pentacles.

Basically, the Four of Pentacles represents financial discipline. In a relationship layout, it can indicate someone who barters personal affection. This is one of the cards for the sign of Taurus. Taureans tend to hold tension in the neck and are prone to issues in the neck and throat area when stressed.

In a general reading, the Four of Pentacles indicates saving money, living within one's means and being realistic about what projects are likely to cost at the outset. If a person is planning to travel, start a business or buy a new home and this Four appears upright in a layout, the next step is financial preparation. Sometimes when I see this card in a general reading, I ask the client if he or she is currently saving towards a specific goal.

The Four of Pentacles describes a person who is not afraid to negotiate to secure the best price on a product or service. This is someone who fundamentally understands money equals choice. The more financial reserves a person has, the more options are available for home environment, choice of car, lifestyle, health maintenance and schools for children.

In a career layout, the Four describes someone who values financial stability. This individual is prepared to work hard and structure life around a reliable source of income. They usually live within financial constraints and still save money to invest. This person is likely to have a secondary source of income, apart from a job, such as a rental property or shares. They understand that work is not meant to be fun. That's why it's called work. It's to provide an income that pays for opportunities for fun – after the bills are paid and savings are set aside.

In a relationship question, the Four of Pentacles indicates an emphasis on financial stability, which is the foundation of a solid relationship for this person. It is a practical approach to love that works. Ongoing monetary issues are one of the top five reasons relationships collapse. When searching for a partner, this individual usually places more importance on a steady income than on beauty or romantic promise.

It sometimes indicates possessiveness, someone who uses money as a tool to control a partner in a relationship. This can be damaging to a partnership in the long-term, especially if the spouse does not have a separate income source. It undermines trust and security.

In a health query, the upright Four of Pentacles indicates the jaw, neck or throat. Sometimes, it signifies tightness across the shoulders. Often, ongoing tension is related to money issues or frustrations with financial plans. It's a card for the sign of Taurus. The other Taurean cards include The Hierophant and the King of Pentacles. Two or three of these cards in the layout confirm issues with health around the jaw, neck, throat and shoulders area.

The upright Four indicates sufficient income to build and maintain physical health. This might include regular massages to reduce tension, gym membership or ongoing support through physiotherapy, chiropractic or yoga sessions.

Four of Pentacles Reversed

The Four of Pentacles reversed indicates depleted financial reserves or the inability to save the money necessary to achieve a goal. Money is slipping through the fingers, now. Spending has accelerated.

However, when this reversed Four appears in a relationship layout, it can suggest the tendency to give generously and wholeheartedly in order to build a solid, lasting partnership. Upright, this card can represent the need to place more value on what is being given to others. When reversed, it's likely that what is offered is taken for granted and will not be cherished. The giver needs to ensure personal efforts are recognised and rewarded. A mother of three children, without paid employment, can work just as diligently as someone who is well-paid for their efforts. However, when it comes to joint financial decisions, she might not have equality. It is worthwhile to return to the previous upright card, the Three of Pentacles, to build lasting personal wealth and stability by establishing strong foundations.

In a layout concerning the purchase of a home or a car, this card describes the money being spent on an item. It can suggest that expenses exceed income at this point. This can be when people travel, as they spend more than usual on accommodation, tours and food.

In a question about starting a new business, it's unlikely the person has sufficient funds to proceed. Financial resources are already stretched thin when the reversed Four of Pentacles is selected for a layout and new businesses often require an injection of funds to ensure viability.

In a general reading, the reversed Four indicates money slipping away. Expenses are greater than income at this point, so it's crucial to be aware of current outlays. It might be a temporary situation that returns to normal in a short time. This occurs when travelling, moving into a new home or during a large purchase, such as a new car, home renovations or an extended holiday.

In a career layout, the Four of Pentacles reversed can describe an underpaid career. The person might be working too hard for the income or travelling many hours each day for work. This card often occurs in a layout when a person is an unpaid intern in an organisation, hoping to be offered a paid position in the company.

For a small business owner, the reversed Four suggests costs currently outstrip income in the venture. It's time to return to the previous upright card, the Three of Pentacles, to establish solid foundations for a profitable business. These fundamentals might include regular advertising and marketing, reassessing the products or services offered or identifying and marketing to target customers.

In a relationship question, the reversed Four of Pentacles describes someone who is capable of giving without considering returns. This generous individual is content to see a partner thrive, regardless of personal cost. Sometimes, it indicates a need to return to the previous upright card, the Three of Pentacles, to ensure a current relationship is on solid footing. This individual might be giving too much, without awareness of a potentially self-destructive pattern being established in a relationship. Perhaps one partner has become reliant on the financial reserves of the other, adding pressure to maintain a lifestyle.

In a health query, this card indicates the neck, jaw and throat. It can also suggest financial concerns impacting on physical health. There may be increased stress, due to money pressures or an inability to pay for regular health maintenance. The reversed Four of Pentacles can indicate unexpected medical expenses, such as a surgical procedure followed by a period of convalescence, a series of sessions with a health practitioner or an annual health fund membership payment. It also points to tension across the shoulders. Occasionally, it highlights stress resulting from financial concerns.

The Fives

The fives in the tarot herald change. The four suits show four different approaches to change. The fives are unique in the tarot in that, when reversed, these cards indicate people accepting change more gracefully than when the cards appear upright.

The wands suit indicates eagerness for transformation and challenge, especially if immediate goals seem impossible. Wands people sometimes see change as a chance to escape current demands or stifling routines. When reversed, wands individuals may claim that a new opportunity is a long-awaited life path beckoning them, when in fact it's simply the lure of success and good fortune without prolonged effort that tempts them away from present goals.

Cups people are unsettled by the loss that often accompanies change. An ending means releasing someone or something to make room for its replacement. Cups people mourn the loss of the familiar, vividly remembering how a person, place or circumstance nourished them in the past. When cups individuals have stable sources of emotional and spiritual nourishment, they accept change more easily. When reversed, cups people are easily lost in memories of the past, often unaware of new options arriving to replace what has gone.

The swords suit is about the need for understanding. The Five of Swords represents negotiating with others after a disagreement. It presents an opportunity to have one's needs met in ways that strengthen bonds between parties for future negotiations. This Five can describe the aftermath of an argument or a separation. Because it's a swords card, sharp words, accusations and recriminations are likely to have been voiced. The individuals involved now have time to reflect and take responsibility for their words and actions. When the dust settles, everyone can begin to find some common ground. This reflection is shown by a return to the upright Four of Swords.

Swords people are sociable so they thrive in communities. These can be based on location, workplace, common interests, politics or aligned business interests. Flourishing in a group usually means offering a meaningful contribution and allowing for differences between existing members.

When reversed, this card shows a person struggling to understand the social landscape. This reflective period can occur after arguments and tension resulting from interactions with others. The fives are cards for change and swords people want to understand the purpose of change. They discover this by asking why a change is happening, where it is leading, what are the advantages of embracing this transformation and whether the changes are the result of something they thought, said or did.

Pentacles indicate a tendency to accept that change is inevitable, realising it can be more comfortable when preparations are made. These are often financial arrangements, such as saving for eventual retirement, purchasing a new home or taking an annual holiday.

When the Five of Pentacles is reversed, people understand the value of money but not the concept of holding on to it. Sometimes, they have such a poor sense of self-worth that they end up in low-paid jobs without opportunities for advancement. Despite a strong work ethic, they cannot build wealth. Thus, they are limited in their ability to build financial stability.

Finding three or more fives (including The Hierophant, the major arcana five) in a layout highlights a period of growth through change. If the fives are reversed, the person is usually much more open to the transformation.

It is sometimes necessary to release current options or circumstances to accept new opportunities. Embracing different possibilities can also require sacrifice. The fives reversed show individuals open to change or searching for opportunities for growth, while upright fives indicate transformation forced upon them without notice.

Five of Wands

The Five of Wands represents enthusiastic anticipation for the opportunities change might bring. Wands people can force upheaval to calm their restlessness. This Five indicates a need to have purpose behind action. The scattered energy resulting from undirected enthusiasm can be exhausting, even to those observing. Here, there are five people waving wands around enthusiastically and carelessly. This card represents the wands' passion and recklessness, which can be awe-inspiring to witness but also bruising for people close to the action. These individuals are better at doing than planning or theorising.

The Five of Wands sometimes represents several facets of one person where each component has a different purpose. Anyone who runs a small business knows what this feels like. Sole traders need to be the marketing manager, bookkeeper, sales manager, receptionist, stock controller and the cleaner.

In a general reading, the Five of Wands describes scattered focus. This can be a person who is juggling too many projects or commitments to be effective with any of them or an organisation that lurches from one near-disaster to the next. It also indicates a team composed of uncompromising individuals. There is often no clear strategy for achieving a desired goal.

These people are often too busy engaged in a project to stop, reflect and plan. Consequently, a lot of energy is wasted due to poor strategies and no pre-action planning. These are the explorers who accidentally burn their only map when they need to start a fire at sunset of day one of a three-month sojourn. A tarot student gave a clear example of this one day. As an eight-year-old, she watched her father saw the leg off the dining room table to make an axe handle. He wanted to chop wood for the fire. The family ate at a foldaway card table from that day onwards.

Basically, the people fighting in this card need to remember they'll have to work or live together after this conflict. How they treat each other now is likely to have lasting consequences.

In answer to a question about achieving a specific goal or purpose, the Five suggests a lack of success due to too many other commitments. It can describe those times when everyone is screaming, demanding time and attention and leaving a person without real focus. It's difficult to concentrate in times of turmoil. Occasionally, this Five indicates unplanned chaos, someone lurching from one impending disaster to another.

In a career layout, the Five of Wands can describe a person who lacks real job focus. Too many other demands surface, distracting the individual from making a clear plan and taking the necessary steps to enjoy a successful career. An example of this was Roy, who handed me his business card one day. The card read: HEALER, ACTOR, GARDENER. My first question to Roy was, "What do you actually do?"

In a relationship layout, the Five of Wands sometimes highlights the juggling of work, social and family commitments so that partners rarely spend undisturbed, quality time with each other. For example, I know a couple who email each other when they are both at home. As she eats breakfast and he takes a shower, rather than walk into the bathroom to talk to her husband, she leaves a message on his email so he can read it on the way to work. They must have the quietest arguments of any couple around.

In a health query, the Five of Wands suggests physical and mental energy are currently being scattered. Arguments or conflicts with others may be a source of exhaustion when this card appears in a health layout. It's also possible this individual is attempting to complete too many different tasks in an average week. This person is trying to maintain a frenetic pace.

Five of Wands Reversed

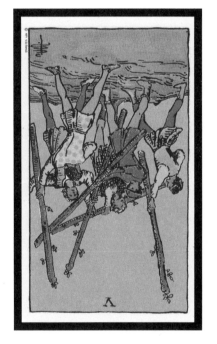

The Five of Wands reversed indicates a realisation that focus is mandatory to achieving a goal. Perhaps due to sheer physical and emotional exhaustion, people are sitting, reflecting upon the appropriate path to take to achieve their objectives. After a period of confusion or scattered focus, they are able to regain their sense of what is important.

When reversed, all the fives in the tarot indicate an openness to change. They suggest that change is seen as an opportunity to explore new directions instead of a threat to current circumstances.

The different coloured tunics worn by the people in this card represent unique approaches to goals, including passionate red, intellectual yellow, spiritual blue and harmonious green. When this card is reversed, it means each aspect is in harmony with the others for a successful outcome.

Also, when the card is reversed, the earth appears above the scattered energy of the wands, suggesting that material or physical (earthy) concerns are forcing a more realistic approach at this time. The Five of Wands reversed suggests a need to focus on a goal. This requires a return to the previous card in the suit, the upright Four of Wands, to regain stability. In that situation, a team of like-minded people can work together towards a common goal for shared success. When each participant has clear goals and responsibilities, complex projects can be achieved more smoothly and in shorter time periods.

In a general reading, the reversed Five of Wands describes increased concentration after a period of scattered focus. A return to the previous upright card, the Four of Wands, enables the person to consolidate plans and focus on each step necessary to complete tasks. It sometimes indicates a brief period of reflection after a conflict. During this thinking process, each participant can consider alternative approaches to the recent struggle.

In a career layout, this card sometimes indicates that a team can work together after a period of discord. The focus has moved from internal competition towards greater cooperation. Each participant's opinion is likely to be heard and considered. This team shares responsibility for solving problems and successfully completing collective goals.

In a relationship question, the reversed Five suggests that after a period of attending to individual needs, partners are prepared to work together towards common goals. By returning to the previous upright card, the Four of Wands, they can consolidate their relationship and strengthen shared focus.

In a health query, the reversed Five of Wands shows an increased focus on building and maintaining robust health. Where energy was previously scattered, it's now channelled into more rewarding directions. It sometimes describes the act of consciously avoiding conflict to reduce blood pressure or ongoing inner tension.

Five of Cups

The Five of Cups is about reminiscing after a loss. It indicates a period of grief needs to occur before the person can fully participate in life again. After a significant disappointment is intellectually and emotionally processed, the individual is often more present and able to focus on the next step in life's journey.

In this card, heavy grey skies blanket what might otherwise be a tranquil scene. The overturned cups hold the attention of the person in black, who is grieving lost opportunities for fulfilment. Due to their narrow focus, this individual is currently blind to other possibilities for happiness.

This card suggests sorrow. There is an acute

sense of isolation, both from the river and from the stability offered by the castle. It's a card of narrow-mindedness because grief can blind us to the opportunities for happiness. The person in this card is unaware of the two upright cups offering ample opportunities for fulfilment, as they are out of view. All is not lost but when this card appears in a layout, the person feels that happiness is elusive.

On the path to the Ten of Cups, grief and loss are unavoidable. Without them, it's not possible to know when life is encouraging. Personal winters are necessary for comparison when summers arrive. After a bleak winter, spring days with warm sunshine and fragrant flowers can elicit smiles from strangers, friends and family.

This card represents grieving the loss of a job, a relationship or even the squandering of wasted years spent with an unsuitable person or in some other hopeless situation. For example, Jasmine plummeted into depression soon after she left her abusive husband of thirty years. Before she could face the task of rebuilding her life, she needed to grieve the years she had spent in what she described as a lifeless relationship.

Although this card indicates grief or loss, it may result in personal growth and a deeper understanding of life. Sometimes a loss is an essential step towards a person's ultimate destiny. Sorrow is unavoidable when we are emotionally attached to people, animals and possessions. When the sadness has passed, most people regain their appreciation of life. When awareness of life's opportunities returns, the bridge over the river is visible. This link offers a steady path back to stability (home, as shown by the castle) and like-minded people (a partner or family). It's necessary to accept the loss while remembering that the next card in this sequence is the Six of Cups, which highlights the castle and suggests emotional balance.

The cups behind the person offer happiness and the castle across the river presents an opportunity for constancy. The firm foundations reflected in the castle are more obvious in the Six of Cups.

In a general reading, the Five of Cups indicates loss and grief. It's time to accept change and process emotions following the end of a situation. Often, the person is in self-exile, reflecting on what has been lost and what remains for the next chapter. When the Five of Cups appears in the outcome position in a layout, it's worthwhile adding a card so the person can be aware of what will emerge from the current sad period. The additional card describes the dawn that follows this harrowing time.

In a career layout, the upright Five of Cups indicates career disappointment.

This might occur if a promised promotion is given to someone else, a person is made redundant or expansion plans are shelved after a difficult financial year. Sometimes, the Five describes the regret that can surface when a person reflects on career plans and is dissatisfied with personal progress. This was Vanessa's dilemma. She had devoted almost twenty years to one company. Instead of being promoted, she was repeatedly passed over for younger people who had limited skills and no genuine interest in the job. They were simply stepping around a chessboard in pursuit of career conquests.

After a period of disillusionment, Vanessa completed some relevant courses and moved to another company. She changed jobs every two years for the next decade, making up for lost time. She ended up heading a department that didn't exist when she began her career. Without this additional training, she would not have been considered for a position as a department head.

In a relationship question, the Five of Cups can indicate the end of a relationship or of a stage within a partnership. Sometimes the loss is not related to the relationship but affects it. This might be grief after the death of a parent, the loss of a dream job, bankruptcy after a difficult period in business or the end of a long-term friendship. Any of these are likely to temporarily affect a relationship if the person withdraws to grieve and reflect on the loss.

This Five can also describe processing the loss of a previous relationship while in a new one. If the individual has not made sense of past events, he or she might not yet be emotionally available, despite being with a new relationship partner. Grief cannot be rushed, so the person's spouse might need to be patient with this situation.

In a health query, the Five of Cups indicates that underlying health issues may be related to grief or loss. Perhaps after a severe setback, the person sinks into depression, unable to process past circumstances while lacking confidence that life might be rewarding again.

In a recent health reading, this Five confirmed Nicky's sadness after the death of her husband. During the grieving process, Nicky retreated socially, lost interest in her daily walking routine and ignored her award-winning garden. Because the Three of Cups appeared in the outcome position, it was apparent that her sorrow would eventually subside and social connections would be re-established.

Five of Cups Reversed

The Five of Cups reversed indicates diminishing loss and grief. It's time to return to the stability of the upright Four of Cups and become reacquainted with inner sources of spiritual and emotional fulfilment. The suffering represented by the upright Five ensures appreciation of the uneventful stability provided by the upright Six of Cups in the future. Security is usually treasured after loss, grief and isolation.

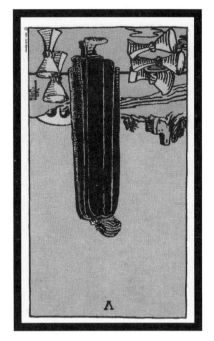

The reversed Five shows a return to open-mindedness after grief subsides and highlights the realisation that there are other cups aside from those that have been overturned. There is also a bridge over the river (representing emotions) leading back to the castle, which symbolises a comfortable structured life. Regardless of how long ago the loss or separation occurred, the Five reversed shows the release of grief or isolation. This person is ready to embrace life again.

An unusual example of this card occurred in a relationship layout for a client who had recently reunited with his former wife after they had resolved their ongoing differences. The reversed Five of Cups sometimes signals that a flame kept burning for a past lover is extinguished when increased awareness emerges of what current opportunities offer.

In a general reading, the reversed Five of Cups indicates a return to life after a period of grief or self-imposed isolation. It's time to discover fresh opportunities, make new acquaintances and reconnect with old friends. There is a renewed awareness of opportunities, with increased confidence that life holds a more rewarding future.

In a career layout, the reversed Five shows a person who is able to focus more clearly on career goals after a period of grief or loss. The bereavement might have involved an unexpected retrenchment from a previous job, a demotion or simply being ignored by management and colleagues for an extended period. With the sadness accepted and processed, this individual becomes more appreciative of current circumstances and opportunities. There are sufficient energy and desire available to pursue career prospects now.

In a relationship question, the reversed Five of Cups describes the end of a period of sorrow and a return to connection with friends and current opportunities. After processing a recent loss, the person is emotionally ready and available for new relationship opportunities. If the individual is already in a relationship, the loss might be related to a previous affiliation. However, it is still likely to affect a current relationship because of a need to retreat to grieve. When past losses have been processed, the individual is emotionally available for love.

In a health query, the reversed Five of Cups can suggest that a period of depression or isolation has passed. This card indicates a return to sound health brings a sense of emotional well-being. Often, dealing with grief or loss expands a person's appreciation for the people and opportunities that are still available.

Five of Swords

The Five of Swords represents the mental acceptance of transformation. Swords people like to know what is happening and why. They also need to understand where current changes might lead. These people need a mental picture of the landscape in their lives. Once they have these internal maps accurately updated, they can scan the environment for opportunities, threat and options. Without a reasonable understanding of why change is occurring, most people oppose it. This resistance is shown in the Five of Swords as arguments and verbal strife.

It is important to realise that sharp words can be every bit as painful as physical blows when groups become polarised. In the heat of the moment, statements are made that cannot be easily forgotten. The mental quickness of swords individuals means there will be just enough accuracy in a claim about another person to make an opinion seem like truth.

This card shows change occurring through words, such as in disagreements, where each party speaks frankly. It can be a card for arguments. Its appearance in answer to a question about the resolution of a dispute suggests ongoing disagreements or a parting of the ways.

The energy-charged clouds sweeping across the sky in this card represent angry or aggressive thinking that results in disagreements and tension. The person in the foreground wears red under a green tunic, suggesting this individual is easily roused to passionate discourse. By speaking without consideration of the consequences, this person forces the issue with three swords (thoughts, arguments and passionately held beliefs). Although it's likely this argument is won, long-term peace is sacrificed. Conflict isn't usually resolved through force but, rather, by skilful negotiation and acknowledging different needs.

The three swords being held represent the pain already felt in the specific card, the Three of Swords. This anguish is manifested outwardly in the form of words and actions that hurt people in close proximity. When a person cannot endure inner suffering, it's often easier to lash out at others instead. Inner torment provokes expressions of anger that hide debilitating fears of feeling powerless. It is difficult to engage the cooperation of others when they feel betrayed or brutalised by this person's actions. Eventually, other people tend to withdraw from this individual, which can be lonely. By being ignored or avoided, there is plenty of time (in the Six of Swords) to reflect on past words, actions and their consequences.

Sometimes, when unable to accept change in our lives, we fight it. This battle can be with those who appear to bring the change or simply with people close to us for allowing the upheaval to happen. When the head of a department announces staff cuts, the backlash is often directed at the messenger instead of at the decision-makers. Staff may believe the department head helped with the decision as to who was to be made redundant or that he should have warned co-workers of the impending threat to their jobs.

Sometimes, this Five represents different aspects of the same person. They may be angry, hurt, abandoned and vulnerable, simultaneously. Antagonising this person might incur a fierce retaliatory response in the form of acrimonious words or harsh actions.

In a general reading, this is a card for arguments that result in a separation. This could occur when a person abruptly quits a job, abandons a relationship or ends a friendship. What is said in the heat of the moment is hard to erase, making it difficult to rebuild trust needed for the relationship to continue in any form.

In a career layout, this upright Five describes a situation boiling over. An abrupt exchange of words might be a way to establish boundaries around what is acceptable in the workplace if someone is feeling bullied or marginalised. This card can also describe a job ending in unpleasant circumstances. Unfounded accusations sometimes arise, resulting in a sudden resignation or termination of employment. This is not necessarily a bad outcome, especially if it leads to a more rewarding position.

In a relationship question, the Five of Swords describes arguments and a possible separation, even if it's temporary. There is a sense of urgency around voicing thoughts and this insistence is a sign that the individual might be emotionally triggered by current circumstances to offload unprocessed emotions from a previous, unrelated situation. Speaking out when emotionally provoked can have devastating effects on a relationship, as words spoken in the heat of the moment can slice through like a sharp sword, inflicting grievous wounds that tend to echo through the brain long after the fighting has ceased.

In a health query, the Five of Swords indicates physical health issues related to ongoing stress and tension at home or in the person's workplace. If the individual is repeatedly subjected to criticism, sarcasm or verbal harassment, physical health symptoms are likely to occur.

In a rare situation, I was subjected to verbal harassment and sarcasm from a medical practitioner who was angry that I didn't recognise a skin eruption I had not seen previously. I returned the volley in a typical swords fashion by coldly saying, "Yes, it's my mistake. There's no need to shout at me. I forgot to go to medical school. That's why I'm consulting a medical doctor. Can you recommend a good doctor in this practice?" He quickly recovered a more professional manner for the rest of my appointment.

Five of Swords Reversed

Reversed, the Five of Swords usually represents a more open-minded approach to change. Perhaps the arguing is over now and there is an opportunity for real negotiation, as the parties involved are finally heard by each other. This is the calm after the storm, and during this ceasefire, it's possible to reflect on what has been said and done.

For example, Maree's ex-husband had been harassing her and disputing the division of property during a vindictive divorce settlement. Having recently found a new partner, he suddenly gave up arguing with Maree, and they reached an agreement in six weeks that they had not previously negotiated in five years. Another example of the Five reversed occurs when parliament passes a bill at 2:30 a.m. After hours of disagreement, exhaustion gradually makes the MPs more agreeable. They're too tired to prolong the battle.

This reversed card suggests it's time to return to the previous card in the swords suit, the upright Four of Swords, to acknowledge personal needs. The stability and tranquillity of the Four of Swords is calming when groups or families negotiate change. After the hasty words or actions shown in the upright Five, the reversed Five usually indicates a more flexible approach. Options that have previously been discounted may now be more acceptable.

People are generally more inclusive after conflict, when they have had time to consider both viewpoints. It's time to put down their swords and resolve differences or make allowances for each other. It's an opportunity to be heard and to negotiate a viable solution that meets a range of demands. It's wise to meet each participant's needs, especially when each stakeholder is also a sword holder.

In a general reading, the reversed Five of Swords describes negotiations after disagreements. Participants have had a chance to cool off and reflect on what was said, different points of view and potential solutions. By resuming dialogue without worrying about not being heard, progress is likely.

In a career layout, this card can describe walking away from a job because of ongoing tension and disagreements. Sometimes, a person realises they do not suit the corporate culture and another workplace is a better solution. It can also indicate negotiated resolutions to employment obstacles. It's possible to plan and implement a strategy to avoid struggles and progress up the career ladder while colleagues are immersed in conflict. The reversed Five highlights an intellectual broad-mindedness. Instead of becoming polarised by obstacles, it's possible to negotiate a reasonable solution given current circumstances.

In a relationship question, this card signifies regret about past words or actions, plus a more flexible approach to finding a solution. Even if a relationship is ending, parents of small children realise they need to be adaptable and civil when dealing with each other over custody arrangements and parental responsibilities. If the relationship is to resume, there may need to be apologies and negotiated changes of habits or behaviour patterns.

The reversed Five of Swords indicates more willingness to listen and to change.

In a health query, the reversed Five of Swords suggests the person doesn't agree with an approach or diagnosis and may search for different options. It can describe the act of walking away from a health treatment or arguments about how to tackle an issue. This card recently highlighted a health question about a client's mother.

Tad's mother was slipping into dementia and he was worried about her living alone in her house. His sister, Kelly, wanted to honour her mother's wishes by keeping her at home but Tad felt it had gone past the point of her being safe at home alone. He wanted her to be in a high-care environment. They had argued about the options and the reversed Five card indicated that both siblings were now receptive to more workable solutions. Their temporary answer was to ensure a part-time nurse visited five days a week and Tad and Kelly were to take turns on weekends. They also agreed to accept the doctor's guidance as to when to move her into higher levels of care.

Sometimes, the reversed Five of Swords suggests health issues stemming from a separation. It can also represent inner stress from an argument that is not yet fully resolved.

Five of Pentacles

The Five of Pentacles suggests that a new approach is necessary before progress can be made. Perhaps there is too much focus on one part of life at the expense of personal or spiritual development. Basically, this card represents a material approach to change. Poverty sometimes forces people to adjust or simplify by re-evaluating what is important to them.

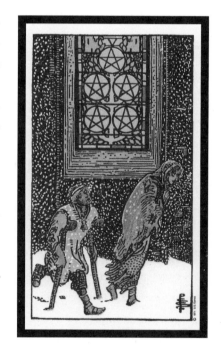

The couple in the card experience poverty to discover the other side of the coin. If they remember these days of deprivation clearly when they are wealthy again (in the Ten of Pentacles), they are likely to be more generous and understanding of others in need. The toughest steel is forged in the intense heat of a raging furnace. Likewise, character is strengthened by challenges met.

Perhaps a period of scarcity is required for full appreciation of wealth. Poverty might be financial, emotional, mental or spiritual. This person feels excluded from a source of fulfilment, like the people in this card feel ostracised from the sanctuary of the church by its thick walls.

As well as economic deprivation, the Five of Pentacles suggests poor health, low vitality and spiritual emptiness. Sometimes, it shows a period without work due to health issues. Ill-health, unemployment or inadequate income can leave people feeling disconnected from their communities.

The people in this card need financial success to improve their lives. However, they also need to reconnect with their spiritual paths for long-term fulfilment. Traditionally, the church offered prayer and contemplation as ways to still the mind and focus on spiritual development but this is not the only option. Today, it's possible to reconnect spiritually through meditation, gardening, writing, drawing, playing or composing music, surfing or cloud-gazing.

In a general reading, the upright Five of Pentacles describes a period of financial hardship. The person might be unemployed or underemployed. This individual could be working hard but without sufficient financial reward for effort. It's a card that shows someone who feels cut off or disconnected from community and without financial stability.

This card can indicate a separation. The individual might be leaving a job, a home environment or a social circle. It sometimes suggests physical health issues that prevent the person from earning a suitable income. One solution is to identify sources of spiritual nourishment before finding a suitable path back to financial stability.

In a career layout, the upright Five of Pentacles can suggest unemployment or conversely, the person is working too hard. It can imply that the present career is not fulfilling or that the pursuit of financial or material success is clouding awareness of a spiritual path. This could be a musician who is playing covers several nights a week while longing to write and present original compositions.

It also describes someone who needs more marketable skills to improve career choices. If the Ten of Pentacles reversed is also present in the layout, it suggests that current financial constraints might be the result of a recession or flat economic conditions. The Five of Pentacles is a card for personal financial constraints, whereas the reversed Ten of Pentacles can indicate economic tightening across the wider community.

In a relationship question, the Five often describes someone who is single and lonely. If already in a relationship, this individual is likely to feel isolated and unhappy in the current situation. It can describe someone leaving or ending a relationship but this is not the only option. If the person identifies other sources of physical, emotional, intellectual and spiritual nourishment, it's possible to rely less on a partner for happiness and more on a range of other sources of joy. These might include fitness activities, social clubs, hobbies, attending courses, yoga, meditation or helping others.

In a health query, the Five of Pentacles often indicates inadequate spiritual nourishment resulting in emotional disconnection and inner emptiness. Sometimes a person who others consider wealthy and successful inwardly feels alone, unhappy or unfulfilled. With discipline, supportive habits can provide the spiritual nourishment needed. Sometimes this Five indicates low income or lack of personal savings are restricting a person's choices when facing a health issue. People living in poverty often don't have the luxury of treating minor ailments. For example, a single mother of three with a part-time job is unlikely to have spare cash for Pilates classes or weekly physiotherapy sessions to strengthen her back.

Five of Pentacles Reversed

The Five of Pentacles reversed indicates a departure from a work environment or a living situation that has been unsupportive. It's time to return to the upright Four of Pentacles to consolidate a stable financial or physical approach to life.

Darryl was working full-time as a waiter when he really wanted to return to woodcarving. He resigned from his job as soon as he was accepted into a wood-carving academy. Leaving an unrewarding situation and moving towards something more satisfying encapsulates the Five reversed.

The Five of Pentacles can suggest a separation that is inevitable. Both partners realise that they will not be fulfilled if they continue the relationship, so they part without too many regrets. It can also describe leaving a job without hesitation. Perhaps it was underpaid or a temporary contract and easily discarded at the right time. Reversed, this card indicates a smoother transition from one situation to another. The person is eager for change and to embrace new opportunities.

In a general reading, the reversed Five of Pentacles describes leaving a situation without hesitation or remorse. They recognise that what is required cannot be found where they are and that new opportunities await. It can signify awareness that better opportunities are ahead and that this change is simply a step towards an improved life.

In a career layout, the reversed Five of Pentacles indicates returning to well-paid work after a period of ill-health or unemployment. It also appears in career layouts when a person leaves an unrewarding job for a better position elsewhere. There are few regrets when this card appears reversed. By returning to the previous upright card, the Four of Pentacles, this person is able to save money or live a more financially secure lifestyle.

In a relationship question, this card indicates an acceptance that a current relationship or type of relationship provides few rewards. It's time to leave and it's necessary to consciously avoid similar relationship patterns in future. Sometimes the reversed Five of Pentacles suggests a couple moving out of a city to a more affordable lifestyle elsewhere. It can indicate that the current location is causing unhappiness, not necessarily the partnership.

In a health query, the reversed Five of Pentacles describes a gradual return to health and stability after a period of ill-health. Perhaps a difficult time provided an opportunity to reassess life direction and reorganise priorities. Now, the individual is acting on this new understanding, moving towards a more balanced lifestyle.

The Sixes

The sixes in the tarot indicate stability. They're a rest stop after the change and chaos of the fives. The four suits show different approaches to stability. The active wands suit represents balance as the period soon after a goal has been achieved and before the urge to pursue another challenge arises. The sentimental cups suit characterises stability as shared emotional contentment in a comfortable home environment.

The cerebral swords focus on mental stability as the gradual change of beliefs settles after a period of mental or physical turmoil. Instead of fighting with friends, siblings or co-workers, this person has found a way to work with others towards a shared goal. The practical pentacles suit emphasises financial security arising from each participant in a project knowing and valuing their place. Each contributor is rewarded for personal efforts — the wealthy man shown in the card by having a stable business and the employees or contractors by having steady income.

When three or more sixes are upright together in a layout, stability in income, home environment and the person's mental state are indicated. When two or more of these three sixes are reversed, growth is suggested. This is because reversed sixes indicate a return to their respective upright fives to embrace change. This occurred with Conrad, who had been offered a promotion. It meant a move from Australia to the United States and he planned to relocate before his family to decide where they might live. His wife and their two children needed to be together to complete the school year before they moved. This career step involved change on almost every level for Conrad and his family, reflected in three reversed sixes in his general reading.

Six of Wands

The Six of Wands indicates harnessing personal energy, focus and enthusiasm to pursue a desired goal. When upright, it usually indicates a successful outcome. The confusion shown in the Five of Wands is replaced by the realisation that to achieve personal objectives, it is necessary to avoid distractions and inspire others to support the quest. This is a card about fulfilling goals.

The card shows an individual riding a horse in a victory parade. Success is due in part to the innate confidence and enthusiasm wands people usually possess. Clothed in red (suggesting passion and physical application for the task), this person is enjoying victory before the next challenge. The clear skies suggest there are few obstacles. This is an example of boldness and effort bringing success.

The person in this card shares this victory with others, who together, have made this achievement possible. Commitment to the task and confident leadership inspired them to help. Wands people often have infectious enthusiasm that can make the impossible seem close enough to be just reachable, with effort.

In a general reading, the upright Six of Wands is a card for success in personal endeavours. This is a goal reached, a job secured or a home successfully purchased. By harnessing focus, enthusiasm and personal energy, this person has successfully reached a goal. Sometimes, their enthusiasm inspires others to help push this individual into a position of leadership, where everyone might benefit from their combination of passion, discipline and vision for what is possible.

In a career question, this card can mean a promotion, a new job, a successful conclusion to a project or a different position within the present company. As the answer to a question, provided there are no conflicting cards accompanying it, the Six of Wands generally means yes.

In a relationship layout, the Six of Wands can mean a new commitment in a relationship, whether it is moving in together, marriage or the birth of a child. This card suggests that, together, a couple can progress happily through life's stages.

In a health query, the upright Six of Wands indicates stable health. It's a card for strong reserves of physical stamina and effective habits that contribute to well-being. It can suggest a speedy recovery after an illness or a surgical procedure. In answer to a question about the outcome of a medical procedure, it highlights a successful conclusion.

Six of Wands Reversed

The Six of Wands reversed indicates a need to return to the previous upright card in the suit, the Five of Wands, to encounter the confusion shown there. This person is attempting too many things at once or giving up on personal goals long before achieving them. Confidence is waning. The support of people who need to be inspired to commit themselves to the goal is also diminishing. Sometimes, this card suggests confusion about life's purpose. Bigger goals become obscured by immediate demands.

For example, Jerome was unsure of what was really meaningful to him. He was working long hours to secure a promotion but his relationship was suffering. He was studying at night to gain further qualifications and trying to keep fit by jogging early each morning. At weekends, he was trying to renovate his house. It was obvious Jerome was attempting too much in a short time. This was confirmed by the three telephone calls he took during his reading, plus his short attention span.

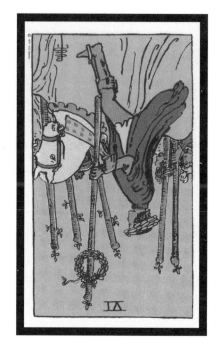

The Six of Wands reversed suggests this person is spending too much time resolving problems involving other people in their careers or relationships. The energy and enthusiasm required for taking any concrete steps towards personal goals are limited. Basically, the Six reversed can signify losing a job, leaving a relationship, missing out on a promotion or a lack of success resulting from poor focus and lack of commitment.

In a general reading, the reversed Six of Wands indicates a lack of concentration, leading to unsuccessful results. It's possible this person is not completely focused on significant goals or isn't confident these objectives are even achievable. Having a backup plan can sometimes decrease pressure from potential disappointment. It can also divert energy from core objectives by reducing focus.

In a career layout, this reversed card describes leaving a position or a job application not resulting in an offer. This can be encouraging news if it helps the person focus on other alternatives. These might include a different career direction, study, starting a business or taking contract work until more precise career goals are established.

In a relationship question, this card suggests a separation or living separate lives. By returning to the previous upright card, the Five of Wands, it's evident these partners don't have the same goals. As an answer to a question about a possible reunion with a former partner, the reversed Six indicates this is unlikely.

In a health query, the reversed Six of Wands can indicate low reserves of physical energy (because it's a reversed wands card) and that recent disappointments have left the person feeling uncertain about the future. In a question about a treatment or a medical procedure, it indicates it's unlikely to result in the desired outcome. It's time to return to the previous upright card, the Five of Wands, to restore clear focus. Perhaps unimportant demands have distracted the person from fundamental goals and personal life purpose. It's crucial to notice what drains our energy or brings conflict instead of rewards.

Diane was exhausted from almost two years of being a carer for her stepmother. Juggling a part-time job and her own family was draining and her stepbrother and stepsister weren't helping. It seemed unfair. When I asked if she had been close to her stepmother, her response was, "Not particularly."

She also explained she wasn't really in touch with her stepbrother and stepsister either. I found myself asking an obvious question. "If she's their biological mother but your stepmother, why are you shouldering all of this burden?" It wasn't necessary for me to receive an answer to this question. Diane simply needed time to consider how she managed her stepmother's affairs from the other side of town, while the elderly woman's son lived only five streets away but seemed unable to contribute to his mother's well-being.

Six of Cups

The Six of Cups represents returning to familiar places, such as a home or town that holds positive childhood memories or to a previous career. It can also be a time of bringing together disconnected spiritual or emotional parts within. When children or teenagers suffer trauma, they sometimes become mentally or emotionally frozen. When this occurs, they may fail to mature psychologically or emotionally for years or even decades. By inwardly revisiting those experiences (often with the support of a supportive friend or a counsellor), it's possible to thaw those frozen aspects and begin to catch up or reunite with the adult person within.

This card highlights a tangible sense of satisfaction derived from stability and comfortable routines. The two people in the card are simultaneously big and small. They are adults and share an adult relationship but are safely surrounded and dwarfed by the castle. Their mature faces and bodies contrast with the children's clothing. They are repotting flowers in a garden; the woman wears a gardening glove. The couple are nurturing the plants and each other through a shared pastime.

The tenderness between the pair in this card suggests a time of recreating purity and innocence. The white flowers being transplanted also symbolise untainted motives with shared tenderness. The individual walking away in the background indicates that others are helping life to run smoothly, contributing to the structure and continuity this scene illustrates. Basically, the couple shown in this card can take time to stop and smell the flowers because they are supported by others. A pentacles person might also suggest they can stop to smell the flowers because they previously planted some.

Often after great change or upheaval (the loss of the Five of Cups), people need a stable period where life is reassuringly familiar. The Six of Cups focuses on an emotional approach to stability, highlighting a time when incidentals are taken care of during a healing period, while the individual rests or plays and builds reserves of energy as they do so.

This card describes a rest on the path to the Ten of Cups. Breathing space is as valuable as the growth represented by other cups cards. It provides a brief glimpse of the Ten of Cups, while reaffirming long-term goals. The potential of the Ten of Cups includes being loved and valued in a nurturing, harmonious family environment. It also promises a supportive community.

In a general reading, the upright Six of Cups represents stability, comfort and peace. The individual has found a like-minded person or people to share life's journey and together they enjoy some simple pleasures. Life is reassuringly familiar and home is a safe haven from the turmoils of the world.

In a career layout, the Six of Cups describes a career that involves nursing or nurturing others. This occupation involves support and tenderness, as opposed to the cut and thrust of big business. The types of work represented by this card include counselling, infant or pre-school teaching, home care support, carers for special needs individuals or the aged, floristry, nannying, social work, massage, reiki or spiritual healing, housekeeping and cooking.

In a relationship question, this Six describes a stable, supportive relationship and a couple with shared history. The initial passion and desire seen in the Ace of Cups have become an enduring friendship with nourishing hobbies and interests. Life is comfortable, home is stable and skies are blue. Each person feels supported by the other and by the immediate environment. Their shared home is a safe place to land and escape the incessant demands of the outside world.

In a health query, the Six of Cups usually indicates stable health. It sometimes arises in a health question to signify a supportive person assisting during convalescence after surgery or an illness. Physical stability contributes to inner harmony and well-being. Sometimes, when surrounding cards show difficulties, this Six indicates a health condition that may have surfaced in childhood. Perhaps childhood asthma has re-emerged in adult years when a person is stressed or living in a polluted environment.

Six of Cups Reversed

The Six of Cups reversed emphasises feeling hemmed in by the constraints of familiar routines. Change and growth are needed, which involves returning to the previous upright card in the suit, the Five of Cups. This might mean leaving a comfortable, familiar or secure environment for new horizons. It's time to get out of a rut and explore new possibilities. Change is inevitable, so look for opportunities within this transition period.

At nineteen years of age, James was feeling frustrated with living at home with his parents. He wanted to share a house with other young people and to embrace life as a young man firsthand, without the rules of his parental home. He saved some money and moved out with two friends. Leaving the security and support of his family home for the freedom of a flat by the sea, he felt a sense of loss and liberation. For several months, he hovered between the two, returning to his parental home for meals and support, while using the flat as the base for his new lifestyle of surfing, partying and meeting friends. The reversed Six indicated his need for fresh horizons.

Fundamentally, the Six of Cups reversed suggests that new patterns of behaviour or unfamiliar territory are about to be embraced because a desire for change has overtaken the need for security. It can indicate leaving a situation without regret or being prepared to accept a personal loss to pursue a new direction. This might be leaving a relationship to accept an interstate career promotion or spending less time with a group of friends to explore new acquaintances.

In a general reading, the reversed Six of Cups describes a desire for change. Familiar routines feel dull and tedious and the person is pushing for change, despite uncertainty. In returning to the previous upright card, the Five of Cups, there is a risk of loss and grief. This is a chance the individual is prepared to take to move forward in life. The upright Six is a time of emotional stability. When reversed, it indicates restlessness for change, fresh ideas and new opportunities.

In a career layout, this card indicates a change of occupation rather than simply a new position. This individual is restless to explore new career horizons and may venture interstate or overseas if the right opportunity arises. If the Three of Pentacles or the Temperance card appears in the same layout, it's likely the person will undergo study to prepare for a new career direction.

In a relationship question, the Six reversed indicates the person is ready to leave behind a relationship or a type of partnership in pursuit of something more. The individual is restless to reach the Ten of Cups and accepts that the next step involves releasing current circumstances. When this card appears reversed in a relationship question, it's likely that a current or new spouse is different from previous partners and the person might have a unique connection as a result.

In a health query, the reversed Six suggests that traditional approaches to health are put aside in favour of something new, different and perhaps unusual. Sometimes, it describes emotional restlessness that may result in health issues, emotional pain and loss (a return to the Five of Cups). This can take the form of giving up prescribed medications without properly consulting a medical practitioner and then being surprised when health issues occur. It can also be the result of revisiting childhood pain to release it, then feeling free to move forward in life.

Six of Swords

The Six of Swords represents a mental approach to the need for stability. The card indicates retreating from disagreements to reflect. Stable emotions are necessary for clear thinking. After the strife of the Five of Swords, a period of reflection allows the individual to examine different points of view and perhaps change or soften a current viewpoint.

In this card, a family steers its boat away from turbulent waters into calmer surrounds. The six swords represent beliefs about life. They are firmly planted in the boat, suggesting that people carry their burdens or views of the world wherever they go. The swords weigh heavily as the person manoeuvres the vessel. Likewise, personal beliefs can weigh us down in daily life. Heavy clouds suggest confused thinking. For swords people, inner peace comes from making sense of personal events.

Cloudy skies restrict views, forcing the people in this card to reflect on past events and current emotions. By reassessing our previous actions and emotional reactions to situations, we realise what beliefs support us and what attitudes don't.

This card image combines three of the four elements or suits. The wooden boat is symbolic of fire, the wands suit. Both the wands in the tarot and the boat in the Six are made of wood. The river represents water, the cups suit. Water traditionally adapts to its surroundings and represents creativity and emotions. The inverted swords in the boat represent air. The swords suit describes the element of air and its corresponding qualities of changeability, mental agility and need for strategy. Progress down the river is slow and steady, just as the process of changing or updating beliefs about life can be. Although the sixes in the tarot describe stability, there is still movement in this card, from emotional upheaval towards calmer waters.

In a general reading, the Six of Swords can represent travel over water, as shown by the image on the card. This is especially so if the layout includes the Ace, Three or Eight of Wands. With The World card, it can indicate overseas travel and with The Star, travel for leisure. With a reversed Star, it suggests business travel or a short trip that is rushed.

The Six of Swords also describes stability after chaos or strife (after the Five of Swords), plus an opportunity to make sense of life and adjust beliefs and attitudes accordingly. A simple analogy for this card is one of leaving a wartorn homeland for a safe haven. There is loss but the next generation might have a better life as a result of this sacrifice. The couple in this card don't want their children to grow up in a war zone and are taking proactive steps to ensure their safety.

The Six of Swords highlights the act of moving away from a source of conflict to make sense of personal beliefs about life. It is a process of allowing life to settle or detaching from an emotionally challenging situation.

In a career layout, this card represents stability, resulting from an insightful understanding of how past decisions and actions have contributed to current circumstances. Improved strategies allow for a calm, more successful career path. It can describe peace after leaving a chaotic job or workplace, with opportunities to reflect on how one's actions may have contributed to frayed tempers or verbal conflict. After action, it is beneficial to reflect, to reach a more thorough understanding of past circumstances.

In a relationship layout, the Six of Swords emphasises settling differences that caused tension. New understanding inspires a more stable relationship. Alternatively, it can describe a new relationship that is different from previous partnerships because the person is more aware of how to negotiate difficult issues.

In a health query, the Six of Swords symbolises slow, steady healing after difficult times. Sometimes, after a serious illness or an accident, people heal physically more rapidly than they do mentally. It takes more time to come to terms with past upheavals.

When the Death card also appears in a health reading, the Six of Swords may signify a tranquil passing from this world to the next. An example of this came up in a reading for Zoe, whose response surprised me when I mentioned a recent quiet passing. It was her mother's death and Zoe explained the way it had happened.

"I don't believe it. She fought with everyone her whole life and then she dies tranquilly in her sleep. She was causing trouble with all of us right up to the end. When I heard she had died peacefully I wanted to slap her."

Six of Swords Reversed

The Six of Swords reversed indicates a need to return to the upright Five of Swords to bring underlying issues to the surface. An argument sometimes clears the air to allow more room for negotiation. This Six reversed represents pursuing emotional upheaval to liberate the energy of a situation. It's a step towards resolution. Forcing change through confrontation is sometimes the best way to shake up a stagnant, unbalanced situation.

In a travel layout, the Six reversed highlights upheaval. An example of this came up in a reading for Michael, who was planning a trip home to visit his parents to tell them he was gay. He expected some emotional conflict as a result of the visit and the Six reversed confirmed this. However, Michael felt it was necessary to tell his parents to have a more honest, open relationship with them.

Sometimes this Six reversed emphasises that a person is not satisfied with a comfortable life, preferring more excitement. This might be a suitable time to examine personal beliefs about life and stability. For some individuals, routine and harmony can be stifling. This is especially so if outer struggle and conflict offer a distraction from inner emptiness, fear or anger. For others, calm always precedes a storm and they feel more tension during harmonious periods than in the midst of upheaval. Reflecting on where these attitudes were formed might help restore inner peace and an appreciation of outer stability.

In a general reading, the reversed Six of Swords indicates a situation reaching a boiling point. If the source of personal tension is confronted, there is likely to be an emotionally charged exchange of words that might cause regret. This could end with an irate boss, a screaming partner or a wild demonstration in the streets where thousands of people shout for change. When returning to the upright Five of Swords, polite manners usually evaporate and people might end up on YouTube if a witness, a fellow diner in the café or a work colleague is quick enough with a camera.

In a career layout, this card can describe an argument that ends a job or even a career. After a conflict like this, colleagues usually await the announcement of a cessation of hostilities before breathing deeply again. As an answer to a question about pursuing a new career direction, the reversed Six can indicate it's unwise to pursue the intended path. It's likely the person will walk away from the new job or career after a conflict or to avoid a stand-up argument.

In a relationship question, the reversed Six of Swords indicates it's time to clear the air, and hopefully, lay some unexplored issues to rest. Perhaps ongoing unfairness requires attention or a longstanding obstacle needs to be removed so the relationship can progress. There is the possibility that a direct approach might end the relationship but this risk could be worth taking.

In a health query, the reversed Six of Swords can indicate symptoms of illness flaring up, demanding immediate attention. It also indicates ongoing health issues, due to undercurrents and unexpressed tension in the person's home or work environment. Occasionally, the reversed Six of Swords can describe cuts or bruises resulting from being in the crossfire of a brawl or a public disturbance (the conflict of the upright Five of Swords). In most readings, however, the reversed Six exposes old issues and clears the air. By assertively stating grievances and setting personal boundaries, a partner or work colleague might release pent-up tension and feel heard. This process can lower internal stress and improve wellbeing.

Six of Pentacles

The Six of Pentacles represents an earthy, practical approach to structure. As pentacles people know the value of money in keeping life materially stable, they are prepared to make long-term sacrifices to enjoy the constancy money affords them. These sacrifices can include extended study in their twenties, when friends are travelling the world or they might save diligently for a home deposit or for an investment, rather than joining friends on an expensive holiday.

This card shows the community looking after its members so everyone can have a reasonable life. It also suggests getting a new job or a loan to pursue plans. In this card, a wealthy individual gives coins to two people kneeling on the ground. The people from the Five of Pentacles are gratefully receiving a portion of what the wealthy person has to offer. Personal abundance is shared with a view to preserving community stability. Without sharing this abundance, they might die or become lawless in order to survive. Therefore, this act of generosity effectively preserves a very comfortable lifestyle and the status quo.

The sixes are cards for stability and the Six of Pentacles represents a financial approach. This card appears when a person is hiring a tradesperson to repair a roof, buying a new car or securing a home loan, funds for a new stage of a business or a new source of income.

In answer to a question about a legal matter, the upright Six of Pentacles can represent a sum of money being awarded. It also signifies a large purchase, such as a house or a car, or borrowing money to invest in a home or a business.

In a general reading, the upright Six of Pentacles indicates securing a new job or a promotion, finding investors for a business idea or establishing a new income stream. In a travel question, it sometimes indicates career-related travel or that the person can afford to travel at this time.

In a career layout, this card describes securing a new job, a promotion or funds to start a new business. As an answer to a question about finding a new occupation or a more suitable position, it indicates that this search is likely to be successful.

In a relationship question, the appearance of this Six can signify that one partner has the role of the wealthy individual, dispensing a small portion of the money/love/energy to the others (partner and children) in the partnership. This person controls the relationship and its direction, while the other partner has a more passive approach. The roles of the interaction are clearly defined, leaving the partners unequal. However, on closer inspection, it becomes obvious that both partners agree consciously or unconsciously to this arrangement to ensure stability.

In a health query, the Six of Pentacles can show an individual spending money on their health. This might mean paying for a surgical procedure, paying an annual membership fee to a gym or to a healthcare fund. Occasionally, it suggests a job is affecting health. This might suggest long working hours that add to stress or physical labour contributing to chronic back pain.

It can also describe beneficial routines, including regular gym, massage or bodywork sessions to maintain physical fitness and reduce personal stress. Sometimes, it suggests that the person is reluctant to leave a job because of the healthcare benefits included with the position.

Six of Pentacles Reversed

The Six of Pentacles reversed suggests being restricted by financial circumstances. It describes insufficient control over income and expenses, resulting in a lack of stability. It can be stressful living hand to mouth and payday to payday. This individual is experiencing difficulties meeting monetary commitments. Perhaps the number of people who are financially dependent upon this individual is over-stretching their budgetary resources. This is indicated by the two dependants who are at the top of the card when it is reversed.

Its appearance in a relationship layout suggests the individual is dominated by another person and that a separation (a return to the Five) might be necessary to reclaim personal power. The way partners earn, spend and generally handle money can be a source of tension in relationships and business partnerships. When reversed, the Six indicates that one person might be influencing the other through control of shared finances.

This card can appear in a business layout to indicate that one partner's financial recklessness is having a damaging impact on the enterprise. Sometimes, it highlights how poor financial choices of the past are restricting the ability of the business to invest well and thrive in the present. Continuing to spend without planning for the future is likely to result in a return to the upright Five of Pentacles and the poverty and restricted choices apparent in that card.

Generally, this reversed Six describes a return to the upright Five of Pentacles to confront the reality of being separated from financial security or an inability to build or control sources of income. This is a monetary winter that will eventually pass. Change is required before returning to economic stability again.

Pentacles people usually accept that money equals choices. Without a sufficient steady income, an individual soon faces limited options in life. From home location to education and food, income determines many of life's decisions. This is why pentacles people need a peace-of-mind account. This is a savings or investment arrangement that can be available at short notice to cover emergencies, such as unexpected illness, retrenchment from a job or storm damage to property. The reversed Six of Pentacles suggests this financial reserve is not available or has already been exhausted.

In relation to a legal matter, it may suggest a sum of money will be awarded in favour of another party or that a case is likely to result in regret and is best avoided.

In a general reading, the reversed Six of Pentacles describes an inability to control spending or that the person lacks a decent income. It's a card that appears in layouts when someone is about to leave a job, even if the individual has not planned to terminate current employment. Sometimes, the reversed Six of Pentacles describes a person whose desires control their expenditure. The need for possessions, toys or trinkets is keeping the person economically stressed. Poor money training needs to be addressed if this individual wants to enjoy wealth and financial prosperity.

In a career layout, the Six of Pentacles reversed can suggest leaving a job or being unemployed. This also occurs in layouts when a person changes jobs or leaves employment to move overseas or to have a baby. It can also highlight putting too much effort into work for insufficient rewards.

In a relationship question, this reversed card indicates one partner is too focused on their career to have time for the relationship. It can describe a job or financial demands that restrict a relationship but this might only be a temporary situation. If one partner is working two jobs to save for a home or a car, or working and studying at the same time, there is likely to be additional stress on the relationship. In a layout for a single person, current career hours may limit the individual's ability to socialise and meet a new partner. Sometimes it indicates being underemployed. This can occur in an economic downturn when businesses reduce the working week for employees.

In a health query, the reversed Six of Pentacles describes a large sum of money being spent on improving health. It sometimes indicates a job or a business is having a significant impact on physical well-being or that the person is currently unable to afford to maintain their health to usual standards.

The Sevens

The sevens in the tarot symbolise the realisation that a new approach is required to achieve goals. When three or more sevens appear in a layout, it suggests that while the method may have to change, ambitions do not have to be abandoned. If the three sevens occurring in a layout are all upright, persistence is likely to bring rewards.

The wands suit highlights having too many irons in the fire. Wands people are sometimes distracted by competing goals or opportunities that divert focus from the main objective. Absolute concentration is required if the primary goal is to be achieved. These are generally individuals who bite off more than they can chew. They are active, enthusiastic, creative people with a zest for life.

The Seven of Cups describes someone searching within for a meaningful life. Cups people naturally reflect on past actions and current needs to discover their motives and reassess feelings about people and situations. This self-scrutiny makes the task of clarifying spiritual and emotional goals easier than it is for wands individuals, who prefer action to contemplation. Wands individuals feel ineffective if they are not achieving goals and conquering obstacles, whereas cups people prefer to avoid haste, conflict and competition. Their energy is more fluid, compassionate and emotional.

The swords suit represents mental adaptability. These people are generally objective, abstract thinkers with well-developed communication skills. However, there is a fine line between changing one's view of the world and self-deception about circumstances. Swords people are usually adept at planning and implementing new strategies to navigate obstacles. The figure in the Seven of Swords card has found a plan that relies on stealth, cunning and adaptable thinking. Some swords individuals are capable of justifying any actions or behaviour in pursuit of a goal.

The pentacles suit indicates a preference for reflection upon career goals, now that financial stability allows current projects to proceed more smoothly. It's difficult to plan for long-term economic and career goals when unpaid bills are mounting up. The upright seven shows a stage when immediate needs are met and it's time to consider longer-term strategies for success. These people are often productive, practical and sensual in their approach to life.

Seven of Wands

The theme of the sevens is *don't give up*. The Seven of Wands emphasises a need to stay ahead of current challenges. These people prefer to be busy, rather than risk being bored. This Seven describes focusing physical energy into one clear purpose to avoid obstacles that might prevent success. When slowed by opposition or challenges, wands people tend to push through. They display a *go-hard-or-go-home* attitude.

In this card, someone is resisting opposing forces that are represented by the six wands below. This individual is standing on higher ground, completely focused on the task of securing coveted territory. Blue skies above confirm that this is not a fight to the death but rather a self-imposed challenge to maintain or improve skills.

Odd shoes suggest the character had to dress hastily to meet a challenge that arrived early or without warning. This unmatched footwear also highlights a personal transition from the Six of Wands to the Eight; one foot rests in the stability of the Six, while the other is positioned in the strength of the Eight. To grow, it is sometimes necessary to relinquish stability and undergo change. When experiencing change or upheaval, the stability of the Six can sometimes seem more tempting than the promise of the Eight. This is why the theme for the sevens is don't give up.

While moving through the Seven towards the Eight of Wands, the person encounters greater challenges. Streamlining or the delegation of responsibilities is needed before they are ready to accept the rewards of the free-flowing energy of the Eight. This individual understands that to be able to ski down a pristine mountain far from the crowd, it is necessary to climb it first.

For example, Brett wanted to compete in an international rowing event. This required fitness training, dawn practice with his rowing team and a full-time job to earn money for airfares. There were cold, dark mornings in winter when he didn't want to get out of bed, let alone row into the low mist over the icy cold river, but he didn't give up. He forced himself to perform the task one day at a time, despite many temptations. This tenacious attitude eventually led to his exhilarating triumph in an international championship event.

The higher ground in the card represents training, discipline and personal achievements. Brett was motivated to compete with and triumph over his peers. With each success, he stepped up to face more skilful competitors. From local to state championships, his ongoing efforts and focus eventually led him to national competitions. After several attempts, Brett's persistence provided an opportunity at an international level. Upon achieving his ultimate sporting goal, Brett realised he'd soon be too old to compete but that he could use his skills of discipline, focus and determination to achieve other career, financial and life goals.

In a general reading, the upright Seven describes someone with plenty of challenges. This individual usually prefers to be busy than bored and enjoys a conquest. It's never a dull moment around this person, although it can sometimes become exhausting to watch. Occasionally, the upright Seven shows someone who is eyeing bigger, more alluring goals that require more focus, discipline and persistence.

In a career layout, the Seven of Wands describes a person who is simultaneously juggling several challenging tasks in career or attempting to balance career with study and family life. Perhaps a full-time job is combined with study to improve career prospects. Keeping up that tough pace now will pay off later.

In a relationship question, this card highlights the pursuit of a commitment despite relentless obstacles. It can describe a person whose persistence in the face of continuous refusal is admirable. However, it sometimes indicates someone who is unable to give a relationship the attention it deserves, due to career, sports or other preoccupations.

In a health query, the Seven of Wands indicates plentiful reserves of physical energy and vitality to build and maintain physical health. Long-term fitness is the focus and there is ample stamina to maintain a robust constitution. This individual is likely to work hard and exercise strenuously to release any residual stress or tension. Uninterrupted, restful sleep at night can be a by-product of this habit.

Seven of Wands Reversed

The Seven of Wands reversed indicates becoming overwhelmed by challenges or responsibilities. It is necessary to return to the previous card in the suit, the upright Six of

Wands, to focus on fewer tasks at a time. The upright Six represents projects or goals a person can cope with simultaneously.

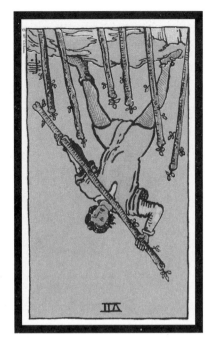

The person on the card wears odd shoes, highlighting a lack of careful preparation that results in chaos and a need for short-term crisis management. It is wise to return to the stability of the upright Six of Wands before preparing for the additional responsibilities of the Seven. Perhaps this individual is overwhelmed by a continuous onslaught of demands and feels unable to control circumstances or effectively manage daily challenges.

Too many people or situations are demanding immediate attention and scattering focus. Continuing in the current direction increases the risk of being swamped by life's demands. There is a need to return to a simpler, more focused path (as shown in the previous card, the Six of Wands). *Don't hold on*, is the message of the Seven reversed. Don't release yourself from all of life's demands but focus on the key areas first.

As this is a wands card, it can indicate growth without strategy. As a business grows or a project becomes more complex, increasingly specific strategies are usually required. Thought and preparation can ensure smooth, steady growth. With planning and effective systems, a small business can grow into a medium-sized company. This transition often requires more staff, new premises, more planning meetings and improved communication amongst staff. Without this strategic preparation (something that wands people usually avoid because it involves meetings) there is a risk of the business collapsing or losing customers through poor service.

When Cindy's home-based business began, she worked three days a week making colourful clothing for small children. She did some photography training to improve the product images on her website. Through the quiet months, she studied new designs and tried out a range of fabrics. The business was growing slowly yet steadily. Then an influencer raved about her range on Instagram. Online orders exploded overnight. Soon she had four months of backorders and decided to hire an assistant. Before she had decided on the right person, Cindy had ten months of orders and was exhausted from responding to email, taking phone calls and mailing parcels.

As Cindy didn't expect the sudden rise in demand, she had no real plan for this positive, yet overwhelming, turn of events. She consulted a business coach who discussed her needs, and together they prepared a clear business plan to grow her venture and service the market that had found her. Her new coach insisted that Cindy take weekly online courses to improve her design and marketing skills and she hired two people to make the clothes from her cut patterns. This is the Seven of Wands. If a person is prepared to persist towards goals in the face of opposition or constant demands, the Eight of Wands awaits. In Cindy's business, the six wands above her are her customers, demanding early delivery. With each order sent, additional photos of her products were uploaded to Instagram, increasing demand even more. By hiring staff and a business coach, Cindy returned to what she loved (the upright Six of Wands), cutting fabrics and making new designs. In doing this, she effectively turned the Seven of Wands upright.

In a general reading, this person is overwhelmed by the demands of life. Perhaps he or she is juggling an arduous working week with a course of study, plus home renovations. It's necessary to return to the upright Six of Wands to make a clear plan and focus on what needs to be done now.

In a career layout, the Seven of Wands reversed can indicate a person who has a job that is unsuitable. Perhaps the individual is not coping with a recent promotion and feels under constant pressure to perform. The person might be facing unfair demands such as covering a colleague's workload while they are away on holiday or on maternity leave, or simply that the job is expanding as the company has grown. Returning to a more familiar or less demanding position (returning to the Six of Wands) might help this individual find a more suitable place amongst the team.

In a relationship question, this card can indicate someone is ignoring their love relationship to focus on career or other pursuits. It's time to reduce distractions and strengthen the current relationship while it's still possible and there's something worth salvaging. Occasionally this reversed Seven can suggest that there is unnecessary drama in a relationship and that it may not be wise to hold on to it any longer. When reversed, the sevens can suggest that it's time to let go.

In a health query, the reversed Seven of Wands can suggest a person is not focusing on maintaining stable health, due to other demands. There is only so long that an individual can run on adrenal energy before collapsing. It's time to shed the workload and focus on health maintenance. When reversed, this card sometimes highlights stress and tension in the neck and shoulders.

Seven of Cups

The Seven of Cups represents an emotional and spiritual need to persevere with the search for meaning and purpose to life. It is about the quiet moments spent looking within to find out who we truly are. By coming to terms with spiritual identity and direction, it's possible to better understand where to find happiness. Profound emotional and spiritual nourishment isn't found in striving but in habits and pastimes that are not achievement-focused. These might involve a few hours each week spent painting, writing, walking in nature or lost in thought while staring out to sea.

Reflection can allow a person to mentally explore more suitable careers or discover what type of relationship might provide greater emotional satisfaction. It can also highlight any personal weaknesses or negative behaviours that require attention while pursuing spiritual purpose.

On the card, an individual examines the contents of seven cups contained within a cloud. This person is searching the different aspects of self to discover which people, situations, habits and hobbies can provide spiritual nourishment.

This Seven represents an inner search for fulfilment. This quest sometimes provides a glimpse of unresolved matters that interrupt inner peace. These issues may include how the individual's persona or the face they show to the world has been shaped by the expectations of parents or friends. It also includes how the opinions of others have shaped self-perception.

Stability and support from the home environment are indicated by the cup containing the castle. The cup with the jewellery highlights personal self-worth and material value. This cup represents the person's ability to establish and maintain sufficient financial and material wealth for a stable life.

The cup containing the wreath shows inner strength and self-confidence. This wreath is also seen in the Six of Wands where a figure can be seen acting with confidence to achieve goals. The individual's subconscious connection to true spiritual purpose is highlighted by the cup with the demon. This demon can indicate frightening dreams at night as the subconscious mind attempts to make sense of daily life in relation to spiritual purpose. The snake cup symbolises sexual and creative energies, while the figure beneath the shroud at the top of the card indicates the person's own spiritual or higher self. This aspect is often obscured to encourage a deliberate search while forging a stronger connection.

Basically, this card highlights an inner quest for one's true self. It represents the act of not giving up the ongoing exploration of one's spiritual self. It describes a time where someone questions personal happiness. This individual is ruminating on past choices while making decisions about future work, relationships and recreation that might bring fulfilment.

In a general reading, the Seven of Cups indicates a process of examining your personal landscape to determine what is necessary and what can be discarded. It's an opportunity to review work choices, friendships, home environment, hobbies and interests to ensure ongoing emotional and spiritual fulfilment.

In a career layout, it is time to acknowledge an intense desire for a meaningful occupation and consider whether the current career suits individual needs. Work without any deeper significance usually only satisfies financial or ego needs. Many career paths can provide a sense of purpose if the person is aware of these possibilities. This card describes finding ways to enjoy one's job so that it means more than a paycheque as there are additional levels of satisfaction. This might include recognising how a routine task benefits others, or that the service provided is meaningful to the customer or end-user.

In a relationship question, this upright Seven represents a time to reflect on a range of surface and unspoken needs in a relationship. If the person is single, it might be beneficial to consider what type of partner would be suitable through the coming years. While a wands person usually competes with others to win a partner that everyone envies, cups individuals value friendship, compassion and selflessness, especially if they plan to have children. This Seven can show someone wondering if children are part of the future and how one might balance career with family life. Sometimes, it indicates someone who is searching for different sources of fulfilment. These might include new friendships, hobbies, interests, self-development courses or reading uplifting books. Basically, it's time to find fresh sources of nourishment without necessarily abandoning current circumstances.

In a health query, the upright Seven of Cups suggests stable health accompanies emotional balance. There are also opportunities to find ways to maintain mental, emotional and spiritual well-being through engaging hobbies, interests and pastimes. It's a time to reassess those activities that support physical and mental welfare and adjust or replace them if necessary.

Seven of Cups Reversed

The Seven of Cups reversed suggests the self-examination necessary for understanding what happiness means is being ignored. Instead of taking a few quiet moments to contemplate, this person is filling every waking hour with activities that might not provide inner satisfaction. It is difficult to know if these pursuits offer any real fulfilment until the individual rests and reflects. It's necessary to consult the different parts within to determine which activities and pastimes are worthwhile.

The Seven reversed depicts someone who is holding on to what is familiar or to what once provided happiness while refusing to update personal perceptions about life and changing needs. It is necessary to return to the previous upright card in the suit, the Six of Cups, to have sufficient security to reflect without collapsing during any adjustment period.

Learning includes periods of action and then contemplation. Effort requires direct involvement, while reflection provides an opportunity to decide what worked and what didn't. The sevens represent a time of introspection. Without effort, life is simply theory. Without consideration, it's not possible to judge which actions were useful and which were wasted. Because this is a cups card, it's natural to associate emotions and creativity with pondering. On the path to achieving a goal, it is necessary to pause to survey past and present actions to ensure steady progress. Effort without reassessment can sometimes be wasted.

When reversed, the Seven of Cups suggests feeling overwhelmed by a range of emotional and creative opportunities that have failed, disappeared or been abandoned. By processing the feelings of loss associated with these past endeavours, it's possible to move forward with a clearer understanding of what is required for more creative and emotional fulfilment. Future steps are taken with a more realistic understanding of the practical steps required in every creative plan.

In a general reading, the reversed Seven of Cups indicates a tendency to hold on to old sources of emotional nourishment that may no longer offer sustenance. It's time to decide which traditional avenues for fulfilment are still effective and those that can be replaced. As people mature, tastes, hobbies, interests and friends change, often requiring new, more suitable sources or nourishment. In one's early twenties, an emotionally satisfying weekend might involve sharing a tent in a field at a music festival. However, an equivalent weekend in one's fifties might be spent at a quiet place with a heated pool, open fire and an extensive menu.

In a career layout, it's likely that the person is unfulfilled with a current job. Perhaps demands and deadlines have suppressed the creative process. Another project may be required by a certain deadline, turning what was a creative endeavour into a production line. A return to the upright Six of Cups might involve a break or a holiday to rest and regroup. Thinking about something else will help the individual remember what it's like to be inspired.

In a relationship question, the Seven of Cups reversed describes a person who is overwhelmed by past emotional losses. It may have been a long time since this individual considered their emotional needs and the possibility of having different sources of happiness. For example, one person might enjoy gardening, whereas another might prefer photography, restoring old furniture or learning to fly. The reversed Seven of Cups can also describe being too busy to allow time and effort for emotional nourishment. It's time to return to the previous upright card, the Six of Cups, to enjoy a period of comfort and stability with familiar habits and pastimes before considering new avenues for happiness.

In a health query, the reversed Seven of Cups describes health symptoms resulting from underlying emotional issues. Health could be improved by returning to the previous card in the suit, the upright Six of Cups, and reconnecting with friends and family or immersing oneself in a group with shared creative goals. It might be a painting class, a choir, a gardener's weekend retreat or a book club. Replenishing those cups with love, joy, creativity or spiritual fulfilment is a path to balanced health.

Seven of Swords

The Seven of Swords signifies deceit, a lack of clear communication or the presence of hidden agendas. However, it can also indicate that this is not the time to give up on personal goals. A new approach is necessary for success.

In this card, golden skies highlight sunrise or sunset, as a person sneaks away with five swords belonging to the military camp in the background. The people in the camp are foreigners and he is using their swords (ideas, plans or military information) for personal advantage.

Sometimes, this Seven suggests a new approach to a problem is available, through thinking about solutions in a different light. For example, Stephen often complained that he needed $300 more a week to rent a small house to live in but he did not have enough money. A friend suggested he really only needed a small place to live in, not necessarily $300 extra each week.

Five months later, we received invitations to his housewarming party. Stephen was caretaking a large, fully-furnished waterfront home for fifteen months for a friend who had been transferred overseas. When he began thinking about a house rather than the sum of money needed to rent one, this housing opportunity emerged. He has now been happily caretaking this home for over two years after his friend added a holiday to his overseas transfer.

The Seven of Swords often means *don't give up,* so don't rule out reaching a solution to a problem. Think the issue through and consider alternative approaches. An unusual viewpoint can produce an excellent solution that has been invisible to a person thinking along traditional lines. Some of the greatest advances in science have resulted from people applying the teachings of one field to another area and arriving at concepts later hailed as breakthrough discoveries.

In a general reading, the Seven of Swords indicates that adaptable thinking may provide unusual answers to current issues. Strategy is half the battle and effective tactics are needed now. Finding new solutions can minimise stress and speed up progress towards goals.

In a career layout, the Seven of Swords can be a constructive card for finding solutions, expanding options or simply keeping up with industry trends. Some industries, like IT, are changing so quickly that what is considered cutting edge today may be redundant technology in five years. The Seven of Swords shows someone keeping ahead of the curve by being mentally adaptable. Sometimes, the Seven of Swords indicates deceit, especially if The Moon is also in the layout. In combination, these two cards can indicate that management is planning redundancies or a restructure but has not yet made anyone aware of this. It's time to investigate unannounced changes to clarify job stability and if needed, start looking for other job options.

In a relationship question, the Seven of Swords suggests someone might be considering making changes but not talking about these plans. It can describe someone who keeps a facet of life secret or hidden from a partner. This occurred with George who kept his interest in meditation hidden from his wife. Helen was scathing in her attitude to such activities and considered it a waste of time, so George told her he was taking an ancient history class as he slipped away to join a weekly meditation group.

In a relationship layout, this Seven can suggest deceit but other cards such as The Moon or the reversed Three of Cups are needed to confirm this. The person could be being dishonest about relationship needs. The Moon indicates unspoken desires and the reversed Three of Cups sometimes signifies a love triangle when the Seven of Swords also occurs in the layout.

For example, Taylor seemed to be a happily married man with two small children. Each Sunday afternoon, he visited his aged mother in a nursing home for a few hours. That is, until his wife, Athena, discovered that his mother had died two years earlier. Taylor had a male lover in another part of town, whom he visited each Wednesday morning and Sunday afternoon. He clearly wasn't being honest about what he wanted in his marriage. In this case, the Seven of Swords and the Knight of Cups alongside the Three of Cups reversed confirmed this.

In a health query, the Seven of Swords can reveal a sense of denial about personal health. It can also indicate that mainstream solutions may not be effective. By researching current health issues and examining personal options carefully, it's possible to build and to maintain buoyant physical health.

Sometimes a seven indicates scattered mental energy that requires physical rest or a pastime that encourages mental stillness. In these instances, each of the seven swords represents a different idea or project demanding attention and dissipating reserves of energy. Regular periods of quiet time with relaxing activities can help to still the mind. These might include watering the garden, light reading, listening to relaxing music or a guided meditation recording, or walking to a local park.

Seven of Swords Reversed

The Seven of Swords reversed suggests that outdated beliefs are accompanied by obsolete patterns of behaviour. It can indicate self-deception. This person refuses to see life as it is or is unable to consider viable alternatives to current frustrations. It requires a return to the previous card in the suit, the upright Six of Swords, to transition gently away from restrictive beliefs and attitudes towards new, more flexible ways of thinking.

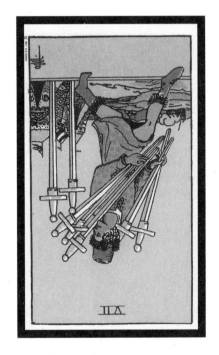

This may require being surrounded by people who encourage growth and personal development, while unworkable beliefs are gradually replaced with ideas that support a more rewarding life. By observing how others resolve issues and tackle obstacles, it's possible to embrace new approaches to daily setbacks.

Sometimes, the reversed Seven describes self-deception. It can indicate a person who does not regularly check their beliefs against reality. When this card appeared reversed in a career question for Rachel, she was desperately waiting for news about a retail job she had applied for more than three months previously. Instead of moving on to apply for other positions, she was clinging to the fading hope that she'd be offered the position. She explained that the company had not contacted the two people who had supplied references. I suggested that she ask a broad question about career generally, before enquiring about this position. I wanted to be able to deliver some good news before the bad news. Her broad question indicated that she needed to complete some study to be prepared for her next job.

In a general reading, the reversed Seven of Swords card indicates a need for adaptability or mental agility to move forward. Old ways of thinking and acting are not helpful now. Although it can be difficult to change obsolete thinking patterns, sometimes a well-written book, sparkling conversation, riveting public talk or podcast can present new avenues and rational solutions for current issues.

Sometimes, this card reversed indicates deceit. Perhaps someone is not being honest and forthcoming about their goals and motives. It might be the person selecting the cards or a friend, co-worker, boss or spouse. It's very difficult to progress with plans when someone is sabotaging one's efforts.

In a career layout, this Seven suggests that the person cannot see a viable way out of their current career. Inflexible thinking is restricting vision and choices. Instead of wondering if they can do something, the person needs to ask, "How can I do that?" If an answer is not forthcoming, it's probably time to read about someone who has achieved a similar goal. Sometimes, the best individual to help you climb a personal summit is someone who has already conquered mountains.

In a relationship question, this card describes a need to be adaptable. If single, the individual might be waiting for a suitor while remaining stuck in restrictive routines that prohibit socialising, such as night work or repeatedly refusing invitations. If the person simply travels to and from work, shops in the same place each week and lives alone, the only strangers to meet are likely to be delivery personnel or tradespeople installing or repairing appliances. It's time to forge some new habits or routines involving single, available, like-minded people. Sometimes this Seven reversed can indicate deceit in a relationship or a union kept secret from friends and family. This meaning is strengthened if the Three of Cups and/or The Moon card occur in the same layout.

In a health question, the reversed Seven of Swords describes a narrow-minded attitude to improving or maintaining health. Sometimes, it can be worth challenging clients to study cutting-edge health research before deciding if their current approach is the best path. An informed choice requires knowledge of the latest discoveries and ongoing investigations.

Seven of Pentacles

The Seven of Pentacles suggests it is not time to give up on financial and career plans. Although less effort is required, more vigilance is necessary until success is achieved. The person is generally considering where life is going regarding career or financial success or a personal relationship.

In this card, someone stands casually, watching a money tree growing. This individual is contemplating possibilities, now that the fruits of personal labour are about to yield rewards. The blue clothing suggests spiritual rewards, yet the person remains torn between the security of the Six of Pentacles and the challenge of the Eight of Pentacles in the future, as shown by the different coloured boots. (Please note that in some later versions of the Rider-Waite Tarot these boots are the same colour).

The pentacles' nature is to become comfortable with what they already have. However, passion, symbolised by an orange boot, propels this person towards the opportunities presented in the Eight of Pentacles. In career terms, that Eight might include additional training to specialise, to manage a team or to improve skills and increase income. The Eight represents a step forward or ascending another rung on the career ladder.

The Seven of Pentacles, however, describes a time where there is money to invest while planning a stable financial future. In a career layout, it can show a person considering to enhance skills through study.

In a general reading, the Seven of Pentacles indicates spare money that can be put towards personal security or long-term plans. It describes a time when financial pressure subsides, allowing for reflection on long-term economic plans. Perhaps stable ongoing investments or business provides a source of income without too much effort.

In a career layout, the individual can relax and consider alternatives without living hand to mouth. Perhaps a business has grown and it's time to plan an exit strategy. This might involve selling a business, borrowing more money to invest in future expansion or training a replacement person before retirement from hands-on management. It can highlight someone considering the next step in career.

In a relationship question, stable finances are allowing the person to plan a more rewarding life. This security has been carefully structured and nurtured because pentacles people understand that money equals choice. Sometimes pentacles individuals wait until they have sufficient wealth before settling down with a long-term partner, to ensure both of them have comfort and financial stability together. Providing stability is a sign of their devotion to a partner.

In a health query, the upright Seven of Pentacles suggests balanced fitness, plus sufficient financial resources to meet any health surprises in the future. This individual has probably set aside additional funds for increased health costs in old age. The Seven shows a person thinking about the health concerns that come with each stage of life. This individual probably lives moderately now so they can maintain stable physical well-being into old age.

Seven of Pentacles Reversed

The Seven of Pentacles reversed sometimes suggests that a person is unaware that the fruits of their labour are about to be delivered. Occasionally, an individual loses sight of long-term plans and needs to return to the calm of the Six of Pentacles. The Six highlights the enjoyment of safe, predictable routines without being burdened by too much responsibility.

This individual eventually tires of humdrum security. Although this person feels most comfortable when life is certain and predictable, the highs are electrifying when risks are involved. Routine is eventually replaced with change, novelty and possibilities when the person moves towards the more expansive Eight of Pentacles.

Don't hold on is the motto for all the reversed Sevens. In the Seven of Pentacles, it refers to not holding on to material possessions, routines and career habits. It's time to step back from the comfortable habits of life to determine where new opportunities lie. It can also describe a job that is not helping the person achieve goals.

A return to the upright Six of Pentacles by changing to another job can bring new opportunities. When the reversed Seven occurred in Adele's reading, she complained that loyalty was not rewarded at her company. She had been in her job for eight years and was now hiring assistants who were just out of university and being paid $20,000 more than she was for easier roles. It was time for her to move from this company. She then deliberately changed jobs every couple of years until she secured a role with ample rewards, acknowledgement and responsibilities.

In a general reading, the Seven of Pentacles reversed indicates a loss of control over finances. Returning to the previous card in the suit, the upright Six of Pentacles, provides an opportunity to reassert control over income and expenses. The Six of Pentacles shows a wealthy individual offering tradespeople a small portion of his wealth for services rendered while retaining the remaining money for private use. Personal dreams and goals are unlikely to be achieved until financial control has been regained.

In a career layout, the reversed Seven of Pentacles describes someone without a clear plan or strategy for success. It's likely there is a limited future in the current organisation and that a return to the previous upright card, the Six of Pentacles, is necessary. The upright Six is a card for securing a new job, a promotion or a new career direction.

It's possible this individual has not considered long-term career prospects and is content to remain comfortable and unchallenged. Instead of evolving steadily, whole industries are changing faster than a grand piano can fall from a clifftop. In the 21st century, staff who drift along until a company is consumed by a competitor can suddenly be lost in a cost-cutting exercise or squeezed out when their skills are no longer required.

Sometimes the reversed Seven can describe someone who is doing the jobs of two people because a company is cutting costs. In some corporate cultures, constant employee burnout and high staff turnover is expected. In sections that require one hundred employees to complete the workload, they routinely hire fifty to sixty.

In a relationship question, lack of control over finances may be adversely influencing a relationship. It's possible that one partner is working too many hours each week to have time or energy for a relationship, or conversely, has been unemployed for an extended period. Lack of income can stress a union. Sometimes, the reversed Seven indicates one partner's restricted income or spending habits are burdening the other spouse.

In a health query, career or financial ambitions may be depleting the person's reserves of energy. It's also possible that they cannot currently afford to improve or maintain their physical health due to financial constraints. Careful thought needs to be given to building and maintaining long-term health and well-being. Although this may require some financial investment in exercise equipment, gym fees or a fitness coach, it is likely to be a wise investment. Sometimes, the reversed Seven of Pentacles indicates that the individual's job is depleting their health and well-being. Long hours or a toxic work environment can have lasting effects on staff.

The Eights

The eights in the tarot represent strength and the four suits show completely different types of courage. The Eight of Wands is about having the nerve to challenge life and to see where it leads. This might be to impulsively accept a new job, relocate to a different city or country or actively pursue a dream.

The Eight of Cups indicates the inner resolve necessary to leave an emotionally unfulfilling situation. Cups people are naturally sentimental, so leaving someone or a situation behind is often unsettling for them. It requires commitment and determination to move forward without a guarantee that they will be happy as a result. The promise of a better life can strengthen resolve to relinquish an unrewarding but safe situation.

The Eight of Swords focuses on having mental courage despite one's doubts and the restrictive beliefs of family, friends and colleagues. It requires great mental fortitude to have different ideas from everyone else and to value personal beliefs in the face of criticism or disinterest. It often involves having a plan and believing in that strategy to escape monotony and carve out a unique path in life.

The Eight of Pentacles represents a strong commitment to achieving results. Persistence in the face of obstacles and one's own doubts eventually brings rewards. Practical, stoic pentacles people display their courage through work, discipline, consistent effort and perseverance. They enjoy working because work often makes them feel worthwhile.

Three or more eights in a layout can signify inner courage and conviction are being tested. Receiving three or more eights reversed indicates that opportunities to learn about the value of inner strength and the role of personal determination in achieving results is being ignored. Consequently, this individual is operating from a position of weakness. He or she may be reacting to circumstances or fears, instead of taking control of a situation. It's time to summon courage. Courage isn't a lack of doubt; it's determination and resolve in the face of uncertainty.

Eight of Wands

The Eight of Wands signals a period of freedom. This is a fundamental desire of most wands people. Life is undemanding and balmy summer days are long and ripe with opportunities when the Eight appears. In this card, eight wands move freely towards their destination. A castle in the distance is visible, yet is close enough to engender anticipation and excitement. The river suggests travel over water (overseas) and clear skies overhead confirm continuing stability. The Eight is a card for voyages that are exciting and rewarding.

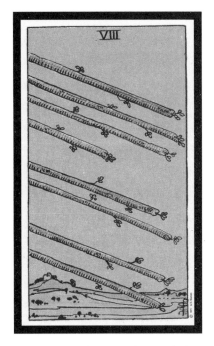

The eights are cards of strength and the wands forté is shown at its best in freedom of spirit, enjoyed during exploration, sports, competition and the pursuit of achievable goals. The moment of unhindered travel towards objectives shown on the card is the one that wands people live for and remember vividly. All the struggling and physical efforts in the past hinged on the hopes that these moments might be achieved.

On journeys, wands people enjoy having a destination to look forward to and an alternative goal in case the desired one doesn't measure up to expectations. They generally prefer travelling to arriving. They are adventurers, willing to go where others might fear. The Eight of Wands shows the wands' dream fulfilled. It's the downhill ski slope, the arrival at a new port with days of exploration ahead or the possibility of an adventure. The air crackles with tension and promise for those ready to take the next step.

The Eight of Wands card appears when a person is steadily rising in career, suggesting few obstacles to success. Achieving ambition is likely at this stage. This card can also indicate the benefits of an uncomplicated romantic relationship with freedom and shared goals.

In a general reading, the Eight of Wands can represent travel and objectives easily reached, plus the freedom to pursue personal aspirations. There are few if any obstacles to progress at the moment, allowing current plans to reach successful conclusions. As an answer to a question, it can indicate clear success with plans.

In a career layout, the Eight of Wands suggests work-related travel, an overseas posting or freedom to achieve career ambitions with minimal interference. The individual feels capable of rising to occupational challenges and achieving personal targets. Positive opportunities await, with minimal obstacles to slow career progress.

In a relationship question, this card describes a partnership formed when travelling or that the partners live apart and periodically travel to be together. It may be a holiday romance or simply an uncomplicated relationship. Sometimes, this card indicates the flexibility to pursue personal interests because finances allow complete freedom. In Calvin's reading, this card occurred after he received a multimillion-dollar inheritance. His windfall meant he didn't have to work again and at age thirty-six, he was free to travel with his wife for extended periods. Sometimes it simply describes a fun, harmonious union.

In a health query, the upright Eight of Wands shows plentiful reserves of energy and vitality that result in strong health and physical fitness. Occasionally, it confirms a period of well-being when on holiday overseas. This card sometimes appears in clients' layouts when they are eagerly anticipating overseas travel in a search for sun and sand during a long bleak winter. These individuals have plenty of physical energy and strong recuperative powers.

Eight of Wands Reversed

The Eight of Wands reversed indicates there are some restrictions now but not enough to prevent the wands from reaching their destination. This individual is likely to achieve personal goals but not as quickly or smoothly as hoped.

When this card is reversed, it might be beneficial to return to the previous upright card in the suit, the Seven of Wands, to control obstacles that are slowing progress in the reversed Eight. It is valuable to make decisions and resolve issues immediately, to avoid having to face them later. The upright Seven of Wands involves having effective systems to maintain momentum towards the fulfilment of projects.

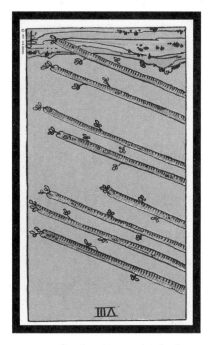

A typical reversed Eight situation occurred with a friend of mine, Tony. On the spur of the moment, Tony decided to leave Australia and travel overseas. He wanted to spend five months travelling across Europe. However, there were only ten weeks between his decision and his departure. In that period, Tony was too busy working and saving money for the trip to think about his possessions and where they would be stored when he left.

He drove his car to the airport, stopping only to collect a load of washing from the laundromat and pack his bags in the airport car park. Handing his keys to a friend, he asked that the car be sold and the money transferred overseas to wherever he was at the time.

Having spent his savings seven weeks later, Tony had to postpone his visit to mainland Europe and work in Scotland in order to have enough money to live on until his car was sold. The car didn't sell. Instead, Tony returned to Australia without having visited many of his desired destinations. By not dealing with all his possessions before he departed, Tony lived through the Eight of Wands reversed. He was not prevented from travelling altogether but his trip was shorter and included more financial constraint than he anticipated.

In a general reading, the reversed Eight indicates a few minor interruptions but progress is still possible. Perhaps the person was ambitious in the planning stage and didn't allow for typical delays. With patience and persistence, objectives can be achieved. In questions about travel, this card can indicate a time to rest on a journey. Sometimes, great discoveries are made when life diverts us from a path.

In a career layout, it pays to be patient when facing minor setbacks. Use this time wisely by returning to the previous card in the suit, the upright Seven of Wands, to focus on improving systems and preparing for opportunities to move forward again. This can also indicate work-related travel for meetings, conferences or to source new merchandise. It's still travel, only with deadlines and demands and no time for lazy days in the sun.

In a relationship question, the reversed Eight of Wands suggests some delays in moving from one stage to the next. One partner might be ready to share a home, while the other isn't able to relinquish a current lifestyle. Patience and persistence are required, as this is only a temporary postponement.

In a health query, the individual's energy levels are sufficient but not brilliant. This can result from strenuous efforts to push a recent project over the line. Delays at this time might provide an opportunity to relax and restore vitality. Any minor health issues are easily remedied, as the person still has reserves of core strength.

Eight of Cups

The cups' strength is in knowing when a situation has yielded all it can, for now. Because cups people are attuned to emotions, they instinctively know when a friendship is ending or when a personal relationship is undergoing a transformation. Although cups people have a tendency to live in the past, they are usually aware of what present circumstances hold for them because they instinctively sense the energy of most situations. They have an intuitive awareness of when it is right to stay or to leave.

On the card, someone in a red cloak and boots is walking away from eight cups arranged to allow for a ninth cup. This person realises that although the Seven of Cups provided a glimpse of life, the picture was incomplete. In the Eight of Cups, the search continues for the ninth cup.

This quest requires energy, passion and commitment, shown by the red cloak and boots. It preoccupies the person for days and nights, signified by the presence of the sun and the moon in this card. Through reading books, asking others and noticing life patterns during the daylight hours and through dreams at night, the individual seeks what is missing within. This person connects with a veiled, hidden, inner self. This is the spiritual self, the part that doesn't sleep at night and is aware of the greater fabric of life.

The Eight is neither a promise of happier times nor a guarantee of success. It simply means that each individual needs to act on their own awareness that present circumstances have little to offer. Perhaps after years of working and living with a partner, the Eight is the realisation that a change is needed for inner fulfilment. This person is walking away from a job, a relationship or a lifestyle, reasoning that it holds no purpose worth exploring. This card might not signal the physical act of walking away but it is a quiet withdrawal into a search for new sources of joy. It's time to discover what brings happiness. For each individual, this quest is unique.

In a general reading, the Eight of Cups shows someone walking away from a partnership or a situation in search of deeper fulfilment. It's accepting that what the person is searching for cannot be found in current circumstances. Although an existing situation might have previously offered fulfilment, this individual now needs more than is presently available. It's acting on the awareness that life has more to offer to those prepared to venture from the safety of the shore.

In a career layout, this card might indicate a job change or retraining to pursue a different type of career. Lucinda's job choices were non-existent in her chosen field of science in Australia, despite her PhD and years of skilful application overseas. Her desire to purchase a home and eventually retire in financially comfortable circumstances meant she had one of two choices: relocate overseas or change career direction. Tired of hoping for opportunities and living hand to mouth, she retrained in engineering.

In a relationship question, the upright Eight of Cups shows an individual stepping away from current partnership opportunities. This might involve ending a relationship or finding other sources of emotional or creative fulfilment to supplement the relationship. This could include courses, creative endeavours or new friendships. This card also suggests someone deciding that a type of relationship cannot offer long-term growth.

In a health query, the upright Eight of Cups indicates walking away from circumstances because they are emotionally draining. Sometimes, is suggests discontinuing current health treatments or methods in pursuit of new solutions. It requires strength and courage to explore new possibilities, plus the inner conviction that there is more to be found by searching elsewhere.

Eight of Cups Reversed

The Eight of Cups reversed highlights confusion and indecision about where suitable opportunities can be found. There is the temptation to explore new horizons but also a fear of missing out on current opportunities. Sometimes, it's necessary to let go of what you have to explore new directions.

The Eight reversed emphasises uncertainty about whether it is better to stay or leave a situation. On Monday, the individual is determined to stay. On Tuesday, resolve has weakened. By Wednesday, this person is ready and willing to leave. However, on Friday, staying becomes more appealing. Understanding one's requirements usually helps identify the circumstances that could best meet those needs. It is necessary to ignore immediate discomfort while focusing on the longer-term rewards of staying or leaving.

An example occurred with Jonathan, who was confused about his job. He complained that it was too far from home, with travel times of up to three hours a day. However, he enjoyed the work and had a range of ideas and plans he wanted to implement over the next eighteen months. He was sometimes ignored by management and felt resentful that he had recently been overlooked for promotion, yet he had flexible hours and time to work on personal projects. He made a list of what constituted his perfect job and then decided which of those requirements represented a *good* job. He determined that ticking seven of those ten boxes would indicate a suitable position. However, his current job only ticked five boxes, so Jonathan began searching for a new occupation.

A return to the previous upright card in the suit, the Seven of Cups, involves reassessing sources of happiness and fulfilment. Jobwise, it might include weighing between travel and working hours, creative fulfilment and financial rewards or free on-site parking and a daily train commute. The individual can reassess personal needs and decide what provides sufficient physical, emotional, mental and spiritual nourishment. By identifying one's requirements, it is possible to determine whether current circumstance or a new horizon is the better choice.

In a general reading, the reversed Eight of Cups usually shows a person unfulfilled by current circumstances. This individual is uncertain whether to stay or leave, unsure of having remained too long or if leaving now is jumping ship too soon. This requires a return to the upright Seven of Cups. It's time to ignore justifications and identify underlying needs. Once emotional and spiritual needs have been clarified, it's easier to determine whether the current partner, job, relationship or circumstances are suitable.

In a career layout, the reversed Eight of Cups shows someone confused about two career directions or between a current position and a new one. Jobs are more than simply ways to earn an income. An occupation can provide a social network, travel and training. It can be a convenient train ride away or a series of crowded bus trips. It might offer work-from-home days or keep a person stuck inside an airless office or a cold factory until late at night for a basic wage. It's time to forget about immediate options and instead focus on long-term personal needs.

In a relationship question, the reversed Eight shows indecision and perhaps a conflict between head and heart. When Alison wanted to leave her long-term partner, she was nervous about being alone. They had been together for almost twelve years and although she was unhappy, Alison didn't know what to expect if she moved. I suggested that she ask the cards, "What does the future hold for me if I move out?" and then ask, "What does the future hold if I remain where I'm living?"

The reversed Eight of Cups appeared in the position of surrounding energies, confirming Alison's confusion. The outcome looked much more rewarding if she made a move, so she followed that question by asking if it was wise to share a rental home with a co-tenant or live alone. Eighteen months later, Alison returned and seemed to be thriving. She was sharing an apartment with two other women but was ready to move out to live with Declan, whom she'd been dating for eight months.

In a health query, the reversed Eight of Cups highlights reconsidering whether a health avenue or medicine is working or not and what can be done about it. This card also indicates someone who is vacillating about the best approach to health. Perhaps this person tries one approach and then abandons it when discovering a different method.

This card appeared reversed in Jeremy's reading when he was unsure if it was time to wean himself off smoking. Although it was a simple, portable method of relaxing, smoking was also affecting his health long-term. Instead of suggesting that he give up cigarettes, I asked him what he might replace them with that was just as portable and effective but without the health consequences. I also asked what he'd do with the $5,000 he'd save each year by not smoking.

Eight of Swords

The Eight of Swords shows us that brute force is no match for clear thinking. In this card, someone is bound, blindfolded and surrounded by swords that point downward, rigidly placed in the ground. This suggests that inflexible personal beliefs are limiting options. Clouds symbolise confused or clouded thinking. Grey skies suggest that even with eyes wide open it is possible to be confused or restricted by one's thoughts and beliefs.

    This individual cannot see the path ahead and is not free to defend ideals or protect against the intentions of others. In the Eight of Swords, strength cannot be found in physical activity. Instead, it must be discovered within. When this card appears in a layout, thoughts, strategies and personal beliefs are required to identify paths to freedom. It's not as easy as leaving a job or a marriage or standing up to an oppressor. The situation requires much more than that.

    This person cannot walk away from circumstances, as shown in the Eight of Cups. Nor is there the personal freedom to explore opportunities like in the Eight of Wands. It is time to reach within to find the inner strength to face the torments of personal thoughts. Fuelled by fear, these self-doubts may be creating worst-case scenarios that are unlikely to occur in reality. It's time to scrutinise the stories you are telling yourself as they may not be based on current circumstances but on past encounters. "There is no choice," could actually mean, "I haven't yet found a suitable choice."

    The person is dressed in red, suggesting passion and courage. The eights are cards of strength and the swords' strength lies in the mental ability to find new solutions. Wands people have to attempt an action physically to determine if it will work or not, whereas swords individuals generally examine a situation mentally, anticipating possible problems before proceeding.

Therefore, the individual's power lies in thinking, coupled with inner reserves of strength and determination. The people who live in the castle on the hill nearby can restrict this person's movement, their sight and their opportunities but they cannot obstruct the person's thinking unless the individual is unconsciously or deliberately complicit. This person is blinded but so are the castle's residents. Everyone has blind spots. When a person identifies a lack of awareness in those who attempt to impose restrictions, it is possible to work around their attempts, turning wardens into prisoners.

In a general reading, the upright Eight of Swords describes physical restrictions. It also suggests that the person needs to view these constraints from a different perspective to find solutions. A change of attitude can improve the awareness of opportunities, whereas circular thinking can limit progress. It's time to reassess assumptions to identify outdated attitudes and beliefs.

In a career layout, this card appears when a person cannot see opportunities and feels stuck or burdened with obligations and responsibilities. It can be difficult to elevate current attitudes and perceptions so as to glimpse new options or possibilities. It's like approaching the summit of a tall mountain when the peak is shrouded in mist and you're uncertain which way to tread.

In a relationship question, this card describes a person who feels as though there are no viable options at present. The Eight of Swords occurred in David's reading when he asked what the future held for a potential relationship with Akriti. They are both spiritually focused people but from different religious backgrounds. Both David's and Akriti's families opposed their relationship. After Akriti's family threatened to disown her, she abandoned her association with David. The outcome didn't look optimistic for an elopement, so it was time for David to explore other relationship options. Suggesting an alternative approach requires delicacy and tact, especially while David believed that Akriti was the only person in the world for him.

In a health query, the Eight of Swords can indicate asthma, chest and lung troubles or even physical stiffness resulting from mental rigidity. The ties in this card bind the chest and torso, suggesting concern around the heart, lungs or digestive system. If The Sun or Strength cards are also in the layout, it emphasises heart issues. If The Chariot or The Moon cards appear, it might be stomach issues. The Death card indicates health imbalance with the abdomen or reproductive organs, while the Ten of Wands can signify spinal tension.

Eight of Swords Reversed

The Eight of Swords reversed suggests it is necessary to return to the previous card in the suit, the upright Seven, to find a solution through personal analysis and thought. The Seven of Swords shows mental agility in solving problems. It's time to think carefully about the current circumstances. When this card is reversed, it shows the swords falling from the ground, indicating that thoughts are less rigid now, allowing for unexpected solutions. Answers might arrive in dreams at night or when completing menial chores and allowing the subconscious mind to sift through possibilities.

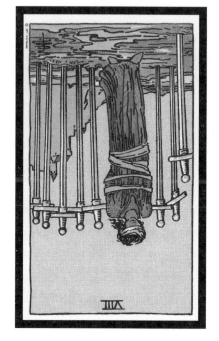

The Eight reversed shows that through analytical thinking, bonds can be severed with the swords (swords represent thoughts). The individual approaches the current situation as a challenge and usually solves puzzles by relentlessly searching the mind for possibilities. The solution is usually in the person's subconscious and can be found more rapidly by exploring diversely from eccentric to more conservative possibilities. Bizarre concepts are worthy of consideration at this stage.

When the Eight is reversed, returning to more adaptable thinking and the perseverance of the Seven allows for unusual solutions. The Eight of Swords is a more encouraging card when reversed. Other swords cards that are more positive when reversed include the Five, Nine and Ten.

In a general reading, the reversed Eight of Swords indicates moving forward from current restrictions. This person often feels relief after a constrictive period. By returning to the previous upright card, the Seven of Swords, it is possible to mentally search for the best way to reach objectives without encountering too much resistance from others. This individual is able to casually slip below the radar and do what is necessary to achieve goals.

In a career layout, the reversed Eight of Swords can show progress based on exploring new solutions and opportunities. This occurred with Brent, who was worried about being retrenched from his company during a recent restructuring. Just as the company's fortunes improved, Brent was offered a new position with a competitor. After twelve months of stress about his job security, he suddenly had several options available.

In a relationship question, this card suggests a workable solution after a period of restriction. It can also highlight a change that has been made with new relationship opportunities. Options and choices are becoming more visible. Ongoing restrictions may have lessened enough for change to be possible. This might involve changing roles or patterns of behaviour in the partnership or introducing fresh options such as a new location or less demanding careers that provide more time together.

In a health query, the Eight of Swords reversed represents improved health after a difficult period. It's time to return to the previous card in the suit, the upright Seven of Swords, to find new, more effective ways to manage health. It can indicate issues with asthma, the chest or lungs. The ties in this card compress the chest and torso, suggesting concern around the heart, lungs or digestive system. If either The Sun or Strength card is also in the layout, it accentuates heart issues. If The Chariot or The Moon card appears, it might represent stomach issues. The Death card indicates health imbalance with the abdomen or reproductive organs. The Ten of Wands suggests spinal tension. This card usually indicates improvements in health when reversed.

Eight of Pentacles

A pentacles individual's strength lies in a practical, organised, common-sense approach to life. When problems arise, pentacles people diligently strive to restore balance through disciplined spending and cautious application of plans. The Eight of Pentacles represents the benefits of common sense and self-discipline. The emphasis is on a commitment to goals. Pentacles people fundamentally understand perseverance. They resist changing course at minor setbacks but continue stoically towards established objectives.

In this card a person is at work, focused

on a task, with some finished products (the six pentacles hanging up) on display and another pentacle incomplete below the workbench. A path leads off to the city where this individual can sell completed products. As they establish a reputation, they can live away from the city and still make a solid living. The blue tunic suggests this individual invests personal work with skill, proficiency and spirit, making each pentacle more than just the product of disciplined hands. The red tights and boots confirm the substantial energy required for this work and suggest abundant physical reserves.

The wealth a person generates benefits their family and others in the community. However, this individual is focused entirely on the work, simply because of the pleasure of seeing a job well done. If problems arise, this person is able to restore balance by tackling each stage with steadfast determination.

In a general reading, the upright Eight indicates a commitment to doing the finest job possible. It can show a person learning new skills and striving to be the best at the current job. This individual feels proud of each carefully completed task and works with skill and confidence. It sometimes highlights adding new skills to existing expertise to increase income and job satisfaction.

In a career question, this card often shows a person who is adding skills to their existing qualifications to specialise in some type of work. It can indicate a course to update expertise in a changing industry or learning through direct application on the job. The person is committed to career progression and is likely to find fulfilment through a chosen occupation. People often give their best efforts when mastering new skills, applying fresh knowledge with focus and enthusiasm.

In a relationship layout, the Eight of Pentacles highlights a commitment to a fulfilling relationship. This person is prepared to build long-lasting connections and has a realistic approach to what makes a partnership last. There is an awareness that sufficient income provides greater choices regarding the home environment, hobbies, travel and socialising opportunities — and that these, in turn, support partners in their long-term union.

In a health query, the individual is committed to building and maintaining robust health when the Eight of Pentacles appears in a layout. This might include regular exercise, eating well and taking supplements to ensure ongoing health and fitness. 'Prevention is better than cure' is the attitude to health when this Eight occurs upright in a health layout. A self-disciplined approach to well-being, coupled with moderation, ensures a balanced state of health.

Eight of Pentacles Reversed

The Eight of Pentacles reversed represents an absence of commitment. It often reveals a lack of direction or not having a worthwhile goal to work towards. Returning to the previous upright card, the Seven of Pentacles, is worthwhile, as it suggests reflecting upon what is personally meaningful. When long-term ambitions are clear, it's easier to plan a path to a central goal. With far-reaching purpose, it's often more apparent what can assist or detract from the current direction.

Sometimes, due to immaturity, the individual has high expectations of achieving ambitions with minimal effort. When the imagined success isn't quickly achieved, the person tends to move on to more promising possibilities. Instead of building steadily and realistically towards each goal, this individual loses interest and avoids disappointment by searching for a bigger, shinier objective. It's a whimsical approach to aspirations, rather than a more practical, resolute perseverance that usually defines the pentacles approach.

In a general reading, the reversed Eight of Pentacles describes someone who is drifting through life without viable goals or purpose. This card appeared in Calvin's layout after he sold his business for a considerable sum of money. He never needed to work again. Two years later, he was bored. Most of his friends were busy working, so weekdays dragged for Calvin. He was tired of taking flying lessons and had recently completed major home renovations. After twenty years of having specific business and financial goals, Calvin was sliding through each week, unable to find a suitable objective and motivation. It was time for him to examine the lesson of the previous upright card in the suit, the Seven of Pentacles, and consider his next long-term plan.

In a career layout, this card indicates shoddy workmanship or poor concentration with a lack of motivation. It represents the job that was offered, rather than the career this person wants to have. A return to the upright Seven of Pentacles allows enough space to stand back and decide if current work, relationship or lifestyle is worth the effort.

In a relationship question, the Eight reversed suggests a lack of commitment to a future with a spouse. Sometimes, it highlights that both partners have lost sight of their shared goals. The relationship might be suffering because career commitments or family demands are consuming all available time and energy.

The reversed Eight of Pentacles sometimes describes an individual who wants to date but not to settle down with anyone. This person might struggle with commitment, due to fear of loss, or they may simply dread the possibility of missing out on a better opportunity.

In a health layout, the reversed Eight of Pentacles can indicate that the individual's current job is affecting physical health. Perhaps workplace conditions expose the individual to danger (such as working on construction sites) or to toxic chemicals.

This card can also suggest that the person is not committed to building and maintaining their physical well-being. Perhaps there is denial about current health issues. This occurred with Gil, a corpulent, diabetic pastry chef, who ignored doctor's orders and routinely sampled his own delightful creations. Following several surgeries on his feet, Gil was unable to stand for long periods, which eventually restricted his ability to work.

The Nines

The nines in the tarot represent a period of reflection before a final commitment to a goal or purpose. The Nine of Wands shows a weary individual examining past decisions and actions. This is the first time in the wands suit that a person looks back to the past. Wands individuals generally favour the excitement of possibilities ahead rather than absorbing valuable lessons from past events.

The Nine of Cups displays a contented person reflecting upon past actions. It is time to review the results of past efforts. Previous decisions and actions have led to this point and it's time to decide whether changes need to be made to move forward successfully.

The Nine of Swords represents someone unable to sleep because unresolved issues are crowding in simultaneously. The need to understand why events unfolded and what decisions led to current pressures can keep this person awake night after night. Sometimes, it describes thinking in circles and resolving nothing.

The Nine of Pentacles shows an individual whose sense of routine allows time for reflection while ensuring present stability continues. Past efforts have been fruitful, affording this person time to consider paths and possibilities. Pentacles people enjoy unhurried moments to ponder life's possibilities, as they usually think deliberately and methodically.

Three or more nines in a layout suggest that a cycle or a chapter is ending and that it is a time to consider necessary changes. By reflecting on past challenges and obstacles, it's possible to know what to pursue and what to avoid in the future. Previous choices and actions have shaped who we are today and every decision or effort that is taken now shapes who we become tomorrow.

Nine of Wands

The nines represent a final reassessment before completion. The Nine of Wands is about re-examination regarding commitment to projects or people. As wands individuals tend to look ahead towards new challenges, they sometimes miss the perspective available to those who also look back at former actions. We are all products of our past events, circumstances and decisions. Realising which choices provided the results we desired may help us plan events more carefully. Basically, the Nine of Wands involves weighing up past successes and failures prior to making a long-term commitment.

The person in this card examines personal history to assess the consequences of previous actions. The head bandage hints at strife endured. This individual looks warily back at historical challenges, hesitant to make any new commitments before being aware of their consequences. There is no longer an easy escape if things don't go well. If problems arise, it is necessary to stay and sort them out. This is difficult for wands people, who prefer moving onto greener pastures when life gets too strenuous, too slow, predictable or monotonous.

The person is aware that lasting success results from persistence. Where life was once a series of short sprints, now it has become a long-distance journey. The prize is greater but the risks and demands have also increased.

To acquire the rewards presented by the Ten of Wands (personal achievement, stability, respect and opportunities to guide or teach others), it is first necessary to become the King or Queen of Wands. The Page and Knight of Wands usually lack the maturity and discipline to plan long-term and pace themselves for extended effort. For success, it is necessary to find new ways to resolve conflict so as to work well as part of a team. Wands people are generally better suited to working alone or being group leaders, due to their naturally competitive tendencies. In group projects, it is necessary for them to curb these inclinations to achieve long-term objectives.

In a general reading, the upright Nine of Wands shows someone reassessing past actions before deciding on the most suitable approach to completing plans. By reviewing the past, it's possible to clarify the likely outcome of a path before taking another step — knowing not every plan succeeds.

In a career layout, this Nine sometimes appears when a person has been overlooked for promotion. It's natural to reassess career options and even explore other job opportunities. In some occupation layouts, the person is re-evaluating the workplace culture after witnessing a bullying incident. The acceptance that all has not been perfect previously includes considering how to deal with similar issues more effectively in the future.

In a relationship question, the individual might be reassessing a partnership after a difficult period. This occurred with Jessica, who asked about her relationship with Charlie. After discovering Charlie was having an affair, Jessica was uncertain about their future together. She was effectively asking if she could find a way to trust Charlie again and how she might protect herself if he was unfaithful in the future.

Sometimes, this card shows the decision to commit to a new partnership after a previous association has ended. It's a commitment made with an awareness of the inherent risks.

In a health query, the Nine of Wands can describe a person who is expecting bad news about their health. It indicates an acceptance that past health priorities have been misguided or inconsistent. The individual is aware of how their future health requires more consistent effort and planning.

Nine of Wands Reversed

The Nine of Wands reversed highlights doubts about making long-term commitments. It is often a card for individuals who feel that life is all work and no play. They endure onerous responsibilities without consistent support, leaving them hesitant to make promises about future obligations. When reviewing the past, this person focuses more on hardship, struggle and endurance. Tangible rewards are sparse in a landscape that is both barren and joyless.

It's necessary to return to the previous card in the suit, the upright Eight of Wands, to enjoy a period where life flows easily and pressures are few. Life doesn't have to be a perpetual struggle. Perhaps rest is overdue. A suitable holiday at this point might not include all-day hiking or adventurous sailing because of exhaustion. Instead, this person needs a hammock, sunshine, the shade of a few palm trees and glistening white sand. As tranquil waters lap at the edge of a tropical island, the big decision of the day is between the lobster and the spicy stir fry. But first, a swim will dissolve personal cares and a snooze is likely to follow.

If a holiday isn't convenient, living more simply can be rejuvenating. It might be time to socialise, spend time in a garden or take an art class or a yoga lesson. When reversed, the Nine of Wands represents focus is on the pain and frustrations of the past rather than personal triumphs. A period of joy is usually an antidote for this. Take time out to relax and enjoy simple pleasures.

In a general reading, the reversed Nine of Wands indicates an acceptance that past efforts have not produced the desired results. It describes the process of asking, "How did I get here?" and "How might I be more effective with less effort in future?" Pain and regret can be powerful motivators for changing life direction.

In a career layout, the reversed Nine describes a person who is exhausted and overwhelmed by career demands. Perhaps the individual has been working while studying, is struggling in a low paid job or is routinely required for unpaid overtime. This card is sometimes found when a person is nearing retirement and realises no provisions have been made for the financial transition ahead.

In a relationship question, the person is reflecting on poor relationship patterns of the past and is wary of pursuing love in future. This card sometimes appears after a bruising divorce settlement, indicating someone who feels relationships are unstable, unreliable investments. These feelings can eventually pass, resulting in the Nine appearing upright in subsequent readings.

In a health layout, physical exhaustion often contributes to health issues. In countries with expensive health care, ageing workers become concerned about retirement and not being able to afford personal health care in old age. It's time to reassess health maintenance. Rest is a vital factor in robust health, along with sufficient sleep, nourishing food, fresh air and regular exercise. A grateful attitude can also contribute to personal well-being.

Wands people are the most likely to forget they are no longer youthful, resulting in sports and physical injuries as they age. When this reversed Nine occurred in sixty-seven-year-old Tony's health layout, he had recently strained his back mowing the lawn. Pushing a heavy mower around an enormous sloping lawn was easier when he first moved into the property, more than forty years previously. It was time for Tony to purchase a ride-on mower or hire a younger man for garden maintenance, who might clear the leaves from his roof at the same time.

Nine of Cups

The Nine of Cups highlights emotional reflection on a situation prior to commitment. While knowing the value of what you provide is essential to self-worth, understanding that love increases in value when it is given away is even more significant. This Nine represents fulfilment resulting from a job well done or an idea seen through to completion. It can also highlight feelings of self-love and self-respect. This is not self-inflation or narcissism but a simple, powerful sense of self-worth and confidence.

Although the individual in the card wears a red hat and socks or stockings, the robe is grey. This

suggests they are surrounded by love but need to connect emotionally with others to be able to give and receive it in a meaningful way. The bright yellow background represents a clear understanding of the value of love and of being valued by others. The blue background signifies the security that comes from being valued by others and knowing one's own spiritual value.

Some students erroneously believe the person in the card appears smug or is filled with self-importance. Sometimes, it can seem this way to people who might lack a well-developed sense of self-worth and who perceive self-respect as smugness. Knowing your true worth is the first step to knowing what you don't want at work, in your heart or in your life, generally. From this realisation, it's possible to discard what is superfluous.

The individual in this card reflects the traditional cups' life perspective. There is generally reticence towards people until they are sure their motives are sincere. Past pain has demonstrated that others do not necessarily have this person's best interests at heart. However, there is also profound understanding that life is a banquet and this person has been invited. The cups journey has taken almost until the Ten of Cups to realise what was known as a small child: that there is a place of belonging in the community and in the world for everyone. Each participant at life's banquet brings something unique to the table.

In a general reading, the upright Nine of Cups describes contentment with life and joy resulting from past opportunities and achievements. Some readers see this as a card of happiness but it more clearly describes fulfilment. Happiness is fleeting, whereas a profound sense of fulfilment is lasting, especially when the concept of gratitude is embraced. Pursuing happiness is like attempting to catch a butterfly with bare hands, whereas well-being relies less on outside factors and favours a sense of stillness and inner contentment.

In a career question, the Nine of Cups describes a satisfying career. It often occurs in layouts with people who have creative careers, because projects allow for unique personal input. As an answer to a question about pursuing a career path, it describes triumph ahead, with a personally nourishing direction.

In a relationship layout, this card indicates feeling happy and fulfilled, partly because a love relationship is only one source of joy in a range of choices. These options might include a close partnership, a loving family, supportive friends and a stable home life. When people value their contribution to love relationships, they are better able to negotiate to have emotional needs met. The upright Nine of Cups suggests that this person is already happy. A love relationship is the icing on the cake and not the cake itself. It is an additional source of joy in a balanced life.

In a health layout, the upright Nine of Cups indicates balanced health, along with emotional and spiritual well-being. As an answer to a question about the effectiveness of a health solution, it suggests the person is likely to be happy with the results. This card also highlights the importance of emotional and spiritual nourishment in maintaining health and well-being.

Nine of Cups Reversed

The Nine of Cups reversed suggests that overlooking one's place in the world and in the community may lead to dissatisfaction. There is a sense of not belonging that sears the heart and soul. Sometimes, people attempt to satiate neediness through worldly distractions. This inner emptiness is both difficult and simple to resolve. The first step is to allow one's heart and soul to become open to nourishment. It might also require returning to the previous card in the suit, the upright Eight of Cups, to determine who or what needs to be left behind.

It can be difficult to understand one's own qualities when friends and work colleagues don't value our traits and talents. It's possible that some friendships, hobbies or circumstances no longer provide the emotional or spiritual sustenance they once did. If so, it's time to find new sources of joy.

The Nine reversed indicates reaching for worldly possessions or activities to satisfy emotional or spiritual emptiness. The person might be engaged in addictive or compulsive behaviours, including anorexia, bulimia, drug and alcohol dependence, gambling, spending or craving anything that creates a buzz. This person's unconscious hunger can uncentre others and become spiritually and emotionally draining for family, friends and colleagues. The reversed Nine describes someone who has not yet addressed the underlying causes of emotional or spiritual starvation.

The reversed Nine of Cups suggests feeling unhappy with life. Spiritual and emotional needs are not being addressed and the person is feeling isolated from friends, meaningful work and life in general. Returning to the previous card, the upright Eight of Cups, to reflect on what is no longer significant in life can be valuable. It is time to plan an adventure or a holiday or undertake a course or pursue an interest that provides spiritual and emotional nourishment. Regular meditation, yoga, prayer, gardening, singing, charitable works or daily walks might provide effective ways to bridge the gap.

In a general reading, the reversed Nine of Cups indicates an emotional or spiritual emptiness leading to a range of symptoms including addictions, compulsive behaviour, restlessness, lack of motivation and sometimes even depression. It basically describes someone who is unhappy and unable to find sufficient emotional or spiritual nourishment.

In a career layout, the person is likely to be unhappy with current work circumstances and unsure about what might offer a more rewarding career direction. It's time to return to the previous upright card, the Eight of Cups and walk away from people, situations or circumstances that don't offer fulfilment. Then it's necessary to examine what career directions offer the most personal growth and knowledge and support a well-rounded life. Sometimes, instead of changing career direction, a person can pursue fresh hobbies or interests outside of work. These new pursuits can provide the missing joy or necessary challenges and focus.

In a relationship question, this individual feels disconnected from other people. Even if relationship opportunities are present, a lack of awareness around the value of their contribution means they are likely to settle for less or fail to have their needs met. An innate lack of self-worth leads to feeling disconnected from the world. When a person is emotionally detached, even a loving relationship partner feels distant or remote.

In a health query, the reversed Nine of Cups suggests that physical symptoms of imbalanced health are the result of spiritual emptiness. Treating the physical symptoms alone is unlikely to be enough to fully restore health and harmony. It's time for the person to examine the underlying emotional and spiritual causes of current health issues. Alternatively, it's time to decide what might make improving personal health worthwhile.

Sometimes, in a health layout, this card signifies a drug, alcohol or gambling addiction is undermining physical and mental health. Instead of just giving up the addiction, the person needs to replace it with more suitable sources of emotional and spiritual nourishment. It can also indicate depression, either reactive (as a reaction to a recent loss) or chronic (ongoing) listlessness and disconnection from friends and circumstances. It's time to discover more joy and happiness in life.

Nine of Swords

The Nine of Swords represents a time of questioning one's commitment to current beliefs. Sometimes, people cling to attitudes that no longer sustain them. This might occur when a small business owner who has spent years working alone in business hires employees to share the workload but is unable to relinquish control. When one insists on managing every task in the business, it cannot grow despite an effective team.

Attitudes can subtly shape a person's life, highlighting some opportunities, while obscuring others. If a belief system is not supportive, then it is time to consider an overhaul of personal judgements.

Margaret believed that if she worked hard continuously, she'd eventually be promoted to a more senior position. Instead, she noticed less experienced colleagues progressed swiftly past her up the corporate ladder. They worked harder at making social connections but were less focused on their daily tasks. Margaret's beliefs about working diligently had made her too valuable at her current level to be considered for promotion.

The individual in this card has been awakened from sleep by a disturbing dream, which is reflective of current life events. The person's subconscious mind is attempting to make sense of life and present solutions for problems. The blue squares on the bedcover suggest a connection with one's spiritual self through sleep and in dreams. The red roses reveal inner desires, unconstrained by the conscious mind. The struggling figures carved into the bed represent the skirmishes that sometimes take place in dreams. The dotted outlines of the planets and the signs of the zodiac suggest planetary influences are also at work and that certain periods in each calendar year are more suitable for clarity of dreams than others.

In a general reading, the Nine of Swords highlights fear, doubt and worry over present or future circumstances. Often, these anxieties are real. If a pentacles card is added to this card in the layout, the concerns are likely to be financial. A cups card indicates emotional or creative issues, whereas a wands card suggests apprehension concerning goals and achievements. If a swords card is added to this card, it indicates a struggle for mental clarity as a range of stresses meld together. There is inner mental turmoil.

In a career question, the upright Nine of Swords indicates worry about job security or unfinished projects. This sometimes occurs when an individual works late into the evening and retires to bed with a list of unfinished items. Disturbing dreams continue the burdensome thinking processes from the day.

In a relationship layout, the Nine of Swords suggests being inwardly unsettled about a relationship. It is possible that night-time dreams offer viable solutions to problems. Poor sleep patterns due to ongoing stress are likely to influence current or potential relationships. Focusing on sources of stress also distracts from the love and support provided by a partner. Occasionally, this card highlights someone who cannot let go of a former partner and who dreams about that person regularly.

In a health layout, the Nine of Swords can signify disturbed sleep, issues with headaches and stress in the neck, upper back and chest. Each part of the body that the swords pierce in the card image is likely to be affected. If The Moon card also occurs in the same layout, the person is likely to face interrupted slumber at night. Strong dreams often influence sleep cycles and a new baby in the house may interrupt usual rest patterns. Mothers of newborns rarely enjoy unbroken slumber in the first few months of a baby's life. Instead, they drowse lightly, ready to be up and moving at the first cry.

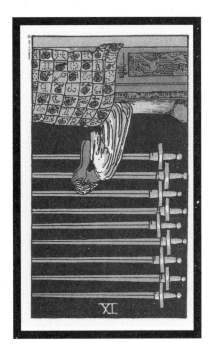

Nine of Swords Reversed

The Nine of Swords reversed highlights awareness of dreams. Although sleep might be disturbed, this person is making sense of the messages from the subconscious mind. Worries and fears are subsiding now, either through a resolution of the problem or resignation to circumstances as shown in the previous card in the suit, the Eight of Swords.

A return to the upright Eight of Swords allows access to inner strength to overcome limiting beliefs or attitudes. It can also represent a retreat within that allows life or others to have control until there is sufficient strength and commitment to make necessary changes to move forward again.

In a general reading, the reversed Nine of Swords indicates vivid dreams that are more likely to be remembered and understood in the waking state. It can also suggest a period of worry and stress is subsiding, as the person discovers suitable solutions to daily issues. It sometimes indicates intuitive dreams that point the way towards a better life. At this time, it's wise to focus on nocturnal dreams. They can provide valuable information.

In a career layout, this card indicates stress with interrupted sleep. It's likely to be financial or work-related anxiety. Decisions are needed before it subsides. It's time to outline possible strategies for a range of eventualities and if the current job is under threat, a new position might be the most suitable alternative.

In a relationship question, the reversed Nine indicates concerns about a current or a past relationship. This card appeared in Atsu's reading and when I suggested his current worries were subsiding, he explained why. For five years, his wife had become increasingly unpredictable and impulsive. She was afraid to leave the house and be among strangers one day but out splurging at a crowded retail sale the next. After a referral to medical practitioners and a psychiatrist, Laura was diagnosed with bipolar disorder. As Laura's new medication began to take effect, their lives settled down. The reversed Nine of Swords reflected this adjustment process.

In a health reading, the reversed Nine of Swords signifies sleep disturbance, headaches, neck, shoulder and upper back problems. It can show a time when the person worries in bed at night, only to awaken exhausted in the morning, despite significant hours of rest. It's time to return to the previous card in the suit, the upright Eight of Swords, to notice how attitudes and perceptions can restrict one's vision of viable options. It can be difficult to pursue effective solutions without a change in thinking or believing that change is possible. Sometimes, reading motivational books, finding a support group, consulting a counsellor or seeing a life coach can help prepare a person for real change. As this is a swords card, transformation begins with a change in thought patterns and beliefs. The upright Eight of Swords shows someone finding viable options within current restrictions. The reversed Nine of Swords suggests that worrying isn't helping now and that rational thought can lead to viable solutions.

Nine of Pentacles

The Nine of Pentacles symbolises financial and material success. It highlights a comfortable life, resulting from practical planning, discipline and commitment to personal goals.

In this card, someone stands outdoors, relaxed and secure in their surroundings. All necessary steps have been taken to ensure that life is stable. This allows time for hobbies and other simple routines, by which the days, weeks and seasons are measured. The snail on the ground suggests that building security and stability takes time. Slow, steady steps are required to develop solid wealth and fulfilment. The fruits on the vine are ripe and represent the rewards of labour. This individual is successful in their chosen career as well as with financial management.

The person has mastered self-discipline throughout the past eight cards and is currently contemplating life. The future has been secured as far as possible. They are now able to extend their talents and abilities to a wider circle of people. It is time to consider group projects and goals, such as a family or plans relating to the local community.

Although the castle in the background of the card represents stability, the person is happiest outside amidst nature. It is rejuvenating. Pentacles people often refresh themselves by walking in forests, in fields or anywhere in the countryside, as nature beckons them from their routines to remember their place in the world. They are often gardeners, bush explorers, surfers and dog walkers outside of working hours.

In a general reading, the upright Nine of Pentacles indicates a financially comfortable life. It can signify a self-made person, whose success results from training, planning and applied effort. From an early age, this practical, risk-averse individual has realised that building wealth is a life's work, not simply a weekend endeavour.

In a career layout, this Nine indicates job stability and can suggest more than one stream of income. It's possible that investments or other sources of revenue supplement earnings, enhancing financial stability. This is a materialistic but realistic perspective. The person is capable of building solid wealth through career and investments. As a result of living within personal means, this individual usually has spare income to invest in low-risk ventures with a view to eventually retiring with several sources of income.

In a relationship layout, the Nine of Pentacles indicates a materially comfortable life but one that involves periods of aloneness. Perhaps this person might be too busy working to spend time sharing goals and hobbies with friends and family. However, the Nine appearing in a relationship layout often suggests that practical and material concerns have been adequately addressed and now it's time to find a life partner. This person is usually reliable, conservative and sensual in relationships.

In a health query, the upright Nine of Pentacles confirms stable health resulting from a moderate life and ongoing health maintenance. It also indicates sufficient financial resources to build and maintain personal well-being. Time spent in nature provides a soothing break from the stresses of daily life. This might include walks in a leafy neighbourhood or local park or weekends spent tending a large private garden. Generally, it suggests balanced health that comes from a harmonious attitude to life. This person is unlikely to be extreme or overly spontaneous where health is concerned. There may be a tendency to overindulge in life's pleasures but this is usually tempered with a need for moderation.

Nine of Pentacles Reversed

The Nine of Pentacles reversed suggests someone who lacks understanding of their personal place in the world and is not aware of the physical, emotional, mental and spiritual value of spending time amidst nature. Walking, hiking or simply having a picnic can be therapeutic in easing the stresses of daily life.

In a career layout, the Nine reversed signifies toiling too hard for the lifestyle they desire. This can mean working evenings, weekends or two jobs, or being poorly paid for one's effort. It can also describe someone who is employed full-time and currently studying to improve career prospects. It is time to return to the upright Eight of Pentacles to gain further skills so as to be able to charge more for one's labour.

With the increasing pace of change in small business and corporate life, remaining relevant by mastering new workplace skills is advisable. The days of completing studies in your twenties and settling into a long and productive career are over. Automation and artificial intelligence routinely reduce the numbers of staff required to run an enterprise effectively. The upright Eight of Pentacles represents upskilling to remain relevant.

Clara looked exhausted, even as I told her that she was working too hard for her lifestyle. She was working six days and three nights at two jobs to save for a house deposit. Her husband was twenty-five years older than she and was content to rent a house. Clara knew she wanted her own home and realised it was necessary to save for it now, while she was young enough to borrow from a bank. The isolation reflected in the Nine is often increased when the card is reversed. Clara felt unsupported by her husband and alone in her pursuit of a financially secure old age.

In a general reading, the reversed Nine of Pentacles describes a time when efforts are insufficiently rewarded. Perhaps the person is being underpaid or is covering the tasks of two people and being paid for only one. As big business realises two of their biggest expenses—rent and wages—can be trimmed, staff numbers are culled and employees are encouraged to work from home. It now seems customary for a company that requires one hundred people to hire only sixty workers. Although this increases staff turnover and requires additional employees in the recruitment process, it still represents significant savings.

In a career layout, it may be time to reassess long-term strategies, because the current extended hours and heavy demands cannot be sustained. Options might include further study for more relevant qualifications or a change of job to a workplace that has a less demanding corporate culture. It's time to return to the upright Eight of Pentacles to show commitment to long-term career goals and not simply to the job at hand.

In a relationship question, this card represents both partners relying on a single source of income. If one individual is studying or caring for children, the limited salary of the other partner is stretched to cover the family's needs. It can also describe a person working both day and evenings or weekends, with limited time and energy to devote to maintaining a relationship.

When Tia asked about her relationship with Tony, the reversed Nine of Pentacles in the layout suggested she needed to be patient, as Tony was likely to be consumed by work demands and exhausted in his spare time.

In a health query, the reversed Nine of Pentacles can suggest that unrelenting work demands are affecting physical health and energy levels. It's time to decide if the current effort is worth the long-term rewards. In rare instances, this card signifies a specific workplace incident that has affected one's health, such as a work-related accident or exposure to toxic materials or chemicals. This occurred with Ted, whose years of renovating houses exposed him to asbestos, resulting in ongoing lung issues in later life.

The Tens

The tens in the tarot describe the completion of the journeys of the four suits. From the earliest beginnings at the aces, these pilgrimages are completed at the tens. The Ten of Wands shows a grand challenge being realised. This might be the sale of a business that was a lifetime's work. It could be a promotion to the company board as the CEO, CIO, CFO or company chairman. It can also involve leaving a long-term career, selling up and starting a new business in a different location that aligns with personal values, such as in renewable energy, an organic café or sustainable farming.

The Ten of Cups shows a complete family unit and the fulfilment that it brings. This can signify a wide group of friends and family members who support each other towards better opportunities. It might take the form of finding a spiritual family or simply a group of people who share emotional and spiritual values.

The Ten of Swords illustrates how personal beliefs lead to consequences; although convictions themselves are invisible, they can be traced by the results they yield. In constructive terms, this Ten can describe releasing ideas, concepts and thinking to surrender to life's plan. It is accepting that life might have a better plan than this individual can construct. Instead of making a clear strategy to achieve an objective, it involves allowing opportunities to surface, unhindered by personal beliefs and expectations.

The Ten of Pentacles indicates a stable home and work environment, where the results of personal and group efforts are visible in the material world. The big house with carefully manicured gardens and the wisteria-covered summer house down by the river provide comfort, privacy and tranquillity, plus an escape from the bustle of city life. When three or more tens occur in a layout, contracts, legal documents or the purchase or sale of a home, car or business are suggested.

Ten of Wands

The Ten of Wands indicates reaching goals but not smoothly. Wands people have difficulty saying no to offers and opportunities. Consequently, by the time they reach the Ten of Wands, they are overloaded but still struggle enthusiastically towards their goals. This Ten is a card of achievement, with more energy being used to reach goals than is necessary. This is success despite the lack of a clear plan and effective systems. The process could have been shortened and streamlined with the help of a swords person.

In this card, someone carries ten wands while struggling determinedly towards the destination: the castle in the background. This individual feels alone in being responsible for achieving a desired outcome. To achieve success, it is necessary to remain aware of each of those wands. If this card represented a small business, the wands might individually signify the marketing responsibilities, new product designs, the accounts payable department, website and IT updates, staff or contractors, manufacturing, shipping and customer service areas of the endeavour.

In answer to a business question, the wands can represent being burdened by different parts of the business: for example, the accounts department, the sales force, the products or the business premises. This Ten can indicate stress or back trouble from undertaking too many physical or mental responsibilities. Fire people tend to take on projects with enthusiasm and minimal consideration for the substantial effort required.

This card indicates an individual is successfully reaching significant goals but that progress could speed up if some tasks were delegated to others. This would allow the person to focus on the fundamental issues while remaining mindful of their goals. Basically, the Ten of Wands highlights a life filled with goals, challenges and commitments. This person is likely to be juggling deadlines while feeling pressured to perform.

In a general reading, the Ten of Wands can describe a person who owns a small business. This person is likely to be busy juggling deadlines and demands. It can suggest that the individual adheres to the idea that if you want a task completed properly, do it yourself. It sometimes describes someone who is burdened by previous commitments made in haste. A task that was expected to take a few weeks now stretches out to months or years.

This was driven home to me during a phone conversation with my editor. I mentioned I had an idea for a new book and that I wanted to begin it immediately.

"How are things progressing with the current six books you're writing," she asked pointedly. I realised that before commencing the new book, I'd first need to complete one or two of my existing projects.

In a career layout, this individual works hard, partly due to their insistence on doing everything themselves to ensure tasks are completed to standard. It shows a reluctance to delegate responsibility to others, plus a tendency to micro-manage subordinates. If this person owns or manages a small business, it is likely to do well because of their innate work ethic. Fiery people are often dynamic work-horses. Current demands are a burden but until effective help is offered, this person does what is necessary to keep everything going.

In a relationship question, the Ten of Wands can represent issues within the relationship or pressure from shared goals, such as buying a house, preparing to travel overseas or saving for retirement. It can also signify that one partner feels fully responsible for the success or failure of the partnership. However, both people in a relationship are responsible for its outcome. Sometimes, this card indicates a partnership that arises in a work environment. Spouses might be work colleagues or meet at a work-related conference.

In a health query, the Ten of Wands indicates the back or neck. The person in the card is hunched over. He has gathered the ten wands slowly and in doing so, has not found a better, more effective way to carry them. This reveals effort without strategy. When younger, it was easy to carry a few wands but now with added demands, maintaining sound health requires a new approach. This individual has plenty of energy but some of this may be squandered inefficiently. It's time to plan and implement new strategies that free up valuable time for longer-term goals. This might mean doing less, delegating tasks to others and ensuring regular time is set aside for checking and tweaking strategies. This can relieve the mental and physical stress that results from too much doing and not enough planning.

Ten of Wands Reversed

The Ten of Wands reversed indicates someone who is unlikely to reach current goals, due to huge commitments and responsibilities. It is usually beneficial to return to the previous upright card, the Nine of Wands, to decide where your exclusive commitment deserves to be. By discarding or delegating anything of lesser importance, this individual frees up time and energy to focus on the steps to their central objectives. It's easy to become distracted by urgent demands and overlook other significant matters when burdened with responsibilities. However, matters that are avoided for long enough will eventually become urgent concerns.

The Ten reversed can also describe using career to avoid emotional issues. Long hours doing something *more important* than nurturing a relationship or home life can improve business at the cost of a relationship. It's time to prioritise.

This card illustrates Ross's dilemma. Starting or expanding a business usually demands complete attention. This suited Ross, as he didn't even want to be aware of the problems lurking in his marriage. The twelve-hour days and the weekends he spent at the office kept him away from his family, as well as the conflicts they represented.

Instead of the issues between him and his wife being resolved, Ross suffered a heart attack and the time he spent in bed recuperating helped him to notice that his wife and children no longer knew him or needed him. He had become a stranger in his own family. They had learned to live without him because he was always working. It was a painful realisation for Ross and he was determined to make restitution. His recuperation at home provided the space for him to notice the rut he was in and a chance to examine possible solutions.

In a general reading, the reversed Ten of Wands describes someone burdened by too many commitments or obligations. This person is unlikely to reach desired goals and may be forced to abandon plans and begin again. The delegation of some tasks might allow the individual to step back and reassess priorities, improve strategies or end the process if it is unlikely to be rewarding.

In a career layout, there are likely to be strong demands on this person's time. This reversed card is sometimes found in a layout when a person is working full-time and studying part-time. If so, this is a temporary situation with an endpoint and viable rewards for current efforts. However, if it describes unreasonable workplace demands, it's time to return to the previous upright card, the Nine of Wands, to reassess current commitments.

In a relationship question, this card indicates a person avoiding relationships by working long hours. Perhaps a demanding job requires evening and weekend work, thus restricting a personal life. This pattern limits the chance of meeting someone new or maintaining a current relationship. Sometimes, the reversed Ten describes someone who feels entirely responsible for the happiness of a partner. Low self-esteem or poor family modelling in childhood leaves some individuals with an overactive sense of responsibility. They blame themselves when a partner isn't happy. By returning to the previous card in the suit, the upright Nine of Wands, it's possible to reassess priorities and clarify the best path forward for both partners in a relationship.

In a health query, the reversed Ten of Wands can describe long working hours or workplace demands that affect the individual's health. This card also highlights the shoulders, back or spine. It sometimes indicates exhaustion from too many demands. In returning to the upright Nine of Wands, it's possible to assess where vitality is being depleted and limiting those activities to conserve energy reserves.

Ten of Cups

The Ten of Cups represents finding the right workplace, one where it's possible to enjoy emotional and spiritual growth. It can also indicate a harmonious family life or the existence of a peaceful love relationship built on commitment and trust. This Ten signifies emotional completion, where the person feels a sense of belonging in a community or a family.

On the card, a couple stands together enjoying their abundant surroundings while children play nearby. Ten cups appear above them in a rainbow. These people know the value of time spent together as a family. They also realise that deep connection often comes from unplanned moments and not the 'quality time' that is carefully factored into a busy schedule. They generally have a less adventurous life, with more room for sentiment and emotional fulfilment.

This card represents being amongst your tribe. These are people who feel like family despite their origins. It describes being amongst a supportive, spiritual group. Each person in this card is appreciated for their contributions. Being seen and valued by others encourages people to do their best.

This card occurred in Marnie's health reading. My friend Marnie was undergoing chemotherapy after a cancer scare and she was physically and emotionally exhausted. Unable to be her usual social self, she gave up many of her hobbies and interests. Eventually, her friends began visiting and asking if the book club and the musical evenings could be held at her place. Her friends set up rosters so that a couple of people arrived ahead of the event and cleaned Marnie's home before setting up chairs and tables. The rest of them arrived and they enjoyed their gatherings as usual. Afterwards, they packed everything away, washed the dishes and left. I visited her one Monday evening after she'd had a sociable weekend and her opening line was, "We need to go out. I need to meet some people."

"But you've just told me that you had more than fifty visitors throughout the weekend," I said.

"Yes. But they were visitors. I already know them. I want to meet new people. I only want to speak to strangers tonight," she replied, reaching for her coat.

"Does this mean I'll need a wig and an accent?" I enquired cheekily.

In a general reading, the Ten of Cups describes a comfortable family life or being with a group of like-minded people at work or during social hours. This network of supportive folk can be a source of strength when the individual faces obstacles.

In a career layout, this card indicates creative opportunities and emotional support from surrounding people are more significant than mere financial rewards. It also suggests that the person is well supported at work. This Ten describes a group of people working together in harmony as they plan, execute and complete projects in the workplace. It's likely to be a creative, relaxed environment where each staff member is valued.

In a relationship question, the Ten describes a partnership of like-minded people. When partners share similar perspectives, it can reduce tension or arguments as they often prefer the same types of homes, friends, holiday destinations and lifestyle choices. This is the life the person dreamed of having when the Ace of Cups was originally presented at the start of the journey.

In a health query, the Ten of Cups suggests harmonious health and emotional stability. This card describes an emotionally balanced home or work life, with a satisfactory sense of belonging. This individual is nourished by friends and family and is likely to enjoy meaningful work.

Ten of Cups Reversed

The Ten of Cups reversed can describe a lack of support from people. Its appearance also suggests that this individual has a pattern of retreating from groups when feeling pressured. This urge to retreat might have begun in childhood if ongoing support from family or friends was lacking.

Oliver spent his childhood avoiding others due to a fear of being teased. As an adult, he still managed to blend in by keeping silent and hiding away, both physically and emotionally, when group activities took place. The appearance of the Ten reversed showed that Oliver felt excluded by people around him. However, he was ostracising himself through his reluctance to participate. Eventually, people stopped encouraging him to join in.

Sometimes, the Ten reversed reveals a clique from which the person is excluded. This sort of situation may occur in country towns, where a newcomer is considered a visitor ten years after arriving. However, this exclusive clan may be part of the person's work environment, peer group, or any gathering that imposes a code of dress or behaviour on its participants.

In a general reading, the reversed Ten of Cups can describe someone who has not yet found their tribe. This person is familiar with being an outsider, being tolerated instead of valued. It sometimes shows someone who has a partner and family but who is not emotionally available for or connected to them. In a recent reading, this reversed Ten indicated that fundamentally, the person expected to be alone in old age. He preferred his own company and avoided his family whenever possible. If an individual feels excluded from a social group, it's time to return to the previous upright card, the Nine of Cups, to value their own talents and traits. Then it's likely to be easier to find a like-minded group that shares common interests.

In a career layout, the reversed Ten describes an unsupportive career environment. Colleagues are not likely to work cooperatively as a team to plan, create and complete projects. Instead, there might be a sense of competition, poisonous politics or the freezing out of anyone who challenges the hierarchy. Creativity is the first casualty of any environment that is teeming with undercurrents or unspoken resentment. It's time to return to the previous card in the suit, the upright Nine of Cups, to reconnect with one's skills and talents before finding a more supportive workplace. When someone values their own talents and abilities, it's harder for others to derail them. People with poorly developed self-worth are usually hired by organisations who are filled with similar people. Confident people usually steer away from such companies.

In a relationship question, the Ten reversed suggests that this person feels excluded or ignored by a partner. It can indicate repeating a family pattern of being physically close but emotionally distant. Perhaps its time to find new opportunities with like-minded people so that a spouse is not the only source of joy. From shared hobbies to sports and social clubs, opportunities for group interests abound for people ready to participate. Sometimes fresh interests can breathe new life into a routine partnership and inspire more shared activities.

In a health query, the reversed Ten of Cups suggests that continual exhaustion is a consequence of being intuitively sensitive. Living or working with people who bury their fears, desires and resentments can be toxic for highly sensitive individuals. Regular spiritual cleansing, through meditation, swimming, walking amidst nature or yoga practice can restore energy levels. Health issues might stem from unmet emotional needs when the reversed Ten of Cups appears in a health layout. The obvious surface symptoms sometimes include listlessness, exhaustion, loneliness or depression. Spending time away from a toxic group might provide temporary relief. Daily spiritual cleansing usually provides stronger relief. Finding new sources of emotional and spiritual nourishment is the best defence for an emotionally draining work or home environment.

Ten of Swords

The Tens represent completion or the end of a cycle. The Ten of Swords shows how one's thinking determines who a person becomes. When your life ends, you are the sum total of your actions and decisions; as you think, so you become. Events can sculpt an individual's perception of the world but it's also possible to reshape personal attitudes through consciously adjusting daily thinking. It's time to assess personal ideas, beliefs and habits, to determine if they are supportive or destructive.

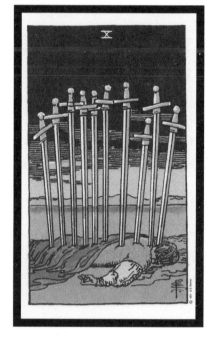

If a person believes that life is dangerous or threatening, deliberately taking note of when life is safe, supportive and nurturing makes it possible to change ingrained perceptions. For instance, our ageing cat fears that food supplies are about to run out at any moment. She constantly chases me for more food, despite her ample proportions. Maybe it has something to do with her previous owner but food definitely dominates her thinking.

When I purchase fresh supplies of cat food, I take her to the cupboard and position the new cans, packets and clean bowls on the lowest shelf where she can see them. One of her favourite activities is a quick stock check while I'm reaching for a bowl and a can. She has a canister for dried food and when I top it up each week from the huge bag stored in her cupboard, she loves to eat directly from the canister. It's as though she has found a crystal clear, cool river after a month in the desert.

Over the years, her food-shortage fear has gradually subsided as she updates her perceptions of life. A few years ago, she learned to reach up to tap me on the arm if she was hungry when I was writing or engrossed in a book or a film. It's as though she has decided, "He's a man. Don't be subtle. Give him a tap and nod when he meets your gaze."

On this card, someone is lying face down on the ground with ten swords plunged into the back and neck. The red cloth symbolises passion and physical energy, both of which are insufficient to change the current situation. The dark sky overhead emphasises the heaviness of this burden. It's the darkest hour before the dawn but the glimmer of light at the horizon heralds the approaching sunrise.

When this card appears, a situation is at its lowest point. However, from death comes rebirth. From the ending of one situation another opportunity appears. By knowing in advance that winter will be colder than usual, a person can prepare for the long haul.

The best course of action for the upright Ten of Swords is to surrender to ongoing conditions and remind yourself that this situation will eventually pass. It is wise to use this time to re-examine one's beliefs about life, as they may have contributed to current circumstances. If the pressure is financial, while the focus is on unpaid bills, there is usually scant attention on new possible sources of income to meet these demands.

In a general reading, this Ten indicates that circumstances have reached their lowest point. Feeling overwhelmed is a natural response to the situation. If this card is in the outcome position, a card can be added for a glimpse of what follows. Despite feeling exhausted and confused, it's worth remembering that personal winters don't last forever.

In a career layout, this Ten signifies a low point. It can represent a recent retrenchment from a job, the collapse of a company or being a scapegoat when the organisation loses a significant contract. It's time to surrender, rest, gather thoughts and examine options before moving forward.

In a relationship question, it's possible that beliefs and attitudes have led to an ending or to the collapse of a relationship. It's worth examining one's thinking before proceeding. It is difficult to assess one's own beliefs but it's possible to notice their results. Sometimes, the Ten of Swords highlights the need for a relationship partner who is more aligned with personal values. When a vegetarian is cooking thick steaks for a partner who feels salad is mere decoration, it can eventually place strain on a relationship.

In a health query, the Ten of Swords highlights spinal issues, along with physical and mental exhaustion. This card sometimes describes back and neck problems. It can also indicate low reserves of energy due to negative beliefs about life. When the reversed Nine of Cups and the reversed Judgement cards also appear in the layout, it can suggest depression. Rest is required to restore energy reserves and it's crucial to guard against circular thinking. This can be a card for obsessively dwelling on past upheavals without any new conclusions. Mental discipline is required at this time.

Ten of Swords Reversed

When the Ten of Swords is reversed, the swords are falling from the person, who appears above the darkness and the burden. This suggests that a difficult period is over but that the individual is unaware of the freedom. It's time to plan a way forward and act on personal goals.

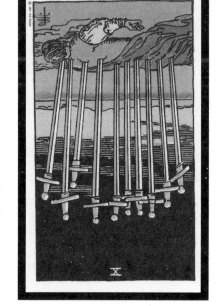

Outdated beliefs or attitudes are stifling potential. It is time to take control. The Ten reversed suggests it is best to return to the upright Nine of Swords to listen to the wisdom of the inner voice through dreams or by consciously using intuition. Accepting that changes are necessary is a significant step towards a return to stability and recognising new opportunities.

The Ten of Swords reversed is like carrying an open umbrella when it has been sunny for days. There is a tendency to react to life as it once was, despite changes in circumstances. It is necessary now to challenge assumptions and beliefs about life so as to see potential opportunities. If an individual cannot see viable options for growth, paying attention to dreams or meditating might provide an inner path forward.

In a general layout, the reversed Ten of Swords describes a low point in a situation. The worst has already happened but the person doesn't yet have sufficient clarity of mind, energy or purpose to get up and move on with life. When Amy asked about her job security, the reversed Ten of Swords suggested she was weary with her position and the workplace. She explained that there had been three rounds of retrenchments and everyone left was exhausted and demoralised. She admitted it didn't matter that she had survived with her job; she was so worn out she no longer cared. I suggested Amy ask if it was wise to apply for new positions with other companies and move on. The cards indicated she'd have a new workplace within three months. Amy emailed the next day to tell me that she had enjoyed her first full night's sleep in eight months.

In a career layout, this card suggests it's time to change a job or career direction. By gracefully surrendering to this ending, it's possible to see new opportunities ahead. Strong dreams and interrupted sleep might persist (a return to the upright Nine of Swords) until the subconscious makes sense of recent events.

In a relationship question, the reversed Ten of Swords represents a low point but that pressure is lifting. It's time to make sense of recent events and move forward. Sometimes, this card indicates the acceptance of an ending of a difficult relationship. In returning to the previous card in the suit, the upright Nine of Swords, dreams can offer clarity that helps resolve unanswered questions.

In a health query, the reversed Ten of Swords indicates that a period of ill-health and low vitality is nearing an end. It's time to think about how life might be in a year from now and how health and vitality can be restored and maintained. Intuitive dreams might offer solutions to health issues at this time.

Ten of Pentacles

The Ten of Pentacles represents material completion. After years or even decades of careful planning and application, the person is able to enjoy the choices associated with personal wealth. Pentacles people generally place great emphasis upon the physical comfort that often accompanies financial security. They work hard to ensure their old age is spent doing what they want and can afford to do.

The card itself highlights material stability. There is a solid house, with family crests on the wall confirming that it is built with old money. The business in the background provides income for a comfortable lifestyle for the family to share. The dogs are focused on the man who is seated; they know the real leader of the household. Being pack animals, they seek out the head of the group or family for guidance, attention and approval.

This individual was once a boy or a Page of Pentacles. He then became the Knight of Pentacles, before finally becoming the King. He sits patiently surveying his domain, clothed in the fine fruits of his persistent effort. However, on the left side of this card, just above the head of the man seated, is a small image of a tower. It suggests this situation has the appearance of stability and permanence but that like everything else in life, it is only transient. The Tower card represents change. It reminds us of the importance of spiritual purpose and suggests that possessions and comforts representing material security are impermanent.

In a general reading, the upright Ten of Pentacles indicates financial stability or a sound investment. There is an awareness that money improves choices, so finance is fundamental to ongoing security. Careful attention is given to how wealth is accumulated and spent to maintain comfort and continuity.

In a career question, this Ten can describe a large organisation with more than 200 employees. Sometimes, it's a corporation, a government department or a smaller branch of a government department such as a hospital. This organisation is multilayered and the person needs to be aware of the structure, the politics and the corporate culture. Large organisations can offer more job security than small businesses, along with bonuses and perks but they don't necessarily suit everyone.

In a career layout, this is an encouraging card, indicating opportunities to advance within a large organisation. Sometimes, in a question about a small business, it can indicate a contract to supply a large organisation that brings regular income.

In a relationship layout, the Ten of Pentacles can signify a strong emphasis on wealth building and financial security. Career and prosperity goals cement a bond with a spouse. It can also describe a relationship based on one partner's financial worth. It can describe a stable relationship built around career goals. Sometimes, the Ten of Pentacles means the couple met through a shared work environment, through a career conference or through one person's occupation. This might be a work colleague, a supplier or a client but the working environment provides the initial meeting place. Despite the image of The Tower, the blue skies shown on the card confirm that life is likely to be balanced for a while. It also describes a partnership that has the benefit of financial wealth and stability.

This is likely to be a comfortable relationship with familiar routines, carefully planned annual holidays and a stable home environment.

In a health query, the Ten of Pentacles suggests being able to afford adequate healthcare or that a workplace pays the staff annual healthcare premiums as part of a wage package. It's also likely that this individual has established a set of constructive health routines that contribute to long-term well-being.

Ten of Pentacles Reversed

The Ten of Pentacles reversed suggests that the tide is receding financially. In a career layout, it can represent a large corporation that is tightening its belt, leading to financial cutbacks and redundancies. In a bid to save money, there may be a freeze on hiring new staff and wage increases. In answer to a question about borrowing money, the appearance of the Ten reversed suggests the loan is not likely to be forthcoming.

The individual is counting on a stability that is ebbing. Bernard invested heavily in his business, counting on the economy to remain in a growth cycle, with demand for his product remaining high. Five months after he had borrowed $600,000, the economy slowed. As a result, demand for his exclusive outdoor furniture halved, leaving him servicing a large debt with high-interest rates and diminished income.

This card reversed represents monetary problems that have far-reaching consequences. However, being aware of a looming financial winter in advance allows deliberate belt-tightening to avoid potential financial burdens.

When the Ten of Pentacles appears reversed in readings for several different clients a week, it can suggest the approach of an economic downturn or confirm an existing recession. The worst week I've seen in over thirty years of tarot readings occurred when, in only two days of readings, this card appeared in layouts at least a dozen times. Between them, six clients had recently lost $23.5 million, mostly in long-term small businesses.

Some had traded successfully for more than twenty-five years and although the tide had turned, they were confronting treacherous conditions ahead.

I instinctively pared back my own spending to weather the approaching storm and in hindsight, I was glad that I did. By postponing large purchases and trimming monthly costs, I was able to ensure a more stable passage through a recession.

In a general reading, the reversed Ten of Pentacles suggests it's time to cut costs and delay major purchases while ensuring several stable sources of income. This card sometimes signifies retrenchment or a period of unemployment. It may indicate under-employment, where a person has two or three part-time jobs but still earns a low wage. It can also describe a period where costs are escalating faster than income.

In a career layout, the reversed ten indicates few opportunities for advancement in an organisation as cost-cutting and staff reductions are likely. In a recession, it can describe the security provided by a large company despite cutbacks and retrenchments. Employees are constricted until the financial storm passes, usually with reduced resources and fewer work colleagues.

In a relationship question, the Ten of Pentacles reversed signifies hectic work demands are restricting opportunities to meet someone new or maintain an existing relationship. Long working hours, regular interstate or overseas travel for work or poor wages and high expenses could be restricting social life. For an existing relationship, the reversed Ten of Pentacles indicates financial difficulties are damaging or undermining a partnership. Monetary issues are a common contributor to relationship breakdowns.

Sometimes, the reversed Ten of Pentacles indicates one or both partners are so consumed with workplace demands they have nothing left for each other at the end of each week. This card appears when one partner works far away and flies home every weekend, or when someone has an overactive sense of duty and responsibility to fulfil a company's unreasonable work demands.

In a health query, the Ten of Pentacles reversed can describe being unable to maintain health and fitness due to unreasonable work demands. It can also suggest that current income is insufficient for building and maintaining stable health. Perhaps workplace practices or office surroundings are depleting one's health. This can range from excessive noise on a nearby construction site to sitting for hours at a desk far from a window beneath acres of fluorescent light in extreme air-conditioning.

The Court Cards:
People, Character Traits and Life Lessons

The court cards are multilayered and combine the four elements in different combinations. It is useful to look at the relationship between the court cards, the suits and the elements of fire, water, air and earth. The suits and court cards are associated with an element.

Fire represents passion, enthusiasm, impatience, an innate desire to shine and a deep sense of competition. It is associated with the suit of Wands. The Knights of each suit represent this element as they display the abundant enthusiasm of fire.

Water represents compassion, empathy, creativity, imagination and a desire for group harmony and support. The suit of Cups is associated with water. The Queens of each suit are linked to water as they are receptive, intuitive and readily adapt to their surroundings.

Air characterises ideas, conversations, the exploration of alternatives, precision and the desire to build networks that thrive through clear communication. This element is associated with the suit of Swords. The Pages of each suit are aligned with air due to their natural curiosity.

Earth symbolises practicality, preserving tradition, financial stability, nourishing food, nature and a desire to thrive financially. Earth is associated with the suit of Pentacles. The Kings of each suit are relatively steadfast and have a practical approach to life and are thus connected to the element of earth.

This means that there are four court cards that contain only one element. These cards represent people who display strong qualities of each element. The Page of Sword is double air, the Knight of Wands represents double fire, the Queen of Cups shows double water while the King of Pentacles is double earth. These cards show the four elements in their purest forms.

	Wands - Fire	Cups - Water	Swords - Air	Pentacles - Earth
The Pages – Air	Page of Wands The airy part of fire. Intellect combined with enthusiasm.	Page of Cups The airy part of water. Intellect combined with compassion.	Page of Swords The airy part of air. Intellect combined with curiosity.	Page of Pentacles The airy part of earth. Intellect combined with practicality.
The Knights - Fire	Knight of Wands The fiery part of fire. Passion combined with enthusiasm.	Knight of Cups The fiery part of water. Enthusiasm combined with compassion.	Knight of Swords The fiery part of air. Enthusiasm combined with intellect.	Knight of Pentacles The fiery part of earth. Enthusiasm combined with practicality.
The Queens - Water	Queen of Wands The watery part of fire. Compassion combined with enthusiasm.	Queen of Cups The watery part of water. Compassion combined with creativity.	Queen of Swords The watery part of air. Compassion combined with curiosity and intellect.	Queen of Pentacles The watery part of earth. Compassion combined with practicality.
The Kings – Earth	King of Wands The earthy part of fire. Practicality combined with enthusiasm.	King of Cups The earthy part of water. Practicality combined with compassion and creativity.	King of Swords The earthy part of air. Practicality combined with intellect.	King of Pentacles The earthy part of earth. Practicality combined with tenacity.

Developing a comprehensive understanding of these elements and how they are combined, allows a proficient tarot reader to decide when a card in a layout describes a person or when it represents an aspect of the client. It also helps the reader to tell the client how these elements apply to the question being asked of the cards.

If I'm describing a King of Pentacles to a client and she can't clearly identify the person, I might list a few of the King's qualities. These include being practical, slow to change, careful with money and someone who thrives on routines. This is a man who'll happily have an identical meal in their preferred restaurant every Saturday evening for five years. He'll want to sit at his regular table, order the same item and arrive and depart at the same times. He enjoys knowing the staff and will be heartbroken if the restaurant closes down. His big adventure in the whole process is alternating between the winter and summer desserts.

In contrast, the Queen of Swords often knows almost everyone at every café she frequents, rarely orders the same dish twice and often asks for food combinations that don't yet exist on the menu. She'll arrive early or late, often pausing to ask a total stranger at a nearby table what they are eating because it looks so tasty and may wander next door to catch up with a friend she noticed through the window. Food for her is simply a backdrop to great conversation.

As the court cards can represent people or situations, they can cause readers confusion. It is the task of a tarot practitioner to decide when a court card represents a person, a situation or an aspect of the individual sitting for a reading. There are a few simple techniques that can help determine the appropriate meaning of these cards when they appear in a layout.

For example, when answering a relationship question for a woman in her early thirties and the upright Page of Pentacles is the answer, there are several possible meanings for this card:

1. It represents a young person. If it is in the outcome position, it may signify a child around the woman or herald the arrival of a baby in the future.

2. The individual might be undertaking some study or mastering unfamiliar tasks at work. When learning new skills, one can feel like a child in the initial stages of applying theory in practice. This card shows the practical application of study that is typically found in the pentacles suit.

3. This card can also highlight an individual's commitment to personal relationships, as well as indicating a change of direction with a partner. This person might feel young or unfamiliar with a new goal but still committed to pursuing it. One client, Jamie, agreed to work for another two years and pay down the mortgage before starting a family with Lucas. Their plan was to be as prepared as possible when she stopped work for a few years to raise children. They decided not to take overseas holidays during this time, to save as much as possible towards the next stage of their lives together.

There are several ways to determine the meaning of a court card in a reading. These include spontaneous decisions, looking at the surrounding cards, adding a qualifier and checking whether your client knows who they are.

Deciding spontaneously

A reader might choose to say silently within, "This King represents ___" and go with the first option that springs to mind. This is an effective intuitive technique for some readers. It becomes more accurate as the reader's intuitive or subconscious mind is increasingly engaged during the reading process.

Look at the surrounding cards

The meaning of a court card can be confirmed by other cards in the layout. In relation to the Page of Pentacles, if there is another page, the person may have two children or be thinking about having a family. If the Eight of Pentacles is also in the layout, it might strengthen the study aspect of the Page of Pentacles. If the Six of Pentacles is also present, the Six might indicate a new job, while the Page suggests that the type of work is different and likely to make the person feel like a novice at first.

Add a qualifier

Add another card to qualify the court card. If it is another court card, it confirms a person. If it is a major arcana card, it can signify that the card represents an aspect of the individual. If the major arcana card reflects the element of the court card, it may provide a clue to the person's identity. For example, the Page of Pentacles combines air and earth. If the qualifying card represents an earth sign (The Hierophant for Taurus, The Hermit for Virgo or The Devil for Capricorn), the card could describe a young person of one of these signs.

If the King of Wands is added to the King of Cups, it could describe two different men or one man with two sides to his nature. He is likely to be cheeky, passionate, impatient and tactless and at other times be compassionate, imaginative and soulful. While he thrives on competitive sports and fast cars, he's also able to run a bath for his partner and add her favourite essential oils when she seems exhausted.

Does your client know them?

Describe the attributes of the court card and ask your client if they sound familiar. If the card is a page, ask whether they or their current partner have any children. If so, then describe the page as a child. If neither has children, consider another meaning for this card.

When a reader decides that a page represents a person and the client disagrees, it is reasonable to remember that initial feeling. For example, when the early instinct suggests a page represents a child, pursue a line of questioning to confirm this intuitive feeling. Sometimes, clients don't consider a teenager to be a child, or the person has a twenty-year-old son who lives at home while completing university. Although the young man has a part-time job and plenty of independence, he still falls within the age and maturity range of a page.

If I sense that a page is a child, I intuitively scan for an image of the child. Sometimes, I'll see a young person playing at home, whereas in other readings I'll only see a few significant features about the individual. These brief images might include curly, dark hair, a soccer ball or a trail of toys and clothes strewn across a living room floor. Sometimes, I'll hear a musical instrument playing or glimpse a child's car seat in the back of a family car.

If I notice an image, I'll usually continue with the reading. If I look within again and the image is still there, I know it's not my imagination. Then I describe what I'm seeing. This intuitive process doesn't usually occur in the first hundred layouts a reader gives. However, with practice, it's possible to train one's intuition to work with the tarot during the interpretation process.

Using intuition isn't a replacement for studying the tarot because the system of the tarot is usually more reliable than clairvoyance. There is a fine line between imagination and intuition, whereas a practical working knowledge of the tarot can help someone give effective readings in almost any circumstances.

The Pages

In the tarot, pages represent children or young people (usually up to about twenty-one years of age). In some circumstances, the age can be extended beyond twenty-one if the person is an immature adult or is feeling young and unskilled when tackling a new situation or project.

The Page of Wands represents a passionate, enthusiastic young person. This is a fearless explorer who is attracted to fire, the outdoors and danger. This individual is likely to be competitive, sporty, messy and self-motivated. Even as young children, they tend to be cheeky and excellent self-marketers.

The Page of Cups symbolises a romantic, emotionally sensitive individual, who anticipates loving someone special and being loved in return. This young person is shy, sensitive, introverted and creative. Cups people are usually patient, kind to animals and inclusive of others.

The Page of Swords reflects a thoughtful or intellectual young person who wants to understand everything. Having a naturally curious nature inclines a swords type towards science, research, history and solving puzzles. This is a sociable individual who thrives in groups, enjoys meeting people and loves reading, talking and debating. They love to ask questions. When my son was five, he was continually asking questions, to the point where I'd say, "Oh, you've been reading the book of questions again."

The Page of Pentacles embodies a realistic, sensible young person who anticipates eventual material rewards of study, effort and commitment. This individual is usually conservative, responsible and moderate in their tastes. Even as children, pentacles people are often practical with finances, saving diligently, working hard and insisting on value for money when making purchases. One eighteen-year-old Page of Pentacles I know prefers to pay cash for everything, so he can see his hard-earned money going out of his wallet as he spends it. It makes him more aware of his spending habits and provides time to reconsider spontaneous purchases.

Traditionally, pages brought correspondence between courtiers, so when three or more appear in a layout, news is imminent. In modern times, news might arrive via a phone call, a letter, SMS, email or social media. When a greater number of these pages are reversed, responses are likely to be delayed.

Page of Wands

The Page of Wands is an enthusiastic, energetic, self-motivated individual who needs to have a goal or a destination for motivation. This person relishes a challenge and without an objective, can become despondent or restless and argumentative. This young child or teenager enjoys sports, outdoor activities and competitive pursuits.

In this image, someone stands grasping a wand, staring off into the distance, anticipating adventures ahead. Blue skies promise a clear path to a goal. A dominant colour in this card is orange, suggesting that this individual is enthusiastic and passionate about achievement.

The salamanders on the tunic represent the element of fire — a traditional symbol for this element. All the court cards in the wands suit have a desert as a backdrop. Traditional desert dwellers in the different parts of the world were nomadic people. The open spaces suited restless natures. In astrology, the fire signs are Aries, Leo and Sagittarius. This Page might not be one of those signs but will usually display fire qualities, including a love of sports or physical activities, self-motivation towards goals, innate competitiveness, impatience, playfulness, hard work, boldness, a desire to travel and a sunny temperament.

PAGE of WANDS.

This is the small child who loves direct involvement and having the freedom to explore. When a friend's son was fifteen months old, we took him to the beach in winter. We thought a walk along the beach might be beneficial, so we rugged up against the wind. As we walked along the deserted beach, Kyle struggled to be released so he could get into the water.

He protested so vigorously that his mum stripped off his clothes and allowed him to walk in. He stumbled towards the oncoming waves, free at last from parental restrictions. As soon as he reached the water, a wave engulfed him and he froze. The icy cold water gushed around him and he shot us a dark, accusing look suggesting, "How could you let me walk into this cold water alone?"

The wands energy made him want to be free but he was unaware of the consequences of his actions. It obviously seemed like a good idea to him at the time. When wands people finally reach their goals, they have often overcome many more obstacles than they first anticipated. However, this rarely prevents them from pursuing another goal. They don't rest on their laurels and savour the moments of achievement but prefer to be preparing the next adventure.

In a general reading, the Page of Wands can represent planning a trip, moving house or changing jobs. It concerns that time in life when movement or change is required to add energy and enthusiasm to life. It can describe a passionate, enthusiastic young person who enjoys outdoor pursuits.

In a career layout, it indicates starting afresh and learning through direct involvement. This is the person who is unafraid to retrain for a new career at any age. "How difficult can it be?" they ask, while spontaneously leaping forward to the next challenge. It sometimes indicates a career involving children or young people, such as school teaching, sports coaching or childcare.

In a relationship question, this card describes innocence and the anticipation and passion for exploring new horizons. It can also suggest a relationship opportunity that is new and unfamiliar. Sometimes it describes a young person influencing the relationship.

In a health reading, this upright Page usually indicates robust health with plenty of energy. Being a wands page, this individual often takes on too much for an extended period, before collapsing with exhaustion for a few days. Then the cycle begins again. Wands people enjoy being busy. It can point to a new health routine, such as a daily walk or regular gym visits.

As a person, this card describes a passionate, enthusiastic and impatient young person. Naturally competitive, this individual can be self-motivated to pursue desired goals and relishes the challenges involved. To motivate this person, simply insist that they are too young, too short or incapable of attempting a challenge and then stand well clear as they leap into it.

As a situation, this Page indicates beginning a new project with enthusiasm and eagerness. It sometimes points to a willingness to learn and gain practical skills by taking action. This is often a venture that is taken without a clear plan. Wands people are usually too impatient to spend time planning an assignment; they prefer doing something active, instead. They enjoy a challenge and the constant movement that new goals provide. To wands people, life is only as good as the next challenge.

As an aspect of the client, this card can describe a person who feels young and unskilled in a new job or situation or when tackling an unfamiliar project. However, this individual is passionate, enthusiastic and eager to begin.

Page of Wands Reversed

The Page of Wands reversed describes an impatient, energetic, restless individual, whose attention span is short and who might even be hyperactive. This Page reversed needs a wholesome diet with plenty of regular exercise, preferably outdoors. A fiery Page of Wands reversed can become troublesome when kept indoors too long, due to excess physical energy that needs an outlet.

Sometimes, the Page of Wands reversed highlights a desire to move on, even though current issues remain unresolved. Wanting a new job may be an attempt at escaping the present one, however there is usually insufficient thought about what exactly is unfulfilling in the current position. It's often easier for wands people to act than to sit around thinking about why they are unfulfilled. They are naturally active, restless people.

The Page of Wands reversed indicates setbacks in plans. This may be due to a delay in news reaching the person or to other commitments needing to be fulfilled prior to taking the next step. Instead of pacing around like a caged animal, this person might ask what can be done here and now, while waiting for the next chapter to begin. Keeping busy reduces the frustration of delays.

When reversed, wands cards highlight the undesirable wands traits of impatience, tactlessness, anger and a cavalier attitude to paperwork. When the Page of Wands appears reversed in a layout, it can suggest current delays are the result of cutting corners, poor planning or ineffectual budgeting.

In a general reading, the Page of Wands reversed indicates poor planning and impatience for results, plus a need for endless goals and challenges. If it describes a client who is over twenty-one years of age, it indicates immaturity. For these individuals, success must be huge, loud and witnessed by all. It's the purple-velour-covered Rolls Royce with a gold-plated radiator. More is always better for these individuals. Subtlety is rarely their style.

In a career layout, the person might be impatient to change jobs or move on to a new project but there are likely to be delays. Better planning might have avoided the current setbacks. Sometimes, restlessness makes this individual prefer short contracts or project work, with regular changes in location, type of work or circumstances. There is an innate fear of routines.

In a relationship question, this Page reversed can describe an individual pursuing a relationship for the challenge, without any real idea of what it might be like to live with that partner long term. The conquest or the process of securing another person's emotional commitment is more alluring than what follows.

In a health query, this card suggests an individual is scattering their reserves of energy in too many directions to be effective in any one area. It's time to slow down, conserve energy and delegate some tasks to others. These fire types usually wear themselves out because they refuse to acknowledge they don't have the same energy levels they once possessed. Even a twenty-year-old wands person doesn't have the same energy levels as a five-year-old.

As a person, the Page of Wands reversed describes someone young, who lacks discipline. This person begins new projects and then abandons them at the first setback or when boredom sets in. Wands individuals often lack the persistence of pentacles (earth) types. Speed and agility are preferred to stoic perseverance.

As a situation, this card indicates a delayed start to a project or a lack of preparation for the specific task. It also suggests someone who has not yet mastered the lesson for fire — pacing oneself to complete undertakings. Impatience makes the person squander energy. This scattered exuberance is not often harnessed towards completing specific projects.

As an aspect of the client, this card indicates someone who is impatient, restless and immature. It sometimes describes a young person who has surplus energy that isn't channelled into productive pursuits, someone who prefers computer games to team sports or dreaming instead of doing.

Page of Cups

When the Page of Cups represents a young person, it is usually someone who is soft-hearted, imaginative and emotionally sensitive to surroundings. Often shy at first meeting, this Page warms to others slowly, valuing friendships and relationships greatly. The card can also describe a young person who is naturally nurturing, and therefore patient with babies or toddlers.

The Page of Cups is physically and emotionally delicate, creative and usually needs time to reflect and restore inner peace every day. The Page on the card stands on the sand, staring into a cup. Cloudy skies above suggest clouded thinking. This Page is romantic and sentimental, with fuzzy thinking that tends to soften reality. The fish in the cup represents the element of water.

This Page can represent a water sign person (Cancer, Scorpio or Pisces) or someone with water qualities, who generally approaches life through feelings, intuition and creativity. This is not an energetic risk-taker like the Page of Wands but a slightly timid person who is intuitively tuned to the current moods of dominant members of the immediate environment.

The Page of Cups can also represent an offer, usually an emotional opportunity. There may be the beginning of a romantic relationship or a chance to join a group of like-minded people who provide inner nourishment.

In a general reading, the Page of Cups can describe a sensitive young person. Naturally creative and sympathetic, these individuals usually prefer one or two close friends rather than crowds of people, unlike the fire Page who loves an audience or mingling with crowds. This water Page is romantic, sentimental, shy and nurturing. This card also represents an emotional opportunity. It might involve a friendship, a creative partnership or a love relationship.

In a career layout, this Page indicates a creative opportunity. This might be a chance for a writer to collaborate with an illustrator or two musicians pairing to write and produce songs. It can indicate an offer that enables this individual to be creative in the workplace. Sometimes, in a specific career question, the upright Page of Cups indicates a job offer.

In a relationship question, this card can suggest a new romantic offer. If this Page describes a male, he is sometimes invisible to women in his twenties because he lacks the passion and charisma of the Page of Wands. However, in his thirties, women wanting to have families are generally more appreciative of his subtle qualities, seek his softness, sensitivity and nurturing strengths. Mature women recognise how patient he (now a Knight or a King of Cups) is with children. Sometimes this page indicates a soft-natured child around this relationship.

In a health query, this card generally indicates that balanced health depends on the person having a harmonious home and workplace. Cups people are extremely sensitive to the emotions of others, so they need to avoid workplaces that make them uncomfortable. In a health reading, this Page suggests problems with the feet. It sometimes highlights stress-related health issues that respond well to regular meditation. It also points to a period of psychic or spiritual development stimulated by a focus on inner needs.

As a person, the Page of Cups describes a sensitive, creative young person. This individual usually has a vivid imagination and enjoys escaping everyday life through books, music or films. Innately shy, this Page warms up to new people slowly and usually has only one or two close friends.

As a situation, this card can indicate an offer. It's usually an emotional or creative opportunity involving a new friendship, relationship or creative partnership. It sometimes describes intuitive development, especially in combination with The High Priestess or The Moon. The High Priestess indicates intuition resulting from calming the conscious mind, whereas The Moon indicates insightful dreams that point the way forward.

As an aspect of the client, the upright Page of Cups emphasises going within to decide what is best when making a major decision. Cups people are usually well-connected to their intuition. It sometimes suggests taking time to reflect on one's needs and motivations. This person does not rush forward to embrace new opportunities but prefers to consider the pros and cons of each new opening.

Page of Cups Reversed

The Page of Cups reversed describes a dreamy, passive young person, who is content to imagine life as they prefer it to be, rather than face harsh reality and physically do what is necessary to create a fulfilling life. Dreaming is easier than action for a reversed Page of Cups.

With encouragement, this individual might find a suitable outlet for their vivid imagination through writing, painting, music or nurturing small children. Basically, when the Page of Cups is reversed, it suggests a more realistic view of life is necessary before achieving personal goals.

The Page of Cups reversed can also signify dissolving a relationship or feeling uncertain about self-worth and personal contribution in a relationship. They might be waiting for news to confirm acceptance of an application to study a creative subject but when the Page is reversed, this news is delayed or is not affirmative. When it appears in response to a question, the Page reversed is a no, suggesting disappointing news or setbacks with plans.

In a general reading, this card indicates obstructions to an offer, usually in a creative endeavour. It describes waiting on news about an opportunity, such as a job application, a bank loan or a marriage proposal. However, all is not straightforward. Perhaps the individual has unrealistic expectations about how much happiness this new opportunity will provide.

In a career question, it can describe delays with news, a rejection of a job application or the cancellation of plans regarding a creative project at work. If the person is nervously awaiting a response to a job application, it might be wise to apply for other positions while marking time. Then, if the news is negative, other opportunities are already being considered.

In a relationship question, this reversed Page suggests uncertainty regarding a partnership or waiting to hear back from someone who is ambivalent about making a commitment. It can also describe someone whose assessment of a current or potential affiliation is based more on hope or fantasy than facts. This individual may be unable to release a previous love so they can focus on a current relationship opportunity. Sentiment about the past is limiting present possibilities. There is generally a nostalgic, soft reminiscence about previous partnerships. It's an example of the term 'distance lends enchantment.'

In a health query, the reversed Page of Cups suggests denial about current health issues or a hope to return to full health without a solid foundation for this unrealistic expectation. Sometimes, it can signify avoiding a medical examination because the person doesn't want to hear bad news. It also indicates avoiding a depressing emotional environment by retreating into dreams and fantasies. While this person is engrossed in a book or a film, current disappointments seem far away. Sometimes, an individual is exhausted from enduring continuous obstacles and more bad news is likely to pre-empt a plunge into despair.

As a person, the reversed Page of Cups can describe a young individual who has retreated within to escape the harsh realities of life. Perhaps this person is depressed or processing an emotional loss or a creative setback. Sometimes, it describes emotional immaturity, whereby a person is dreaming of a creative life without making sufficient practical effort to ensure it happens.

As a situation, this card can indicate waiting for an offer, such as a new job or hoping for a text or an email after a first date. The offer is delayed or unlikely when this Page is reversed in a layout. Sometimes it describes the process of engaging in fantasies instead of taking practical steps towards building a comfortable life.

As an aspect of the client, this card can describe someone who is unrealistic about the likely outcome of a situation. This person is hoping for a clear-cut conclusion without having put in the required effort. They are wishing rather than being proactive. There isn't a solid foundation upon which to build when this card occurs reversed.

Page of Swords

The Page of Swords represents a talkative, curious, mentally restless young individual, whose mind is constantly searching for new information and understanding. This person usually benefits from time spent away from a television or a computer screen, perhaps venturing outdoors to do something physical. However, swords people are less inclined to physical pursuits, so supervision might be required to ensure they discharge some of their excess mental energy in a physical way. These individuals might benefit from playing sports, exercising, walking a dog or helping out in the garden.

PAGE of SWORDS.

A self-reliant side to this Page (and to all the swords court cards) is that when they want advice, a discount on a purchase or some information, they are rarely shy in asking others for assistance. They know the value of communicating their needs.

In this image, the earth beneath the person's feet is out of proportion, suggesting that the ground is a long way down and the individual is up in the air. Birds fly overhead and clouds hover, as the Page clasps a sword in both hands and gazes wistfully off into the distance. The birds signify the mind's capacity to perceive challenges from an objective viewpoint (a bird's eye view) when searching for solutions.

The red boots suggest passion, while the purple tunic shows the need to still the mind (purple being a colour for spirituality) in order to comprehend universal truths. The yellow clothing signifies mental energy, while the trees bending in the wind in the background symbolise that mental energy is best harnessed or disciplined to be effective. Wild, chaotic thinking needs to be calmed. Although imagination is a powerful tool for inspiration, allowing it to soar unchecked can fuel confusion and fantasy.

If this card appears in answer to a question, the Page of Swords indicates that the person is dreaming of solutions without a solid grounding in reality. Perhaps intellectual energy is being dissipated by talking endlessly about goals, rather than acting to achieve them. This Page can highlight the value of making a list of ideas or choices for moving towards a suitable solution. Practical results are much more likely after considering all options.

The Page of Swords also represents tossing ideas around and playing with words and concepts until a different viewpoint is reached. Sometimes, a misheard sentence can completely change the meaning. I recently overheard a four-year-old state, "A lemon can't change its spots." I immediately thought that as the leopard risks becoming extinct, that saying might enter common usage.

In a general reading, the Page of Swords can suggest a flight interstate or overseas. It also describes a person with a healthy curiosity and excellent social skills. It suggests ideas that haven't yet been tested or developed into plans. This card sometimes describes a workable idea that requires refinement before it can be applied. It's the broad brushstrokes but without the finer detail.

In a career layout, this Page can signify job-related travel. This may be an overseas or interstate trip for a conference, or the individual could work as a pilot or a flight attendant. It sometimes signifies career-related news that is likely to be encouraging, as the card is upright. It also indicates exploring employment options before deciding on a direction.

In a relationship question, this card describes someone young (up to twenty-one years of age), who is talkative, curious and adept at negotiating to have their needs met. This person values communication skills, clever use of language and is best suited to a quick-minded, sociable partner. Sometimes this page indicates news regarding a relationship or a young person who is influencing a partnership.

In a health query, the upright Page of Swords is a beneficial card, indicating encouraging news about health or a personal network to discover ways of building and maintaining health. Sometimes, this card indicates the person knows what to do to maintain stable health but finds it difficult to translate this knowledge into daily habits.

As a person, the Page of Swords describes a quick-minded individual with plenty of ideas but limited practical knowledge. This sociable person is competent at networking, in conversation and when developing theories but there is often insufficient effort when attempting goals. This young person wants to be a manager or a consultant rather than someone who exerts themselves to apply theories.

As a situation, this card describes an idea or a concept that may require more refinement before it works as planned. It can also indicate a phone call, letter, text or email communication. As an answer to a question, it usually suggests an affirmative response.

As an aspect of the client, this card shows someone with plenty of ideas, effective social skills and the ability to communicate concepts and plans through the written or spoken word. It can describe the process of negotiating to have one's needs met. This is a person who is capable of finding solutions to obstacles and negotiating workable outcomes with people who oppose their personal plans.

Page of Swords Reversed

The Page of Swords reversed represents undisciplined thinking resulting in chaos or dissipated energy. It symbolises someone using words without sufficient thought of the power they have to hurt or confuse others. This card can describe gossip or conversation for its own sake. This young person can be extremely talkative, making family members wish there was a mute button.

It can also represent ideas that are poorly thought out. In written form, this is the five-page feature story that would have more impact and clarity if presented as a single, succinct paragraph. It's the long, rambling talk or lecture that leaves the audience wondering if the speaker is being paid by the word. Or, the fifteen-page resume sent to a potential employer who receives 280 applicants for one position.

An example of the kind of idea represented by this Page reversed is the concept a friend laughingly presented to me. It was that humankind is too obsessed with the pursuit of money and that we should be more like the birds in a forest. The birds don't worry about money and yet still survive. This overlooks the reality that birds spend most of their waking time feeding themselves while trying to avoid predators.

As humans have fewer predators, we have more waking time to devote to other pursuits, such as learning to speak and write, travelling or building a house that isn't twenty metres up a tree. Another example is an acquaintance of mine saying recently, "I never repeat gossip, so listen carefully."

In answer to a question, the Page of Swords reversed suggests delays in receiving news (similar to all the pages), a poorly thought-out plan or a presentation that is too wordy. It's time to revise plans. The sword in this card needs to be used to cull unnecessary words, ideas and concepts, distilling a carefully crafted plan into a useable form.

In a general reading, the reversed Page of Swords can represent travel by air. It also indicates delayed news or unrealistic expectations about the acceptance of an application. If describing a person, this card represents a young person who is talkative, curious, mentally agile and sociable, who prefers ideas to action.

In a career layout, this reversed Page describes a poorly thought-out plan or unrealistic expectations. The theory has little connection with reality. This occurred one day on a business trip interstate. I ordered a typical bacon, eggs, toast and tea breakfast in a hotel restaurant and it was served in a slightly curved bowl. I wondered if the chef had ever seen people eat bacon and eggs before. It was so absurd that I took a photo of it and emailed it to a few friends. One swords person ran with the absurdity of the situation by suggesting that I ask for it to be put through a blender and served in a tall glass, toast included. Sometimes it indicates delayed news regarding a job or a career project.

In a relationship question, this reversed card sometimes describes words that don't match actions. It might indicate a partner who is quick to make promises but slow to deliver. This person might be keen to make plans for the weekend but then cancel at the last minute. Reversed, the swords court cards can describe people who are flaky and personify the phrase, 'Talk is cheap.'

In a health query, the Page reversed can indicate waiting for news about health, chaotic thinking or anxiety, plus a need for physical exercise to bring the person from a purely abstract perspective back to the physical body. It can also describe incessant worrying about health problems without undergoing tests to confirm or eliminate issues. Swords people often feel anxious when stressed, so this is sometimes a card for worry, pressure and mental confusion in a health question.

As a person, the reversed Page of Swords describes someone who is erratic, mentally quick but unfocused and unable to plan a project to its conclusion. This young person might be anxious, nervous and quick to think of worst-case scenarios when attempting something new. This is an individual who might exhibit a very short attention span, constantly fidget and is easily overstimulated. It's not unusual for this person to have three or four electronic devices going simultaneously, while not being properly focused on any of them.

As a situation, this card can describe awaiting a delayed response. Perhaps a project cannot move forward until the person receives a go-ahead from a bank, a supplier or a partner. It also describes a hastily structured scheme that is unlikely to succeed without revisions to the original plans.

As an aspect of the client, the reversed Page of Swords describes someone who is ungrounded or not centred in reality. This individual might have ideas and schemes that are simply not achievable without more careful planning and preparation. It could be a person who sells everything to buy a small hotel, having never previously worked in hospitality. When the shock of what is required sets in, this individual replaces this goal with a new idea. This person needs to realise that ideas are worthless unless they can work practically in the physical world.

The reversed Page of Swords sometimes describes someone who is endlessly hopeful, despite previous mistakes. It was described simply by a swords friend at the fourth marriage of his brother: "It's a triumph of hope over experience," he said, "but it's nice to dress up and the champagne is always first-rate."

Page of Pentacles

The Page of Pentacles represents a serious, responsible young person who is prepared to work diligently and study to secure a solid income. Pentacles people enjoy material comforts, such as food and belongings that accord them status. They usually maintain their possessions carefully.

In this image, a young person stands in a field holding one pentacle and examining it closely. The bright sky above suggests that all is well with the world and that this is a tranquil moment spent planning a path to prosperity. The red hat and scarf highlight the passionate pursuit of material prosperity. Even at a young age, this Page is practical and financially sensible. The green tunic suggests awareness of the need for balance and harmony between work and rest.

This is a card for a conservative young person. The suit of pentacles describes the earth signs in astrology. These include Taurus, Virgo and Capricorn people. However, this card can describe a young person of any astrological sign who is practical by nature. It simply means that basic pragmatic, earthy characteristics are prominent.

PAGE of PENTACLES.

When this card appears in answer to a question, the Page of Pentacles suggests that success usually comes after mastering new skills. This card indicates a dedication to developing the expertise necessary to achieve goals. The appearance of the Page shows a novice who is dedicated to mastering additional skills. For example, when commencing a new job, many people may feel like the Page of Pentacles while attempting to gain the required expertise for the position.

In a general reading, the Page describes a young person (usually up to twenty-one years of age) with a mature, sensible, responsible attitude to life. This person enjoys nature, regular routines and thrives where there are clear rules and boundaries. Sometimes this is a card for commitment to study, in order to advance in career. It can also describe a person who is saving for an important goal, such as a new home, a course of study or an investment.

In a career layout, the Page of Pentacles indicates study or dedication to learning new skills, with a view to long-term career success. It sometimes describes a person who feels unfamiliar with workplace systems and requirements and is steadily acquiring the necessary skills for performing well in the job.

In a relationship question, this Page can suggest a child in the relationship or someone thinking of having a family. It's a card for considering commitment for the long term. If it represents a relationship partner, this person is often mature and usually considers the long-term consequences of decisions and actions.

In a health query, this card indicates a commitment to learning how to balance and maintain stable health. It involves a sensible approach to diet and exercise. Determination to build and maintain lasting health can involve regular physical activity, ensuring sufficient sleep every night, plus disciplined food intake. This person is aware that moderate living and consistent exercise can improve long-term health.

As a person, the Page of Pentacles represents a serious, responsible young person. This cautious individual has a strong work ethic and understands the value of money. He or she carefully maintains personal belongings, keeps promises and is usually a motivated student. This is the eight-year-old who whispers discreetly into a parent's ear, "Mum, that is your third drink and we do have guests."

As a situation, this card can indicate news about employment, such as a job offer or a promotion. It sometimes describes study and learning, especially in an unfamiliar subject. The person might be forty-five years of age but feels young and unskilled when returning to study to improve career prospects. It can also indicate commitment to saving towards a worthwhile goal. This might be a car or a home purchase or an investment to secure a better financial future.

As an aspect of the client, the upright Page of Pentacles indicates a focus on financial matters or career-related study to improve income. It can indicate commitment to learning new skills (we sometimes feel young or page-like when we are unfamiliar with a new process). It represents practical commitment with an awareness of the sustained effort required to achieve goals. It also shows an awareness that money allows for choices. The greater the income or net worth, the broader range of choices are available in life.

Page of Pentacles Reversed

The Page of Pentacles reversed represents a young person who is materially hungry, often mistaking material wealth for peace of mind. However, it can also suggest a need to lighten the workload to achieve goals. Sometimes, it implies immaturity; perhaps this is the child who is given toys and trinkets instead of time, attention and love and soon learns to manipulate the innate guilt of parents to secure even more valuables.

When upright, the image in this card shows a circle containing a star with the tip pointing upwards. This highlights the need to keep private passions and desires in check while pursuing goals. When the card is reversed, the star points downwards, suggesting desires presently dominate thinking. In the short term, this individual might decide that social life is more important than study or other long-term goals.

It shows a lack of commitment to mastering the necessary skills to achieve objectives. This person might have taken on too much or be unclear about the right path to achieve desired results. Sometimes, immediate desires are leading this individual away from long-term aims.

When this card appears in answer to a question, the Page of Pentacles reversed suggests being unsuccessful in the pursuit of goals because of intermittent commitment to purpose. Time spent engaged in physical activities such as exercise, sports or gardening can help to rebalance this person.

In a general reading, the reversed Page of Pentacles indicates a lack of success due to inadequate commitment to objectives. It can represent concluding a course or abandoning study in favour of short-term desires. Sometimes it shows a person who pursues short-term rewards over long-term objectives.

In a career layout, the reversed Page of Pentacles describes a lack of purpose or sense of obligation regarding a current occupation. This individual is simply passing through and has no intention of pursuing long-term employment with the current organisation. It can also indicate unrealistic career expectations. The person expects a smooth ride all the way to the top with minimal effort. It's often someone who expects to be discovered and mentored by leaders in the field. The dedication and commitment necessary to build and maintain skills are sometimes missing when the card is reversed.

In a relationship question, this reversed Page can signify a lack of ongoing commitment to a partnership or to relationships generally. It can indicate a child or the desire for a child or a family. It occasionally describes a young person who is causing upheaval in a relationship. It might be a child from a previous relationship attempting to derail a new parental relationship. In rare instances, the reversed Page of Pentacles might point to a person who is considering ending a marriage or a long-term relationship because the spouse is a financial drain. Perhaps the partner is a chronic gambler or has poor financial habits.

In a health query, there is limited effort or planning regarding fitness. Short-term solutions are often favoured over discovering causes of health issues. It's easier for this individual to take antacid tablets after every meal than make fundamental dietary changes. It shows an unrealistic perspective in the areas of physical health and well-being.

As a person, the reversed Page of Pentacles describes someone who desires material possessions but is not aware of the effort required to earn and then maintain them. In a tarot reading, a client agreed she had been interested in investing in rental property but after purchasing two houses, she was disappointed to discover they required maintenance. She sold them two years later without making any profit. Finally, in her late sixties, she wondered how she might secure her financial future. I pondered how much those houses might be worth today and what annual rents they'd command.

A young pentacles person enjoys routines and stability when provided by someone else. This individual is likely to tell friends that investing is easy, overlooking the assistance received while still living with parents, rent-free for decades. When reversed, this Page lacks the practicality of the upright Page, wanting luxuries without the resolve and persistent effort needed to acquire and maintain them.

As a situation, this card indicates a lack of commitment to a job or to financial plans. This is the person who embarks on a spending spree after abandoning a five-year budget, twelve weeks into the process. It sometimes describes someone who is worried about job security or whether a workplace contract will be renewed when it expires. Sometimes this reversed Page simply describes someone who has given up on a current job or income source and is search for something new.

As an aspect of the client, this card can describe a person who is experiencing financial upheaval or is considering leaving a job. The individual is usually worried about impending change, particularly financial upheaval, as pentacles people thrive on financial stability, routines and continuity.

The Knights

The four knights of the tarot represent people, aspects of a client or situations. As people, they are usually young men between twenty and thirty years of age. When a man in his fifties appears in a reading as a knight, he is usually emotionally immature.

The Knight of Wands is enthusiastic, energetic and forthright. The Knight of Cups is romantic, emotional and sensitive. The Knight of Swords is a talkative, curious communicator and the Knight of Pentacles is serious, practical and responsible.

When the knights represent situations rather than people, the Knight of Wands can suggest movement and travel. Wands symbolise fire energy which is an inspirational, outgoing, active, warm, sociable perspective.

The Knight of Cups represents an offer or an emotional opportunity. This Knight can also symbolise the choice between the cups and the wands paths in life. If this young person chooses the path of the cups, he'll eventually mature into a King of Cups. He'll also learn to discipline inspiration and creativity to produce tangible products or services. If instead the wands path is chosen, he'll eventually mature into a King of Wands. This means he'll struggle with pacing himself until he understands how to discipline passion and enthusiasm to pursue projects to completion.

The Knight of Swords represents the need to act swiftly or to *carpe diem* (seize the day). This card represents a combination of fire (the knights) and air (swords). As air fans fire, this individual is successful when they have an idea first and run with it to market before competitors know what is happening.

This knight can also symbolise the choice between the swords and the wands paths. If he chooses the path of the swords, he'll eventually mature into a King of Swords. He'll realise the power of words to inspire, provoke, soothe or win an argument. This path also involves understanding that ideas are powerful only when they are acted upon with precise planning. If he chooses the wands path, he'll eventually mature into a King of Wands. This path involves discovering how inspiration and action can bring about surprising results.

The Knight of Pentacles signifies remaining aware of the long-term consequences of actions. This combination of fire (the knight cards) and earth (the pentacles suit) makes this Knight the hardest working and most persistent of the four in pursuit of goals. While other knights are thinking a day, a week or a year ahead, before his twenty-fifth birthday, this knight has carefully planned a career and investment path right through to his well-funded retirement. He usually combines action with practical purpose. He'll work hard to earn money to invest, build wealth and ensure security and stability in old age.

The Knight of Pentacles is unlikely to be as close to the forefront of change as the Knight of Swords, partly because he understands that serious return on investment occurs when a product or service is offered to the mainstream, not the trend-setters.

Three or more knights in a layout represent academies, study and learning. Their appearance signifies undertaking study, a part-time course or even a correspondence course. It is organised study, rather than learning through reading books or gaining practical, personal skills.

Knight of Wands

The Knight of Wands is an enthusiastic, forthright man, usually under thirty years of age, who is impatient and hasty. If he is older in years but displays the same characteristics, he is likely to be immature. Sometimes this knight represents a Sagittarian person, especially if the Temperance card is also in the layout. In these instances, the person may be male, female and of any age. This Knight is better suited to short bursts of activity than to prolonged application, as his attention wanes when goals seem too far away. He doesn't yet have the maturity or discipline to pace himself for the long haul. When he has developed this sense of

KNIGHT of WANDS.

self-discipline, he'll eventually become the King of Wands.

The image on the card shows a young person straddling a rearing horse. The Knight of Wands is energetically pursuing dreams or goals, clothed in a tunic covered in salamanders, representing the element of fire. The predominant colour in this card is orange, suggesting passion and enthusiasm, playfulness and inspiration. This individual usually has these qualities well developed. The Knight is generally assertive, sometimes bossy, warm, optimistic and competitive. This person is a risk-taker with a short attention span and sometimes a quick fuse.

All the knights represent the fire part of their suit, and since the wands suit is the sign of fire, this Knight is the fiery part of fire. This means he exhibits most fire-sign qualities. These include enthusiasm, eagerness for adventure, a need to pursue goals and often a level of honesty that borders on tactlessness. The Knight of Wands describes a Sagittarian person when accompanied by the Temperance card. This Knight is dynamic, idealistic and independent.

This card represents moving to another place to live or to work. It is an optimistic card, one for pursuing goals and rising to challenges. It can represent travel overseas when accompanied by the Eight of Wands, Six of Swords or The World card, or travel with work if it appears in a career layout.

In a general reading, this Knight describes action and the pursuit of goals with abundant self-confidence. It is a card of movement, appearing when a person leaves a home, changes job or sets off travelling. This is someone who rarely takes no for an answer. Sometimes, being told something can't be done is perceived as a challenge to do exactly that. It's also a card for travel, especially in a layout with Temperance, The World, The Star, the Ace of Wands, the Three of Wands, the Eight of Wands, the Six of Swords or the Page of Swords.

In a career layout, this card can describe a job conducted outdoors or a career where regular travel is required. Sales or marketing are suitable careers for wands people because they appeal to their sense of competition to achieve more sales than their peers or colleagues. Fire people are naturally competitive. Sometimes this Knight indicates a change of jobs.

In a relationship question, this Knight describes a cheeky, passionate, enthusiastic young person who enjoys the thrill of the chase more than the commitment of a relationship. Potential partners find this individual reckless and even slightly dangerous but usually believe training and taming is possible. A Knight of Wands is basically a risk-taker. This person usually enjoys travelling and spending time outdoors with a partner in challenging pursuits, such as hang gliding, parachuting, hiking, rock climbing, canoeing and white-water rafting.

In a health query, the Knight of Wands represents the hips and thighs. Accidents resulting from clumsiness are also likely with this card. Generally, it is an encouraging card for health when upright. It shows the stamina and vitality to bounce back from illness. Because wands people enjoy risky outdoor pursuits, they often suffer cuts, bruises and occasionally broken limbs when calculated risks fail. However, they usually bounce back, as they are naturally fit types with plenty of energy and exuberance. This individual is likely to attend the gym or have other regular fitness routines.

As a person, the Knight of Wands describes a young individual, usually between twenty-one and thirty years, who is passionate and competitive and who relishes taking risks. This person usually enjoys travel and learning through direct experience and can be cheeky, impatient and forthright. Some people are attracted to his wild, untamed persona, believing they can smooth away any rough edges. These individuals are often successful in careers that involve sales, marketing, teaching or coaching, as they are motivated self-starters who love a challenge.

As a situation, this card can describe a trip or a relocation to a new home. It can also highlight a person who is actively working towards their goals. It can indicate a Sagittarius person, especially if the Temperance card also appears in the layout. In response to repeated frustrations or a lack of achievable objectives, this card suggests it is time to look beyond one's circumstances for new opportunities. This might involve looking outside a current organisation for a new job, beyond a present city for a new home or to foreign shores for a new relationship.

As an aspect of the client, the upright Knight of Wands describes movement from one job to another or from one home to a different location or even from one relationship to another. As an answer to a question, it sometimes indicates that a forthright, active approach is required to achieve success.

Knight of Wands Reversed

The Knight of Wands reversed is extremely impatient, with a limited attention span. This person is often only capable of commitment to really short-term goals, needing immediate rewards for personal effort. When this card is reversed, it highlights someone who is immature, preferring to scatter energy recklessly and talk about goals rather than reaching for them. The reversed Knight of Wands describes a person who is rarely thorough or cautious. When frustrated, this person can become tactless, angry and impulsive.

Delays in travel or in reaching goals are shown by the Knight reversed. Sometimes, this is due to the lack of a steady pace. This individual is easily distracted and tends to work hard in fits and starts, rashly scattering energy. It can also describe a course of action that is foolhardy or irresponsible. When faced with obstacles or the need for greater commitment, this person often moves on to a new, more promising goal, justifying actions by claiming the new objective is part of his destiny. Abandoning a situation is still running away, no matter whether it is dressed up as destiny or the pursuit of spiritual purpose.

For example, Conrad was attempting to complete a novel. To support himself, he wrote feature stories for magazines that paid him on a per-word basis. This gave Conrad a reasonable income but it slowed progress on his book. When I read for him, Conrad was writing a story for a magazine that wasn't paying him at all. Therefore, he was devoting his time and energy to writing features that were not supporting him financially and were depleting his energy for writing his novel. I asked him about his long-term goals.

"I want to complete and publish this novel," he replied.

"Then how is writing a free story for a magazine that can afford to pay you helping you towards your goal?"

"It isn't," he muttered dolefully. After this conversation, Conrad set more solid, realistic goals about his book and eventually completed his novel. The Knight of Wands reversed can represent uncertainty about the appropriate action in a given situation. This can delay results when energy is syphoned off into other pursuits.

In a general reading, the reversed Knight of Wands describes setbacks due to scattered focus and inconsistent effort. When the going gets tough, this person is the first to get going — out the door and into a taxi. Occasionally, this process is varied by them being the first out the door — and into the arms of someone new.

In a career layout, the reversed Knight of Wands describes a job involving lots of rushing around. Perhaps the person is a sales representative who is expected to cover a wide territory or a flight attendant who doesn't know their intended ports of call more than a week ahead. The reversed Knight sometimes describes a lack of focus in a career layout. It's often because this individual is living in the moment without sufficient thought for the future.

In a relationship question, the reversed Knight is usually a person aged between twenty and thirty who enjoys relationships but not commitment. This is someone who often has two or three partners on the go simultaneously while pursuing a fourth possibility. Relationships usually last longer if this person regularly travels for work, lives interstate or overseas from a partner or is granted freedom to roam at will.

In a health query, the Knight of Wands reversed indicates the hips or thighs. It can sometimes describe exhaustion from too much partying or attempting to cram too many events into a social calendar. At their core, this person has an urge to run: from the past, from commitments and from current expectations. Responsibility and tenacity are not strong features for this reversed Knight. Sometimes, this individual suffers health issues in later life resulting from an excessive intake of food or drink. These health issues can include weight gain, gout and ongoing pain from old sports injuries. Outdoor adventures that went wrong decades ago can cast a long shadow over the person's health but this can offer a valuable lesson in actions and consequences.

As a person, the reversed Knight of Wands describes someone who prefers freedom to commitment. When faced with long-term commitment or comfortable routines, this individual has an urge to run away. While escaping, this person usually justifies their actions as an overwhelming desire to pursue true spiritual purpose. In reality, it's still running away.

This reversed Knight can describe someone who enjoys beginning new projects, relationship or plans but soon tires of the effort required to sustain them. Passion and excitement quickly wear thin and routines seem like drudgery. Soon, the promise of new horizons beckons and present plans are abandoned. This is someone who loves a party without the preparation or cleaning up afterwards. In extreme instances, this is the person who arrives late for a group dinner at a restaurant and then orders the best of everything.

"This was fun. We must do this again soon," he says handing $30 to the organiser for his share as he leaves early. Others are left to pay his full share long after he has gone.

As a situation, this card can indicate that current instability is caused by restlessness. This person might change jobs every time boredom sets in and soon discover that it's difficult to secure a new position during a recession. Casual or contract work appeals to the reversed Knight of Wands, as does project work that offers plenty of variety. This card can indicate a changing landscape, such as retrenchments at work or that a home has been sold and it's time to move again.

As an aspect of the client, this card usually describes someone who thrives on change and variety. Short-term goals are possible, whereas long-term plans often feel overwhelming, as the person lacks the sheer tenacity needed to complete a project. It's time to step back, pause and remember the longer-term objectives. It's also necessary to ask if current actions are leading towards or away from long-term goals.

Knight of Cups

The Knight of Cups describes a soft-hearted, creative person, who is both romantic and enthusiastic. Like the Page of Cups, this card can also represent a creative or emotional opportunity.

On the card, someone sits in the saddle, holding the horse's reins with one hand and a cup in the other. This horse moves at a slower pace than the horse being ridden by the Knight of Wands. The tunic is decorated with fish, representing the element of water and thus signifying emotions and creativity.

KNIGHT of CUPS.

The knights are the fiery characters of the court cards. Cups are the suit of water, and therefore, the Knight of Cups represents the fiery part of water. This person, if a male, has a choice to become the King of Cups (Water) or to become the King of Wands (Fire). This decision is made during his twenties and usually by thirty years of age he knows which direction is most suitable. More often, this person matures into a King of Cups, leaving behind some of the passion of youth when entering his thirties.

Both paths offer opportunities and restrictions. The fire direction is one of challenges, adventure, achievement, trophies, competition and success measured in what is achieved or conquered. This generally makes it a social but also lonely path, because people who continuously compete with others often find it difficult to allow even their loved ones to get close to them, as they unconsciously measure themselves against everyone.

The water path is one of creativity, romance, intimacy, shared group activities and inspiration. It includes a profound need to find a comfortable place within a community. The opportunities for worldly achievement the fire path offers are not usually desired for people on the water journey. Emotional and spiritual fulfilment or tranquillity are often greater priorities than trophies and financial rewards. These individuals are content to choose a career that pays less if it can be more meaningful to them. If they are helping or inspiring others, this is a suitable reward.

The Knight of Cups must choose between these two different paths in order to become the king of one of them. Once a direction is taken, it is difficult to go back to the other. I have seen men in their forties surrender the path taken for the one left behind and it usually cost them everything they had in life. Relationships, family, friendships, career and material possessions are often sacrificed when a person decides to choose the other route because one journey leads to achievement, while the other to stillness.

Conquests in achievement are everywhere, from personal bests to breaking international records, whereas the only triumph in stillness is a mastery of the self. The fire path requires an audience to applaud and stiff competition to make the race a close finish, whereas the water path is a private accomplishment, leading slowly, sometimes imperceptibly, towards inner peace and contentment. Fire seeks constant movement, change and new challenges, whereas water only moves when pressured by an outside force, such as gravity. Without an external influence, water is still.

In a general reading, the upright Knight of Cups can describe a person deciding how to apply passion and enthusiasm to a creative idea to push it towards a tangible result. It can also indicate an attempt to balance the need for stillness with a desire for achievement. Both offer rewarding outcomes. Sometimes it's not a choice between them but a decision of which to pursue right now. After achievement comes rest. After respite there is often sufficient energy to reach for another goal.

In a career layout, this card describes a young person who prefers to pursue a creative career rather than corporate life. This individual is not suited to political or competitive business life, preferring instead to design a website, write a book or compose a song. The Knight of Cups is not as ambitious as the Knight of Wands or the Knight of Pentacles and values occupational enjoyment above management perks or career advancement.

In a relationship question, this Knight describes a young individual (twenty to thirty years of age) or an immature older person who is romantic, sensitive, creative and kind-hearted but sulky when crossed. A potential spouse might overlook this person early in life, due to a lack of charisma but in the thirties when more men and women are ready for family life, this person's attributes are more obvious. This is someone who is likely to be kind, patient and gentle with a partner and young children.

In a health query, the Knight of Cups indicates balanced health that comes from taking care of emotional and physical needs. This card suggests involvement in hobbies, interests and activities that reduce stress and inspire creativity. This person is usually drawn to yoga, meditation or creative outlets including painting, drawing or playing a musical instrument and these pastimes often reduce stress and contribute to well-being.

As a person, the Knight of Cups describes someone who is creative, sentimental, kind-hearted and sometimes shy. He prefers a job that makes a difference in the lives of others and will sacrifice part of his income to pursue emotionally rewarding work. Women sometimes overlook this man in his twenties because he is shy and doesn't always make a strong first impression, yet when they want to start a family, some women search for this type of partner because he values shared goals. He also makes a kind, understanding father to small children. He is an artist at heart, a storyteller and sometimes a poet, whatever his chosen career.

As a situation, this card describes someone trying to balance emotional and spiritual needs. It can describe a compassionate, sentimental person who might be a friend, partner or co-worker. It sometimes indicates an emotional or artistic offer, either for a relationship or for a creative partnership. Occasionally, this card focuses on the choice between the cups' need to be still and the wands' desire to push on towards new goals. In a recent reading, I asked the client to add two cards, one to each side of this card, to explore the cups and wands options. Before he selected these cards, I decided that the first additional card would represent the cups' need, and the second, the wands option. It was a way to help him explore two underlying needs without sacrificing one for the other.

As an aspect of the client, this Knight describes someone reassessing emotional needs while attempting to balance the demands of life with creative hobbies and interests. As the fiery part of water, this card suggests a desire to act, while wanting to feel calm and serene. Each motivation is meaningful but pursuing one instead of the other is likely to result in a lack of fulfilment later on. Sometimes, the answer is as simple as combining action with imagination, such as producing a creative idea. The process of writing a song, painting a picture or landscaping a garden can address both needs simultaneously.

Knight of Cups Reversed

The Knight of Cups reversed can describe the disillusionment that comes from realising an offer is not what it initially appeared to be. This is a romantic approach to life, where hopes and desires cloud the vision of what circumstances are actually offering. Sometimes this individual feels stuck. This card can also represent immaturity — indicating that this reversed Knight is emotionally still a page.

This person can be sulky, moody and overly sensitive. There is an inclination to brood on past frustrations, with a tendency to become passive-aggressive when thwarted. It's someone who struggles to make the most of opportunities because of a disposition to live in the past. This individual tends to review past events almost obsessively, finding it difficult to forgive and forget the past misdemeanours of others.

When reversed, this card describes a person between twenty and thirty years of age or an older immature individual who cannot deliver on promises because of emotional immaturity. This individual dreams of what life would be like in a relationship but is unaware of the effort required to make a relationship work in day-to-day living. A reversed Knight of Cups prefers to mentally replay romantic interactions, where the risks of rejection are low and imagination is the only requirement. This allows for perfect endings without the risk of rejection. Often, while thoughts and hopes are directed towards past or missed opportunity, current avenues for joy are ignored.

A reversed card can indicate a passing set of circumstances. An upright Knight of

Cups may become temporarily reversed after a serious disappointment. It's possible that the reversal is reflecting current circumstances and a year later the same card will present upright in a subsequent reading. This occurred with David, a 26-year-old TV producer who had worked diligently for eight months on a television series that he eventually pitched to the head of programming. His hopes were dashed when he was told a similar concept was pitched three weeks previously. He suddenly felt mediocre and unoriginal. I reminded him that the lightbulb was invented in two locations at around the same time by people in different countries who had never met and suggested he examine the other concept to see the similarities and the differences. His concept might bring an inventive twist to the existing TV pilot.

Two years later, in another reading, he selected the upright Knight of Cups in his career layout. He explained that after examining the competing series concept he asked if he could work with the series producer. They thrived in their partnership as co-producers and when David wanted to pitch another idea for a different series, the head of the department was keen to meet with him.

The Knight of Cups reversed reflects the inability to choose a path (active or creative) towards desired goals. The choice between the fire direction of action or the water route of feelings and creativity may be confusing at this point. However, commitment to one path is required before being able to move towards achieving objectives.

In a general reading, this reversed card can describe a creative or romantic person who lacks the practicality to turn ideas into products or outcomes. This individual is more comfortable with the inspiration part of a project and finds the action required to make an idea happen slightly overwhelming.

Sometimes, this card shows a lack of familiarity with turning ideas into tangible outcomes. This Knight might benefit from a partnership with a more practical and capable individual who can effectively manage creative projects towards successful conclusions. This card sometimes describes a creative offer that fizzles. It arrives with the promise of success but fades before being pursued.

In a career layout, the reversed Knight of Cups shows someone who is being unrealistic about a creative career. Talent and inspiration are only the first steps towards success. At some point, the person needs effort (wands), a strategy (swords) and hard work and investment (pentacles) to take the idea to market. This card can describe a young individual who believes a perfect creative job will be offered to them with minimum effort. While waiting to be discovered, decades slip away. If this person doesn't take a more practical approach, a likely destiny is as a reversed King of Cups, with a manuscript gathering dust in a drawer or an untouched musical instrument crammed into a dusty cupboard.

In a relationship question, the reversed Knight of Cups sometimes describes an inability to resolve and release a past relationship to be ready and available for present opportunities. This person is sometimes confused by conflicting needs between pursuing an opportunity for love and an innate desire to run away and explore the world.

In a health query, this card indicates an imaginative approach to health. Sometimes the individual believes that meditation or merely thinking about improved health can cure everything. Although these approaches have their place, it's unlikely that meditation alone will heal a broken leg.

As a person, the reversed Knight of Cups describes a young man who is dreamy, creative and sensitive. He is easily dissuaded from his goals, especially when faced with strong competition. Whereas the Knight of Wands thrives on competition, the Knight of Cups prefers cooperation to rivalry. He is likely to live in the past, vividly remembering when life was safe, secure and even cosy. He sometimes struggles to make his ideas real and when this occurs, he escapes into memory, imagination and fantasy. In a relationship, it's likely he secretly yearns for a past love, especially an unrequited one. Everything is perfect in his imagination until reality intrudes and a current partner demands he produces some art or gets a regular job.

As a situation, the reversed Knight indicates someone waiting for an opportunity. Either it is not forthcoming or it is delayed. Because this card represents the fiery part of water, it's possible to activate the fiery part of this Knight's nature and motivate him to work on a new project while awaiting news. Perhaps while anticipating acceptance into an art exhibition, he can raise his public profile on social media with effective personal designs and images, design a course and take on some students or begin a new creative project.

As an aspect of the client, this card indicates someone focused on a reply. This individual might be hoping for a second date, a job confirmation or news about being shortlisted for a writing competition. He is unlikely to keep himself busy with a new project while waiting, yet this is a viable way to limit disappointment if he receives an unfavourable response.

Knight of Swords

The Knight of Swords represents an intellectual young man who aims to understand the world cerebrally. He has well-developed communication skills and he thrives where he can ask questions and provide personal opinions. If words alone could put the world to rights, this man would be in great demand. However, as the Knight of Wands is quick to point out, it is our deeds by which we are mostly judged.

KNIGHT of SWORDS.

In this card, a young man rides furiously, clutching the reins in one hand with an upright sword in the other. Wind-blown trees and clouds streaking across the sky provide evidence of a powerful gale. There are birds on the horse's bridle and butterflies on its saddle, both representing the element of air (thought, analysis and ideas). The butterflies also symbolise the way thoughts and ideas can transform a person's understanding of life and circumstances.

The Knight of Swords represents a young man quick to think and act, who is well suited to short-term projects and to careers where he can use his communication skills. He has yet to fully comprehend the power of words to heal but also to inflict pain. This is shown by the way the person in the card rides with his sword outstretched.

As the knights represent the fire part of the suit and swords represent air, he is the fiery part of air. As air fans fire, he is the quickest thinking and acting of all the knights. He is restless. Basically, he is an ideas man who is detached, reasonable, observant and objective. He likes to talk and has plenty of sound ideas but can be indecisive. Thinking and conceptualising are his favourite pastimes.

This man has the choice of two paths: those of fire and air. If he chooses the fire path, he will become the King of Wands. This leads to an active, adventurous life, filled with achievement and struggle towards goals.

If he chooses the air path, he will become the King of Swords. This path leads to a rational life, filled with study, precision in thought and in action and often a professional career. By using his mind, he usually doesn't have to work as physically hard for an income.

In a general reading, the Knight of Swords suggests it's time to act swiftly to avert disaster or secure an opportunity. This is a 'seize the day' moment. A quick solution to an issue may be required and swift action now can save the day. It sometimes describes the client or someone around the client who is impatient, quick-minded and mentally agile.

In a career layout, this card suggests there could be a window of opportunity to forge ahead towards a new job or a career goal. There is no time for hesitation, as circumstances may change rapidly. This is a card for noticing career or business opportunities before others and rapidly seizing them while they are available. This Knight can sense a trend or a market opening for a product earlier than competitors.

In a relationship question, the Knight of Swords can represent a quick-minded man who values a partner's mind. This is someone who begins and sometimes abandons relationships without hesitation. He lives in the moment, so promises he has made in the past don't always apply to the present moment. He's likely to take on too many projects at once, eventually abandoning some to focus on others.

In a health query, the Knight of Swords can indicate headaches and nervous exhaustion, due to tackling too many tasks at once. If the exhaustion is due to work demands, more planning and less rushing around might restore energy reserves. This individual might benefit from techniques that provide inner stillness or calm, such as meditation, a day without electronic devices and social media or a swim in the sea.

As a person, the Knight of Swords describes a mercurial young man. He is quick in thought and deed, with an agile mind and talkative to the point of being loquacious. He is adept at winning a debate, rationalising away his bad conduct and breaking the ice with conversation. He usually believes that the way to a girl's heart is through her ear. I mentioned a voice-training sentence to a swords friend, who soon used it to his advantage. Having struck up a conversation with a young lady at a crowded party, he disappeared to secure some drinks. Upon his return, he stared soulfully at her and declared, "Since we briefly parted, my heart has cried out for you like the moan of doves in immemorial elms amidst the murmuring of innumerable bees," before presenting her a champagne flute. She found it charming. I simply heard an actor practising some new lines.

As a situation, this card suggests it is time to seize the day and act swiftly to secure victory. Sometimes, a clear idea acted on at the right moment can change a person's destiny. This describes the ability to survey a situation and quickly grasp the opportunity contained within. Sometimes, being first is essential to success.

As an aspect of the client, this card indicates that the person is quick-minded and likely to be an early adopter. Not bound by tradition or what is familiar, swords people tend to adapt to change easily. This individual can quickly see an advantage in having the latest model phone, software or device and can profit from being ahead of competitors. This card may indicate it is time to act swiftly in pursuit of goals.

Knight of Swords Reversed

The Knight of Swords reversed represents scattered thoughts and action with insufficient planning. This man rushes into situations without thinking things through, often resulting in him being cut by his own sword. His words and deeds cause him pain that careful reflection might prevent. In a bid not to over-assess a plan, he tends to underthink it. Sometimes, his quick mind lacks direction and discipline, resulting in scattered focus.

As the fiery part of air, he's impatient and often acts on a plan before he has considered it carefully. The process of rendering an idea into physical form soon highlights its flaws and shows that more in-depth thinking is required to resolve problems.

The Knight reversed indicates a man who is more generous in talk than in action, seemingly unaware that words alone do not produce results. He is eager to promise, yet just as quick to forget his commitments. He can be unpredictable, restless and continually searching for stimulation. His beliefs about life have probably been hastily gathered and not yet tested.

Peter is an example of how swords people love playing with words. He was giving a one-day talk in the country, training a group of farmers on business management. They were paying him for his time with two sheep. He liked the idea that 'talk is sheep.'

I overheard a young woman at a party tell a Knight of Swords, who was flirting with her, "You're all talk."

"Yes, I am," he replied immediately with a laugh, "… t-o-r-q-u-e."

In a general reading, the reversed Knight of Swords suggests a person might be rushing around without any true purpose. More planning, clear systems and persistent effort are required to reduce the sense of urgency and become more effective.

In a career layout, it can describe the urge to bolt from a job in reaction to a setback or a momentary frustration. This issue will pass and the person will then have the mental clarity to make more effective decisions. Acting on the urge to jump ship sometimes leads to regret. Take more time with important decisions when this card appears reversed in a career layout.

In a relationship question, it describes a man who is unreliable. This is someone whose words do not match his actions. He begins new relationships while already in existing commitments and might eventually disappear without a trace. When Annette separated from Kyle, he was quick to meet someone new and they lost contact. Almost a year later, she received a lengthy text message from him late one night. This was followed by two more in the following week before he phoned to invite her to a friend's engagement party. Then Kyle ended the contact as abruptly as he began it. When he texted Annette again several months later, she ignored his approach. It's not unusual for a reversed Knight of Swords to blow hot and then cold around friendships and relationships. They can be impulsive and changeable.

In a health query, the reversed Knight of Swords can describe someone who is continually anxious or fretful. It also shows mental confusion and physical exhaustion resulting from juggling too many ideas, plans or tasks at once. When Lara asked about writing a book, it turned out she was partway through writing seven different books. Instead of completing an existing work, Lara wanted to pursue a new idea. She was more at home with the promise of an unexplored concept than with the act of physically completing an existing one.

She explained she found the actual writing process dull and time-consuming, so I suggested she hire a ghostwriter. This might be a professional writer who would interview her about her idea over a few weeks, recording their conversations before shaping the concept into a readable book. An accomplished writer might need to contain Laura's tendency to leap from one idea to another and insist only one book is completed at a time but this presented a much more realistic option. Lara was better at commencing books than completing them. A ghostwriter might complete her unfinished works.

As a person, the reversed Knight of Swords describes a man with myriad conflicting ideas and concepts. Sometimes, he'll finish a friend's sentences to shorten a conversation or interject with a random sentence related to a word the other person has just said. He is unlikely to achieve his objectives unless he has support from more practical people, as he has not yet discovered that words do not make deeds. Talking about climbing Mt. Everest is not the same as putting on the boots, training for months and then attempting to ascend the mountain while facing blizzards. In business, he's a better starter than a finisher. He can secure new clients but others need to deliver on his promises.

As a situation, this card can describe chaos resulting from poor planning or too many different goals in conflict with each other. The mind is scattered, making it difficult to focus on immediate demands and underlying issues. A map is required to determine what the goals are and how they can be effectively achieved. In rare situations, it can describe the consequences of hasty actions, such as being arrested following the spontaneous decision to drive after consuming a bottle of wine at dinner.

As an aspect of the client, this card sometimes describes someone who is mentally scattered, anxiety-ridden and impatient for results. This person wants precise answers to sixty of his most pressing issues in a thirty-minute Skype reading while supervising three hyperactive children at home. In one such reading, I watched the family dog eat my client's dinner from his desk, as he searched for his questions list and his reading glasses, while two children repeatedly bounced a basketball off a nearby internal wall. This is not a time for action but it is worth carefully considering the likely consequences of intended actions. By engaging the mind before the hands and feet, it's possible to avoid acting on impulse and living with regrets.

Knight of Pentacles

The Knight of Pentacles can represent a young person who is hard-working and career-minded. This is someone who is prepared to work long hours while studying in personal time for career advancement. While the other knights are out enjoying themselves, this serious young person is often working hard to build a career and financial

KNIGHT of PENTACLES.

security for the future. There is a tendency to relax more in retirement with greater rewards for their effort.

In the card image, someone sits on a stationary horse, examining a pentacle in one hand and the path ahead. The sense of urgency evident with the other knights is not present here. This person has an earthy, practical approach to life. Both horse and person are stationary because he is aware that one step in the wrong direction usually requires another step back to the right path. This individual knows how to pace himself. Being naturally cautious, conservative and realistic, this earthy knight is pragmatic, methodical and materialistic. He doesn't expect his job to be fun — that's why it's called work. He does however, expect to be paid well for his efforts.

As the knights represent the fire aspect of the court cards and the pentacles element is earth, this Knight represents the fiery part of earth. This is translated into enthusiasm and passion channelled into practical concerns, such as career and long-term plans. This young person understands business and is patient and persistent.

The card symbolises a hard-working, mature young man. This person is serious, practical, diligent and cautious in the pursuit of new paths. Old-fashioned at heart, he has a preference for a relationship partner who is realistic, loyal and hard-working, who will assist with achieving career plans.

This person prefers self-employment and detests being told what to do. Not the most sociable of the knights, this individual often meets partners through a work environment rather than at clubs or social events.

Work, study, planning and saving are constructive attributes of this earthy knight. This person is not spontaneous or adventurous like the Knights of Swords or Wands, preferring the same holiday destination each year — if taking holidays at all. It is necessary for this person not to become work-obsessed, by remembering that rest and play help to ensure a well-rounded life.

Pentacles individuals understand that money provides choices around home location, clothing, motor vehicles, holiday and the level of education provided for children. The Knight of Pentacles usually takes care of this fundamental need from which all other options depend. This person accepts that work is not fun and doesn't yearn to be happy with his work like the Knight of Cups. Personal happiness stems from a job well done, a stable home and work life and money carefully invested for the future.

This card represents long-term planning, commitment to career goals and financial discipline. The element of earth ensures hard work but also requires a realistic material return for effort. Safe investments provide sound sleep at night for earthy people.

In a general reading, this card indicates success through persistence and hard work. It sometimes describes a Capricorn person, especially when The Devil card also occurs in the layout. If a Capricorn person is represented, it may not be a man. The person in this card is motionless, unprepared to move until sure about a long-term destination.

In a career layout, this is an encouraging card for carefully considered, long-term plans. This individual has a strong work ethic and is often promoted into positions of responsibility at an early age. It's not unusual for the Knight of Pentacles to become the youngest state manager or director of a company in the organisation's history, partly because of being a safe choice. Mentally, this person is sixty-five years of age long before their thirtieth birthday. Sometimes, the upright Knight of Pentacles indicates a responsible attitude to career plans and a belief that if you want a job done properly, do it yourself.

In a relationship question, the Knight of Pentacles describes a serious, responsible man who is ambitious. This individual feels a need to be financially stable before being an attractive proposition to potential partners. It is someone who wants a life partner who values stability and routine and who doesn't become bored when life is comfortable. This person rarely rushes into commitments and works long hours to provide for the family. Careful consideration is given to the long-term consequences of marriage or any emotional commitment because the possibility of an expensive and crushing divorce can derail career and financial plans.

In a health query, the Knight can suggest issues with the skin, such as dry, flaky skin or intolerance to soaps and moisturisers. It can also signify concerns about the knees or teeth. In a health layout that also includes the King of Swords and the Ace of Swords, it can suggest knee surgery. Generally, the upright Knight of Pentacles indicates a set of long-term strategies to build and maintain personal health. These might include walking, gym visits and a balanced diet that becomes part of a regular health routine. Health fads rarely appeal to this person. Instead, the attitude is to eat less and do more if weight or stamina become issues.

As a person, the Knight of Pentacles card usually describes a sensible, practical, hard-working man. As the fiery part of earth, this individual is prepared to work tirelessly towards long-term goals. Paced for a marathon instead of a sprint, this individual approaches career and marriage prepared for a lifetime commitment.

The Knight of Pentacles represents the fiery part of earth. Fire thrives on action and activity, while earth requires reward for consistent effort. In combination, this individual is usually able to make long-term financial or career plans and stick to them. This shows the ability to harness the passion of fire with the ambition and financial understanding of earth. It highlights someone who works diligently to build wealth. This person is unadventurous but dependable, responsible and unafraid of hard work.

The innate sense of duty and responsibility means this individual is often promoted well beyond peers in early life. Basically, this person is moderate, conservative and prefers routines to novelty. Marrying young is not a realistic choice for earth knights as they usually realise divorce is expensive and not tax-deductible. Sometimes this person marries young after recognising a life partner early on. When this happens, he is reassured that she loved him before he was wealthy.

As a situation, this card points to a focus on long-term career or financial plans. It can represent study and learning new skills to improve career prospects. It's a practical approach to money, whereby the individual sets aside some funds for a rainy day. If that emergency fund is never spent throughout the decades, this person realises how fortunate they are.

As an aspect of the client, this card shows the person thinking about long-term goals and deciding if current actions are heading towards the fulfilment of those objectives. It indicates a responsible, cautious approach to the future. It sometimes shows a person taking time to ensure stability in old age, based on sound financial reserves. Pentacles people understand that viable, steady sources of income are fundamental to a stable life. They prefer low-risk investments, such as real estate, so they can sleep peacefully at night.

Knight of Pentacles Reversed

The Knight of Pentacles reversed can describe a young person who is lazy and without any real purpose. They are usually not idle in all areas and have the potential for hard work when the right rewards are available. An example of this was Trent, who couldn't be bothered looking for work but who diligently practised his guitar for several hours every day. Music inspired him, whereas the jobs he was qualified for did not provide sufficient motivation.

The Knight reversed needs an outlet for his fire energy but one that appeals to a basic need for earthly rewards. Sometimes, it can describe someone who values material possessions but is unprepared to work for them and prefers to rely on others for financial support.

A reversed court card can describe a temporary situation or a rut that the person has created. This reversal might result from losing a dream job, the collapse of a business or the loss of a relationship resulting from career priorities.

When Lyle selected the Knight of Pentacles reversed in a general reading, his circumstances contributed to this period of frustration. His father, a lawyer, virtually forced Lyle towards a career in law and he loathed the work. He wanted to become an engineer and after ten years of law studies and practice, he pursued an engineering degree. Lyle's frustration at not being able to determine his life direction was palpable. When he changed to his preferred career, he moved closer to becoming an upright Knight and eventually a King of Pentacles.

Sometimes, a reversed Knight is still living at home at age thirty-five, while driving an expensive car and owning one or two investment properties. By avoiding personal rent or mortgage expenses, this person can save and invest, knowing there will be a hot meal on the table every night, with laundry washed and carefully folded on the bed twice a week.

An example of the reversed Knight of Pentacles was Julian, who travelled the world funded by two credit cards paid for by his father. His father's terms were that he could travel free for two years and then he was to return home to take over the family business. Julian was avoiding the dismal prospect of working for a living by finding ways to extend his two-year holiday. An upright Knight would have had a clear plan before he began the holiday. The reversed Knight was shocked when the 24 months ended and it was time to return home to pay for this holiday for the next forty years.

In a general reading, this reversed Knight can indicate working in a job that is not a career. This position is unlikely to lead the person towards a desired goal, as it's simply to earn money. It sometimes describes someone who has not yet decided where a career will lead or a person who doesn't know how to learn the required skills for an occupation.

In a career layout, the reversed Knight of Pentacles shows an individual unsure about future career direction. As it becomes more common for people to retrain into second and third careers, this card can describe a person of any age. The reversed Knight sometimes suggests someone who has been recently retrenched and feels too old to continue in a current career. It's as though this individual has reached the end of a personal career map. A new plan needs to be prepared.

In a relationship question, this card describes someone whose career is more important than anything else in life. A relationship partner comes a distant second to ambition. Sometimes, it's the complete opposite: someone who has no career goals and is unlikely to be working. This individual wants a relationship partner for support after parents have declared it was time for him to become self-sufficient.

In a health query, it can indicate health issues resulting from workplace upheavals. From a poorly designed office chair to unbearable stress from job demands, it might be time to find a more suitable and less stressful work environment. It can also indicate issues with skin, such as dry, flaky skin or even psoriasis. It sometimes suggests intolerance to soaps and moisturisers. This card also highlights concern around the knees or teeth. When reversed, the Knight of Pentacles can sometimes indicate postponing surgery, possibly making current health issues even more serious.

As a person, the reversed Knight of Pentacles can describe someone who is working days, evenings and weekends. Perhaps a lack of confidence or insufficient education restricts this individual's choices. Sometimes, it can describe someone who is unfocused with greater career direction while concentrating intently on current responsibilities and obligations. This can be someone who is too busy cutting down trees to sharpen his saw. It might show an individual who is under-employed in casual or part-time jobs, due to inadequate training or skills to apply for better-paid work.

This reversed Knight doesn't respond well to being directed by others and yet hasn't sufficient self-discipline to work unsupervised or in self-employment. Sometimes, this card reversed describes someone who isn't sure about long-term career direction. Occasionally, seeing this card in a layout prompts the cheeky response, "It's okay that you don't yet know what you want to be when you grow up. You're only fifty-eight. There's still plenty of time."

As a situation, this card can describe someone who is burdened by responsibilities and the demands of others. This person feels stuck, hampered by existing commitments in a life that is all work and no play. The reversed Knight can suggest a dead-end job or someone who has been pushed into a loathsome career. Financial obligations, such as a large credit card debt, keep the individual stuck when this card is reversed. Debt is bondage, and yet currently, this person lacks the sheer determination to improve their personal circumstances. After an exhausting day of work, it can feel overwhelming to sit down and study at night, even if more skills will eventually offer a wider range of job opportunities.

As an aspect of the client, this card can indicate no real career direction or frustration at financial obligations and job demands. Sometimes, it highlights an individual who has material desires that exceed current income. This person may be working long hours or several jobs to pay off loans for past purchases. Occasionally, this reversed Knight indicates someone who has never been guided towards a suitable career and has no awareness of how to find a mentally and emotionally rewarding occupation.

The Queens

The queens in the tarot usually represent women, aspects of a person (male or female) or approaches to life. The Queen of Wands is enthusiastic, intuitive, warm and forthright, whereas the Queen of Cups is someone who is sensitive, imaginative, compassionate and intuitive. The Queen of Swords describes an individual who is talkative, impartial and quick thinking. The Queen of Pentacles is usually practical, conservative, stable and moderate.

The aspects represented by the cards are as follows: The Queen of Wands signifies inner strength and the courage to face life, whereas the Queen of Cups represents powerful intuitive and creative connections with the subconscious mind. The Queen of Swords has an organised, sociable and perceptive approach to life, while the Queen of Pentacles represents success through practical planning and sustained effort to complete projects. This card can also suggest being connected to nature through walking or gardening, leading to inner balance and harmony.

When three or more upright queens appear in a layout, they highlight the presence of powerful women in a person's life. These can include strong, independent females who are in the public eye due to their business, career or political achievements. These individuals might be advisors, colleagues or mentors and their influence is supportive.

Queen of Wands

The Queen of Wands can represent a Leo person, especially when The Sun or The Strength card appear in the same layout. It can also describe any passionate, independent or outspoken woman.

This Queen is forthright, courageous and she enjoys a challenge. Therefore, any career with demanding goals is likely to suit her. She is an achiever, a natural leader and organiser and is capable of motivating a team or a workforce towards a target.

QUEEN of WANDS.

The Queen of Wands thrives on competition, as it spurs her on to greater achievements. This woman needs variety, as routine stifles her. In the card, the Queen of Wands is seated on her throne, her wand in one hand and a sunflower in the other. A black cat sits alert at her feet and lions surround her — a male and a female lion are carved in stone beneath her and there is a pair above her head.

The cat at her feet and the cat-head clasp securing her cape represent her intuition and her untamed, passionate nature. The clasp is an Egyptian symbol of Bastet, a lioness and warrior goddess. In more recent times, she has been depicted as a cat. In ancient Egypt, cats were seen as protectors, keeping vermin away from homes. This woman will vigorously defend herself and loved ones if necessary. When bullied, she can respond with fury. Even domesticated cats retain a little of their wild origins, like this Queen, who treasures her intense independence.

The predominant colours in the card are yellow and orange, suggesting a combination of intellect and passion. The Queen is an enthusiastic woman who can mentally direct her energies towards useful, creative purposes. The sunflowers in her hand and on her throne represent the joy she brings to others through her optimistic attitude to life. But beware, for under that sunny disposition lurks a mighty temper. When roused to anger, she can be blunt, explosive and forthright. This person has no need for assertiveness training.

When the Queen of Wands appears as an influence (the fourth card in a seven-card layout), it describes a woman who is coaching, supporting or helping an individual towards a desired goal. This Queen also represents a situation where success is achieved through inner strength and the courage of personal conviction.

In a general reading, this card indicates success through inner strength and courage. Self-belief in the outcome of a project will increase persistence in the face of obstacles. Sometimes, burning ambition and the drive to succeed is a result of being repeatedly told a goal is unachievable. When told they can't do something, wands people usually have an urge to say, "Watch me." This card can also indicate support from an assertive, forthright woman.

In a career layout, this card indicates that career success is the result of self-belief. It can also suggest that a strong, assertive woman has assisted the individual towards their career goals. This is someone who, after being told she could not possibly achieve a goal, deliberately sets out to prove everyone wrong. Her reply to someone who tells her she cannot do something is usually, "Watch and learn." She is suited to careers in teaching, sales, marketing and politics, as she's usually a self-starter with plenty of ambition and determination. This individual is not afraid of hard work. As a manager, she's happy to roll up her sleeves and help out on the shop floor when required. As a result, she's usually admired and feared by her subordinates.

In a relationship question, the Queen of Wands describes a strong, independent, straightforward woman. As a modern female, she does not hesitate to secure the number of a person she's attracted to and then phone later to arrange a dinner date. This Queen doesn't have the patience to sit around, hoping that he'll phone. She'd rather know if he's interested or not. If not, she pushes forward towards her next opportunities without regret. She's an active, goal-oriented individual who is passionate about life. She's also likely to coach, push and motivate her partner to achieve more than that person thought possible. The Queen of Wands often has an eye for potential.

In a health query, the upright Queen of Wands can suggest issues with the heart or the spine. Leo individuals usually have supple spines but sometimes suffer ongoing back issues. Generally, the upright Queen indicates buoyant health and sufficient energy to bounce back from setbacks.

As a person, the Queen of Wands can represent a Leo individual, especially if

The Sun or Strength cards appear in the layout. As a woman, she is bold, assertive and outspoken. She's passionate, a natural leader and an enthusiastic, playful teacher. She can be competitive and impatient when teams take too long to reach consensus. She sometimes feels that by the time a team or a committee come to an agreement, she could have completed the task. She is better suited to the doing rather than the planning part of a project.

As a situation, this Queen can represent success through inner strength, courage and self-belief. This individual persists long after others have given up, often to prove friends or colleagues wrong when they have said she couldn't achieve a goal. This card describes success that is the result of inner strength and persistence.

As an aspect of the client, the Queen of Wands suggests there are sufficient courage and self-belief to reach the desired objective. It sometimes highlights the ability to give a project a unique look and feel by injecting personal flair and creativity into the finished product. This person is likely to have excellent marketing instincts. In job interviews she is an effective self-marketer.

Queen of Wands Reversed

The Queen of Wands reversed indicates that confidence and inner strength are waning or there is a temporary lack of courage. The person's nerve in facing obstacles is currently diminished. He or she is more likely to act from fear than from a position of strength. Therefore, decisions being made at this time might not be the best ones.

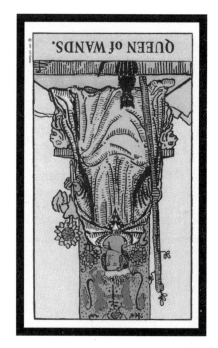

When reversed, the card still represents a Leo person or any enthusiastic, passionate woman whose energies are presently low, due to ill-health or exhaustion. Wands people often push themselves too hard and end up collapsing with fatigue, influenza or some other illness. It's life's way of reminding them to rest and pace themselves more carefully. They are prone to burning the candle at both ends.

As an answer to a question, the reversed Queen of Wands can indicate a lack of success in a venture, due to low energy or insufficient inner strength and courage. Perhaps the person is feeling overwhelmed by life and needs to restore reserves of vitality before pursuing personal goals.

It's a reader's task to determine whether a reversed court card represents a response to temporary setbacks and frustrations, or a long-standing character trait. If it's temporary, the client may have this card upright in a subsequent reading several months or years later. If it's an established approach to life, it will appear reversed until the person changes. A temporarily reversed Queen of Wands could be the result of an unresolved argument from the previous day, if the person has a range of unexpressed emotions. Given a chance to vent her anger out loud, this Queen soon settles down to the positive, passionate woman she is. I like to think of it as her reading aloud from her favourite newspaper, *The Daily Rant*.

In a general reading, this is a card for lack of success due to limited inner strength and poor self-confidence. At this time, the individual lacks the necessary courage and determination to forge ahead with plans. Sometimes this reversed Queen describes a bossy woman interfering in the client's life.

In a career layout, this card describes delayed or a lack of success, due to the absence of inner strength and self-confidence. Unlike the upright Queen, if others tell her she cannot do something, she is inclined to believe them and abandon her goals. When frustrated in career, she sometimes initiates conflicts with co-workers and makes enemies of people who could have been her friends. Starting fights and arguments makes this person feel alive. As a result, they can be magnets for trouble.

In a relationship question, the reversed Queen of Wands describes a passionate, independent and enthusiastic woman who thrives on challenge, travel and working towards goals. Competitive by nature, she needs to admire her partner and feel proud of his achievements, while simultaneously accomplishing her own goals. She can become bossy and when channelling her inner headmistress, she's likely to tell everyone who listens what they are doing wrong in life.

In a health query, the reversed Queen of Wands can indicate temporary physical exhaustion, due to working too hard or pursuing too many projects simultaneously. She believes that increased effort will clear the way to pursuing personal goals. As a result of her efforts, people around her sometimes offload their responsibilities on to her, burdening her even further.

As a person, the reversed Queen of Wands describes someone who is reckless, impatient and bossy. This individual usually has poor negotiation skills, preferring instead to push personal plans and agendas, regardless of group consensus. Sometimes, this card suggests someone who is exhausted after completing a demanding challenge or project. Although needing rest, this person is unlikely to pause to catch up. The pace can be brutal.

As a situation, this card describes a lack of success due to insufficient strength, courage or self-belief. This individual needs to be encouraged before reaching their peak potential. A small amount of support can help develop the innate strength of this fiery Queen. Sometimes, the reversed Queen of Wands shows a person who has alienated friends and colleagues who might have supported her goals. By insisting on doing everything herself, she has become bogged down with tasks.

As an aspect of the person, this card highlights a tendency to fight with others. This is sometimes caused by constant criticism in childhood and poor self-esteem. This individual needs to learn to value personal contributions to situations and notice when others are appreciative. Instead, there is a tendency to brag about personal strengths and belittle others in a bid to feel superior. This can be a symptom of insufficient inner strength and self-worth.

Confidence needs to be built slowly and patiently. This person is likely to lack endurance, tranquillity and the ability to pause and reflect on past actions. By not reviewing the past, mistakes are repeated. The fire signs (Aries, Leo and Sagittarius) are usually more adventurous and excitable by nature. As a result, new goals and opportunities beckon and reflective pauses are swept aside. Doing brings results but reflection sometimes helps generate better results with less effort.

Queen of Cups

The Queen of Cups is intuitive, emotional, creative and sensitive to the feelings of people around her. She can unconsciously 'read' or intuitively assess the energy of a room full of people when entering it. She often makes judgements based on how she feels or what she senses.

In this card, a woman is seated on an ornate throne holding an elaborate cup with both hands. This cup has two angels on it with a cross on the lid. She sits patiently but her strong gaze highlights emotional strength and determination that is often unnoticed at first meeting.

Careers in counselling, psychology, writing, human resources, working with children or any support role are suitable options for this individual. The Queen of Cups doesn't crave the limelight; she is happy to leave centre stage for the Queen of Wands. Instead, she needs to know she makes a difference to the emotional quality of life of people around her.

QUEEN of CUPS.

She can thrive as a personal assistant but in such a role she is not necessarily as organised as the Queen of Swords. Creative, harmonious surroundings are necessary if she is to perform to her best. She is sensitive to the energies of her work environment and to people around her. When a colleague is angry or anxious, she can feel that person's emotions within her own body. This is physically and emotionally draining and reduces her ability to work effectively.

She is a natural listener. Strangers often feel safe confiding in her and divulging their troubles. She is also sought out by children or anyone who needs to be heard and understood, as she is naturally nurturing, tactful and intuitive. She is capable of facing great pain in life. Her personal strength is her emotional depth and patience.

The Queen of Cups is a card representing success through personal creativity and intuition. This card can also signify accomplishment that comes from patiently awaiting opportunities and moving when the time is right. She instinctively understands the art of timing.

In a general reading, this card describes a sensitive, introverted woman with a vivid imagination and powerful intuition. She is naturally creative, inclusive rather than competitive and she appreciates kindness. It can describe success in a creative endeavour through intuition and quiet persistence.

In a career layout, the Queen of Cups describes a creative career or a job involving listening to others. This person is a natural healer, clairvoyant, counsellor or nurse and usually possesses a strong desire to alleviate the suffering of others. Any role that involves supporting people in their life journeys requires the natural strengths of this Queen.

Sometimes, this card indicates a time of patiently awaiting new opportunities. By focusing on the elaborate cup in her hands, she has time to notice where future job opportunities might lead her. This card usually describes someone who is more focused on emotionally and spiritually meaningful work than an attractive salary package.

In a relationship question, this person is happiest with a supportive partner. Basically, a cups type is an effective listener and is discreet when privy to a partner's secrets. Unlike the Queen of Wands, who actively pursues relationship opportunities, the Queen of Cups instinctively knows when a new partner is approaching, sometimes months before a first meeting. The new partner might feature in her dreams at night. The water Queen waits patiently, knowing not to rush life.

Cups people are capable of attracting opportunities to themselves or pushing outdated relationships away simply by focusing on their desired outcomes. Life does the rest for them. When balanced, they understand that anything that can be achieved through physical effort can also be mastered with energy and focused desire. The pace is calm, patient and involves quiet focus.

In a health question, the upright Queen of Cups indicates balanced health, due to personal, emotional and spiritual nourishment. This card also describes a soft, compassionate individual, like a nurse or a carer who might assist this person towards balanced health. Cups individuals understand the value of spending time in emotionally and spiritually uplifting surroundings as part of ensuring ongoing health. They do not usually function well in noisy, competitive, unsupportive environments and tend to avoid them.

As a person, the upright Queen of Cups describes a shy, sensitive, creative and intuitive individual, who listens more than speaks, a natural counsellor for friends and colleagues. This person is usually kind, patient and nurturing, preferring to socialise with one or two people than within a noisy crowd.

As a situation, this card represents success through creative discipline. It also highlights intuition in making major decisions. It is a card for reflection. This individual regularly takes time to think about the past while emotionally processing recent events. Contemplation is valued. She generally avoids rushing around in pursuit of deadlines.

As an aspect of the client, the Queen of Cups can indicate a need to identify sources of emotional and spiritual nourishment. From creative hobbies to spiritual practices, this person understands the value inner harmony contributes towards a fulfilling life.

Queen of Cups Reversed

When the Queen of Cups is reversed, unresolved emotional pain sometimes makes her bitter or vengeful. Problematic past issues obscure her vision of the present, making her an unreliable counsellor or confidant. Personal attitudes often isolate her from life and from opportunities for healing. Sometimes, she has more invested in blaming others than in healing herself of past upheavals.

Reversed cups people tend to hold on to emotional pain, remembering every intricate detail of past suffering as though the video replay is on a continuous loop. It's as if maintaining the memory of past anguish is more meaningful than the natural healing process. By repeatedly remembering old wounds, these injuries cannot heal naturally. Recuperation often requires time and emotional and spiritual nourishment. Eventually, the ability to forgive past hurts and embrace the present occurs naturally.

Deanne's marriage of twelve years collapsed when she discovered her husband had been cheating on her. The betrayal was so painful for Deanne that she drifted into despair and then depression. Five years later, she was still distrustful of men, believing that all men cheat on women; her unresolved grief and anger were preventing new opportunities for love.

It was suggested to Deanne that for her husband to lie to her successfully for such a long time, it was possible she might have been subconsciously deceiving herself. This struck a chord with her. Deanne needed to listen to her intuition more closely to know which men are trustworthy. She had been unable to connect with her intuition throughout the twelve years with her husband, suggesting that perhaps she was a Queen of Cups reversed before her marriage collapsed. An upright Queen of Cups is rarely deceived, due to intuitively sensing the motives of others within her own body.

The Queen of Cups reversed tends to sulk when she doesn't get her way. She also has a very long memory for emotional pain. She can quote back verbatim what was said and done to upset her sixteen years ago as though it was yesterday. This person is effectively stuck in the past. Eventually, she'll face the difficult task of releasing the pain while grieving the loss of the intervening years when she refused suitable opportunities for happiness.

The Queen of Cups reversed can suggest a need to forgive someone and let go of the past. This act of forgiveness allows new opportunities for emotional fulfilment. While holding on to the past, it's unlikely this person will be open to new avenues to happiness. It's difficult to be clear-thinking and optimistic when burdened by unresolved betrayals — the pain of the past colours one's view of the world. What was once a glass half full has become a cracked glass with a chipped rim containing muddy water.

Years ago, I worked beside a tarot reader whose readings were influenced by her own unresolved pain. In her sessions, she rarely predicted happiness ahead, even as clients embarked on marriages and settled into new homes. She felt she had made an impact only when her clients were crying. To achieve this, she listed each one of their past disappointments. When setbacks are listed without including past opportunities to balance them, life suddenly seems bleak. I privately referred to her as Pessimistic Meg.

If this is a temporary set of circumstances, the reversed Queen of Cups suggests that the person is likely to be currently overwhelmed by pain or grief. She feels stuck and unable to process her emotions. If this is an ongoing chain of events, the individual feels powerless to find a peaceful life. When faced with opportunities for joy or love, she sees the risk of pain and emotional hunger instead. When she can process her loss and resolve her grief, this person is likely to appear as an upright queen in subsequent readings.

In a general reading, the reversed Queen of Cups describes emotional baggage colouring a person's current perceptions of life. This card indicates someone who is presently grieving, processing a loss or cannot lay the past to rest. There is a risk becoming embittered because of past betrayals. Sometimes, if it feels appropriate, the question to ask the client might be: 'What would you need to release the past and move forward?'

In a career layout, this reversed Queen describes someone feeling dispirited after being overlooked for promotion. Perhaps this person's input is unappreciated when creative projects are distributed. Maybe someone in the workplace has taken credit for this individual's original ideas. She lacks the innate passion and force for self-promotion. This card indicates a lack of fulfilment from the work environment. When unable to find suitable creative or meaningful work, it is useful to have hobbies and outlets for personal creativity and inner nourishment.

In a relationship question, this card represents someone who is not yet available in the present moment. This person might be yearning to resume a past relationship or to hear from a previous partner who was once loved and valued. Sometimes, a water individual loves a person more post-separation than when they were together. There is an inclination to continuously review the past rather than process it and move on.

Sentiment and intense emotional yearning combine, leaving this person hungry and fed only through imagination. It's safer to imagine a perfect relationship than to risk more pain by engaging in one. She is likely to read romance novels or watch sentimental films to fill the emptiness that might have existed even before her previous partner arrived.

Sometimes, the reversed Queen of Cups describes an individual who is emotionally unavailable for a current partner, despite being in a long-term relationship. She is emotionally frozen in time, perhaps due to a past loss or trauma.

In a health query, the reversed Queen of Cups can indicate emotional or psychic disturbance influencing health. It often suggests listlessness or depression. If it is reactive depression (a reaction to a loss or a major disappointment), time might heal it. If it's chronic, this person might benefit from the assistance of a counsellor, psychologist, psychiatrist or medical doctor.

Sometimes, the individual is simply in need of an ear. Being the one who listens to others, a Queen of Cups is often ignored when she needs to be heard. This occurred with a counselling client of mine who arrived one day looking tired. I sensed she was feeling invisible, so I said, "It seems I could be the first person to actually see and hear you all week." She nodded affirmatively before correcting me. "All year basically." It was August and despite having a husband and three children, she felt inconspicuous at home.

The reversed Queen of Cups also describes someone who needs emotional and spiritual nourishment. The heart might be fed by a swim in the ocean, daily meditation or prayer, or through spending time with supportive, nurturing friends. Sometimes, a simple afternoon with old friends, nourishing food and interesting conversation can refuel one's heart and soul.

As a person, the reversed Queen of Cups suggests someone who is depressed or emotionally exhausted. This person is probably unable to make sense of past trauma or loss in order to resolve it. This limbo state can inhibit the individual's awareness of present opportunities. It's also possible there are insufficient sources of reliable emotional and spiritual nourishment to balance life's demands. It might be time to take a yoga class, dive into the sea, join a book club, learn to play an instrument, spend an hour with a colouring-in book and some pencils or grow a garden.

As a situation, this card sometimes describes someone who is not heeding intuition. This individual probably feels unhappy due to not engaging in activities that provide nourishment. Sometimes a Queen of Cups card appears reversed when the person is supporting someone with ongoing health issues while juggling a job and family. In these circumstances, options like an ocean swim or a yoga class are off the table. There simply isn't time. This occurred with Antonia, whose mother was in the early stages of dementia. Antonia knew that although managing her time was difficult, not caring for her mother might mean years of guilt when she eventually died.

From a hectic job to long-forgotten hobbies, sources of happiness are diminishing when the Queen of Cups appears reversed. A creative outlet or an attentive friend or counsellor might help this person reconnect with suppressed creative and spiritual desires.

As an aspect of the client, the reversed Queen of Cups describes exhaustion and resentment resulting from always listening to and meeting the needs of others while their own wishes are ignored. It's a price this person pays for intuitive sensitivity. She is conscious of when others need encouragement, providing help before they ask. When needing assistance or kindness themselves, this person is shy about asking for help and others are often too busy to notice her struggling. Although it feels unfair, it's worth realising that being ignored by others is probably more related to their intuitive insensitivity than selfishness.

When a Queen of Wands needs help, she asks, even shouts, if necessary. When a Queen of Swords needs assistance, she knows who to ask, how to ask and she often negotiates to have her needs met. When a Queen of Pentacles requires support, she is usually prepared to find the best person to provide that support and pay for it if necessary, whereas the Queen of Cups is shy. Instead of asking, shouting, negotiating or searching online for support, she sits quietly, hoping someone will notice her needs and offer to meet them.

Queen of Swords

The Queen of Swords is a quick thinker, organised, perceptive and able to cut through the confusion to arrive at the truth or essence of a person or situation. This Queen represents the water part of the suit of swords. The swords suit is the element of air. Consequently, the Queen of Swords represents the watery part of air. This means she is basically compassionate in her judgements and allows for human nature and unresolved emotional issues when considering people's motivations in acting a certain way.

QUEEN of SWORDS.

In this card, a woman sits on a throne with an upright sword in one hand and the other hand outstretched with a tassel hanging from it (a reminder of being tied up in the Eight of Swords); her tunic is covered with clouds. The clear skies above and the clouds below her head suggest she is clear-thinking. Her upright sword symbolises mental clarity, plus the double edge shows an awareness of the dual nature of life.

As the water part of air, this Queen is a combination of sympathy and rational thought. The bird above the queen's head symbolises the mind's ability to soar above day-to-day problems in order to perceive solutions. Butterflies adorn her crown and there is a large butterfly carved into the base of her throne. These creatures represent the capacity of the mind to transform our personal understanding of life. By comprehending the decisions and actions that have resulted in current situations, it's possible to alter behaviour or make different choices that will result in more suitable consequences in future.

The butterflies also represent the ability to renew oneself by seeing how thoughts lead to actions and actions produce consequences. This is one of the purposes of counselling, as it can help clients untie the mental and emotional knots they are in as a result of damaging life experiences.

The Queen of Swords needs to know why, what, when, where and who. Until she makes sense of her circumstances, she can find sleep at night difficult. She usually has a reliable memory, is an exceptional conversationalist and enjoys social occasions, as she is naturally curious about people. Swords individuals get a dinner party or a social gathering started through conversation, with the ability to discuss subjects that cups people wouldn't dare approach.

An example of this was something my friend Bethany, an adept conversationalist, once said. We were standing (talking, naturally) together at a party when a man limped into the room. His twisted torso suggested he had limped since birth. We nodded politely to him and after a cursory glance at his twisted leg, I resolved not to look again. Bethany had no such intention.

"Hi, I'm Beth, and what happened to your leg?" she asked, stretching out her hand warmly to him.

"I'm Robert and I was born with this," he replied. They started discussing his leg, when Robert mentioned that his hips were lopsided, making walking over uneven surfaces difficult. At this point, Bethany disappeared and returned with a tape to measure the distance between each of Robert's hips and the floor.

"You're right, you know. The right hip is at least three centimetres higher than the left."

Bethany was genuinely interested and Robert seemed content to be measured by a stranger. Curious swords people like to find out what the rest of us secretly want to know but can be too embarrassed to ask. They usually don't offend because they are tactful and genuinely curious. At the end of this process, three more people had gathered to see why Robert was being measured. One asked if it was for a new suit. He was suddenly the centre of the conversation. A shy person, accompanied by a swords friend to a social event, is likely to meet more people in a night than in the previous few months.

In a general reading, the Queen of Swords indicates success through clarity of thought and thorough planning. It also describes a quick-minded, sociable person with excellent skills in project management. This card suggests someone with fine people skills, plus a wide range of contacts who can assist with ideas, supplies or discounts. This individual can quickly see the flaws in a plan.

In a career layout, the Queen of Swords indicates success that comes through preparing and implementing a careful strategy. From delicately negotiating workplace relations to networking within and outside the organisation, this individual is usually widely known in her industry. As a consequence, when they consider changing jobs, this individual is sought after by organisations and competitors.

In a relationship question, the upright Queen of Swords represents someone who enjoys conversation and exploring new ideas. She desires a partner who provides intellectual stimulation. A spouse doesn't have to be an intellectual powerhouse but it will help to be quirky and curious about life. This person admires a partner who is open to negotiating solutions to issues and can argue a case for their perspective when necessary.

In a health query, the Queen of Swords can describe a medical person and sometimes a surgeon. When this card represents a health advisor, they are usually organised, precise and trustworthy. This individual is well-read on a chosen speciality, quick to assess an individual's state of mind and physical health and ready to offer the most appropriate treatment for the circumstances. Sometimes this card can indicate a person who is exploring new approaches to health, weighing up the best avenue for ongoing wellbeing.

As a person, the Queen of Swords represents a quick-minded individual who is a natural negotiator. A talented networker, this person usually enjoys mingling in a crowded room in search of interesting conversations, new ideas and riveting discussions. This card suggests someone who has a powerful memory for details and enjoys reading books. Unlike the Queen of Cups, who has an interest in historical romances, this Queen typifies someone who reads more for knowledge than to escape current circumstances.

As a situation, this card describes success that comes from careful planning and adapting to changing circumstances as the need arises. It represents being able to restructure a strategy according to current location, the team involved or the desired outcomes. This person values input from everyone involved, which often saves time and helps avoid disaster when participants reveal flaws in current methods. This is a card for success through clarity of thought.

As an aspect of the client, this Queen indicates clear thinking with effective analysis of the strengths and weaknesses of a partnership, career or project. This individual comprehensively understands what skills need to be applied to reach the desired goal, plus the likely setbacks that exist on the path ahead.

Queen of Swords Reversed

The Queen of Swords reversed can be extremely self-critical, selectively reviewing the past and focusing only on what did not go according to plan. She is a perfectionist and resents making mistakes. Her desire to understand what went wrong and how she might have avoided an obstacle can lead to confusion between her thoughts and feelings. It's difficult to review past efforts objectively while berating yourself with negative self-talk.

It's a reader's task to determine whether a reversed court card is a brief reversal resulting from temporary setbacks or frustrations, or if it represents a long-standing character trait. If it's temporary, the client may have this card upright in a subsequent reading several months or years later. If it's an entrenched character trait, it's likely to appear reversed until the person changes.

A temporarily reversed Queen of Swords can be the result of recent criticism. If she feels that someone has been unreasonable, she can become sharp, impatient and alert to the flaws of others. When she has answered the 'why' question (Why did he treat me that way?), she usually returns to the (upright) alert, sociable, quick-minded queen that she is.

The Queen reversed often prefers time alone to clarify her thoughts and process her feelings in a bid to restore inner peace and mental clarity. Sometimes, she cannot understand why, despite having clear strategies, plans unravel before they are achieved. She retreats to make sense of events. This need for solitude is perhaps why some traditional tarot writers have dubbed her 'the widow'.

It is true she often has more than her share of loss and pain when reversed but she is capable of returning to the upright position when she makes sense of what life has delivered. Sometimes, the best approach to her past is to accept that life is neither fair nor just. Starting points in life are different for every individual, making comparisons futile.

The appearance of the Queen reversed can suggest being released from the restrictions connected to the Eight of Swords. Old memories and pain are triggered by incidental events, causing a retreat from life and from what is perceived as dangerous. The clouds are now above the Queen's head when reversed, blurring her vision and perception of life.

In a general reading, this card describes self-criticism and a quest for perfection that leaves the person disappointed. This individual seems critical, sharp and prickly when threatened. A single raised eyebrow can signify impatience with perceived incompetence. This person is capable of inflicting severe damage with minimum words when crossed.

Sometimes, this individual is scathing when assessing others. I overheard a comment at a local government meeting where lack of planning had allowed an irate resident to hijack the agenda. The panel sat confused about how to control the meeting when a reversed Queen of Swords turned to a friend and said, "Who are these elected clowns and will the school bus be along soon to collect them?"

In a career layout, this card describes self-doubt about one's abilities or someone around the person who is continually critical of their job performance. Perfection is the unrealistic yet desired starting point for this individual. It can describe a colleague who instils doubts about a team's ability to complete a project. This is someone who usually doesn't play well with others.

In a relationship question, the reversed Queen of Swords describes someone who is anxious, indecisive and consumed by doubts. Constant internal criticism can become debilitating. Sometimes, in a relationship, this person directs inner criticism outwards, becoming scornful of a partner and undermining the bond between them.

In a health query, the reversed Queen of Swords can indicate periods of anxiety, mental confusion and exhaustion, resulting from continual self-criticism. This person has a quick but undisciplined mind. It runs rampant in any and all directions, often seizing on perceived flaws and imperfections. The card reversed can also signify hypochondria. When reversed, the Queen of Swords is ever alert for symptoms of ill-health, every sneeze marks the onset of influenza and each cough the sign of a chronic lung condition. Researching symptoms on the internet can become a habit.

As a person, the reversed Queen of Swords can describe someone who is anxious, mentally scattered or self-critical. There is a tendency to overthink potential problems and become distracted from immediate issues and decisions. This person usually has an internal voice that is scolding and judgemental and which undermines their efforts. This may echo criticisms of a parent, a former schoolteacher or another demanding person from the past.

As a situation, this card represents a lack of success due to poor planning or fuzzy, circular reasoning. Clouded thinking, too many distractions or an inability to focus on tasks may lead to poorly executed plans. It sometimes indicates that too many doubts are consuming valuable thinking time and distracting the person from goals.

As an aspect of the client, this card describes self-critical thinking patterns. This individual cannot appreciate past personal successes due to minor imperfections. A quest for perfection can spoil sound friendships, long-term love relationships and enjoyment of life. When this Queen is reversed in a layout, there is a belief that every silver lining has a cloud.

Sometimes, the reversed Queen of Swords indicates that the individual is attempting to understand the motives of someone else. This might involve thinking in circles and retracing old conversations in a bid to comprehend why someone has acted in an unexpected way. This process can be a recipe for stress or anxiety that interrupts sleep and wastes time and energy.

Queen of Pentacles

This card represents a practical woman whose approach to life is realistic, conservative and routine. While the other Queens dream of the future, this Queen is aware that the future starts right now. She plans each step carefully, aware of the effort involved while planting her feet firmly on the ground.

In this card, a woman sits patiently on a throne in a garden examining a pentacle. The skull of an animal is carved into the throne, along with various fruits and several human figures. The rabbit in the foreground reminds us of this woman's connection with animals and nature. She wears a red tunic, suggesting a passionate but sensible approach to life. The sky is gold, symbolising good times.

The Queen of Pentacles represents the water part of the earthy suit of pentacles. This combination of earth and water means she has emotional depth (water), plus the practical application to realise goals (earth). She needs time amidst nature to restore her energy. Time spent with animals also makes her feel happy.

The Queen of Pentacles is suited to a range of careers, including accountancy, banking, financial controlling and growing crops, herbs, fruit and vegetables. She also enjoys working with therapeutic massage (the sense of touch being natural to pentacles people), real estate, food or general business management. The pentacles queen is usually a diligent worker and takes a steady, considered approach to her career responsibilities. She soon develops a reputation for being thorough and reliable. As a result, she often moves steadily up the career ladder.

She is practical, nurturing and methodical and, as a mother, she lends an air of stability to her environment through establishing solid routines and a healthy lifestyle. For example, Alison insists her five-year-old daughter, Clara, take a long walk every day. At first Clara (a Page of Swords) moaned through the whole walk but soon Alison learned to distract her with stories about plants and animals along the way. Eventually, Clara began to look forward to the walks and their time spent together talking. Gradually, Alison increased the distance they walked, to strengthen her daughter physically and help discharge some of her restless energy, to ensure she slept soundly at night.

Alison realises Clara is not an earthy, practical person but she insists on providing an opportunity for her to spend time with nature so as to learn to appreciate the outdoors. The balance between Clara's mental energy and her physical body is improved through regular exercise.

The Queen of Pentacles is a card for success as a result of thorough planning with a realistic approach to personal goals. It describes accomplishing objectives through physical effort combined with financial discipline and emotional balance. She's basically a sensible, reasonable person who forms productive habits that serve her well over the years. She lacks some of the curiosity of the Queen of Swords and the passion of the Queens of Wands because she believes the road less travelled is often less travelled for a very good reason. She's conservative and traditional, preferring a well-trodden path. The glamour and excitement of exotic places do not entice this person from her path.

In a general reading, this card describes a successful person who enjoys nature. This individual finds purpose through work and understands that income is the foundation of choices in life. Sometimes, the upright Queen of Pentacles describes a supportive person in the client's life who is steadfast and reliable.

In a career layout, the Queen of Pentacles can suggest a practical, no-nonsense approach to long-term career success. It also describes a supportive, realistic individual assisting with career plans. It indicates career success that is achieved steadily because pentacles people understand wealth is best built gradually to avoid upheaval. They are generally not risk-takers, preferring to advance wealth slowly and deliberately rather than rush in fearlessly.

In a relationship question, this Queen is practical, realistic and appreciates stability with comfortable routines. She doesn't become bored when life runs smoothly. Instead, she prefers to have an emergency fund and admires a partner who can minimise debt and save steadily towards goals. If a partner belongs to the wands or cups suits, this person usually balances the business accounts and helps make budgets when planning the future. This is someone who lives within their means and works hard towards meaningful shared goals.

In a health question, this card usually confirms stable health. It can emphasise spending time in nature to relieve stress and indicates sufficient financial resources to maintain ongoing good health. Areas of the body to watch when the upright Queen of Pentacles appears in a health layout include the kidneys and the pancreas. The digestive system is also an area to consider when stressed.

As a person, the upright Queen of Pentacles describes someone who is realistic and conservative and who understands the value of money. This is a natural business person who appreciates being surrounded by nature, plants and animals. The card highlights an individual who enjoys making a garden thrive and feels more at peace with an emergency fund in place for a rainy day. This is someone who prefers stability and likes comfortable routines, who is not bored by constancy but realises how stable habits consolidate feelings of safety, peace and support.

As a situation, this card indicates success through the practical application of plans. In a question about a business venture, it sometimes suggests the person has sufficient funds to begin a project successfully. It also highlights a realistic assessment of how much effort a plan needs to reach the end goal. The upright Queen of Pentacles indicates that the person will have sufficient stamina and persistence to achieve objectives.

As an aspect of the client, this card represents a quiet confidence, usually resulting from personal accomplishments. It suggests patience, perseverance and the ability to pace oneself for the long haul. It sometimes describes someone making decisions to secure long-term financial security. It highlights a desire for stability over change at this time.

Queen of Pentacles Reversed

The Queen of Pentacles reversed suggests someone who has lost connection with nature and is too focused on job prospects or financial issues. Sometimes, it indicates a lack of self-confidence, someone whose self-worth depends on career achievements rather than actual personal self-worth. Driven to succeed, this person values the control that wealth affords them in life above the closeness relationships or family can offer. This is sometimes with good reason.

During Dana's twenty-two-year marriage to Giorgio, he constantly told her that he was a successful businessman and without him she'd be poor. This was despite Dana managing staff, business banking and marketing for their joint business. During an economic downturn, Giorgio overspent on advertising and upgrading business equipment and they had to sell the business to cover their rapidly escalating debts.

He blamed her, so Dana left him and began her own business. She freely admitted that the ensuing ten years were spent working too hard to prove to Giorgio she was a better business person than he. She built up a thriving homewares store and sold it to buy a home and begin a new venture. After losing a close friend to illness, Dana realised it was crucial to enjoy a full life as well as being financially stable.

This reversed Queen may appear as ambitious, overly career-minded and determined to get ahead financially at all costs but on closer inspection, sometimes this person is still a child emotionally. She has lost her balance, favouring the earthy (practical) part of her nature over her watery (emotional) instincts. She clings to the structure of career to compensate for the inner chaos or turmoil in other parts of her life. This individual is less likely to be intuitive, creative or compassionate, perhaps due to unresolved emotional issues that interrupt her instinctive connections.

The reversed state of this card might only be temporary. Resolving outstanding issues helps reinstate the upright Queen of Pentacles again. Time spent amidst nature provides a broader perspective, enabling this individual to recognise the true importance of career in the greater scheme.

In a general reading, the reversed Queen of Pentacles describes a practical, hard-working person whose low self-worth limits her to working for minimum wage. This is the qualified accountant working as a bookkeeper for low rewards and doing the work of two people. It might be the result of poor money training as a child. This individual tends to live hand-to-mouth while working hard.

Alternatively, the reversed Queen of Pentacles can describe an ambitious person whose approach to financial stability is to marry well. This can be a profitable approach, provided the partner doesn't die suddenly leaving huge debts or elope with a work colleague. The upright Queen doesn't usually rely on others for income and stability because this person understands how changeable life can be.

In a relationship question, this card describes someone who doesn't fully value their contributions to relationships. Perhaps the individual is worried about being dull or lacking charisma instead of finding a partner who appreciates stability and comfort. Sometimes, the person is driven to make money but lacks sufficient training to earn a reasonable income for hard work.

In a career layout, the reversed Queen of Pentacles suggests a lack of success with career or financial plans. This might be the result of poor planning, a lack of hard work or insufficient tenacity in pursuit of goals. Often, however, despite hard work, lack of self-confidence is holding this person back from career success. Sometimes, the reversed card highlights a lack of confidence in study, improving career prospects or moving up the career ladder. The person might not believe they are capable of improving their qualifications and might need a coach or a mentor for guidance through the process.

In a health query, this card describes a career that affects health. It might be a toxic work environment (physically or emotionally), lack of sleep or insufficient rest on weekends due to commuting times or extreme workplace demands.

The reversed Queen of Pentacles appeared in Carol's health layout and she mentioned that anyone who left her office before 7:00 p.m. was teased about taking a half-day off. She worked every second weekend without pay and estimated that the eleven people in her workplace did the work of 28 people, year after year. She didn't have time to apply for a new job because there was too much to do.

Physically, the reversed Queen can suggest problems with the pancreas and the kidneys. This card sometimes represents issues with the digestive system, often due to overwhelming responsibilities. It can also suggest that money needs to be spent on improving health for long-term rewards. It's time to build solid, regular health habits.

As a person, the reversed Queen of Pentacles often describes someone who works hard for little or no reward. Fear of change can keep this individual entrenched in an underpaid job. A lack of self-confidence prevents this person from studying to improve skills and employment opportunities. This person is a bit resistant to change and, instead of embracing it, constantly remembers life could be worse. Greater self-belief leads to more opportunities.

In contrast, the reversed card sometimes points to an ambitious person who searches for a wealthy partner to secure a solid position in life. Disinterested in a love match, the person is constantly assessing a potential partner's financial worth. For them, money equals power and comfort.

As a situation, the reversed Queen of Pentacles indicates poor attitudes to money and building financial wealth. Parental training around finances might have been inadequate or chaotic, restricting the person from enjoying a stable life as an adult. It can suggest a lack of success due to insufficient funds to support plans.

As an aspect of the client, the reversed Queen indicates a lack of confidence or an inability to value personal contributions. It might be reflected in financial scarcity when an individual works extremely hard at an underpaid job. Sometimes, it describes a partner or a dependant who cannot seem to earn sufficient income or live within their means.

The Kings

The kings in the tarot represent four mature masculine approaches to life. The king is the earthy part of each suit, so his focus is usually on tangible, practical results. This is why when his partner feels sad or upset, he wants to do something about it. He wants to fix it rather than simply sit with her and allow her to feel her emotions while she finds her own solutions.

It's unlikely for a woman to appear as a king in a layout but when it occasionally happens it is usually to confirm an astrological sign. The King of Wands is Aries (the accompanying card being The Emperor), the King of Cups is Scorpio (along with the Death card), the King of Swords is Aquarius (along with The Star) and the King of Pentacles is Taurus (the other cards being The Hierophant and the Four of Pentacles).

When pairing each of the suits' kings and queens together, a clear picture emerges. The King and Queen of Wands gaze directly into each other's eyes. Their relationship is intense, straightforward and honest. The King of Cups glances away from the Queen of Cups, while she looks into her cup (a chalice) to sense what he is thinking and feeling. No words are needed, as they both intuit what is unsaid between them.

The Queen of Swords gazes directly at the King of Swords as though awaiting an answer to a question. The King is lost in his own thoughts of fathoming the world. This suggests that concepts and ideas preoccupy them. The King of Pentacles looks down at his pentacle, keeping an eye on practical concerns to ensure stability. The Queen of Pentacles does the same but with less of the air of pride in her achievements that the King displays through his posture. Instead, she realises that by investing her resources wisely she can protect the generations to come.

Examined alone, the kings look in directions that reveal their natures. The King of Wands looks to his right for what is traditionally the path of action. The King of Cups glances to his left, at an emotional and creative direction. The King of Swords stares straight ahead to decipher what is real and what is perceived to be genuine in life, while the King of Pentacles looks downwards at practical concerns in the material world.

King of Wands

The King of Wands represents a forthright man who is suited to any task or career that offers goals and challenges. Routines don't appeal to him; in fact, when habits start to develop, he knows it is time to move on to another challenge. He is not afraid to speak his mind and so is usually unsuited to delicate negotiations. Generally, this King favours the commando-style surprise raid to protracted telephone discussions. This is why sales managers refer to sales territories and treat weekly meetings as a chance to marshal troops and capture the market or hold the line when competitors begin discounting. This King lives for the next conquest, be it a career move, a fitness challenge or a marriage proposal.

KING of WANDS.

In this card, the person seated on the throne stares off into the distance in search of the anticipated arrival of someone or something to excite or challenge him. He holds a wand in his right hand. The salamanders covering his cloak and the lions carved into the back of his seat, highlight the King's inner strength and confidence in his abilities. His orange robe indicates a passionate, excitable nature but he is seated (and not rushing towards his goal, like the exuberant Knight), which suggests that in maturity he is disciplined in his excitement.

The element for the wands suit is fire and the kings represent the earth element. As the earthy aspect of fire, this King is practical and tempers his enthusiasms. He restrains himself, so as not to commence projects he is unable to complete. The elements of earth and fire often oppose each another. Where earth wants to maintain the stability of current circumstances and resist change, fire prefers to abandon the existing situation in favour of new opportunities and the promise of better circumstances elsewhere. This King resists ruts and routines quickly bore him. He is sometimes torn between preserving current stability and forging ahead in search of stimulating new opportunities. He thrives on excitement and challenges and is a risk-taker.

The King of Wands is suited to a career in sales, teaching, coaching sports teams, acting, singing, professional sports and most outdoor jobs that provide plenty of freedom to walk or drive around. For example, if this person has a career in sales and is promoted to a position where he is locked away in an office all day, he is likely to go a bit stir-crazy as he needs to be outdoors with plenty of space. As a manager, he has a hands-on style. King of Wands people usually start new businesses and then sell them to other, less adventurous, kings and queens.

In answer to a question, this fiery King can indicate success resulting from self-discipline and controlled enthusiasm. In a health reading, the King of Wands can represent headaches or illnesses that affect the head area. Wands people resent anything that impedes their mobility or their ability to pursue their goals, so thoughts of ill-health rarely occur to them until they are physically sick. Consequently, they are poor patients, sometimes rushing back into life before they have fully recovered.

In a general reading, the King of Wands describes success resulting from self-discipline. By harnessing excitement and enthusiasm for a goal, a person can work tirelessly until it's within reach. This card can also indicate support from a passionate, forthright individual who is a helpful influence in the person's life, inspiring, coaching or supporting wherever possible.

In a relationship question, this individual is excited by the chase in love. The more challenging the circumstances, the more it appeals. This is someone who prefers a bold, straightforward approach with cheeky, playful, self-confidence that appeals to potential partners.

In a career layout, the King of Wands is a card of success, especially in sales, marketing, managing a business and competitive sports. The individual is likely to be passionate, competitive and motivated to achieve more when competing with co-workers. This person needs goals, sales targets and rewards for objectives achieved.

The King of Wands is naturally competitive. A four per cent annual bonus is not likely to be the best reward for this person. There is a great desire for something tangible that covers shorter time periods. A monthly prize of a weekend away for two or an afternoon sailing the harbour followed by a lavish dinner for two at a waterside restaurant are more likely to have this enthusiastic fire King regularly breaking sales records. This individual is impatient to achieve goals and reap immediate rewards. Someone with this level of dynamism usually prefers to live spontaneously than to carefully guard shares while waiting patiently for their value to increase. The King of Wands lacks the patience of the King of Pentacles.

In a health query, the King of Wands indicates headaches and sometimes sports injuries due to carelessness and reckless impatience. Burns often feature in health issues, due to an attraction to fire but also to impatience and hastiness when dealing with it. Generally, the upright King suggests robust health with ample reserves of energy and passion for life. This is a warm, lively person with an optimistic outlook.

As a person, the King of Wands describes a forthright, passionate individual who is competitive, playful and thrives on goals and achievements. This is someone who enjoys the outdoors, sports, walking and exploring nature. Suited to careers in sales, marketing or as a self-employed tradesman, this person prefers to spend part of each day outside. Paperwork holds little appeal to this fire person, so for a business to succeed, it is necessary to have an assistant or a partner who dispatches invoices and pays bills. Small-to-medium-sized businesses suit someone who loathes endless meetings and is not suited to delicate negotiations. Stand-up meetings were probably designed for a King of Wands, who wants every meeting to be brief.

As a situation, this card represents success through self-discipline. This upright King is a person who has mastered the fire within and learned to adjust to a less frenetic pace for long, complicated projects. He mostly keeps control over his impatience. Sometimes, however, frustrations bubble to the surface, resulting in short, angry outbursts. After venting anger, the person is quickly able to return to the task.

As an aspect of the client, this card indicates an ability to remain focused on the goal and not become distracted by obstacles. Periodically, the person remembers that if his objective was easy to achieve everyone would have already accomplished it. This individual understands that few people enjoy the view from the mountain's summit because most who attempt the climb, don't reach the top.

The King of Wands shows someone whose previous achievements are testament to their abilities. This person doesn't look back and reflect because there is usually a bigger goal ahead to inspire and motivate more action. It represents an individual who has mastered the fire within but not extinguished it. As a consequence, there is a natural thrust to continually move forward to new conquests.

King of Wands Reversed

The King of Wands reversed suggests an immature person whose need for action betrays a restless spirit and inner discontent. There is an inclination to be careless with the feelings of others, as he is tactless, impatient and reckless. Sensitivity and depth of feeling are not qualities the reversed King enjoys. Instead, this person can be a bully with a surly temper and a short attention span.

Randy's desire to teach his nine-year-old son to ski comprised a brief, sharp lesson. It involved strapping boots and skis to the boy's feet before leaving him behind at the top of a snow-covered mountain while skiing off down to the lodge, two kilometres away.

"It will toughen him up a bit," was Randy's reasoning. An hour later, a shivering little Page of Cups arrived at the lodge where his father was drinking brandy by the fire.

This reversed card represents a lack of success due to attempting too many projects at once. Sometimes, inadequate follow-through is the reason for failure. A reversed King of Wands is generally impatient, fickle and lacks persistence. The King of Wands reversed is basically acting like a Knight of Wands. This person needs to master the Knight's lesson of harnessing enthusiasm to complete personal projects, before becoming an upright King.

The upright King displays a more tempered enthusiasm and persistence with longer-term goals. When mature, the upright King can harness his energy with a more practical view and enjoy lasting results.

In a general reading, this card indicates a lack of success, often due to inadequate self-discipline. Scant consideration is given to what is required for achieving a goal when initial commitments are made. This individual can be rash, impatient and lack long-term vision. "How difficult can it be?" is the question often asked before discovering exactly how arduous a project can become, especially when the end is obscured by a punishing workload.

What initially seemed simple usually turns out to be more complicated. An example of this was the U.S. president whose electoral platform consisted of dismantling Obamacare and replacing it with a 'fairer' health system. After weeks of discussions and passionate negotiations with various factions, he said, "Who thought healthcare was so complicated?" Almost everyone else in the country, as it turned out.

When the reversed King of Wands has discovered, through direct experience, what everyone else already knew, he is the first to erect a warning sign for others. Sometimes, this individual is a proud and perfect director of the Department of the Bleeding Obvious!

In a career layout, this reversed King describes someone who is pursuing too many avenues to ensure success in any particular direction. It's time to focus attention and effort on one clear objective and then set a steady pace towards that goal. The reversed King of Wands often quarrels with co-workers, customers and management and sometimes bullies staff, is tactless and impatient. If not asked to leave jobs, this person often quits after a fight.

In a relationship question, this card suggests an urgency to begin new relationships, followed by a desire to escape the confines of long-term commitment once they have begun. The promise is often more appealing than the delivery for a reversed King of Wands. What appeared to be a butterfly in the store window looks like a moth at home. This person is usually restless, discontent and pessimistic, continuously searching for immediate gratification or an escape clause.

In a health query, this card indicates exhaustion. It's time to simplify life by abandoning projects that are unnecessary or unlikely to be completed in favour of a few personal objectives. Preserving energy is vital for rebuilding health and stamina. Headaches are suggested by this card in a health reading. Until the reversed King learns to negotiate calmly to find solutions that work for everyone, stress is likely to lead to high blood pressure.

Destructive spontaneous reactions can sometimes cause self-injury. Angry outbursts often impair judgement.

As a person, the reversed King of Wands describes an impatient, egocentric individual who is easily distracted and angered when delayed. Instead of focusing on personal goals, this individual becomes overwhelmed or distracted by obstacles and is sometimes tempted to abandon difficult objectives for instant results elsewhere. The reversed fire King often has a short attention span and seeks instant gratification.

This person is often better at beginning new projects than completing existing commitments and isn't usually a team player due to innate competitiveness. At heart, this reversed King is still twenty-three years old and cannot imagine the consequences of actions, until they loom large. Often in a hurry and dismissive of boring details, this individual is also accident-prone.

As a situation, this card indicates limited success, due to the lack of self-discipline. The person is likely to give up at the first hurdle and blame others while hurtling forward to begin another new project. There is a tendency to repeat past mistakes and learn slowly, usually through tackling obstacles directly. Sometimes, the King of Wands reversed suggests it's time to respect boundaries. Pushing too hard now could undo past efforts. This might mean that forcing a situation at work could lead to being dismissed or aggressively asserting an opinion in a bar could result in an arrest.

As an aspect of the client, the reversed King of Wands indicates that patience is required. If the person is unable to sit still, it's best they walk away and release pent up anger effectively. From angrily chopping firewood or working out at the gym to visiting a gun club, a non-harmful outlet for aggression might be needed. Sometimes, the reversed King of Wands suggests the person is tackling too many projects at once. It is necessary to focus by completing some tasks while jettisoning others. It's judicious to avoid commencing new projects at this stage.

The reversed King of Wands may describe a person who believes that daily struggles and strife are part of a noble quest for truth, fairness and justice. In extremis, this person feels fated to vanquish the opposition. There are no shades of grey in his perceptions of life. There is only black and white, truth or falsehood and right or wrong. Unfortunately, family members and work colleagues usually see this individual as antagonistic, combative and unable to work in a team to complete projects effectively.

King of Cups

The King of Cups represents an emotionally mature man who appreciates a creative life but who is earthy enough to make a living from inspired pursuits. This card represents creative success through a disciplined, practical approach to artistic goals. It can also indicate the presence of a supportive, imaginative person.

In this card, a man sits on a throne that rests on a platform surrounded by water. He holds a cup in his right hand and a sceptre in his left. The clasp around his neck contains a fish, symbolic of the element of water. He is quietly strong-willed, as shown by his intense stare. He understands the necessity of being clear about personal desires to avoid attracting undesirable events.

As the element of the suit of cups is water, the King of Cups is an earth-water combination. This person has a practical approach to creativity. He is inspired, inventive yet grounded in reality. When stirred by a creative idea, this person usually takes practical steps to give the concept form. He might produce paintings, gardens, designs, books or songs. From making short films to carefully restoring old furniture, a vintage car or a dilapidated building, the King of Cups can be passionate about preserving history. The past is ever-present for these people.

As this person is naturally sensitive to the emotions of others, time alone is required for rest and to restore inner balance. When friends or colleagues are upset, angry or resentful, this person can feel their emotions intensely. When this happens, spiritual cleansing techniques can restore inner peace. These include swimming in the ocean or in a salt-water pool, meditation or sitting beside the sea. Cups people need to avoid using alcohol to suppress awareness of the collected energies of others, as this only removes conscious awareness and does not clear absorbed energy.

This King is suited to careers in counselling, psychology, psychiatry, music, art, writing or psychic readings. He often has an interest in history, genealogy or hypnosis and is usually attracted to the sea. As this King is an excellent listener, guiding or caring for others are natural career choices. He effortlessly reads the energy of a room and is quick to sense when people he loves are hurt or in emotional pain. He tends to be a calming influence in such circumstances.

This person can be compassionately aware of the shy aspects of other people, choosing words or actions carefully so as not to offend. For this individual to fulfil personal potential, a stable love relationship is essential. This person treasures being loved. Emotional depths and mystery are attractive facets of the earth and water combination.

In a general reading, the upright King describes success in inspired endeavours due to creative discipline. This individual usually proceeds quietly and steadily towards personal goals without fanfare, whether it involves completing a painting, a book, composing an original piece of music or designing a website. This King is usually willing to assist other people towards their artistic goals.

In a career layout, this card can indicate a unique and inspiring occupation. This person doesn't usually show a burning desire to climb the corporate ladder or conquer the competition to take over a market. This is a vocation centred on artistic pursuits that allows room for family life. It indicates creative success, sometimes as a secondary career. After the daily job, the person might be a part-time musician, writing a book or working as a designer in the evenings and on weekends.

In a relationship question, the King of Cups describes an easy-going person who is private, intuitive, creative and romantic by nature. Other people are attracted to this sensitive individual's thoughtfulness. There is a tendency to be shy in large groups of people and this individual usually doesn't actively pursue relationships with the same forthright intensity as King of Wands.

Sensitivity makes this person fear rejection and this can dampen enthusiasm for initiating the first steps towards new relationships. When Sophie asked about a man in her workplace that she was attracted to, the King of Cups was selected in her layout. Sophie explained that they had spent time together on a three-day corporate training at a country retreat and she enjoyed his company. She was waiting for him to ask her out but weeks had passed.

When I suggested she might need to invite him to an event, lunch or a meetup, she shook her head.

"I can't. What if he says no?"

"If he says no, you won't have spent the next three months living in hope. You'll know where you stand."

She looked dejected, so I took a different approach. "Are you a modern woman?" I asked.

"Yes, I like to think so."

"I think so, too. You are successful in corporate life, have purchased your own apartment, drive a new car and manage your life very well. You've completed university studies plus some post-graduate study and your career is on track. It seems as though the only piece of your puzzle missing right now is a life partner."

"You're right," she replied.

"If a modern woman can manage all those goals and tasks successfully, why can't she ask a shy man out on a date? Why can't she cross the floor and ask him to dance? It's no different from applying for a new job."

The following year Sophie returned for another reading. Her first question was "When will he propose to me?" She had invited the King of Cups to a day at the races with friends and their relationship had blossomed from there. It was time for me to suggest she steer him towards her local jewellery store. After all, a girl can't always trust a man to pick a suitable ring to last a lifetime.

In a health query, the King of Cups indicates the importance of an emotionally supportive environment for maintaining health. This individual is attuned to the feelings of others, so it's necessary to avoid environments filled with conflict, resentment or deceit. There is a tendency to absorb the negativity from other people, which influences an inner sense of well-being. In physical health terms, this King can represent the lower back, bladder, bowel or prostate in men and reproductive organs in women.

As a person, the upright King of Cups describes someone who is creative, private and a deep thinker. This individual is sensitive and prefers a career where it's possible to make a difference in the lives of others. Naturally inspired, hobbies usually include creative pursuits such as photography, design, drawing, painting, wine-making and furniture, car or home restoration. This individual is interested in what motivates people so psychology, counselling and coaching appeal as career choices. There is an inclination to be sentimental and sometimes emotionally intense, with a long memory for past hurts. This person rarely argues with others in group activities or in the workplace and is an effective listener when people want to share their troubles.

As a situation, this card indicates success due to creative self-discipline. This is the person who is inspired to form a writer's group, a filmmaker's resource centre or restore a crumbling local theatre and then steadily completes the task. It's also a card for inner peace and calm resulting from a balanced emotional life.

As an aspect of the client, this card can signify an individual waiting patiently for the next opportunity to arrive. Whereas the King of Wands actively searches for prospects, the King of Cups waits patiently for suitable circumstances to appear. During delays, this person usually strengthens the skills relevant to their goals, so the time is not wasted. This is a card for having faith that the Universe will provide.

King of Cups Reversed

The King of Cups reversed combines earth and water in an unfavourable way. It sometimes represents a bank of earth preventing the natural flow of water. Stagnant water can become toxic. Likewise, this King reversed can become embittered unless he learns to resolve the past and allow his emotions to flow unimpeded again.

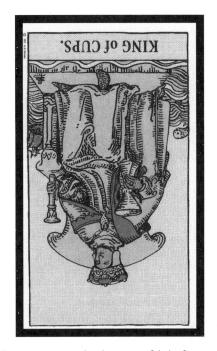

He is still a strong, quiet individual but darker and more sullen than the upright King. Bouts of sulking are more frequent and emotional withdrawal is common when things don't go his way. He is also vengeful if crossed and his creativity is likely to be focused on punishment for those whom he feels are responsible for his circumstances. Alternatively, he seeks out drugs and alcohol to alleviate the immense suffering he believes no-one else has ever felt before. He uses his powerful imagination to deceive himself about life and cannot see that his burdens and suffering are often self-induced. Given a chance, this person is capable of misleading others into seeing life from his gloomy perspective.

Sometimes, beneath apathy and mild depression lurks powerful anger which, if triggered, has all the fury of a hurricane. This rage needs a constructive outlet before creative energies can flow freely again. This is someone who is habitually deceitful, manipulative and constantly seeking power over others in subtle ways. When controlling those around him, this person deliberately remains in the background to manipulate their strings like a puppeteer. There is a fundamental understanding that real influence is often felt but rarely seen.

This card indicates a lack of success due to hidden motives and blocked creativity. The individual represented by the King of Cups reversed unconsciously sabotages personal attempts at success and will spoil others' endeavours too, given half a chance.

In a general reading, the reversed King of Cups can describe a lack of success due to poor creative discipline. This person considers the inspiration part of creativity to be the entire process and often stumbles when it's time to make a concept real. Refining prototypes or managing a personal project can become overwhelming and cause plans to be abandoned. A lack of tenacity influences the outcomes of inspired schemes.

This person might benefit from consulting an upright King or Queen of Swords, who could easily map out a creative project, engage supportive people with skills and talents and prepare a budget for the process. When this card is reversed, emotions cloud thinking, planning and the ability to face the hurdles that many artistic projects encounter before completion.

In a career layout, the reversed King describes an individual who is unhappy in a mainstream career but cannot see a way to earn a reasonable living from creative pursuits. This is the artist whose parents discouraged art or design classes and actively encouraged a career in engineering, accountancy or the technical end of IT. Although this person makes a comfortable living from a current career, the heart is heavy from not pursuing a personal dream.

One upright King of Cups I know maintained a conservative career to support his family while taking weekly painting classes for thirty years. When he retired, he moved away from the city and became a full-time painter. Living by the ocean (a cups person's dream), his expenses are low and he sets annual exhibition dates in art galleries. Now he paints to ensure he has enough for each exhibition. He usually sells out before the exhibitions conclude.

In a relationship question, this individual can be depressed. It sometimes describes a previous emotional loss that has not been accepted or released. The past situation casts a long shadow over current life events, reducing trust and openness to a partner. It also limits awareness of everyday opportunities to be happy together. In extreme circumstances, the reversed King of Cups describes someone who is jealous, secretive and unable or unwilling to forgive any perceived misdeeds of past or current partners. This person can eventually create a toxic environment of secrets, fear and doubt that erode trust and engulf everyone involved.

In a health layout, this card represents difficulties with the lower back, abdomen, bowel and reproductive organs. It sometimes indicates an issue with the prostate. It can also suggest health problems resulting from suppressed emotions. Perhaps this person is unable to get past a recent loss and finds it impossible to find nourishment from books, films, music or an artistic outlet. Instead, there is a pervasive sense of dread at facing life's daily demands, coupled with a persistent feeling of powerlessness.

As a person, the reversed King of Cups describes a mature individual who might feel stuck in life. Unable to find a creative outlet or enjoy emotional sources of nourishment, there is a tendency to withdraw from people or situations. Dreams of a creative life have been replaced by bitterness and pessimism. This person is usually secretive and has a long memory for details of past hurts. Seeking revenge is a poor use of creativity.

As a situation, this card can indicate a lack of success due to inadequate creative discipline. In group projects, it sometimes shows delaying tactics to ensure progress is slow or eventually abandoned. If unchecked, this passive-aggressive behaviour can control the direction of a project, an event or a workplace.

As an aspect of the client, this card sometimes indicates poor results because the individual didn't devote sufficient commitment to a key objective. Instead of acknowledging that a goal isn't desired or worthwhile, the person subconsciously sets out to fail. Perhaps this individual feels powerless to say *no* to a project and to ensure a similar task isn't set in future, he or she fails to complete it in time or successfully. If asked to bake a cake for an event, the person produces a large, round, flat biscuit. Thus, they are unlikely to be given a similar responsibility in the future.

King of Swords

The King of Swords represents the earthy part of air, making this individual clear-thinking and practical. He is attracted to science and logic. This person has a sharp mind, communicates with others easily and enjoys learning. He usually remains curious about the world throughout his entire life.

In this card, a man sits on a throne, holding an upward-pointing sword in his right hand. The ring on the Saturn (second) finger of his left hand suggests he takes his responsibilities seriously. Sometimes, it also indicates unresolved issues with his father or a father figure. It's possible that responsibilities were thrust upon him early in life and as a result, he has learned a range of effective strategies for setting goals.

The King's blue tunic represents a desire for spiritual understanding. His purple cloak signifies compassion in the way he uses his mind. His sword is slightly tilted, suggesting he has not yet the clarity of thought possessed by the Queen. He is, however, still far ahead of the other kings in the amount of energy he devotes to learning, reading, conversation and mental stimulation.

KING of SWORDS.

The butterflies on the back of his throne are a reminder that thinking can be transformative because beliefs and attitudes influence what you become. The clouds are below his head indicating crystal clear thinking which is not obscured by past issues but free to analyse and communicate easily. The birds in the background symbolise the mind's ability to soar above problems of the material and emotional worlds for a more expanded perspective.

Career-wise, this King is a professional man, who prefers to keep his hands clean in the pursuit of an income. He is suited to the law, medicine, writing (non-fiction), strategic business planning, sales, counselling (modes that favour a change in beliefs rather than a compassionate approach) and business administration. Any situation that requires clear-thinking, planning or problem-solving suits this King. He also enjoys puzzles and likes to play with words. Languages usually appeal to him.

This card represents success through planning and the ability to remain focused on objectives. Asking for assistance or for advice when pursuing goals is helpful, as other people might be able to provide what is needed or direct the person towards information to simplify the process.

Swords people tend to know the value of requesting help and are aware of the opportunities that may arise through communication. An example of this kind of opportunity occurred recently when a client telephoned me to reschedule an appointment and mentioned she had transcribed my last tarot reading for her.

"That was diligent of you," I said.

"Well, I played the tape into a microphone linked to my computer and a software package did the rest. Out came pages of details that I tidied up afterwards." I was intrigued.

"I need a program like that. I could write a book in a third of the time it usually takes me," I said. She gave me the relevant details. Simple conversations often present opportunities for people who are attentive. The internet was designed for swords people, who sometimes enjoy being able to communicate without being interrupted by those receiving the information. Via e-mail, Facebook and other social spaces, swords people can keep in touch with ten times as many people as they might otherwise see in the course of an average day.

The King of Swords does not need to be in a romantic relationship in the same way the King of Cups does. The Swords King may even be content to have a part-time or a long-distance relationship. The way to his heart is through his mind and a way to garner his full attention is through interesting conversation. Unlike the King of Cups, the King of Swords would rather discuss a book he's read or a documentary he loves than quietly cuddle up beside a fire with his partner.

He loves ideas and concepts, no matter how quirky. A King of Swords friend recently asked me, "If a tree falls in a forest and nobody hears it, where the hell is everybody?"

In a general reading, this card indicates success through clear planning. The King of Swords usually enlists the support of friends or colleagues towards goals, as he is a natural networker and negotiator. It can also describe support for an endeavour from someone talkative whose network might prove useful.

In a career layout, the King of Swords indicates success through having a comprehensive strategy. This person always has a back-up in case original plans are derailed. This individual usually succeeds in any profession that requires keeping up with the latest research, reading or writing reports and teaching or mentoring others. Communication is one of this person's strengths.

In a relationship question, the upright King of Swords describes a curious, mentally agile person over thirty who enjoys conversation, debating and social events. At dinner in a restaurant, he is likely to be continuously waving at people he recognises: friends, colleagues and acquaintances. This person is not shy, is capable of taking a conversation in any direction at a moment's notice and is usually attracted to original-thinking in a partner.

In a health query, the King of Swords can describe a surgeon or a medical practitioner who is focused on daily tasks. The physical health areas symbolised by this King include the lungs and arms, especially if The Lovers card accompanies the King of Swords, the kidneys if The Empress card appears and the ankles or the retinas of the eyes if The Star is found in the layout. As an answer to a question about the outcome of surgery or a medical procedure, the upright King indicates a successful conclusion.

As a person, the King of Swords describes an organised, analytical individual with well-developed networking skills and persistent curiosity about life. This card highlights someone who usually enjoys learning, reading and debating and is an effective manager in the workplace. The King of Swords might describe a doctor, lawyer, coach or advisor who is mentally agile and effective at finding suitable solutions. When upright, this person is a worthwhile consultant or guide to have when pursuing major goals. A unique strength is being able to quickly assess a situation and suggest a realistic course of action for progress.

As a situation, this card points to success through mental clarity and the effective application of well-thought-out plans. The Swords King indicates a person capable of adapting a concept to suit an environment. It describes the ability to think, plan, manage people and modify plans fluidly as required in pursuit of desired objectives.

As an aspect of the client, the King of Swords indicates clear thinking is contributing to success. This person is capable of making an idea or a concept into a tangible product or service. Adept at managing people, finding solutions on the go and asking others for support when necessary, these people are natural communicators.

King of Swords Reversed

The King of Swords reversed can be sharp-tongued and condescending to those who do not share an ability with words or comprehend a wide vocabulary. This individual might use certain words to obscure their intentions or impress other people. Sometimes, the King reversed represents someone who is confused and unable to choose between the alternatives that life is offering. This individual can be reluctant to commit to relationships, preferring personal freedom.

The King of Swords reversed enjoys conversation but it doesn't have to be about anything significant or even make sense in the end. This person is brimming with ideas that might not amount to very much, partly because he doesn't yet understand that words are not as effective as actions for achieving objectives.

In a general reading, this King suggests someone who can describe in intricate detail, the process of suiting up to climb Mount Everest and the best way to be prepared for the changeable weather, despite having never even worn climbing boots. This person might have seen such a climb late one night in a documentary while eating noodles on the sofa. Sometimes, this individual is unreliable, loquacious and much faster to promise than to act on commitments.

In a career layout, this person is the most likely of the four kings to be wondering what to be when they grow up when already physically mature. This is someone who pays scant attention to any area of life, preferring to blend work, home, travel and relationships into a one-act ensemble piece. There's often no time for intermission, as there is always something dramatic or exciting happening. This individual is usually more skilful at networking than actually doing any of the work.

In a relationship question, this person is likely to feel that commitment to one partner is simply too difficult. There is a tendency to tire quickly of routines in work, home and relationships, becoming restless to explore what might be missing. Commitment is easily promised but rarely delivered with this individual. Sometimes, partners forgive actions because this King is adept at painting a vivid picture of how good being together will be, *soon*. That can mean directly after the partner has paid this person's debts, a divorce is finalised or after an urgent, unexpected trip overseas. However, soon is never quite now.

In a health query, this reversed King sometimes describes a medical practitioner who is distracted, careless or focused on too many directions at once. It's time to secure a second opinion before proceeding with suggested treatment. It can also indicate anxiety and scattered thinking. This person might benefit from regular meditation or any activity that stills the mind, such as yoga, fishing, surfing, walking, gardening or running. In physical health, the reversed King of Swords can indicate the lungs, the ankles or the kidneys. Sometimes, this individual suffers from cuts or bruises resulting from hasty actions.

As a person, the reversed King of Swords can describe someone more attracted to concepts than outcomes. Passion for new ideas soon fades, replaced by another novel plan. This individual is happy to talk endlessly about goals, but in doing so, dissipates the urgency necessary to make them real. In the extreme, this individual is capable of overhearing an adventure story and appropriating it as a personal encounter when re-telling it over lunch. In business, he can be successful if someone else more capable, practical and physical delivers on his grand promises.

As a situation, this card indicates a lack of success resulting from ill-considered plans. Hasty action following superficial thinking is, at best, a viral moment on social media that rarely leads to anything worthwhile. If this person is a medical, dental, legal or financial advisor, secure a second opinion because his words lack substance.

As an aspect of the client, the reversed King of Swords indicates confusion, chaotic thinking or lack of mental focus on goals. This individual is usually clear about core objectives but has no clue about how to create a path to achieve them. The effort for turning an idea into something tangible is missing. Achieving goals usually takes time, but before then the reversed King has moved on to another 'brilliant idea.' This person can 'talk the talk' but not 'walk the walk.'

Sometimes, this card describes someone who is usually clear-thinking but is briefly experiencing mental chaos after a setback or a disappointment. If so, it's best not to make critical decisions until the mental storm passes.

King of Pentacles

The King of Pentacles is a moderate, conservative, practical man who prefers tradition to innovation. He can be technology-resistant, especially when compared with the King of Wands or the King of Swords. This King possesses a reliability that is attractive to the Queen of Cups and the Queen of Pentacles. However, this quality is likely to irritate the Queen of Wands, who prefers excitement and adventure to dependability.

In this card, the King of Pentacles is clothed in grapes (the fruits of his labours) and sits on a throne from which the heads of bulls protrude, suggesting the sign of Taurus. He holds a sceptre in his right hand and a pentacle in the left. Sitting proudly, this individual is aware of their material achievements and ready to measure others by their worldly success. A solid castle stands in the background and the beast beneath the King's feet has been subdued. The same discipline is applied in his pursuit of material stability and security. This is someone who likes routine, who is not afraid of hard work and who rewards himself well for his efforts and persistence.

As the pentacles' element is earth, the King of Pentacles is the earthy part of earth, making him very practical, realistic and concerned with worldly pursuits. This person wants to be comfortable for his ride through life, leaving philosophical questions about a possible afterlife to the other kings.

KING of PENTACLES.

The King of Pentacles represents the typical individual who starts a business because they don't like being told what to do by others. Alternatively, this person runs a branch of a company where they are left alone by upper management. This individual usually rewards himself with material possessions, such as a new car, a swimming pool, a holiday home, or some other suitable toy, when successful.

There is a tendency to return each year to the same holiday destination, so it makes sense to purchase a small weekender home or a timeshare in a holiday village. His friends the Kings of Cups, Wands and Swords are happy to spend the occasional vacation with him but wouldn't consider repeating the experience every year. However, the King of Pentacles' love of routine makes returning to the same place each year a satisfying event.

The King of Pentacles represents success through the practical application of procedures. Through doggedly sticking to goals and plans and taking each necessary step to achieve them, success is likely through sheer persistence and hard work, rather than innovation.

In a general reading, the King of Pentacles indicates financial or practical support from a reliable, conservative individual. It sometimes represents a personal career or financial success and ongoing stability in life. It's likely that this person started their first job (even a part-time position) at an early age. There is a basic understanding of the value of prudent plans and hard work.

In a career layout, the King of Pentacles indicates solid career success. This person chooses an occupation that is safe and one that rewards his efforts solidly. Banking, insurance, finance and residential or commercial real estate appeal as career options. If this individual buys a residential rental property, there is a preference for it to be close to home so as to be able to maintain a watchful eye on this investment when walking the dog each day.

In a relationship question, this person provides a stable, comfortable lifestyle. This individual usually delivers on promises and is always considering a secure, comfortable retirement. There is a tendency to be slow to pursue new relationships, needing to be sure that one's efforts will be worthwhile in the long term. This person is aware that a poor choice of partner can be an expensive mistake.

In a health query, the King of Pentacles can indicate job stress or money worries that cause anxiety, although this person generally has the financial reserves to maintain good physical health. This individual usually has sufficient income for gym membership, a fitness trainer, a well-balanced diet and medical attention when required. This King can indicate issues with the neck, throat, jaw and shoulders as this is where tension is stored. This is especially so when accompanied by the other cards for Taurus, such as The Hierophant or the Four of Pentacles.

As a person, the upright King of Pentacles represents a practical, conservative, responsible individual who understands that money equals choices. This person usually doesn't expect work to be fun but he takes it very seriously, with an attitude that play is when you spend money and work is where you earn it. Unlike the fire types, the King of Pentacles enjoys routines and stability and usually works hard for personal rewards, such as a comfortable car, an expensive watch or a few other physical objects. This individual demonstrates commitment, effort and persistence.

At work, there is a preference to be in charge, either by being self-employed or managing a department of a large organisation. This individual prefers low-risk investments, such as real estate, to risky money-making schemes and usually lives moderately, builds wealth slowly and retires in comfort.

As a situation, the King of Pentacles card describes success through hard work and sound financial management. It also highlights being in a powerful position by having cash or savings when negotiating a large purchase. This is the individual who patiently waits until the recession hits a low point before acquiring a long-desired property or business. As a result, he can expect to pay less than the healthy market value. It involves the awareness that sometimes profit is made when you buy a property or a business, not when you sell it.

As an aspect of the client, this card can indicate remaining stoic in the face of surrounding change or diligently saving towards an objective. In a business or investment question, the upright King sometimes suggests spending cautiously, having saved carefully towards a significant goal. This is a thorough investor who is dogged in pursuit of his long-term ambitions.

King of Pentacles Reversed

The King of Pentacles reversed sometimes gives a false impression of being a practical, financially disciplined man. However, it isn't long before people close to him realise that he is, in fact, impractical and undisciplined with money. His changeability interrupts his path to his goals, forcing him to begin again.

Although he is still keenly aware of money and material comforts, he is unable to earn and hold onto them over an extended period. He searches for a shortcut to the good life, which can bring him to financial ruin or into conflict with the law. This person wants to live beyond his means and to do this, he sometimes cuts corners or becomes burdened by debt.

The King of Pentacles reversed often works in an occupation that is entirely unsuitable. His choice of occupation is frequently designed to please a parent or to prove he is practical. Yet beneath the veneer of common sense, he can be unhappy and long to change the course of his life. However, his lack of financial discipline often limits his attempts to change career direction towards something more personally fulfilling. Because he is unhappy, there is a tendency to spend all earned income on trinkets or rewards for persisting with an unsuitable job, leaving no funds aside to fund another business venture.

When reversed, the King of Pentacles sometimes describes a successful man who is currently under financial pressure. He might have recently been retrenched or be struggling to keep a business afloat in a difficult economic climate. He's basically floundering as a result of economic hardship. When surrounding circumstances improve, his finances will rally too.

Generally, this card reversed describes someone who has a steady job but dreams of working for himself. Because he is inconsistent, any small business he starts or buys is likely to end badly. Throughout his working life, the permanently reversed King of Pentacles who insists on owning a business is likely to tackle a bankruptcy. He simply doesn't understand how to make money or how to hold on to it. He tends to reward himself too liberally for his achievements without keeping a firm eye on the cash flow.

Many years ago, a reversed King of Pentacles in his late thirties asked about a business idea he had. He had a dream of starting his own enterprise as a natural therapist and making enough to support a sumptuous lifestyle. To fund the idea, he was planning to sell some real estate. His parents, who arrived in Australia penniless after World War II, had worked tirelessly and when they died, he inherited two apartment blocks on one of Sydney's popular beaches.

These 24 apartments were paid off and at that time (the 1980s), I estimated his income from rentals to be around $8,600 per week or almost $450,000 per year. I asked him how much profit he'd need each week from his business to support himself and he said he'd need $3,000.

I asked the obvious question. "Why would you give up earning more than $8,000 per week for doing absolutely nothing, to work hard for less than half of that?" He had no answer to this question. He explained that since his father had died, a wealthy man had taken him to lunch every month to ask him if he was ready to sell the apartments. I smiled at the mental image of a patient upright King of Pentacles with a chequebook in his suit jacket, paying for a tax-deductible lunch, while waiting to buy a dream piece of real estate from someone who lacked the vision of its true worth.

Today those apartments would be worth north of $30 million and return over $1 million per year in rent after management fees. I don't know many natural therapists who earn that much, especially without effort.

In a general reading, the reversed King of Pentacles can describe reckless investment in business or poor money habits leading to financial hardship from frivolous speculation.

This is not a valuable business partner to have, especially if this person has control of the finances.

In a career layout, the reversed King of Pentacles can indicate someone who is bored with their current job and restless to become self-employed. Usually, this individual has not carefully considered the many benefits of working for a corporation. Thus, there isn't an appreciation for the annual paid leave, sick pay, superannuation or pension benefits, plus the social benefits of working within a team. The reality of being self-employed, (no annual leave, scant superannuation, limited times off and no sick leave) is unnoticed or overlooked.

In a relationship question, this card can describe someone whose work or career is more significant than personal relationships. This person enjoys working long hours — if only to avoid home or family life. In some layouts, this reversed card describes an individual whose desire to run a business is adding pressure to personal relationships. Financial issues are a major cause of family stress, especially when one partner's poor money habits are impacting on the other spouse.

In a health query, this card describes financial issues restricting the person's ability to build and maintain robust health. It also indicates a current job might be affecting the individual's health or vitality. In terms of physical health, this card can suggest tension with the neck, jaw, throat or shoulders.

As a person, the reversed King of Pentacles describes someone who has more self-confidence than ability in business. Financially, this person is alternately miserly and then eager to spend, borrow and splurge. Although he is aware that money and cash flow are fundamental to a successful business, he cannot delay gratification. As a result, income that should be used to pay suppliers or invested in the growth of the business is spent on living expenses, landing him with serious business debt.

Sometimes, the reversed King of Pentacles describes someone who is mean. This person goes to great lengths to save a dollar. This is the landowner who never repairs or maintains rental properties, underpays staff and lives in constant fear of poverty.

As a situation, this card indicates inadequate control over finances that might lead to financial stress if not immediately addressed. Desires governing spending can lead to debt and even bankruptcy if not controlled. A simple question to ask when this card appears reversed is: "Where is the money to pay for this plan?"

As an aspect of the client, the reversed King of Pentacles can point to someone who lives beyond financial means, often relying on only one income stream. If this source of revenue dries up, the individual is unlikely to survive current circumstances for more than a few weeks. Despite the outward appearance of wealth and comfort, this person is usually burdened by substantial debt.

Sometimes, the reversed King of Pentacles describes a successful person in retirement who buys a few toys as rewards for past efforts. The new car, boat or ski chalet is paid for by a range of existing investment income streams and is sometimes a tax-deductible expense.

The Major Arcana

Underlying Spiritual Lessons

The major arcana is a series of twenty-two cards numbered from zero to twenty-one. They describe the spiritual lessons of life in twenty-two opportunities or steps. The specific challenges of the zodiac signs are interwoven throughout the major arcana. These cards highlight underlying trials and opportunities in career, relationships, health and family.

By being aware of the insights contained within a set of circumstances, it is possible to gain valuable wisdom while resolving a challenge being faced. For example, if the reversed Emperor card appears as the answer to why a person was not promoted in his career, this card suggests there is a need to develop more practical self-discipline. Therefore, consciously improving personal motivation and self-control is likely to increase the chances of career success.

When more than half the cards in a layout are major arcana cards, it is worth asking the client to select an extra card to add to each of the major arcana cards. This helps avoid a reading becoming overly slanted towards a spiritual perspective, which can make it difficult for the client to apply the information to practical issues.

Although readers are well placed to highlight underlying opportunities for spiritual and emotional development, clients still have to face a bullying boss, an unreliable partner or unruly children in their daily lives. In a recent reading where a client was being bullied on a daily basis by her boss, identifying the lesson was only part of her solution. I explained that her mother had bullied her, pushing her to achieve high grades at school and her boss was another strong woman demanding more and more from her. Carol agreed but seeing the pattern wasn't enough. Carol had to stand up to her boss and be more assertive from that day forward. I suggested she undergo some assertiveness training and when she hesitated, I proposed judo lessons, "There's nothing like knowing you can put a bully on the ground in under two seconds to help you feel more assertive. You never need to raise your voice when you know you can defend yourself." She smiled and nodded.

Having five major arcana cards in a seven-card spread presents a strongly spiritual reading that few clients can appreciate as the content seems distant from their immediate concerns and struggles. By adding extra cards, a tarot reader can reveal the underlying thoughts, beliefs and opportunities in everyday life.

When a major arcana card appears reversed, it is worth returning to the learning opportunity of the previous upright card, as it is with the minor arcana. When the Empress is reversed, it's time to revisit to the spiritual lesson of the upright High Priestess card and reflect on long-term goals.

In advanced tarot courses, students are asked to decide which major arcana card represents them at the present time. They write down the name of this card. Then they select from a face-down array of major arcana cards to see how accurate their assessments were. This exercise can be extended to which major arcana card characterises a person financially, emotionally, spiritually, in relationships and in career. By deciding on cards to represent each area before selecting any cards, students are encouraged to think about their personal lives and the card meanings in more depth. Try the exercise below.

- Slide the major arcana cards, facing downward, into a line on a table while asking which card most accurately represents you at this point.

- Select one card from the line of cards and place it face down on the table.

- Before viewing the card, consider your personal conditions and decide which major arcana card most accurately reflects those circumstances.

- Turn the card over to see if what you thought most reflected your current circumstances is the card you've selected.

- Carefully examine the card.

If the card is significantly different from the card you had in your mind, read up on the card you picked and determine how it applies to your current life. Try to notice five things in this card you had not previously seen before putting it back into the pack. This helps broaden your understanding of the card.

The Fool

The Fool represents a time in life when an individual knows within that a goal is achievable, despite any logical reasons to the contrary. There is something alluring about the kind of innocence and trust suggested by The Fool: it enables a person to tackle goals and challenges that might not even be considered with the wisdom of hindsight.

THE FOOL.

Others might caution the individual against intended actions. However, when The Fool is upright, this person instinctively knows opportunities await. With the purity and naivety of The Fool, it's possible to gain valuable life knowledge. For example, it is often the lack of self-reflection or blind faith that prompts people to pursue new relationships after previous unsuccessful ones. In those moments, when people have conviction in life's possibilities, opportunities abound and almost all goals seem possible.

Basically, The Fool is how the average person perceives the wise individual who doesn't follow convention and is considered eccentric. The Fool is an original. This individual can perceive opportunities that friends and colleagues cannot. He's not necessarily wrong, merely different. The Fool represents an individual who dances to their own tune rather than obeying convention. Creative opportunities are sometimes available to people who are prepared to step beyond conformist boundaries.

An example of The Fool at play occurred during a meeting with a commissioning editor in 2010. We were discussing a manuscript and Vesna was tactfully explaining that she didn't believe the book had a place in the market without significant changes. She asked me to take the first three chapters and make them into a book. She then gave me the title she wanted.

I was appalled at the suggestion. She was effectively asking for a lightweight book for readers who had nothing more than a passing interest in the subject. She then asked me to tell more of my life story. My heart sank. If I purchased a book about intuitive development and it turned out to be a tome on how fabulous the author's life was as a clairvoyant, I'd be using it to light the barbeque within a week. I left that meeting despondent. My instinct was that it would be a worthwhile book, just as it was. Despite not having a fall-back plan, a few days later I emailed Vesna to say I'd pass on her offer and suggested she find a columnist to write her preferred book. She found someone else. When I found the book in a bookstore with the title she had suggested, I was glad my name wasn't on the cover.

A month later, one of Australia's leading designers, Cristina Re, asked if I'd like to work with her on a project. I sent her the manuscript and together we produced a full-colour book. Nine years later, *Intuition: keys to unlocking your inner wisdom* is my strongest selling title. I knew the book had a readership and I believed it had to be produced in full colour because most readers are used to the Internet, now. Everything on screen is in colour.

The Fool represents a window of opportunity that a person can see that might not be visible to others. Trusting your instincts is essential to developing personal intuition.

In a general reading, The Fool upright indicates a window of opportunity to seize an opening or pursue a plan. It is an awareness of the possibilities available in the moment. It sometimes describes action before thought that usually ends well. The individual who has learned to trust instincts is usually best placed to seize opportunities when they arrive.

In a career layout, this card describes taking a risk with a work project or maybe applying for a position without previous expertise. The job might be interstate, overseas or unexpected. Sometimes, even the person taking decisive action doesn't have a rational reason for doing so, apart from the intense conviction that it is right.

In a relationship question, The Fool can describe taking actions to pursue a new relationship or to change the direction of an existing one. On the surface, this move appears foolish. This is the day when a person decides to abandon a job and a home to move overseas to live with a new partner in an untested environment, based only on the faith that everything will be okay.

In a health query, this card indicates someone who is living in the moment, without thought for maintaining their long-term health. This individual has no serious concern about future health issues or for making preparations for old age. Living in the moment has the distinct advantage of leaving one unburdened by worries about the future.

The Fool Reversed

The Fool reversed represents a need to follow convention, taking advice even when it does not immediately apply to personal circumstances. An individual might want to conform, even though life suggests a more spontaneous approach is necessary at this time.

Alternatively, The Fool can suggest trying to live in the moment in spite of responsibilities that require long-term planning and reliable strategies. The Fool reversed sometimes indicates an adult who is unaware of the likely consequences of personal actions. This person's ongoing success or stability relies on a partner or a supportive organisation to supply structure and financial security. Proclaiming yourself an artist is not the same as producing a body of work that financially supports your lifestyle. Everyone can be an artist if someone else pays the bills.

There is a lack of desire to examine the instruments of The Magician, the following card. It might be that past disappointments have made this person shrink from opportunities and their corresponding responsibilities. The Magician's tools include a wand (the passion to pursue a goal), a cup (creative inspiration), a sword (planning and enlisting support from others) and a pentacle (financial investment for economic gain). They symbolise the wisdom contained in the paths or four suits of the minor arcana. These aids are useful and necessary for navigating the rest of the major arcana. They are contained in the cloth carried on the rod (or wand) by the person on the card.

The Fool reversed sometimes reverts to the upright World card. It can indicate a period where it may be safe to trust the Universe to support you in choosing a wise course of action. The major arcana is a series of cards forming a circle. The Fool can represent arriving in life as a newborn, innocent and pure while The World can signify leaving this life at its end, for the next world. When The Fool card is reversed, it's sometimes possible for a person to draw inspiration or guidance from the other world, even without training or practice.

When Derek asked about marrying for the fourth time, he explained that Tanya was actually his second wife. After a long break, during which Derek married Nadia, Derek and Tanya had met overseas during a business trip. Derek realised he was still in love with Tanya and commenced the process of divorcing Nadia.

"How will this be different from your previous marriage to Tanya?" I asked.

"It will be great," he stated confidently.

I probed carefully. "Have you both changed since you were last married? If so, how?"

The reversed Fool suggested Derek's second opportunity with her might involve re-discovering exactly how incompatible he was with Tanya.

In a general reading, The Fool reversed describes ill-considered plans. This can be a person who leaps from one chaotic situation into another without considering personal contribution to the surrounding chaos. Sometimes, this card appears when someone who is burdened with debt applies for an additional credit card to cover personal expenses. At best, this person is finding short-term solutions.

In a career layout, the reversed Fool suggests hasty action without sufficient thought. The person might have left a job without the safety net of another position and risks unemployment until a new job is secured. It can also indicate accepting a different position without doing any basic research on the company, the workplace location or the corporate culture. The Fool appeared reversed in a layout for Bradley, who quit his job after a long lunch with a friend who boasted about the success of her new business. He decided to launch his own company and set his own working hours. Two years later, he was back working in an identical job after his enterprise had failed to generate a profit. It's an example of inspiration without due diligence.

In a relationship question, this card indicates a lack of experience or the inability to learn from past relationships and avoid repeating negative patterns. When The Fool is reversed, the white snow, the dog and the rose are all above the person's head, indicating that innocence and spontaneity are currently triumphing over reason. In the romance of the moment, this person is acting impulsively without properly considering the possible consequences. These impetuous actions are likely to be proven foolish in time.

In a health query, this card can describe a lack of consideration for how current habits and behaviours might affect personal health. Regularly bringing a large box of doughnuts to share at work might make a person popular in the short term but there could be longer-term consequences. The reversed Fool may be encouraging a second opinion or that more information is needed regarding a health matter.

The Magician

The Magician represents being effective at planning and achieving personal goals. It can involve changing jobs, starting a new business or simply remaining aware of prospects. It is time to choose a path and focus on the pursuit of goals. Good luck is where preparation meets opportunity and this partly describes the Magician.

Outwardly, the Magician is confident, capable and successful; inwardly he plans, rehearses his moves and patiently awaits appropriate circumstances. When a favourable moment arrives, he moves resolutely towards achieving his aims.

We are all Magicians at various times in our lives. For example, when as small children we took our first steps or, later, mastered a musical instrument or graduated from school. A child learning to read is The Magician in action. A whole new world opens up to young readers. Many parents have driven around with a young child in the back seat who is reading signs and shop names aloud while enthusiastically practising new skills.

Pursuing study, a career or any other project is usually a successful enterprise when The Magician appears in the answer position in a layout. This card represents being effective due to practical grounding in reality while remaining aware of life's spiritual dimension.

In a general reading, The Magician can indicate a supportive person who gives useful advice or someone who is well-placed to move a project forward towards a successful conclusion. The time is right to act on plans when the Magician appears upright as an answer to a question.

In a career layout, The Magician indicates that professional success is likely, partly due to the focus and attention this person is giving to the goal and their acute awareness of how best to structure the process. This person makes things happen in their job. An example of this occurred with Helena, who had a successful career as a project manager but somehow organised time to start a fashion design business in the evenings at home. I asked how she managed to juggle these two jobs. She explained that to create a private fashion label she didn't watch television and refused all invitations that distracted her from her purpose. This was a woman on a mission and her daily job only served to sharpen her focus on her small, flourishing business.

In a relationship question, it describes an effective person, usually a man, with a well-developed sense of purpose, who makes difficult tasks look easy. This is partly from being completely focused on what is required to achieve goals. These individuals pay attention to what supports plans, what might interrupt the process and alternative methods needed if a roadblock appears.

In a health query, the upright Magician indicates sound health through a combination of nourishing the physical and the spiritual parts of the person. This individual can maintain balance with diet and exercise, work and play, responsibilities and fun while working diligently towards rewarding life goals. In a question about a medical procedure, the upright Magician can indicate a positive outcome. It might also describe the surgeon as a focused, skilful professional.

The Magician Reversed

The Magician reversed often describes a lack of success due to being out of touch with reality. Confusion, impatience and the absence of a clear plan are highlighted. The timing of a plan or project may be wrong, or the person may be pushing something that is not likely to succeed.

When reversed, The Magician suggests a need to take some time to reassess a situation. It is necessary to return to the lesson of The Fool, to be free from the pressures of the current situation, to see it more objectively. Stepping back from an issue can give a clearer perspective. While enjoying the moment, it's possible for the subconscious mind to sort through potential solutions. It's also possible that a person can discover new methods that can be applied to an incomplete venture while taking a break from the project.

This card can also suggest an unbalanced, wilful person whose desires and goals keep changing. Headstrong behaviour is no substitute for pursuing a worthwhile opportunity with steady application, yet sometimes, The Magician reversed resists being shown a better way. An example of The Magician reversed is the small child who seeks to control parents with tears and tantrums.

In answer to a relationship issue, The Magician reversed may represent a partner who is possessive, domineering and unreliable. One day he is focused, passionate and talkative, while the next he's sullen and passive-aggressive. It highlights several distinct personalities in one individual. It might be helpful for people who live or work with a reversed Magician to name the different parts or personalities in that individual. In this way, it's marginally easier to know who you are dealing with at any given time.

Sometimes, the reversed Magician is depressed or frustrated at not being able to achieve personal objectives. Perhaps colleagues or family members are disrupting attempts to achieve a goal. However, the sabotage can also be within.

When The Magician card appeared reversed in Wayne's reading, it reflected his temporary state of depression. Fifty-five-year-old Wayne loved surfing, running and hiking. Being outside in all weather conditions suited him, which is why he chose to work as a gardener. An old surfing injury flared up, requiring knee surgery. He was told to take some time away from work and rest completely for five weeks. Being indoors resting all day was driving him crazy but he was under strict orders not to walk, hike or surf. "I feel like an old man, limping around the house when it's sunny outside," he said. "I even had to be driven here today by my daughter. If this is what retirement looks like, shoot me now." It is likely The Magician will be upright in Wayne's next reading, after his leg has healed.

In extreme instances, the reversed Magician describes someone who is unpredictable and constantly moving the goalposts. As a partner or a parent, this person may have issues with anger management resulting in those around them walking on eggshells. This individual may benefit from seeing a counsellor, mindfulness training or otherwise working on themselves.

The reversed Magician is like a boss who insists that an employee print and bind five copies of a document in time for a Monday morning meeting, only to suggest the time spent completing the task was wasted. The part of the boss that was present when they requested the copying is absent when the employee supplies them. There may be no recollection of requesting the documents. In some situations, the reversed Magician demands to know where the documents are a week after the meeting. This individual can be unreliable, inconsistent and easily swayed. As a result, they rarely achieve their goals.

In a general reading, the reversed Magician represents someone who is ungrounded or disconnected from reality or spiritual purpose. They are usually very controlling. When people are experiencing continual inner chaos, they might compensate by micro-managing external circumstances. They attempt to control as much as possible, including other people or personal home and work environments.

In a question about a new project, the reversed Magician suggests it's likely to end in disaster. This might be due to poor timing, such as starting a new business venture during the onset of an economic recession. It could end badly because of poor communication, someone constantly changing the direction of the venture or careless planning.

I noticed an expensive sandwich shop had opened in a neighbourhood where most of the locals were living in government housing and few working-age adults were employed. It closed within six months because of its poor location. If the business owners had spent a day or two standing outside the vacant shop, observing the passing locals, they'd have known this wasn't a suitable position for a lunch shop that sold extravagant sandwiches.

In a career layout, the reversed Magician describes a boss or a co-worker who makes life hell for everyone in the environment. As a supervisor, this person bullies staff, plays people off against each other and generally destroys any sense of harmony in a workplace. One client explained that in her small office of twelve people, there were only eleven desks and chairs. Everyone was expected to work in the office every day and the last person to arrive had to make do with whatever work surface was available. They usually ended up working standing up at the small benchtop in the staff kitchen. It was the manager's way of ensuring everyone arrived early.

When someone resigned, the boss inadvertently hired another reversed Magician, who promptly threw the manager's chair out with the garbage one evening. When it was replaced with a bigger chair, the new staff member brought a small handsaw to work and trimmed two of the legs of his desk, so it rocked continuously when the manager leaned on it. The reversed Magician wants to win at all costs, so when caught in the line of fire, step back. When conflict arises, a reversed Magician throws all the rules out the window. A squabble over a parking spot can soon become a life-and-death struggle. This person gets even with others when crossed and enjoys waiting for the perfect moment to inflict revenge.

Sometimes, the person selecting the cards is the reversed Magician, suggesting this individual is currently ungrounded, chaotic in thought and lurching from one idea to the next without any real focus. This might be the result of being bullied at work or having been recently retrenched from a coveted job. It can stem from continual stress and demands in the workplace.

In a relationship question, this card usually describes a person who is unpredictable, unreliable and possibly unaware of having a changeable personal disposition. This individual is likely to be alternately passionate and cold, helpful and obstinate or loving but sometimes cruel. This behaviour erodes trust, resulting in short friendships and relationships, partly due to deficient social skills.

Although the reversed Magician is the one with emotional issues or poor social skills, it is often the spouse who seeks counselling or medical advice. The partner of a reversed Magician may have trouble sleeping, be 'walking on eggshells' and routinely be adapting to unexpected and irrational demands. Eventually, this can take a toll on someone's health to a point where a medical specialist suggests antidepressants or something for anxiety. Attempting to be the voice of reason around a reversed Magician is exhausting, unrewarding work. It is sometimes better to walk away than to try to make a relationship work with this type of individual.

As a spurned former partner, the reversed Magician can be vengeful, toxic and intent on causing havoc. An example of this was the man who, after a bitter divorce and a protracted court battle, was forced to hand ownership of one of the family properties to his wife. The day before he was to sign the deed, he burned the property to the ground. When separating from a partner like this, it can be wise to move away and fade to grey. In extreme circumstances, your life might depend on it because when locked into battle, rules don't apply to this person. Winning at all costs is paramount.

In a health query, the reversed Magician describes an imbalance between spiritual needs and physical desires. These competing requirements can sometimes lead to a wide range of health issues, including inconsistent sleep patterns, erratic thinking and depressive periods or angry outbursts and scattered focus on tasks.

Poor decisions around personal health suggest it is time to return to basics. These include wholesome foods, daily exercise, abstaining from recreational drugs and alcohol, taking time each day for reflection through prayer, meditation, or simply staring out to sea and ensuring sufficient sleep at night. In a question about a medical procedure, the reversed Magician suggests caution. It might be wise to get a second opinion.

The High Priestess

Reflection is necessary, if only to establish individual goals and discover what is fulfilling. The High Priestess is about contemplating purpose, through meditation or by spending time alone in quiet surroundings. Holidays were originally 'holy days' — times set aside to reflect on our creator and spiritual purpose. However, with the hectic pace of life today, holidays are often spent maximising precious time. Reflection, if it takes place at all, could be squeezed into a short meditation each working day.

In this card, the scroll in the hands of The High Priestess represents inner knowledge about spiritual purpose. Our inner spiritual selves remember this deeper resolve, which is interwoven with our destiny. However, our conscious minds forget it in the struggle to achieve goals in the physical world. The moon at The High Priestess's feet symbolises the recall of spiritual direction at night when sleeping.

In dreams, people reacquaint themselves with principles that have lasting spiritual value. Upon waking, some individuals attempt to apply some of that spiritual purpose into their daily lives. More often, however, they stumble into the practical demands of the day ahead, as spiritual values become submerged beneath work deadlines, physical hunger, family demands and the daily commute.

The veil behind The High Priestess limits her view of the pool of water, encouraging her to focus on the physical world. Her natural intuition and spiritual nature make the hidden world behind her more attractive than the harsh realities of physical life.

This card represents the lesson for Pisces: to remember one's true purpose while living in the material world. This can be a difficult balancing act, especially when faced with having to learn to walk, talk, read, study, socialise and as an adult, earn an income. However, it is possible to balance practical and spiritual needs, especially when surrounded by like-minded people. When friends and family routinely take time to pray, meditate, attend yoga classes or include other contemplative practices in daily life, it models nourishing behaviour.

It's also possible to take a spiritual approach to career, especially if it involves helping other people. Service to others comes in many guises, including medicine, accountancy, cleaning homes or offices, driving a bus, teaching a course, designing websites or painting signs. To the ravenous crowd gathered at a busy sandwich shop, the person preparing a crusty ham, mustard and lettuce roll is providing a vital service.

Sometimes, artists carry their memories of spiritual purpose into the physical world, transferring ethereal energy into sculptures, paintings or music. Others may then be spiritually nourished when viewing or hearing these creations and inspired to pursue their own creative endeavours.

In a general reading, The High Priestess indicates it's time to retreat from life to consider personal direction. This is an opportunity to remember life's purpose and to determine which goals are in harmony with important spiritual values. This solitude might occur through a weekend away in the country or time alone spent in meditation or contemplation.

This card can suggest a Piscean person, especially if the Page of Cups also appears in the layout. It also describes a decision (the twos in the tarot are generally cards representing decisions). Choices are made after mentally examining practical issues and influences (the white pillar in this card) and then sleeping on the decision to consider unseen influences (the dark pillar in this card). Dreams offer valuable information from the subconscious to the conscious mind for those who heed them and take time to decipher their personal symbology.

In a career layout, The High Priestess sometimes describes a person with an idea for a business or a vocational direction. It's still in the concept stage and requires further consideration, yet it has potential. The idea is like an acorn and as the old saying goes, "From little acorns, mighty oaks grow."

Carefully considering how to implement and nurture a career idea through the infancy stage until it is strong enough to support the person financially, requires patience and persistence. The more time spent on the creative idea at the beginning, the more potholes can be avoided along the path to success. The High Priestess reveals the conceptual stage.

In a relationship question, The High Priestess signifies stepping back from a relationship to spend time considering individual options. Perhaps the person is deciding what needs the relationship can meet and what requirements are better met through creative, social or spiritual practices. The Two of Cups shows a close friendship or partnership, in which each participant brings something to the relationship and both are nourished by it. The High Priestess suggests that some of what is contributed to relationships is from a hidden, spiritual source of energy.

In a health query, this card is associated with the feet and the glands of the body. When found with the Page of Cups in a health layout, it suggests innate sensitivity to surrounding emotions. For stable health, this person needs to avoid environments filled with strife, negative undertones or too much pressure. This individual is sometimes a sponge for the emotions of others. However, unlike a sponge that can be squeezed at the end of a gruelling day, tension and emotions are absorbed and stored. Daily processes for spiritual and emotional cleansing are required to maintain balanced health and a confident attitude for this individual.

Creative nourishment usually benefits personal health, along with quiet time such as daily periods of prayer, meditation, contemplation or reading uplifting stories. Hobbies such as light gardening, painting, yoga or even twenty minutes with a colouring-in book can offer a necessary diversion for the conscious mind, allowing the subconscious mind to make sense of current circumstances. When this card appears upright, health generally improves from a period of quiet contemplation, away from the stresses and emotions of others.

The High Priestess Reversed

The High Priestess reversed represents a stage when a person happily walks away from a period spent in reflection to actively pursue opportunities offered in the physical world. It is time to return to the previous card, The Magician, to focus energy on achieving tangible objectives. Sometimes, The High Priestess reversed suggests it is the right moment to find people who can help put plans into action. This could include a successful musician who provides mentoring or another knowledgeable professional who assists with some of the steps required to achieve a goal.

After withdrawing for a while to contemplate deeper purpose, this person needs to return to life to physically live it. The message of the reversed card is to keep your eyes open for opportunities while remembering your spiritual purpose as glimpsed in the upright card. In this way, it's possible to be focused, identify opportunities when they arrive and be ready to act to pursue authentic goals, just as the upright Magician does.

In a general reading, this card represents a need to return to the upright Magician, to focus on opportunities in the present moment. The period of reflection has passed and it's now time for action. Contemplating a goal is important but it's only one step in a long process towards the fulfilment of a dream.

In a career layout, this card indicates a perfect time to enlarge one's network when searching for suitable career options. It's possible that a viable opportunity will arrive through personal contacts or social media, rather than traditional methods. Associating with others increases the range of opportunities ordinarily hidden from view. Suitable circumstances are found in social settings, such as attending a meetup, a book launch, a gallery opening or drinks after work with friends.

Sally is a dog walker who takes her own dog to the park wearing a T-shirt emblazoned with her dog-walking-business logo and details. It has brought her new business and she meets fellow animal lovers for conversations and online chats. She has built up regular website visitors as well as discovering what customers in her neighbourhood require, such as sympathetic veterinary clinics or puppy training, dog-sitting and dog-bathing services. Although an online presence is valuable for her business, the reversed High Priestess in a reading indicates it's also worthwhile for her to meet people in the park while walking dogs on a regular basis.

In a relationship question, the reversed High Priestess indicates emerging from isolation to widen one's social circle. This can help in the search for a suitable partner or provide social opportunities if already in a relationship. It is a suitable time to move forward in the search for a compatible partner and new friendships.

In a health query, the reversed High Priestess can indicate an increase in physical exercise after a period of rest or reflection. It sometimes suggests that a friend or an acquaintance might provide contact details of a health practitioner who can effectively treat a current condition. In answer to a specific health issue, the reversed High Priestess suggests that rebalancing health might involve asking other people for additional information about an issue or searching online. It's time to explore outside your comfort zone for more details and options.

The Empress

The Empress represents living life to the full, in an uncomplicated way. This can mean something as straightforward as taking pleasure in a sunny afternoon. The Empress finds many reasons to feel content with life. She typically brings joy to people around her. Years ago, a receptionist at a healing centre where I worked demonstrated Empress behaviour. Jessica loved people and often brought homemade biscuits, scones and cakes for the clients to eat before their appointments. I'd step into the waiting room to greet my next client and find the person with a face full of chocolate cake or settling down to some scones and tea while Jessica stood back, looking rather satisfied.

"You know, I'm very lucky these days," she said to me during a break one afternoon.

"Oh, yes? How's that?"

"I love to bake and my husband can only eat so much but a few months ago I discovered a house full of university students living next door. Now when I bake, I pop over to give them what we can't finish. They're always happy to help out."

I had to stop myself from laughing while envisaging a group of hungry students whose previous meals were two-minute noodles with their noses pressed up against the window saying, "Another ten minutes and she'll be over, so put on some coffee, will you?"

THE EMPRESS.

In a general or relationship layout, this card can suggest pregnancy or a woman who is comfortable with lots of children. If she has two children of her own, there are usually seven or eight other local children using her home as a base or a playground. They'll often be well-fed and looked after in her care.

In a career layout, the Empress card indicates that the person may work from home, even part-time, as the Empress represents domestic harmony and stability. The Empress 'makes a house into a home' with unmistakable touches, such as fresh flowers or herbs from the garden, indoor plants and warm colours in fabrics and paintings. She's connected to the earth and understands that a strong association with nature is beneficial for ongoing health.

The Empress suggests growth or progress towards personal goals. The threes in the tarot basically represent progress. It generally describes an enjoyable home environment where a person can relax and thrive.

In a general reading, The Empress indicates growth and progress with personal plans because it's a number three card. It also describes a generous, earthy person who loves life and enjoys gardening, preparing and eating food and who is usually at ease in social situations. It suggests a stable, warm home environment.

In a career layout, The Empress indicates someone who works from home or has a home office for part of the week. It also highlights focusing on other people, such as a career in hospitality or in the human resources department of an organisation. In a question about a career project, a client recently asked, "What is my role in this project?" In the answer position, The Empress indicated that his role was to support others, helping them to feel confident about the project and themselves so they could work together as a team. The Empress represents teamwork, harmony and shared rewards.

In a relationship question or a query about family, this card can indicate pregnancy. It signifies growth and progress in a love relationship plus a harmonious, supportive household. This stable environment provides a solid foundation for a relationship.

In a health query, this card usually indicates balanced health. Occasionally, it can suggest the digestive system or the kidneys. Food intolerances are sometimes ignored by The Empress, as she is often savouring the flavour in the moment rather than thinking about the repercussions later on.

The Empress Reversed

The Empress reversed suggests domestic instability. This individual is not nourishing themselves through food, exercise or the physical comforts of life. Instead, there is a retreat into personal thoughts. When surrounded by bleak views or pessimistic undertones, the reversed Empress finds it easier to withdraw from feelings into thoughts rather than attempt to improve the situation. If this occurs repeatedly, there is a risk of understanding life only through theories, with limited direct practice. Theories are no substitute for proficiency developed from doing. Wisdom is often the result of forming theories based on direct experience.

When progress is blocked or restricted (as it can be with a reversed number three card), it is time to examine plans. This means returning to the previous upright card, The High Priestess, to review options. Basically, it's time to reflect on underlying needs. Perhaps the current path is not the most effective method of addressing fundamental needs.

When Carly asked about a potential promotion at work, I enquired how this new position might improve her life. She explained that it meant an increased income, more status and a chance to be heard at team meetings. We then explored other ways to achieve these outcomes without a promotion. Potential avenues for increasing disposable income included reducing current expenses or working part-time as a consultant. Becoming a consultant might also increase her status in her chosen career. Delays or obstacles to achieving goals are not necessarily damaging if they offer a chance to explore new ways to meet the underlying needs.

In a career spread, the reversed Empress card means using the domestic environment as a base for work, which is disrupting the usual peaceful feeling. During a question about her home life, Hayley selected the reversed Empress card. She explained that her brother Tim ran a furniture restoration business from the family garage. Potential customers arrived, often unannounced, seven days a week. In the eight years that he'd run the business, her parents and Hayley had not felt completely relaxed in their own residence. She was extremely annoyed that Tim had recently moved into his own house to ensure his personal privacy while enjoying the free use of the family garage and back garden for his work.

This is an example of where the reversed Empress would indicate a home environment that feels uncomfortable. Others include neighbours renovating, new construction increasing noise, dust and heavy vehicles on the street and adult children returning home to an already crowded house.

In a question about fertility, the reversed Empress can suggest problems around pregnancy. If the reading occurs during the final stage of a person's pregnancy, it can indicate the birth and can be used to discover what day the baby will be born.

In general terms, the reversed Empress card signifies an unsuitable or disharmonious home environment. This can include situations such as significant property renovations or living next door to a construction zone. Sometimes, it indicates losing privacy or daily sunlight due to a high-rise building being constructed directly beside the home. Basically, the current living situation lacks peace and pleasant ambience.

In a career layout, this card describes someone with a home office in a house that is not working effectively. The office might be poorly located, too close to noisy living areas, too small or simply crammed into the corner of a bedroom or onto one end of the dining table. The reversed Empress indicates slow growth of career progress. It's time to return to the upright High Priestess and contemplate long-term career direction.

In a relationship question, The Empress reversed can indicate a home environment is contributing to relationship issues. It may be too many people crammed into a small space, teenage children from previous relationships causing chaos or reduced income restricting the choice of neighbourhood. Sometimes, an inability to become pregnant can be a source of tension in a partnership. The Empress reversed can also suggest a reluctance to pursue a partnership to its next natural stage. This individual needs to return to the lesson of the previous card, The High Priestess, to consider personal needs in relationships. Perhaps a period of reflection or time spent in meditation might reveal the benefits of a transition towards a more mature partnership.

In a health query, this reversed card can suggest an undesirable influence in the home environment. When Edna developed severe arthritis, the steps in her home became a challenge. There were twenty-three steps leading up to the front door and three flights of steps inside the tri-level house. She eventually replaced the outdoor steps with a path and restricted herself to two floors of her home.

Occasionally, a person's home environment affects health more subtly. When Trisha began her strict diet, she became aware of the temptations around her shared home. Three fellow tenants left half-eaten pizzas on the kitchen bench, bowls of sweets on the coffee table and opened bottles of wine in the refrigerator. The most difficult times occurred when someone arrived home with Indian or Thai take-out. The steaming scents of exotic spices filled the home, weakening her resolve. It was time to return to the upright previous card, The High Priestess and retreat to her room, away from temptation, to think about strategies for avoiding poor food choices in a shared household.

The Emperor

True freedom is closely aligned with self-discipline. The Emperor represents a methodical, well-organised individual, whose success in the material world is the direct result of personal self-discipline and determination. He is not usually a contemplative person, so his struggles in life are mostly physical. Rarely does he give any thought to the meaning of life or spiritual purpose. It won't pay his bills. This is a practical, hard-working individual. He believes in only what he can see, touch, measure and prove. Clad in armour, he's ready and willing to fight for personal beliefs, challenging those who obstruct progress.

The orange backdrop in the card and The Emperor's red clothing highlight passion and enthusiasm for life and the challenges it presents. This individual's world is black and white. He understands life from personal actions and conquests — he is not a theorist. When seeking this individual's opinion, be prepared, as tact is not usually a high priority. This person is forthright and not necessarily diplomatic but will tell it as he sees it.

Although the Emperor is not an emotional or romantic person, he is reliable and practical, an antidote to the King of Wands reversed, who leaves a job half-finished, or the King of Swords reversed, who doesn't even start a task because he's too busy talking about it. The Emperor describes someone who enlists the help of others and gets on with the job.

In romantic relationships, this individual doesn't send flowers or write poetry. His way of showing his partner that he cares is to keep her front gate oiled and car running properly or to change all her lightbulbs soon after they stop working. He is usually a solid material provider. His attitude is that work is work — it's not meant to be fun. For him, fun is what happens at the weekend, after all the work is completed. He's basically an engineer at heart, thrilled to discover how things are constructed and eager to be useful. If this person has a shed full of tools, they'll usually be put to effective use. He does not amass sentimental heirlooms (cups) or interesting talking points (swords) or flashy baubles (wands) but keeps functional, pragmatic implements that are used regularly.

In answer to a specific question, the appearance of The Emperor card suggests success due to self-discipline and practical application. Through working longer hours and remaining focused on the job, this person can achieve a position of power and make a significant impact.

In a general reading, The Emperor represents success through self-discipline. This individual knows the value of hard work in the pursuit of goals and is realistic, practical and focused on completing each task. The Emperor can also represent a father or a father figure, such as a judge, teacher, boss, policeman or any person in a position of authority. This individual usually believes in what is measurable and provable. There is a fundamental disregard for theories until they are seen in a practical form. Creative imagination is left to others. The Emperor prefers to work from a plan towards a finite goal or finish line. He appreciates outstanding examples of fine engineering. From a well-designed chair to an enormous bridge, there is fascination with how different materials fit together seamlessly, combining form and function.

In a career layout, this person is usually successful due to self-discipline and hard work. With natural leadership skills, he is competent, although not usually the best choice for delicate mediations because of not being politically correct or sensitive to nuanced negotiations. When hiring a tradesperson to complete a task, this is the person suitable for the job. An Emperor has pride in personal work and usually won't cut corners.

In a relationship question, the card describes a practical, unromantic, yet reliable individual who keeps personal promises. The Emperor's word is sound, meaning that a handshake seals a pledge. This is someone who is usually honourable in business. This person brings practical skills to a relationship. If a partner wants a retaining wall constructed, The Emperor will build it or hire an engineer and then assist that person to get it done in half the time. If a spouse wants a swing, a back porch or a line of climbing roses across the back fence, The Emperor makes sure it's done properly.

In relationship, this person likes practical routines, can be strict with disciplining children and doesn't easily accept it when others disappoint. On the bright side, if a partner enjoys camping, The Emperor usually ensures that everything is set up promptly upon arrival and that each item is placed where it can be easily found. The Emperor represents someone who is adept at planning for an adventure or a long trip, usually making one list of what is required and another list of the order to pack everything into the car or suitcase.

In a health query, The Emperor can indicate headaches, small cuts and bruises due to impatience and occasional clumsiness. Sometimes, there are issues with iron levels in the blood. Generally, it suggests robust health due to supportive routines and self-discipline. This person is aware of the benefits of a moderate lifestyle. If a medical or health practitioner instructs an Emperor to increase exercise or avoid certain foods, this individual will rigidly adhere to a committed routine.

The Emperor Reversed

There are several possibilities when The Emperor is reversed. The first is that it represents an individual who has been disciplined and is now mellowing, realising that structures exist to provide freedom to live. This is the upright Emperor in retirement, discovering life's subtleties. The second option is that this person is undisciplined and when faced with a difficult decision, shrinks away from it. The Emperor reversed can be argumentative but when pressed, usually backs down. Basically, this person is 'all bark and no bite.'

When The Emperor card is reversed in a layout, it sometimes describes someone who is not successful yet. This individual prefers to have plenty of choices without having to choose one specific option. Basically, it involves enjoying the promise of several paths without having to commit to a specific direction. This person is apprehensive that a chosen option might not bring happiness and that going back to other possibilities won't be an option. As long as choices are avoided, there is always hope that the current alternatives will remain available. Perhaps in his fifties, this individual is still aged twenty-five emotionally.

For a reversed Emperor, happiness usually involves looking ahead at the possibilities of an adventurous life without ever having to make a commitment. This person dreads commitment, knowing what follows it: effort. There is the awareness that even with determination and commitment, there are no guarantees of success. It's as if this individual set out to climb a tall mountain and instead, spent the next thirty years working in a general store at its base. The card reveals potential that may not be fulfilled. Despite worthwhile opportunities arriving periodically, they are rarely seized and pursued.

When this card is reversed, it is helpful to look back to the preceding upright card to discover the wisdom of The Empress. This undisciplined person can succeed if involved with an Empress partner, whose practical approach to life ensures tasks are completed. The spouse usually manages the finances, organises holidays and books tradespeople to repair the home. If this individual does attempt home repairs, they're often abandoned prior to completion.

As an answer to a question, The Emperor reversed can suggest returning to the previous upright card, The Empress, to fill a need for sensual fulfilment or to receive physical nurturing that may have been missing earlier in life. It can indicate that the person is emotionally stuck at an early stage of development, needing a mother or mother figure to help with the process of emotional growth and maturity. When reversed, this individual is likely to seek more than one partner at a time. A relationship with a nurturing, sensual person like The Empress might enable this person to mature into the upright Emperor, a person who has developed self-discipline and who can set a steady pace to complete complex, long-term life goals.

The Emperor reversed can also suggest a lack of success due to poor self-discipline. This person has a sense of entitlement and wants a partner who'll provide a high level of support. An alternative meaning for The Emperor is a person who has retired from a successful career and is financially supported by past efforts. In retirement, this person sometimes feels overwhelmed. Without the daily demands of a job or a business, there is suddenly no meaningful reason to get out of bed each day. A return to the upright Empress card can help this person to discover that enjoying each day is the reason to get out of bed. Growing a garden and spending time with friends and personal hobbies are rewards for past efforts. Retirement isn't the end but a transition to a new life.

In a general reading, this card reversed can indicate intermittent success due to a lack of strategy or poor concentration on the tasks at hand. This individual begins a project with passion and enthusiasm but soon falters and abandons the process at the first serious hurdle. A return to the previous card, the upright Empress, can help this individual benefit from being supervised by a person who is a practical, efficient organiser. This person can complete a project if it's broken down into smaller tasks. With careful management, a more organised individual can bring out the best in a reversed Emperor.

In a career layout, the reversed Emperor is usually a restless individual who yearns for self-employment. There is often a range of mistakes that might cost this person a business unless there is someone else present to supervise. When closely managed, a reversed Emperor can work hard but usually in short bursts. When working with others, this person is likely to fight with co-workers due to a lack of discipline and a feisty temper.

A career that involves working in the open air is generally more suitable for this person. Careers in the construction industry, mining, driving a truck or a car, running an open-air market stall, gardening or as a tour guide might be most fitting. Sometimes, the reversed Emperor represents a boss or a manager who has been promoted beyond personal capabilities. This individual lacks the leadership skills required to motivate and manage a team.

In a relationship question, this person learns by direct encounters and only then after several repeated attempts. By his third marriage, he's learned what most men discover after their first relationship ends. He realises that if a partner is ignored, criticised and taken for granted, they usually become a former partner. Eventually, there is the realisation that a partner is not a mother — simply there for the sole purpose of attending to personal needs.

In romantic relationships, this person is usually undisciplined, shrinking from major decisions and searching for a strong partner to take care of the details. The reversed Emperor sometimes represents a mother-child relationship between marriage partners. When reversed, the Emperor enjoys being in charge but doesn't like responsibilities and feels overly burdened by oppressive duties. This can be a workable arrangement if the individual is capable of ignoring personal pride and deferring to a better, more capable manager. If governed by ego or a need to be in charge, chaos results from poor decisions and lack of follow-through.

In a health query, this person is likely to face issues related to lack of discipline. This individual is childlike and often lacks moderation. Over-indulgence in food, exercise or pain medication after a physical injury is common. The reversed Emperor has limited awareness of the long-term consequences of actions, habits and personal indulgences. Like a child, there is a desire to stay up late, eat and drink too much, invest in wild ideas and constantly test personal limits.

This is the person who sets off to sail around the world and has to be rescued three days into the voyage. A month later, another vessel is launched and another rescue is required. Five years on, this person is on first-name terms with all the search-and-rescue teams up and down the coast, having never successfully sailed the globe.

In one reading, this card described a man who was unable to hold down a job after a workplace injury. As the Emperor usually relates self-worth to personal achievements, this man had lost self-confidence. Lack of meaningful work made him temporarily depressed, undisciplined and without focus. Eventually, with the help of physical therapists, he was able to return to work but in a supervising capacity. Once back at work, his confidence returned and it's likely he'll appear as an upright Emperor again in a future reading.

The Hierophant

The Hierophant represents a teacher, institute or organisation that favours a traditional approach. The Hierophant's task is to preserve knowledge and pass it on intact to those who want to benefit from past insights.

The Hierophant (or Pope or High Priest) is an authority figure, shown on the card by him seated above the disciples as a role model for them. The followers surrender free will to their teacher to benefit from his knowledge. However, in reality, a teacher cannot teach by enforcing personal will. An instructor can make the learning process more palatable and interesting and possibly spark a lifelong interest in the subject but students have free will to follow that path or choose another. The Hierophant can make mystical information more applicable to daily life but is unable to teach people unless they are open to learning. A willingness to acquire knowledge and challenge old, outdated beliefs can provide insightful understanding of life and spirituality.

The disciple on the left has the passion to learn, shown by the red roses on his tunic, whereas the follower on the right displays pure motives in the form of the white lilies. The ancients used the cross as a symbol of human compassion, shown by the horizontal bar located at the height of the human heart. Enthusiasm, integrity and kindness lead people to a profound understanding of life, although this can be concealed from view to the unaware. Empathy for the human condition is required before people can be truly equal and emotionally close to others.

In a relationship question, The Hierophant describes a Taurean person, as this card represents the lesson for the sign of Taurus: that *mine is not the only way*. It's a process of discovering that there are many different paths to enlightenment. This card can also indicate pressure from friends or relatives to select a 'suitable' partner. In this context, 'appropriate' might mean someone from the same cultural background, with the same religion or with an acceptable job.

It can also suggest a steadfast role model. We all have mentors in different areas of our lives. More accomplished people can model behaviour when a person begins a new job, enrols in a course or joins a new community. The Hierophant describes a patient, proficient teacher or instructor.

Having a teacher, guide or a progressive role model is valuable until a person is familiar enough with a subject to explore it alone. Once an individual can do this, it is possible to choose a path different from previous teachers, even rebelling against them to establish a personal sense of identity. This resistance is shown in The Hierophant reversed, where it's possible to study a subject or process from different viewpoints before arriving at a unique understanding of a subject.

In a general reading, The Hierophant represents a conservative path that is tempered by other's expectations. There are teachers or leaders who preserve the rules or guidelines in most areas of life. Gaining a solid grasp of the rules makes progress more predictable and enjoyable. Whether it's learning to swim, play tennis or use a keyboard, there are guidelines or rules to follow to ensure improved proficiency with the process.

This card indicates that the individual finds it easier to follow established religious or spiritual guidelines than to take responsibility for personal development. This is fine as long as the person is tolerant of others who choose entirely different paths. The shadow side of The Hierophant is an *us* and *them* mentality. This is the process of noticing what makes us different from others instead of realising what we have in common. Despite personal differences, individuals with dissimilar religions, philosophies or life beliefs can share common attributes, goals and community interests, from sports and food to family life or ecological preservation.

In a career layout, this card describes a conservative, practical approach is likely to result in steady steps up the corporate ladder. It sometimes indicates an occupation involving teaching, training others or in academia. The Hierophant can also indicate a mentor in the company who is committed to encouraging this individual to improve and thrive in the workplace.

In a relationship question, The Hierophant describes a liaison that is acceptable to friends and family. It's an attitude that the person 'has married one of us.' Having similar backgrounds can improve the flow of life for those in long-term partnerships. However, these relationships sometimes become more predictable and less spontaneous for the same reason.

This card can indicate a Taurean person, especially if the King of Pentacles or the Four of Pentacles also appear in the same layout. In non-love relationships, it can indicate a teacher and pupil. This might be an ageing artist teaching a younger person core techniques and skills while also acting as a mentor for progressing and succeeding within the art world.

In a health query, The Hierophant can indicate the neck, jaw, shoulders and the throat, as this is a card for the sign of Taurus, and these are traditional Taurean health areas to watch. If a client is considering an alternative approach to a health issue, the upright Hierophant indicates a conservative approach might be more effective.

When Megan asked about her chronic back pain, she explained she had recently tried acupuncture, chiropractic adjustments, massage, herbal medicine and spiritual healing, but nothing had fixed it. She had a list of possible alternative therapies, whereas the cards suggested it was time to try modern medicine.

"Have you had a CT or a CAT scan of your back?" I asked her.

She hadn't. "I don't want to go down that route. I had a friend who had shoulder surgery and her shoulder has never been the same. She's had limited movement ever since."

"That's fine. I'm not suggesting you have surgery. I'm suggesting you have a scan to eliminate any serious issues. After you ask about having a scan, we can consider other options." The answer card for the scan was the upright Hierophant, confirming a more conservative approach was likely to help.

Megan came for another reading several months later, after a diagnosis of bone cancer in her spine. During her second session, she was looking for ways to manage her pain and in that reading, alternative therapies were more likely to help. The upright Ace of Swords indicated acupuncture was a possibility and the Nine of Cups confirmed hypnosis as a viable pain-management tool. Other options offered Megan short-term remedies but were likely to be less effective in the long term as her illness progressed.

The Hierophant, like the other fives in the tarot, indicates a tendency towards single-mindedness. When reversed, it can be a more positive card, suggesting a more open-minded approach to life.

The Hierophant Reversed

The Hierophant reversed represents searching for fresh ideas and possibilities, including potential new paths to tread in pursuit of spiritual wholeness. This is the opposite of the upright Hierophant, which represents a more basic belief that the current direction is the only one. A certain path may seem an obvious choice but each person eventually walks many trails when pursuing personal truths.

Different perspectives are required to gain a broader understanding of life. Consider an apple: a big, juicy green apple may trigger hunger in one person and allergies in another. To a dietician, it might be a source of vitamins and iron. To a worm, it might be home. To a dog, it may seem to be an oddly-shaped ball. They are all viewpoints, and they are all correct, yet each of these represents only one aspect of the apple. To the apple tree, an apple is a chance to reproduce itself, for the seeds contain generations of apple trees. Therefore, the pursuit of new ideas represented by The Hierophant reversed is necessary to increase awareness. This also helps with achieving spiritual wholeness by preventing stagnation or closed-mindedness.

The Hierophant reversed reflects an opportunity to take responsibility for spiritual direction by presenting many paths beyond the current, familiar one. In a relationship layout, the reversed Hierophant suggests an unconventional relationship. Perhaps gender roles are reversed.

In a general reading, the reversed Hierophant indicates an unusual approach might be worthwhile. Returning to the previous card, the upright Emperor, to ensure sufficient discipline to see plans through or to adjust methods when facing obstacles can be beneficial. This reversed card describes taking responsibility for personal direction, in career, relationships and spiritual development.

In a career layout, the reversed Hierophant can describe a job or a business that is not traditional. This might include working unusual hours, being self-employed, working as a contractor or shaping a unique career direction. It suggests a vocation in alternative therapies, artistic expression or as an actor, juggler, yoga teacher or writer. It's often a career that requires effort outside normal office hours.

Starting a small business, especially tarot reading or alternative therapies, requires a strong sense of inner structure. Corporations provide frameworks for stable business, whereas sole traders have to set up and maintain those structures.

For people unfamiliar with business systems, a mentor or a business coach might help with a business plan, marketing plan, setting up a website and social media presence. An accountant can assist with tax compliance and a graphic designer with producing brochures or web design.

In a small start-up, the sole trader is the person who does almost all of the work. Being able to do all these tasks while effectively growing the business requires the discipline of the upright Emperor. If a person lacks that focus, the alternative is a job, perhaps as an employee in a large organisation. This is shown in the upright Hierophant card. There are benefits for working for a large company that may not be found as a sole trader, including holiday pay, sick pay, superannuation or a pension plan.

In a relationship question, the reversed Hierophant indicates an unusual partnership that works well. It is often a pairing that facilitates spiritual growth in one or both partners. While the upright Hierophant card describes a conservative, stable relationship, the partnership is usually much less conventional when the card is reversed. This relationship might include people of diverse backgrounds, cultures, religions or different approaches to life. It might require open-mindedness and adaptability but the rewards are usually worth it. It could include partners of the same gender or with a 25-year age gap. Often, both partners feel these differences are part of the relationship's unique charm.

Kenneth explained that he stays home and raises the children while his wife Marion is a corporate high-flyer. This seems a perfectly reasonable arrangement. However, his male friends sometimes treat him like he's a second-rate citizen. Kenneth doesn't care. He believes that he's 100 years ahead of his mates.

In a health query, the reversed Hierophant suggests alternative therapies may provide effective treatment for a current issue. It sometimes indicates that the cause of a physical issue is spiritually based. Perhaps the person is not pursuing a beneficial spiritual path or yearns to break free from the restrictive expectations of friends and family to enjoy a unique life.

This card is associated with the neck, throat, jaw and shoulders. Some problems in these areas might be relieved through alternative or non-traditional means. Alternative therapies might include yoga sessions or stretching exercises, meditation, energy balancing work or walking in nature. Other options are massage, naturopathy, acupuncture, counselling or hypnosis to trace the origins of the current issues or energy balancing to reset the person. This card reversed might suggest it's time to look outside usual health avenues to find a solution.

The Lovers

Many readers don't look beyond the image of the couple in this card to see its concealed significance. The Lovers card represents combining masculine and feminine energies to move forward in life. The masculine urge is towards action and achievement, whereas the feminine potency is more focused on receiving what life has to offer.

When The Lovers card appears upright, it's time to move forward. It signifies awareness of both physical and spiritual needs when making a decision. "Am I ready to move forward in my life, or is it better to stay where I am?" is the dilemma depicted by The Lovers card.

In this card, physical needs are represented by the tree of knowledge, behind the woman, and spiritual requirements are shown by the tree of life, behind the man. Although the man in this card looks to the woman for comfort and contentment, she gazes up at the angel for hers, realising that lasting fulfilment can only come from within. The cloud stretching between them suggests their spirits are already connected despite their physical distance.

The masculine part of a person continuously thrusts towards possible challenges and achievements, whereas the feminine aspect appreciates the stillness required to explore feelings, hopes and unspoken needs. The Lovers card indicates it is time to decide whether to buy a house, marry a person, take a trip overseas or relocate to another town. It's decision time.

Several years ago, I decided to move within Sydney, away from the eastern suburbs to the north shore of the city. I was nervous about this prospect, as the north shore seemed to be light years away from the nightlife I once enjoyed and the people I mixed with. One afternoon, before even looking for somewhere to live, I sat down and reflected on the reasons behind this significant decision: I no longer enjoyed the inner-city nightlife, my friends lived all over Sydney, not only in the eastern suburbs and I wanted a garden again. Therefore, I looked around and found a suitable home on the north shore.

However, it took me another six months to be sure I had made the right decision. This realisation occurred when I visited a friend in the eastern suburbs one weekend and had to park three streets away from his house. His back garden consisted of a slab of concrete with two deck chairs.

"You should have been here an hour ago. The sun was right on these chairs," he said, as I sat in the shade listening to four different stereos from neighbouring houses. When deciding to move, I had trusted my instincts and as we sat in that tiny backyard, I knew I'd made the right decision.

Sometimes, the appearance of The Lovers card indicates the first or romantic stage of a love relationship. It can also suggest a decision to move forward with personal plans or a Gemini person. The lesson for the sign of Gemini is to make a suitable decision without becoming exhausted from exploring endless alternatives. These individuals may fear they have not looked at all the possibilities and worry they may regret a decision when better options surface. Decisiveness can be difficult for Gemini people because they readily examine all options in everyday choices.

In a general reading, The Lovers card describes a decision to move forward with plans. It suggests beneficial timing, as the person is ready to proceed at that stage. This card represents the process of examining available options but not the action of moving forward. Sometimes, The Lovers indicates the influence of a Gemini person. This might be a friend, partner or someone with sway regarding the topic of the layout.

In a career layout, the individual is examining options to determine which path will lead towards long-term career goals. This card can indicate choices such as taking a new job or remaining at a current organisation. The upright card suggests it's an appropriate time to move forward to new opportunities.

In a relationship question, this card often describes a new relationship or the beginning of a different stage of an existing one. Perhaps the person is considering a lasting commitment or planning to move in with a partner. The risks and possibilities that come with each new chapter in a relationship need to be carefully considered to determine whether the time is right to move forward. Once children arrive, it's not possible to go back to being free to travel and stay up late, as people do when they are childless. There are fresh opportunities but also sacrifices to be made when embracing each new chapter.

In a health query, The Lovers can indicate decisions about health or concern regarding the chest, lungs or arms. If the question is about a medical specialist or a path of action to address a health concern, the upright Lovers card indicates that this is a wise choice if not contradicted by other cards in the layout. It is best practice to always consider the surrounding cards, rather than the card in the answer position in isolation.

In a recent health question, Karin asked if it was wise to undergo laser surgery for her eyesight. Although the card in the answer position was the upright Lovers, the card in the outcome was the reversed Nine of Swords. It suggested that although the procedure was worthwhile, Karin's fear of the process was likely to motivate her to postpone the surgery and continue to wear glasses instead.

The Lovers Reversed

The Lovers reversed suggests that a person is not ready to move on from current circumstances. There may be more to learn from the present situation or it is simply not the right time to move forward.

In 1980, I moved from my hometown to Sydney. The move was prompted mostly by a friend who had been badgering me about it for two years. I left town on a complete high, feeling my life had never been so rewarding. However, I entered four hard years. I was unable to find where I fitted but was not prepared to return home. I had a bad start because I had left my hometown too soon. I was extremely young, naive and needed more support. Timing can be critical. I don't regret the move but I probably should have allowed myself more time to mature before launching into an unfamiliar, busy city.

Another example of the reversed Lovers card occurred when students badgered me to conduct a palmistry course. I had not planned to teach one until later but because of their enthusiasm, I decided to schedule one for the middle of that year. The course filled up before my assistant even had time to telephone the list of people who had requested course brochures.

When I reached the maximum number of students for the room capacity I would be using for the class, I asked the cards if it would be wise to hold it at a larger venue. The reversed Lovers card appeared in the answer, suggesting it was not wise for me to change venue at this point. However, applications for the course continued to arrive, so I ignored my reading and hired a larger venue to accommodate them.

I pondered this card reading later when four students had to cancel for various reasons. New applications covered the cancellations, leaving me with a full course, plus two additional students. However, the cost of a larger venue totalled the course fees of the extra students, so, The Lovers card was accurate. It was not time to move forward yet.

In a relationship question, The Lovers reversed can suggest a desire for romance but not necessarily for an emotionally intense relationship. Sometimes, this card indicates wanting change to escape an unpleasant feeling or situation. The reversed Lovers card suggests it is advisable to return to the previous upright card, The Hierophant, to savour safety, security and predictability.

This reversed card indicates it's not the best time to move in together, purchase a new home or get married. It doesn't mean these natural progressions won't occur in the relationship but that now is not the best timing for the next step. Ignoring this reversed card might result in purchasing a new home just prior to a real estate price collapse or leaving for a honeymoon destination that's in 'lockdown' due to a hurricane. However, the friendships forged in a hurricane shelter being bombarded by the relentless shrieks of the howling wind might make great dinner conversation, later.

In a general reading, the reversed Lovers card indicates it is better to stay with current circumstances than to push forward with new plans. It is time to return to the previous card, the upright Hierophant, to enjoy stability. Security can sometimes be misrepresented as boring or as being trapped in a rut but pentacles people, such as Taureans (the sign for The Hierophant) usually understand that predictability allows a person to take calculated risks and thrive. Stability often improves sleep at night, too.

In a career layout, the reversed Lovers describes indecision regarding career. The individual might be confused about whether to remain in a current career or pursue a new direction. At this point, it is better to continue in the present situation. Opportunities for career progression are slim at this time. This card appeared reversed in Zac's career layout. During his annual appraisal, Zac's boss had given his work a mediocre evaluation, thus eliminating him from applying for a new position being created in the department.

Zac was angry and wanted to quit immediately. The reversed Lovers indicated that leaving at that time could mean being unemployed for a period before securing a new position. The surrounding cards (Eight of Wands and Ace of Swords) suggested it might be better for him to accept the criticism and commit to improving his skills and performance. He did apply himself and seven months later he was poached by another department head for a more suitable position within the same company.

In a relationship question, this card describes the process of deciding to pursue or abandon a current relationship. At this point, it's better to remain in the situation and attempt to build or maintain stability (returning to the upright Hierophant). It's not yet time to move forward. This reversed card sometimes indicates that the person is unable to make a commitment, preferring to hold on to the romantic promise of life ahead than to take practical steps to build that life. This individual might be afraid of the burdens of responsibility, routines and commitment involved in the next stage of a love relationship.

In a health query, the reversed Lovers card indicates the chest, lungs or arms. It sometimes suggests that relationship conflicts are affecting health. It can also highlight indecision about the best way to rebuild or maintain stable health. A return to the upright Hierophant can indicate that mainstream medicine might provide a smooth path towards improved health.

The Chariot

The Chariot is a multi-layered card that highlights the struggle between thoughts and desires. It represents a time when a person maintains self-control through mental discipline, while on the inside, they long to be supported. It's a time to make a choice, despite internal anxiety or deep-seated fears about what might go wrong. This card is a seven and the theme for all the sevens in the tarot is *don't give up*.

The blue-faced moons on the shoulders of the person in the chariot emphasise this individual's innate softness, despite being in charge. This card describes a disciplined person who is often in a leadership or supervisory position, that involves making regular, significant decisions that affect others. Many separate aspects of The Chariot also indicate life's duality, including the black and the white sphinxes; the armour and the blue moons; the land and the water; and the city behind the chariot and the country in front of it.

The Chariot represents the strategic qualities of The Magician combined with emotion. The Magician grasps life from a black-and-white perspective while maintaining control of emotions. This is not so easy to do, especially when feelings surge forward. The Chariot shows a more mature approach to disciplining emotions with mental control.

An example of this conflict between head and heart occurred with Lloyd. Over the six years he was married to Karen, he had become more and more immersed in his job until Karen felt she was alone in the marriage. Gradually, she felt less and less visible to Lloyd, and when Mike began showering her with attention, she found him irresistible. Karen had a short affair and Lloyd found out. They went through a bitter separation, during which, Lloyd's angry outbursts covered his pain.

During their marriage, he struggled to be what he thought Karen wanted him to be: strong and controlled, while concealing his emotional side and suppressing his feelings. After the recriminations settled down, Lloyd discovered it was his soft, gentle nature that had attracted Karen in the first place. It was a challenge for Lloyd to acknowledge his creative, emotional side without suppressing his desire to achieve goals and succeed in his personal endeavours.

Gradually, he began acknowledging his creativity, taking guitar lessons, yoga and a photography course. Swapping his Wednesday evenings at the gym for a yoga class was advantageous, as it was where he met Sandy and began a new relationship.

The challenge of The Chariot card is to use logic and mental clarity to make decisions, while simultaneously considering personal feelings. This may not seem like a difficult task but Cancerians often find it challenging, as it is the underlying lesson for the sign of Cancer. It can be challenging to find balance when immersed in feelings or even weighed down by sentiment. When under pressure, some people retreat into their minds to escape turbulent emotions. However, ignored or suppressed emotions can build up and eventually surge free, wreaking internal havoc while swamping logical thinking. This is shown in the reversed Chariot card.

In a general reading, The Chariot card describes maintaining a balance between mental strength and emotions when pursuing life goals. By accepting the importance of feelings while not being governed by them, it's possible to make plans and achieve beneficial, tangible results. Effective leaders usually have this ability and having learned to direct themselves, can manage others. It's a card for the sign of Cancer, especially when The Moon card is also in the layout. As it is a seven card, it also indicates success through persistence.

In a career layout, this card suggests that persistence brings rewards. This individual routinely remembers that if the chosen path was easy, it would be congested. Personal determination is fuelled by the understanding that it's never crowded at the top because so few people reach the summit. Being resolute doesn't mean doggedly sticking to a job or a career that won't lead to meaningful rewards but instead knowing when to change direction while steadfastly pursuing long-term goals.

In a relationship question, The Chariot can describe a focused, practical individual who is persistent with personal plans. The blue-faced moons on the shoulders indicate innate sensitivity to the feelings of others, as the moon is associated with sensitivity and creativity. The armour hints at the strategies developed for self-protection from criticism and judgement. Although outwardly tough and motivated, this person is also creative and imaginative. A relationship partner needs to be patient to discover this silent, softer side of this person, as it's often concealed beneath emotional armour.

In a health query, this card highlights the stomach and the breasts. This person might encounter digestive issues when anxious, especially when obsessively remembering past emotional upheavals. When imagination is running wild, it's worth focusing on the best choices ahead, to reduce stress and ensure ongoing good health.

The Chariot Reversed

The Chariot reversed represents being completely absorbed by emotions while losing clarity of thought. This can mean experiencing explosive outbursts or becoming overwhelmed with grief for times past.

When The Chariot card is reversed, the body of water (emotions) in the card image is above the head (logic) of the individual. It suggests that feelings are dominating thinking. There is no balance between emotions and thoughts. This person easily becomes emotionally overwhelmed and is then unable to maintain mental detachment. Intense passions distort perception, reducing the ability to make logical decisions. When this card is reversed in a layout, the person might have recently made a poor decision or be about to make one.

The Chariot represents the astrological sign of Cancer and when reversed, it highlights a negative trait of this sign, a tendency to live in the past. Sometimes, Cancerians love a person more when a friendship or relationship has concluded than when it was available. This suggests that past events, even those that were difficult, are remembered as perfect and may stifle realistic opportunities in the present.

The reversed sevens in the tarot can be summarised by the phrase 'don't hold on.' It's time to release the past and move forward. This usually requires returning to the previous upright card, The Lovers. This card suggests it's time to decide to pursue a new or different relationship and this decision may require detachment from a previous relationship. Ghosts from the past are not helpful when developing new friendships, especially if earlier struggles have been airbrushed from the memory, leaving a biased perception of previous events.

Sometimes, The Chariot reversed describes a powerful businessperson who arrives home, closes the front door and goes to pieces, overwhelmed by life and its demands. For an individual like this, it can be beneficial to return to the previous card, The Lovers. If someone special in this individual's life can provide the love and support needed to heal, it can help this person move forward.

The major arcana cards are stepping stones on the fool's journey from innocence to the wisdom provided in The World card. Some of these steps must be shared with another person. These joint portions of life's underlying spiritual journey, as shown in The Lovers card, serve a range of purposes. It is time to provide support for another person and receive insights, assistance, love and care in return. There is also the opportunity to observe how others deal with life's challenges.

In answer to a question, The Chariot reversed can suggest the person is overreacting to something or choosing unwisely. Perhaps there is the burden of too much responsibility or the person is becoming overwhelmed. This could be an appropriate moment to retreat to a safe place or pattern of behaviour. For example, if walking along the side of a river in the afternoon has brought peace in the past, this might reinforce feelings of inner peace. Finding a sanctuary to reflect on choices and actions allows aroused emotions to settle and inner balance to be restored.

In a general reading, the reversed Chariot can indicate being overwhelmed by emotions. When reversed, the sphinxes are at the top of the card, pulling in different directions. This is often a tug of war between thoughts and feelings. When thinking is clouded by passion, decision-making can be poor. The person is more aware of what is being left behind than what will replace it, so it's time to return to the upright Lovers card and make a decision. This involves accepting that stepping forward into a new situation usually requires releasing old patterns and habits. The theme of the reversed sevens is *don't hold on*. It's time to let go.

In a career layout, the reversed Chariot sometimes describes a person who is fielding constant demands from others and feels overwhelmed by the burden of responsibility. It's time to return to the previous upright card, The Lovers, to make some constructive choices about more effective strategies. These decisions might include finding ways to empower others to take responsibility for their own solutions or delegating these responsibilities.

In a relationship question, this is the shadow side of Cancerians — the tendency to hold on to the past through dreams, vivid memories and sentimentality. Fear of new circumstances or of releasing what is familiar might prevent the person from making effective decisions when the Chariot appears reversed in a layout. There is a tendency at this stage to feel emotionally overwhelmed.

In a health query, the reversed Chariot indicates the stomach or the breasts. It can also highlight emotional stress and worry affecting personal health. A return to the lesson of the upright Lovers card may alleviate anxiety, especially after decisions are made. There is a sense of relief at having options while becoming aware of a more clear-cut direction.

The Chariot reversed can indicate excessive worry about health, even when it's unwarranted. With a vivid imagination, a small rash can transform instantly into an exotic illness requiring quarantine and urgent medical care. Unrestrained thinking can create worst-case health scenarios that rival an award-winning film. When the card appears reversed, the water in this card is above the chariot driver's head, indicating that emotions dominate thinking. Fears and hopes can run riot with logic, while rational thinking becomes momentarily abandoned.

When stress affects personal health, this individual can usually benefit from returning to the previous upright card, The Lovers. The Lovers represents a retreat to logic. This can help turn a potentially overwhelming issue into a choice. In deciding how and when to move forward, it's possible to build and maintain better health. The decision might be as simple as committing to a short walk every day or as complex as consulting a medical practitioner to explore health options regarding a chronic condition.

Strength

The Strength card represents a time of inner conviction, of displaying courage despite doubts. Acting with courage isn't always about saving someone from a burning building. There are many forms of inner resolve represented by the Strength card.

Sometimes determination is required to get up in the morning. When a child loses a fight with cancer, facing friends and fellow parents or simple things like feeding yourself can take genuine fortitude. Nonetheless, sometimes people find vast reserves of inner resolve and perseverance to keep going until a compelling reason to do so arises.

Strength may be required to tell a close friend who is leaving that you'll miss her and that she has made a difference in your life. When I was young, our family spent what seemed like every Sunday at the home of my aunts. They were generous hosts, giving up half of almost every weekend to host our large family.

Some years ago, I learned that one of my aunts was dying in hospital. I was unable to visit her, so I sat down and wrote her a letter, telling her she had made a difference in my life and that I was thankful to have known her. Although I was young and wild at the time of writing the letter, I instinctively knew it was one of those rare opportunities to convey my kindest thoughts to someone who deserved to hear them. I knew the opportunity would soon pass and I didn't want to live with regret.

When we forge ahead and are setting new frontiers in a chosen career, our courage may inspire others. If the Strength card appears in an answer position, it suggests success through inner strength.

When Roger decided to give up alcohol, he knew it was going to be a long, arduous journey. Alcoholism had cost him his marriage, his relationship with his daughters and several jobs. He joined a support group and immediately felt overwhelmed by the demands of his decision.

Each time Roger broke his promise, members of his support group provided a lifeline and helped him make a new commitment. They reminded him not to compare himself with people who already had the life he desired but to focus on each step before him. They urged him to find courage, despite his reservations.

At each weekly meeting, he heard how others were struggling with doubts about achieving the long-term goal of a successful, sober life. Gradually, he realised that when his courage was as constant as his doubts, success was much more likely. More than twenty years later, Roger has a new partner and a more stable life.

He described his journey this way: "It's almost eighteen years since my last drink. It sounds strange when I say it but I feel I've travelled for eighteen years to end up with a small house in the suburbs. This long path hasn't led me to a mountaintop. It's led me to the middle and the middle agrees with me. I'm finally content with my life and family."

In a general reading, Strength describes having the determination and confidence to face life and trust it will provide support with personal plans. This card represents the spiritual aspects of an individual having control over the animal or instinctive parts. It sometimes highlights awareness of the unintended consequences of surrendering to every whim or desire.

This is a card for the sign of Leo, especially if The Sun or Queen of Wands appears in the same layout. The first part of the spiritual purpose for Leo people is to find inner-courage to be themselves. The second part is to express themselves creatively.

The predominant colours in this card are yellow, orange and white. Yellow represents intellect, while orange signifies passion and enthusiasm. The woman in this card is clothed in white, indicating her pure motives in soothing the lion. This suggests that the person is addressing both physical and spiritual needs.

In a career layout, this card describes someone who is quietly confident of long-term occupational success. This means that if a current workplace is not supportive or there is limited chance of achieving established career goals in the environment, this individual can map out a new direction and move on without feeling disappointed. Strong talent and ability usually rise to the top, especially when the person has conviction with their plans.

In a relationship question, Strength can indicate a Leo person in a partnership or influencing a love affiliation. It also describes confidence in what is being offered to others and optimistic expectations that personal needs will be met. It suggests that the person is not necessarily aiming to control a spouse but wanting to direct shared passions towards desired goals.

In a health query, this card usually indicates robust health. Physically, it can signify the heart or the spine. In spiritual terms, Strength is a constructive card, suggesting spiritual courage and connection that help maintain a clear, long-term perspective. When upright, Strength indicates robust health and confidence in ongoing well-being. It can highlight appropriate balance between work and play.

Strength Reversed

Strength reversed can represent fear or erosion of confidence. This person might be overreacting to a situation due to anxiety and, as a result, attempting to control others. When this card appears reversed, it is time to return to the previous upright card, The Chariot, to tackle inner opposing forces. This individual could be battling internal demons so the separation of mental and emotional reactions is likely to offer a clearer perspective.

The lion in this card represents enthusiasm and inner strength. Passion is indicated by the colour orange, and traditionally, the lion is a symbol of courage. When upright, this card suggests that enthusiasm is governed by intellect (a skill learned in the previous card, The Chariot) and directed towards rewarding goals. However, the reversed card suggests spiritual requirements are being ignored in favour of physical or emotional needs and desires. This might include a yearning to be famous, successful, admired by others, wealthy or free from the burdens of their current life.

When worldly desires are stripped away, most people search for peace or happiness. Individuals who have suffered great turmoil or trauma usually yearn for inner calm, whereas people who have endured intense sadness crave joy. When these profound needs are addressed, the Strength card appears upright again in tarot layouts.

In answer to a question, Strength reversed can indicate a lack of success results from insufficient inner strength or confidence. When belief in a successful outcome dissipates, a person is less likely to give a goal the effort required for success. The attitude can be one of, "What's the point?" Conversely, optimism in the desired outcome often strengthens courage to pursue individual dreams.

Sometimes the reversed Strength card suggests a person has a meaningful goal but doesn't know how to achieve it. Encouraging the individual to find knowledgeable people for guidance towards a successful outcome can be helpful. This could involve finding a coach, a mentor or someone who has already accomplished that goal.

In a general reading, Strength reversed indicates a lack of self-worth and low confidence in abilities. Short-term desires might be a constant distraction from longer-term goals or the pursuit of spiritual purpose. When this card is reversed, the lion appears above the woman, indicating passions are overruling clear judgement. It's time to return to the wisdom of the previous upright card, The Chariot. In The Chariot, it's possible to learn how to control emotions and wants. Without discipline, desire can take an individual in dozens of short-term directions without long-term reward. Without any definite purpose, an individual's energy and attention can be fragmented and wasted.

In a career layout, the reversed Strength card indicates an individual has not yet identified their personal power in the work environment. Perhaps this person is overwhelmed by current responsibilities and is not confident of mastering all the job requirements.

When Dana received a promotion, it meant more work, almost double her current responsibilities and a paltry reward for the additional effort. As a school teacher, she was already busy and her new position meant she was also in a coordinator role for the English department. A few months into the role, she felt exhausted. Dana received no training; limited resources and the extra work took an additional fifteen to twenty hours a week. She had less time for her own family, for marking exams and assessments or for lesson preparation. Dana felt overwhelmed by the mountain of work. She explained that if she asked to be relieved of the new role, she might never receive another promotion. She felt stuck and the Strength card appeared reversed in her career question, reflecting this powerlessness.

Together, we explored possible options, including applying for positions in other schools or even leaving teaching for a new career. Dana usually had confidence in her skills but the added workload without training was taking its toll. She eventually accepted a position in another school in a more supportive work environment where she blossomed.

The reversed Strength card can also indicate being bullied in the workplace or not being heard or acknowledged by colleagues and management. This person's knowledge and personal opinions are being dismissed or undervalued in the planning stage of projects.

In a relationship question, Strength reversed sometimes describes someone who attempts to dominate personal relationships and friendships. This could be based on an unacknowledged fear of being controlled by others. Alternatively, this person might have surrendered to the dominant will of a partner and is now lacking the self-worth to know that leaving an unfulfilling situation creates the possibility that another, more suitable partner could eventually provide solid love and support.

This card can also describe a Leo person, especially if The Sun or the Queen of Wands appear in the layout. Strength represents one part of the lesson for the sign of Leo: to understand ego boundaries. By being mindful of where your personal boundaries end and another person's boundaries begin, it's possible to recognise two sets of needs and negotiate to meet these requirements. Without strong boundaries, it's likely that one partner will eventually abandon personal goals to please another. This cannot be sustained for long without one partner becoming emotionally and spiritually hungry.

In a health query, the Strength reversed is a card for the heart or spine. In later years, many people take medication for heart issues and lead normal lives, so it's not to be read as an urgent health warning. It can also indicate ongoing back difficulties, sometimes caused by stress or an injury.

There is sometimes a lack of confidence that personal well-being can be improved. Unresolved fears around health might require a return to the previous upright card, The Chariot, to find strategies to keep the mind in control of the emotions. It's not always easy to find the balance between intense opposing forces.

The reversed Strength can sometimes signify the anticipation of disaster or memories of past trauma that can deplete physical health. The key to redressing this is to focus on present obstacles, choices and opportunities, without allowing past fears and phobias to spiral out of control. A hyperactive imagination can be a hindrance if it is not directed and focused. The reversed Strength card suggests it's time to monitor self-talk to ensure it's encouraging, rather than destructive or overly critical.

The Hermit

The Hermit card represents a personal winter. When it appears in a layout, it is time to sit and reflect, to realise how you have arrived at a current point in life. Time spent alone in contemplation is beneficial for understanding past actions. Wherever a person is in life, is often a direct result of past choices, actions, decisions and planning — or a lack thereof.

While others are actively achieving goals in the physical world, The Hermit is passively reflecting. Contemplation is necessary because understanding the consequences of past choices and actions can help to shape plans for future happiness. If you don't like your current circumstances, think carefully about choices that led you here and what

THE HERMIT.

alternatives might make for more rewarding directions.

However, when inner growth is carefully considered, The Hermit represents understanding and self-reconciliation. It is necessary to be realistic about where the current path is leading. Focus is sharpened by the realisation that time is the most fundamental non-renewable resource in life. Many people resist spending periods alone to reflect, fearful that what they might see within will be disturbing. Accepting selfish, greedy or cold-hearted motivations for past actions is necessary for balanced self-awareness. Everyone has an unpleasant shadow side and denial only leads to suppression, which can result in unexpected detrimental outbursts. Being aware of this basic instinct allows one to learn to accept it for what it is, without judgement.

The shadow side is primitive, selfish and reacts to circumstances from fear or anger. It still deserves attention. Time spent in quiet contemplation can acknowledge this basic voice. If suppressed, an individual's shadow side can have more control of outcomes because it remains unseen but subtly active. Hidden motivations and actions are potent forces in derailing a person's life, especially when left unacknowledged.

An example of suppressed beliefs overshadowing perceptions occurred with Cody, who grew up believing that no-one helps others towards their goals. As an adult, it was difficult for Cody to accept offers of help from others, or even to believe they were genuine. Instead, he was unconsciously competitive with colleagues, friends and also with his partner, Stacey. By consciously reminding himself that life is not a competition and that more can be accomplished through cooperation, Cody gradually began to notice opportunities for working together with others on shared goals. It took several years of constant vigilance before Cody released this old attitude. As a result, his career has soared.

For some people, pausing to reflect means they risk realising how much change is required for them to feel fulfilled. With television, electronic media and hand-held devices, an individual never needs to feel alone, despite more people living in single-person dwellings than ever before. Without a spiritual and emotional connection to others, an individual might easily feel unseen or forgotten. Taking time to remember spiritual purpose can alleviate numbing feelings of invisibility while providing inner stillness, acceptance and calm.

Avoiding reflection can have unwanted consequences, including the repetition of undesirable actions and unwanted results. Knowing where you have come from, where you are now and where you are going is a powerful motivator. Being aware of the journey allows a person to remain centred in the present, where all power in life resides. It's unlikely that an individual can alter the past or anticipate all future possibilities and problems. However, it is possible to make changes in the current moment that allow a different perception of the past, while clarifying a range of rewarding possible future directions. It's sometimes difficult to see new opportunities when burdened by past beliefs and experiences.

Although The Hermit is not concerned with physical action and movement, it does indicate personal strength being used to resolve inner conflicts. Increased contemplation can mean less action is required to achieve the same goal. Thoughtful planning can reduce unnecessary effort. By reviewing past actions, it's possible to refine an approach to a challenge, so less effort is required for future success.

The Hermit sometimes suggests a period of counselling can help make sense of the past. Alternatively, a person might keep a diary of thoughts and feelings or spend time alone in nature, meditating or focusing inward.

The subdued colours in this card emphasise the retreat from life to a place where there are fewer distractions. The yellow staff in the figure's left hand and the yellow, six-pointed star inside the lantern suggest that although the person in the image is physically still, the mind remains active.

The star consists of upward and downward pointing triangles. The upward triangle represents fire — the wands habit of setting goals and striving to achieve them. It's the process of acting on inspiration to improve life circumstances. After reflection and planning, the individual usually focuses on doing the hard work necessary to achieve personal goals.

The downward triangle represents water — the cups process of drawing down spiritual light to share with others through creative projects. The water approach to solving personal problems is to sense the way forward. This can require contemplation for stilling the mind and allowing the body to illuminate what feels right. In combination, fire and water represent compassionate action.

Compassionate action occurs when a person is fully aware of how their activities affect others. The two triangles are not always easy to balance. Fire is impatient to make headway, competing with others for available resources, attention and glory, whereas water increases the desire to work with others for shared success. While fire perceives group efforts as leaderless chaos, water attempts to focus on the talents of all participants for a more harmonious result. Fire wants to get it done. Water wants everyone to feel happy when it is done. Fire shouts enthusiastically, "I did it!" Water softly declares, "We did it together."

The hermit stands alone in the snow. The figure is isolated but personal winters provide opportunities to retreat, reflect and prepare for another rewarding summer ahead. Those reluctant to reflect can find ways to keep very busy, often exhausting themselves in the process. This is indicated by the reversed Hermit card, which can highlight an inability to be still, to reassess past actions and their consequences or to know when previous efforts were wasted.

In a general reading, The Hermit card indicates that reflecting on the consequences of past decisions and actions is beneficial. If a person is unhappy with results, it's time to consider a different approach. When an individual stumbles in life, there is an opportunity to make better choices or actions next time. Consequently, life improves as different plans are made.

The Hermit is a card for the sign of Virgo and can indicate a significant Virgo person around the situation. It's also a card for different forms of reflection, including meditation, keeping a personal diary, taking long walks in nature or engaging in counselling sessions to make sense of past or current circumstances. Time spent reassessing the past can save an individual from repetitive mistakes and generally improves personal outcomes.

In a career layout, this card sometimes describes a career as a counsellor, an advisor, a mentor or a coach. The person's role might be to help others reflect on personal actions, habits and choices to make rewarding life changes. It can indicate the need to reconsider career direction. This often happens when an individual is passed over for a job or a promotion or someone close dies unexpectedly. The reaction to the loss is to reassess career direction.

In a relationship question, The Hermit describes the process of taking time away from a relationship, or relationships generally, to reflect on how you arrived where you are and where you'd like to go next. It's also an opportunity to learn how to be alone without being lonely. This card highlights the reassessment of a person's relationship with the self. How kind, forgiving and encouraging are you with yourself?

In a health query, The Hermit is a card for the pancreas and the intestines. The appearance of The Hermit in a health reading can also indicate food intolerances and sensitivity to additives. It sometimes suggests that meditation or daily periods of reflection can be an antidote to constant worrying and thus assist with reducing stress and improving health.

The Hermit Reversed

The Hermit reversed can suggest that a person has begun to reflect on life and become overwhelmed or overburdened by previous actions and their consequences. This card redirects people to the previous card, Strength, to witness those parts of their lives where they have some control. It's an opportunity to find the courage to confront aspects of one's life that are not working.

It requires real commitment to look within and admit who you are, acknowledging both the light and the shadows. Inner strength helps an individual have compassion for the shadow components that may have been twisted out of shape by trauma or challenging circumstances. However, when an individual reclaims aspects that were previously hidden away in the shadows, they become free to accept other people more fully and without judgement, knowing that their shadow sides might have also been forged in torturous fires. When calm within, it's easier to reflect and tackle feelings of insignificance or regret one at a time, to avoid becoming overwhelmed.

The Hermit reversed suggests someone is keeping busy with work or practical tasks to avoid confronting painful emotional issues. It sometimes describes a job that takes up the evenings and weekends, depriving the individual of valuable reflection time. It's not always a conscious decision to work so hard. However, creating space for contemplation might help the person decide if a life-consuming job is worth the rewards.

When reversed, this card indicates a demanding job or that an individual is working full-time and studying in the evenings or every weekend. Although the work/study combination is short-lived and for a specific goal, it still inhibits reflection. It's easy to become swamped by work commitments and lose sight of life's bigger picture: that we are all passing through and taking only knowledge and understanding with us when we finally depart from the world.

In a general reading, the reversed Hermit suggests that a return to the previous upright card, Strength, is required. It's necessary to find personal strength to consider current life demands and plan effective strategies that allow life to flow more smoothly. Without periods of reflection, it's common to repeat unrewarding patterns or invest too much personal energy into maintaining a hectic pace. Sometimes, this card reversed indicates a person undergoing counselling to make sense of past events. When an individual is unable to understand incidents through reflection, an outsider may help clarify circumstances and choices.

In a career layout, this card describes an occupation that demands long working days. Evenings, weekends and even public holidays are spent toiling away, resulting in an imbalanced life. This is especially so when the Nine of Pentacles reversed also appears in the layout. It's not possible to adequately assess career choices when every moment is filled with unrelenting work tasks and demands. There's no time for contemplating work satisfaction.

In a relationship question, the reversed Hermit card indicates someone who might be afraid of being alone. Instead of taking time to consider emotional needs, the individual is fearful of losing a relationship. This, in turn, contributes to a fundamental sense of ongoing loneliness. It's possible to feel lonelier with a partner who doesn't see or hear you on a profound level than when you are physically alone.

Sometimes, the reversed Hermit describes someone who is working long hours to avoid a partner. Tackling ongoing issues is unlikely, as resolution requires communication. This person's approach is avoidance. He or she might provide financial support but is emotionally absent in the relationship.

In a health query, the reversed Hermit can indicate a need to take a break and relax. If work stress has contributed to ongoing health issues, a short rest is usually insufficient for deeper reflection and relaxation. The first three or four days of a break are likely to be spent in bed, catching up on lost sleep to restore physical well-being. When meeting work demands becomes a habit, it can be difficult to take a break, as the workload piles up. It's sometimes necessary to remind people that if they don't own the business that employs them, they don't need to take on the burdens of a business owner. The reversed Hermit suggests that it's time to take a break and explore better systems to reduce personal workload or responsibilities.

Wheel of Fortune

The Wheel of Fortune card represents the circle of life, which involves constant motion. As the wheel turns upwards, events in a person's life appear to improve. As it moves downward, cycles appear to finish, fall away or lose their momentum. After a personal summer, an individual winter usually beckons. Following the darkest day of a personal midwinter, the wheel keeps turning and eventually another summer arrives. During this low-energy cycle, it's beneficial to reflect on past actions. During a high-energy phase, it's better to act on prospects as career, social and creative opportunities are often more plentiful.

WHEEL of FORTUNE.

The beings illustrated on the card (the eagle represents water, the winged lion symbolises fire, the winged bull stands for earth and the angel for air) represent the knowledge learned in the four suits of the minor arcana. They are shown in yellow because, although the four suits or four paths to fulfilment have been understood intellectually, it is not until The World card that these animals are in their full colours. At that point, the four paths are understood comprehensively — physically, emotionally, mentally, spiritually or energetically.

When someone has embraced wisdom, they can see changes in circumstance for what they are: revolutions of the wheel of life. It's possible to anticipate forthcoming seasons and to know when to begin projects and when it's time to end associations, career paths or to move on from goals that are no longer suitable. As capable gardeners know, it's much more productive to work with the seasons than against them.

In life, there are seasons for pain, loss, joy, renewal and growth. By charting previous years, it's possible to discover that every year had a time for each emotional season. People generally don't rage against God or nature when the leaves start falling from the trees in autumn because they understand winter is coming and after winter, spring will follow. Soon summer will arrive again, as the wheel of life turns continuously. These are natural cycles.

A person's emotional life is similar to the seasons. Starting a new relationship is like spring, with glorious green shoots and abundant flowers. The blossoming of that relationship is summer's harvest. Reasserting boundaries, plus a partial return to behaviour patterns formed before the commencement of the relationship, is represented by autumn. The end of the relationship or a time when one or both partners becomes intensely immersed in personal issues is like a cold winter.

Ben is a clairvoyant and colleague who complained to me one afternoon about his client load. As a psychic, he felt he ought to know why his business was quieter than usual, despite his escalating advertising budget. I asked him to tell me when his previous busy time was. He said it had been two years since business had flourished.

"And before that? When were you very busy prior to two years ago?"

"Oh, about five years ago."

"Could it be that you are in your career winter and you need to slow down? Perhaps it's time to draw breath and reflect on the past and your future career direction?"

He pondered this for a moment and released a long sigh. Charting the pattern in his mind allowed him to realise he *was* in a career winter but it also reassured him that summer was on its way. Tracking personal seasons can make an individual more successful in their endeavours because precious time is not wasted planting seeds or starting new projects in a wintery depression when the chances of success are diminished. Ben might have saved himself the extra money he spent on advertising by realising he was in a low period. Increased marketing at this time was unlikely to make much difference to his income.

In this card, the sphinx above the wheel guards the secret of an individual's seasons. People who understand this mystery generally make better use of their time and energy. Winter is a period to conserve energy, whereas spring is the perfect opportunity to plant seeds, plan ventures and begin new projects.

When the Wheel of Fortune appears upright in a layout, it is time to realise what is happening in the greater scheme of life because this overall perspective is likely to bring peace of mind. An awareness of personal cycles means individual improvements in circumstances are seen in balance and lost ground can be salvaged at that time. In the bigger scheme, comparing personal progress against the advancement of others is not so helpful.

The Wheel of Fortune represents the passing of personal seasons. It's a way of measuring time. During one's life and hopefully before it concludes, it's vital to pause and remember that time is all we have. It's a non-renewable resource. Use it wisely.

In a general reading, the upright Wheel of Fortune suggests a period of improving opportunities, choices and possibilities. As a personal summer approaches (the wheel is rotating upwards), the individual can expect increased success, plus a range of viable opportunities ahead. It makes sense to enjoy while remembering it won't last. When summer has reached its peak, the days will gradually begin to grow shorter as the wheel turns downward towards a personal winter, which is the reversed Wheel of Fortune card.

In a career layout, this card highlights a need to combine the four basic elements of fire, water, air and earth (the four beings in yellow at the corners of this card) to push ahead towards career goals. That means combining passion (fire or wands), teamwork (water or cups), a clear strategy (air or swords) and persistence and hard work (earth or pentacles) to achieve career objectives. It also suggests that summer is approaching in terms of employment, so it's time to be on the lookout for opportunities to move ahead.

In a relationship question, this card describes improvements in a current relationship or opportunities to begin a new one. Perhaps the person's social life is expanding as they discover new community circles through work, move to a new location or increase activities such as meetups, working out at the gym, volunteering or attending courses.

In a health query, the upright Wheel of Fortune shows improvement in health. It can also indicate a developing awareness of the most effective ways to build and maintain physical health after a recent personal winter. During reflection periods, energy reserves are often low, restricting activity and encouraging contemplation. These are worthwhile periods for assessing which strategies or habits are beneficial and identifying those that are restricting health and well-being. When the Wheel of Fortune is upright, it can also signify a recent period of low physical vitality.

Wheel of Fortune Reversed

The Wheel of Fortune reversed represents a downturn in circumstances. However, on reaching the lowest point on the wheel, there is only one direction ahead: upwards. The reversed card suggests a need to return to the previous upright card, The Hermit, to reflect upon life patterns. The seasons are moving towards winter and the snow on the ground in The Hermit card.

By thinking ahead to the next summer, a person can decide on the paths that will lead to a more rewarding season ahead. Without the reflective winter period of The Hermit, life's summers begin to look increasingly similar. There is a risk that growth and development will stall while life stagnates. It's a time of hibernation, to rest and contemplate past choices and their consequences while planning to meet and embrace future possibilities.

When the Wheel of Fortune appears reversed in a layout, opportunities are decreasing. It suggests a business is shrinking or a relationship might be losing its appeal. It is wise to remember that the wheel is continually turning, so in time new prospects will arise. Low tide is eventually replaced by a high tide, as the wheel of life turns. Winter approaches to provide reflection time. Look within and make sense of the actions taken in the previous spring and summer. An awareness of life's bigger picture is valuable on the path to reaching The World card. It is worthwhile to remember that when entering a personal winter, the start of summer is only two seasons away.

In a general reading, the reversed Wheel of Fortune indicates a personal winter is approaching. It is wise to return to the previous upright card, The Hermit, for contemplation. This card represents a period of reflection to reassess current plans, hopes and strategies before pushing ahead towards personal goals. It's time to process past losses, frustrations and disappointments. Reflection will lighten the emotional and mental load for the journey ahead.

In a career layout, the Wheel of Fortune reversed indicates that career progress is stagnant or sluggish. The coming months are not the best time to change jobs or seek promotion. If a person has asked about current job prospects in the present organisation and this card appears reversed, looking for a position outside the organisation might be a better option. If the individual has asked if it is wise to pursue an occupation long term, the Wheel of Fortune reversed suggests that it's time to consider other viable career options.

In a relationship question, the reversed Wheel of Fortune signifies a steep path ahead is likely to test a partnership. Facing obstacles together can either tighten the bonds between partners or highlight weaknesses. If the person is single, opportunities for a new romance are likely to be sparse for a period. This reflection time can increase awareness of what is most suitable in new relationships, compared with previous ones. By deciding what you don't want in a partnership, it's possible to enjoy more successful relationships when the wheel eventually turns towards summer.

In a health query, this card reversed can indicate that the person is unaware of the importance of rest and reflection. Sleep at night serves several functions, including a chance to repair the body after daily stresses and give the spirit a chance to be released from the physical world and recharge. Periods of contemplation are also worthwhile to reassess your efforts and reaffirm goals. They provide an opportunity to pull off the road and check the map to ensure you are still heading in the right direction. Small corrections en route are often more productive than hurtling towards a destination only to discover that the strategy doesn't suit the end goal.

During personal winters, energy reserves are often low, restricting activity and encouraging thought. These are quiet periods for assessing what strategies or habits are worthwhile and what are limiting health and well-being. In physical health terms, the reversed Wheel of Fortune can indicate weakening health for a period, plus the need for more rest than usual. Meditate, keep a daily journal and take time to nurture yourself, so you're refreshed and prepared when spring arrives. It is not a time to push the envelope but an opportunity to pause and reassess personal direction.

Justice

The Justice card represents an awareness that personal decisions and actions have consequences. It suggests current circumstances may be the result of poor choices in the past. When people realise that they have choices, they are less likely to blame others for their unhappiness. Individuals can generally change the directions of their lives through increasingly thoughtful decisions.

Justice is cloaked in red — a colour used to signify passion and action. This person can take action but the white shoe (purity of motive) and the blue sword (spiritual awareness) show careful consideration of the consequences. The one white shoe reminds us of spiritual outcomes (white is used throughout the tarot to signify spiritual purity). The blue sword symbolises mental clarity. The purple cloth suggests compassion, while the grey pillars represent the constraints of the physical world. Despite restrictions, this person can reach an appropriate conclusion for the current circumstances and long-term goals. Weighing up possible actions and their likely outcomes requires time and patience. Rushing this process can result in repeating mistakes.

Traditionally, Justice is shown wearing a blindfold. This is to encourage the use of the third eye when making judgements. The third eye, or spiritual eye, is capable of seeing the underlying spiritual lessons contained within ongoing struggles. It also enables a person to have compassion for individuals who cause pain as a result of spiritual blindness, immaturity and selfishness. Basically, it helps a person to forgive and move on without a heavy heart.

In a general reading, the Justice card can describe legalities, the signing of documents or negotiations. When people buy homes, apply for jobs or sign agreements, this card often appears to confirm straightforward negotiations and the associated paperwork. It also indicates someone taking responsibility for personal circumstances. This individual realises that past decisions and actions are impacting the present situation. In the answer position to a question about the outcome of a legal dispute, the person is likely to be happy with the result. It can signify a Libran person (especially if The Empress card also appears in the layout).

In a career layout, the Justice card describes contracts being signed or even the necessary paperwork required when accepting a new position. Justice can also signify someone who works in law or law enforcement. This can include legal work, employment with the police or in the Department of Justice or the Office of the Director of Public Prosecutions. As this is a card for accepting personal responsibility for current circumstances, Justice can indicate someone who is making decisions about career direction, while also considering long-term consequences.

In a relationship question, the Justice card indicates a legal commitment between partners, such as a marriage or purchasing a home together. It sometimes describes a Libran person in a relationship, particularly if The Empress appears in the same layout. If there have been arguments or upheavals in a relationship, the upright Justice card highlights a negotiated resolution. The Justice card represents decisions. The person might be deciding to make the marriage work, before taking all the necessary steps towards this desired goal. Those steps might include resolving past issues with the partner or carefully assessing role changes within the relationship while taking some responsibility for existing problems.

In a health query, the Justice card suggests someone is prepared to take responsibility for personal health and is making decisions about the best approach to well-being. It can indicate the kidneys or the digestive system as these areas are associated with Librans.

Justice Reversed

When Justice appears reversed in a layout, a person might feel life has been unfair. There is an urge to blame someone else for current circumstances. Sometimes, there is an unequal situation occurring, especially when it involves comparison with others who seem to be better off. We each have different starting points in life and come with unique skills and talents. It is not possible to truly know what another person is experiencing, even in their successful moments.

Unresolved arguments and ongoing litigation are also indicated by Justice reversed. An example of the kind of situation suggested by the reversed card happened several years ago. My next-door neighbour complained to me one day that his rear neighbour's dog was driving him mad by barking incessantly. I suggested he have a word with the neighbour. He just shook his head. Later that day, I phoned a dog-training business that advertised they could humanely silence annoying dogs using simple training techniques.

The company sent me out a brochure, which I took over to my neighbour, Robert. He explained that the rear neighbour probably wouldn't spend $240 training the dog. I suggested they each pay $120 and that it would be worth it for Robert's peace of mind. He took the brochure but he didn't seem to understand my perspective. I couldn't hear the dog from my house. Robert seemed more intent on maintaining his rage than resolving the problem. He felt the situation was unfair, whereas I believed it was simply unfinished.

In a general reading, the reversed Justice card can describe ongoing disagreements or a legal battle that drags on for months or years. If this card appears as the answer to a question about pursuing legal channels to resolve a disagreement, it suggests that course of action is best avoided. It's likely to result in an expensive, convoluted process with an unfavourable outcome.

Before becoming bogged down in thoughts of who is responsible for events in life, there is a need to return to the knowledge of the previous upright card, the Wheel of Fortune, to be reminded that everything has its own timing. It's much easier to work with personal seasons than against them. The focus can then shift to the spring that will eventually arrive with fresh opportunities.

In a career layout, the reversed Justice card can indicate ongoing unfairness in the workplace. This may involve bullying, unreasonable demands from management or blatant favouritism. When this card appeared in Jayne's career question, she explained that she worked in an old-fashioned company where the men were in management while the women did the work. As the executives played golf or took long lunches, she was in meetings, negotiating with suppliers and quoting new projects. When the supervisors received generous annual bonuses, she was handed a bunch of flowers, which she usually gave to a colleague who worked in the warehouse. Because this attitude was company-wide, Jayne accepted she needed to move to another organisation to progress with her career. In some situations, only one person is on the receiving end of bullying or mistreatment, whereas in others entire sections of staff are treated poorly.

In a relationship layout, this card sometimes appears to describe protracted wrangling during a divorce. In a question about legally pursuing a partner or a former partner, the reversed Justice suggests it's not wise. It is likely to be a long, drawn-out process with an unsatisfactory outcome. The person might lose many months or years in this futile process. Time is a non-renewable resource and pursuit of legal justice is not wise at this point. Occasionally, it's better to walk away.

Where someone is unable to let go of the desire to fight to the end, it is worth encouraging them to consider releasing the situation and focusing on improving their circumstances. Sometimes, it is necessary to learn from an incident and move on. Worldly resolution is not the same as universal justice.

To use the analogy of a boat for a relationship, both partners agreed at some point to climb into the vessel and set sail for uncharted shores. By reflecting on how unprepared they may have been for turbulent seas, each person can be better equipped for future expeditions with new shipmates.

In a health query, the reversed Justice card can indicate an inability to take personal responsibility for current health issues. This individual might blame others or bad luck for health problems, instead of accepting they might be the result of inadequate diet, lack of exercise or poor personal habits, such as insufficient sleep, overeating or indulging in alcohol or other recreational drugs. This card can indicate issues with the kidneys or the digestive system. Sometimes, it describes an ongoing legal dispute following malpractice by medical or other health professionals. This is generally a slow, protracted process. A resolution might take years instead of months, after which the person might prefer to forget the whole ordeal.

The Hanged Man

The Hanged Man describes times of feeling tied up or constricted. It is difficult to change current circumstances or choose a better path. When The Hanged Man card appears in a layout, it is time to look within for personal fulfilment and to take note of the sources of emotional and spiritual nourishment that are still available.

Meditation can provide inner peace and sanctuary at this obstructive time. When life weighs heavily, leaving a person feeling alone to face burdens, slowing down to reflect and meditate can reconnect one to a higher source of energy and increase mindfulness of the bigger picture. Being aware that this period will pass can momentarily release a person from internal struggles. A profound meditation can offer the realisation of being stronger than the current test. This reminder is necessary to maintain faith in the face of life's challenges.

When a person habitually glimpses a unique spiritual direction, The Hanged Man represents a welcome rest on the path of personal development. It highlights the importance of inner communion that is treasured by those who know its mystical value: inner peace and stillness.

THE HANGED MAN.

Wise individuals are aware that their journey through life is only temporary and tend not to become overly attached to worldly goals or specific outcomes. The Hanged Man contemplates his true purpose here on earth to prepare for the time in the future when a physical body is no longer necessary.

When The Devil card also appears in this layout, material possessions and goals promise increased happiness. However, when compared with lasting spiritual fulfilment, their rewards are fleeting, like shiny baubles in a shop window. The bright yellow aura around the person's head in this card suggests an awareness that divine sources of personal nourishment are beneficial for a balanced life. The Hanged Man is another period of reflection, a time to focus on the inner world while experiencing restrictions within the physical world. Without time for reflection, personal growth is slowed because repetitive mistakes can become habits, especially if they go unnoticed for any length of time.

In a question about career or love relationships, this card indicates prospects are sparse now. It's time to be still and look beyond current constraints in preparation for when new opportunities arrive. Resisting the temptation to struggle against the tide can conserve energy that will be necessary later when the time is right to move forward with purpose.

In Conrad's relationship layout, his wife was ill and had been for several years. Although he loved and supported her, he felt alone in facing her likely departure in the coming year. Doctors had suggested she had no more than six months to live. Although he described her as a warrior, he noticed the fight waning as she struggled for breath every single day. The Hanged Man described Conrad's powerlessness in this circumstance. He was reminded that we are all here temporarily and he seemed utterly weary with the battle ahead.

When his partner eventually passed over, he would face a period of grief and sadness. However, he might be reassured to know he would join her at the conclusion of his journey. I scanned ahead clairvoyantly to glimpse two relatives and a friend who were likely to meet his wife when she passed and described these people to Conrad. He recognised two of them and seemed to relax slightly but was acutely aware of the pain and loss to come. After the reading, I recommended two books that might help him understand the bigger picture of many lives and spiritual development. The understanding wouldn't spare Conrad the pain of his wife's departure but it might provide some context to help him accept that gruelling change.

In a general reading, this card appears when it is time to surrender to life and current constraints. With patience, one can observe present circumstances, reflect on past decisions and plan a more suitable path for when restrictions diminish. If existing limitations do not wane, it's time to adapt. After serious heart surgery, Colin had to accept permanent dietary and lifestyle changes. It was immediately apparent that the price of continuing with old habits would be further surgery or a shortened lifespan. A few years later, he felt fitter than he had in decades. Initially, adapting to circumstances felt like a constriction but eventually, it was perceived as a liberation.

In a career layout, The Hanged Man represents a period of limitations and acceptance. It's time to prepare for when circumstances change by conserving energy, making plans, and reflecting on past career decisions and forthcoming opportunities. When Junka's company put a hold on hiring new staff and didn't replace people after they left, morale plummeted. Colleagues began to wonder if the company might go out of business. Because Junka worked in sales, she knew the whole industry was in a slump. Her competitors were also suffering, so a job in another company in the industry wasn't the answer. During the slow period, she enrolled in a night course in digital marketing and made the most of her time. She completed her certificate course before the turnaround and when it arrived, she applied for a better-paid position and moved on.

In a relationship question, The Hanged Man signals a time to retreat and reflect on life and the journey beyond. The Lovers card reminds us that part of each individual's expedition up the mountain is shared by another, whereas The Hanged Man represents the part of the process that must be tackled unaccompanied. Aloneness is a fundamental part of the human odyssey, a reminder that people, circumstances and possessions are fleeting in the greater scheme.

By reconnecting with spiritual sources of nourishment, it's possible to reduce one's dependence on other people for personal happiness. The term 'reconnecting' is deliberately chosen, as we come into the physical world from Spirit and return to it afterwards. We sometimes visit other realms during sleep at night and it's also possible to do so consciously through meditation. The Hanged Man represents an opportunity to be spiritually awake in life and to remember one's unique purpose.

In a health query, this card describes low reserves of physical energy. Ongoing exhaustion is likely to affect muscle tone, restrict socialising and cloud thinking. It's time to examine what might be contributing to this physical, emotional, mental or spiritual fatigue by reviewing diet, sleep patterns, exercise routines and mental health regimes or undergoing blood tests or trying different vitamins or supplements. It's an opportunity to research and reassess health issues.

Sometimes, The Hanged Man appears in a health layout when the individual is about to undergo surgery and will be bedridden or convalescing for several weeks. Although this is a short-term physical restriction, it is still an opportunity to reflect on current circumstances and life direction.

The Hanged Man Reversed

The Hanged Man reversed indicates loss of faith in one's ability to combat life's obstacles. The individual might be refusing or forgetting to go within to find spiritual nourishment, or may be struggling with weakened mental and emotional reserves. When The Hanged Man appears reversed, the person needs a reminder that the spirit is greater than the flesh and that in some place and time current problems are already resolved.

The darkest hour is just before the dawn and while the inner peace found in meditation may not change physical circumstances, it can restore faith in one's ability to adapt when the right moment arrives. It is a reminder to avoid comparison with those who are enjoying personal summers. We all embrace our cycles differently. It's part of the unique journey of being human.

When this card appears reversed, there is an increased urgency to struggle against the tide, usually without success. The process of expanding awareness towards the bigger picture of life can remind us that the tide will eventually turn, bringing with it new opportunities. When it does, it is vital to be rested, focused and prepared to act with purpose.

This card represents an opportunity to take stock and remember that this difficult period will pass. Stop, reflect and find inner peace and acceptance of life's circumstances. By returning to the lesson of the previous upright card, Justice, and taking some responsibility for current circumstances, it is possible to see how a present situation is the result of past decisions and actions. It's time to be patient. Postpone projects that require energy and commitment and wait calmly for circumstances to change.

In a general reading, The Hanged Man reversed describes a time to be still. Avoid comparisons with people around you and reduce the temptation to struggle against the tide. If friends or colleagues are enjoying personal summers, don't be resentful. Know that your time for fun will come. Although it may not feel like it, current circumstances will pass. It's time to return to the previous upright card, Justice, to understand what decisions or actions may have led to present circumstances. It's also an opportunity to be still and consider how to approach life differently, for better results. It's time to surrender to life, allowing it to reveal your next step in its own time.

In a career layout, The Hanged Man reversed suggests that opportunities for promotion or to change jobs are scarce. It's better to wait than to push for new horizons at this time. To minimise frustration, it might help to look at areas of life where there are fewer restrictions and explore these. Treat this as a rest stop on your life path.

In a relationship question, this card describes someone who cannot accept a loss or the end of a relationship. By refusing to surrender a past situation, new opportunities for love and happiness can be missed. Sometimes, there is even a sense of martyrdom about the person, who has difficulty trusting again, having lost a cherished love. By returning to the upright Justice card, it's possible to review the personal decisions or actions that led to current circumstances. It's time to accept the consequences of past choices. Surrendering to life and allowing for new possibilities is an effective way forward.

In a health query, this card describes a time of convalescence after an illness. It sometimes indicates a long period of low energy or exhaustion. This can be a symptom of depression but sometimes it's an illness that weakens the physical body for a time such as malaria, Ross River virus or dengue fever. A check with a medical professional can confirm or rule out any health concerns.

Death

The Death card represents clearing away old systems to make room for new ones. This includes outdated habits, behaviours and even patterns of thought. Smaller deaths come to us all, many times in an average life, almost as if to prepare us and help us cope with the final death. In grieving and releasing the losses we face, we are free to return to life again. The Death card heralds an internal and external spring clean in preparation for new ideas, habits and opportunities.

Imagine if death called for you and took you away, only to return to you after a year, explaining it was a mistake. You're suddenly free to resume life with your rejuvenated physical body but many aspects of your life have become unavailable. You have no job and no home and all your belongings have been sold or dispersed amongst your friends and family. While you might want to return to your life, everything has changed.

This scenario occurs many times throughout a single life. When a relationship concludes, no matter how much you stare into your ex-partner's eyes, there is no longer any place for you in this person's heart. When resigning from a job, memories of what was achieved in that position are all that's left. It seems sensible to live without regrets as much as possible.

The Death card heralds sweeping changes. It is time to release what is no longer required, allowing an end to occur naturally. No matter how the end arrives, it is often accompanied by a sense of finality. After the dust has settled, it is possible to see the long-term vision of the Temperance card, that follows the Death card. It is not death nor change that shape us but how we deal with the transformations that accompany them. The underlying lesson here is to surrender to the changes life presents. Only when old, outdated patterns are swept away, can new opportunities arrive.

When this card appears in a layout, it's usually not about a sudden change. Often, the individual is anticipating new opportunities. When Carla completed her accounting degree, the Death card appeared in a career layout. University studies were concluding. She completed two years of supervision in a busy accounting company, after which Death appeared in a career question, again. It was time for Carla to change companies. She secured a position in forensic accounting, her desired speciality. With every step towards her career targets, the Death card highlighted the ending of each chapter. These weren't difficult endings because she was ready to release the old and make way for the new.

Endings can be more difficult when someone is reluctant to release an old pattern or situation or when they lack the faith that something better is coming. This is more often signified by the reversed Death card.

In a general reading, the Death card signifies an ending, such as the completion of study, the conclusion of a job, a separation in a relationship or a relocation to a new city or a new part of a city. Sometimes, the Death card signifies a Scorpio person. The spiritual lesson for Scorpio people is to surrender to the many intense changes and chapters in their lives. As a fixed sign of the zodiac, Scorpio individuals tend to resist change. It's not the ending itself that is significant as much as how a person deals with it. For every inward breath, there must be an outward one. It's easy to breathe out because we know we can take another breath when required. If life was a book, the Death card shows the endings of each chapter contained within it.

In a career layout, Death usually signifies the end of a job or a career direction. When Tony retired from the police force, he wanted a career with less stress and aggravation. He dreamed of having an occupation where people smiled at him when they saw him, instead of making demands, excuses or threats. It was a planned change and his new career in finance suited him. Sometimes this card indicates the end of a role in a company or a transfer to a new department with different responsibilities.

In a relationship question, the Death card sometimes suggests a Scorpio partner or the influence of a Scorpio person on a relationship. It also describes the death or end of a relationship or a stage of a relationship. For example, when a new baby arrives, the dynamic in the home can change rapidly. A partnership may be transformed by decisions made by either partner or even by outside events. A job promotion, a new home, an elderly parent coming to live with a couple or even grandchildren moving in can significantly alter a relationship, ending an old chapter and commencing a new one.

In a health query, this card can indicate issues with the bladder, bowel, lower back and the prostate in men and the ovaries in women. It can also signify a physical death but only when in combination with other cards (see: *The Meanings of Cards in Combination*). Sometimes it indicates stress associated with an ending, such as retrenchment, the conclusion of a love relationship or the loss of a friendship.

Death Reversed

Death reversed indicates a need to have faith that life will provide new opportunities to replace what is being left behind. It can be difficult to build confidence when confronted by loss. One way to strengthen trust in the arrival of new choices is to reflect on the previous chapters or events in your life. After past situations ended, they were eventually replaced by different prospects. This card reversed indicates the act of physically or emotionally holding on to people, situations or behaviours, despite their obsolescence.

The Death card appeared reversed in Kevin's career layout because he was holding on to a job he didn't like. He wasn't confident to leave it behind. Kevin worked night-shift in a factory assembling windows. It was physically demanding work and everyone on the assembly line worked as casual labourers. He'd have to ask the boss every Friday how many days they needed him next week and it ranged from two to four days on average.

Kevin was not paid well and had no job security. Sometimes, they halved the number of assemblers during slower months, so he knew it was time to move on to better-paid and more secure employment. I encouraged him to check the job ads. When he resisted, I asked him to treat it as research. He'd research how many suitable jobs appeared online each week and then he'd practice his interview skills by applying for a few jobs each month.

Six weeks later, Kevin had a new job. His wages more than doubled and he was working nine to five, allowing for a social life. Four months later, he returned for another reading where the Death card appeared reversed again. He had resigned from the new job and returned to the factory because he missed his friends on the assembly line. Shortly afterwards, the factory owners invested in a machine to assemble the windows and everyone on the line lost their jobs. It was time for Kevin to move forward. I suggested he return to viewing job ads online and arranging as many 'practice interviews' as possible. I pointed out that when he was working nine to five for better wages, he'd be able to organise an assembly line reunion lunch on a Saturday or Sunday. When releasing the past seems overwhelming, it may be necessary to take a moment to review the new options available. Sometimes, the best option is to focus on potential opportunities ahead.

When resisting the release of what death seems to snatch from us, or grieving a loss, it is difficult to return to life with confidence in the future. In the darkest hours, beyond tears, while numb and alone in the world, innate faith in the greater scheme is vital. This reinforces the concept that death usually removes what is no longer needed for personal growth. Withered leaves must fall in the autumn so new shoots can appear in spring.

Instead of holding on to what is fading away, try to focus on where the next opportunities lie and what form they might take. Returning to the previous upright card, The Hanged Man, is a reminder to surrender to life because personal transformation is a natural process. Go easy on yourself and allow for a period of healing and acceptance.

The Death card reversed can signify a Scorpio person. More often, however, it describes a slow ending of a situation with continuous delays before new opportunities finally arrive.

In a general reading, the reversed Death card shows a gradual, sometimes interrupted conclusion to a set of circumstances. It can also indicate completing one chapter, followed by a period of waiting before new opportunities emerge. It's necessary to return to the previous upright card, The Hanged Man, to be still and reflect until the next chapter or path is ready. During the waiting period, it can be beneficial to ask, "How can

I best approach new opportunities for more rewarding results?" The reversed Death card can also highlight a Scorpio person who is significant.

Sometimes, a reversed Death card indicates a change avoided. In some circumstances, it is possible to hold on to a situation but the transformation isn't stopped, it's merely postponed. By avoiding a retrenchment in the workplace, a person might feel relieved, until other changes occur within the organisation. Remaining with the company might involve a greater workload as there are fewer staff members to complete the jobs of the recently departed. When a period of growth eventually arrives in the company or the greater economy, existing staff often leave for less demanding roles elsewhere.

In a career layout, this card describes limited options ahead in a current occupation. The company might be downsizing, retrenching staff or about to enter voluntary liquidation or bankruptcy proceedings. Sometimes, it signifies the ending of a profession and not simply a job. As more industries are disrupted by advances in technology, workers may have to retrain several times in a career span.

In a relationship question, the reversed Death card describes the slow conclusion of a situation. Perhaps one or both partners are reluctant to release the liaison but it is finishing anyway. Sometimes, this card indicates that a Scorpio person is influential in this relationship, or it may describe one partner processing a loss, such as the death of a parent or the end of a career.

When Rosalie asked about love relationships, the reversed Death card described a recent partnership ending but nothing on the horizon to immediately replace it. She was desperately lonely, so I asked her to add two additional cards to the outcome position. The first was the Ten of Cups reversed and the second was the King of Cups. I explained to her there was another man in the future but that he was currently extracting himself from a long-term relationship. If she pushed him to begin a liaison immediately, he'd probably leave her in a few months, associating her with the end of the previous relationship. If she waited, she might meet him at a better time, when he had grieved his loss and was ready for love.

Sometimes, the reversed Death card is like waiting at a railway station for the next train. As you watch the previous carriage depart, you need patience and faith that the next train will arrive soon.

In a health query, the reversed Death card is associated with the lower digestive system, bladder, bowel or reproductive organs. It can describe being physically and emotionally depleted by a protracted ending. Judy's aged mother was ill but insisted on living out her final days in her own home. This required Judy to make three visits to her mother's house every day to provide food, clean up and help her bathe. Twenty-five months of this routine took its toll on Judy and when her mother was hospitalised, dying soon after, Judy slept for a week. It took two years for her to feel normal again. Although it was Judy's mother who was ill, running two homes, working a full-time job and taking her mother to doctors' appointments depleted her reserves of energy.

Temperance

The Temperance card provides a glimpse of a person's longer-term purpose. Temperance shows the awareness that there is a path for the spiritual and the human side to coexist harmoniously. Temperance is a card for Sagittarius, a sign that usually values a strong sense of purpose that is evident in careers, relationships or major choices.

This card also represents learning, whether through completing formal courses or through travelling and exploring life. In career questions, the Temperance card can describe teaching or an occupation that includes regular travel. Teaching might take the form of mentoring subordinates or team members.

The auric energy shown around the head of the person in this card represents spiritual understanding attained. The path behind leads to the sun, symbolising purpose. Although the track looks appealing, the person is content to stand still, finding peace through balancing the cups, which represent emotions. In this balanced state, clear choices can be made with an eye on the likely consequences.

Also shown on the card is an orange triangle, which signifies the element of fire, or passion and enthusiasm. It is surrounded by a white square, representing the element of earth or the practical application of ideas. When passion for a goal is enclosed in a measured, practical approach, objectives are more likely to be achieved.

The yellow circle at the centre of the brow suggests a well-developed third eye chakra. This represents the element of air and indicates a preference for an intellectual perception and understanding of life. In combination, the four suits of fire (triangle), water (the cups), air (circle at the brow) and earth (white square) are combined with mindfulness of profound spiritual purpose. This individual is often aware of how personal actions affect others in the bigger picture.

When Temperance represents an answer to a question, it suggests success through maintaining a balanced approach. Temperance is a card that signifies moderate action while maintaining a broader perspective. This individual is aware of the desired consequences and regulates their efforts accordingly.

In a general reading, the Temperance card highlights self-control, self-discipline and moderation. By attending to both physical and spiritual needs, it's possible to remain aware of life purpose and avoid excess or self-indulgence. This card can represent travel, especially if the Eight of Wands or the Ace of Wands appear in the same layout. It sometimes describes teaching or attending a course, particularly if the Three of Pentacles appears in the spread.

In a career layout, this is a card for teaching or studying towards a new occupation. Teaching can take place in a school, a private course, university, an independent academy, hospital or in workplace training and assessment. Temperance is a card for travel, sometimes indicating regular trips as part of a career, such as a pilot, flight attendant or ship's crewmember. It can also signify someone whose job involves frequent interstate travel, such as a wholesale buyer for a department store, a train driver or a long-haul trucker.

In a relationship question, it can indicate a Sagittarian person in the relationship or influencing the partnership. The underlying spiritual lesson for Sagittarius is temperance or moderation. As this sign is ruled by fire, Sagittarians can be passionate, enthusiastic and impatient for results. The upright Temperance card describes being able to see the consequences of actions while realising the importance of meeting physical and spiritual needs for a balanced life.

In a question about an existing love relationship, Temperance indicates a harmonious partnership, with opportunities for personal growth and learning. It can also suggest that one or both partners are flourishing spiritually as a result of this relationship.

In a health query, the Temperance card can suggest learning about physical well-being to improve personal fitness. In physical body terms, this card highlights the hips or thighs. Upright, this card is generally an indication of stable health. It indicates a balance between meeting spiritual and physical requirements for ongoing health and well-being.

Temperance Reversed

Temperance reversed describes a person who is acting without any long-term vision. 'You only live once' is the prevailing attitude when this card appears inverted. It usually indicates living with the consequences of excessive, self-indulgent actions such as losing a job after fighting with the boss, abandoning a relationship when circumstances were difficult or enduring poor health after years of alcohol abuse. This direct-experience way of learning can be a slow, painful process. When reversed, Temperance indicates a lack of restraint, with an inability to delay gratification. Buy now, pay later. The need to have it immediately ignores the extra cost of postponing payment.

Holly typifies this reckless behaviour. She is overindulgent, eating whatever she feels like whenever the urge surfaces. Her philosophy is 'I'll have to die of something.' It was a phrase she used to dismiss any helpful suggestions from her doctor and close friends. However, if dying was as simple as keeling over one day and passing immediately, we'd probably all live like there was no tomorrow. It wasn't death that caused Holly to suffer, so much as living for seventeen years with severe diabetes. Carers who observe the lives of others realise that old age is often spent according to decisions, excessive or otherwise, made in younger years.

An example of the hasty action of Temperance reversed is a man who leaves his fourth wife for his secretary, unaware that he is repeating a hurtful pattern of behaviour. His desire to be free from the restrictions of relationship could constrain him for years afterwards. Supporting children from four relationships was probably not what he was thinking about when he chose to be spontaneous and reckless.

When the Temperance card appears reversed, it is time to consider the lesson of the previous upright card, Death, to release whatever is obscuring the bigger picture. The aim here is to clear the path to make way for personal destiny. When Temperance is reversed, the individual cannot see ahead to The Sun card, shown at the end of the path behind the person on this card. Without a specific goal to focus attention, the individual becomes easily distracted, resulting in a life lived without purpose. Speedy action is not necessary, as the Death card, like the tides, gradually removes impediments or blockages that are no longer useful. The individual needs faith that life will leave them enough for their survival.

In a general reading, this reversed card can indicate excessive indulgence in food, drugs, alcohol or simply living in the moment, without thought for tomorrow. Risky behaviour that provides constant excitement can also shorten life expectancy. It describes a cavalier attitude to life, with a lack of awareness of the spiritual dimension of existence. This person nourishes only the physical self and not the spirit.

In a career layout, Temperance reversed describes teaching and sometimes indicates a person who is not thinking about a long-term career. A current job is simply that, a job. It provides an income but it's not a calling or vocation. This card can also signify chaos in the workplace, with a lack of strategic planning, disorganisation or a lack of temperance.

In a relationship question, a reversed Temperance card can indicate a lack of awareness of the consequences of behaviour. During a secret love affair, little consideration is given to the pain caused to current partners. Sometimes, this card reversed describes an individual who wants company without commitment. It can also indicate that one partner's habits or behaviour might eventually derail a relationship. This can occur with an alcoholic spouse or someone with other addictive or compulsive behaviours.

In a health query, reversed Temperance shows the results of an excessive lifestyle. By living only to gratify immediate needs and desires, a person can expect poor health, eventually. In terms of physical wellness, this card can indicate the hips or thighs. It also highlights injuries from accidents, reckless behaviour or clumsiness.

The Devil

The Devil card represents being seduced by the material world. This is shown by the reversed five-pointed star above the main figure's head. When upright, the five-pointed star represents the ability to keep desires in check through rational thinking. However, when reversed, personal desires overrule intellect and govern life choices. There might be a longing to be successful in a career, to be wealthy or to own more material assets than friends or relatives. While passionately pursuing worldly possessions, people can lose sight of spiritual direction.

Overly regimented routines foster stagnation and mediocrity, especially when stifling a thirst for knowledge. The Devil card represents the process of learning that fulfilment is not related to ownership. This card is more progressive when reversed because the five-pointed star is then upright. (Other cards that are also more positive reversed include all the fives and the Eight and Ten of Swords.)

Each new object acquired brings a fleeting period of excitement that rapidly passes as the gadget loses its novelty. By pursuing ownership of more and more chattels, a person's time becomes taken up with procuring objects and then with maintaining them, rather than living an abundant life.

In time, we become possessed by the chattels we own. It is helpful to be aware that belongings do not bring fulfilment. Ironically, a natural way to learn this is to accumulate personal effects. An old friend, Carl, loves to buy business shirts. Whenever he feels stuck or frustrated by circumstances, he picks up his phone or a device and looks online for new shirts. Although he usually only wears the same five shirts until they begin to fall apart, he confessed that he had sixty-six business shirts in his closet. That's not including T-shirts, turtlenecks or casual shirts. Sometimes, he purchased an identical shirt to one already on a hanger because he hadn't seen it for a while. To wean himself from this expensive and unfulfilling pattern, Carl found that when he felt like buying a new shirt, all he had to do was to select one already on a hanger and begin to wear it as if it was a recent purchase. He even momentarily considered wrapping it up and posting it to himself for the excitement of opening a parcel.

In this card, there are two people in front of the Devil. They have heavy chains around their necks, yet they enjoy a level of security in their bondage. The philosophy here is better the devil you know than the devil you don't. This card shows an attempt to quell their spiritual hunger. Without an ongoing sense of purpose, they only have work, fun and daily obligations. The harder they work, the easier it is to forget any yearning to discover life's veiled purpose.

To avoid the drudgery of striving to survive, they long to fall asleep at night so their spirits can leave their physical bodies and the limiting beliefs held in their conscious minds. Memories of the Death card and the losses they have experienced make them determined to avoid change at all costs. They are unaware that the spirit cannot be destroyed and they only risk losing restrictive beliefs. Instead of searching for meaning, they find ways to control their lives, making themselves more physically comfortable. They fill each waking moment with activities, leaving no time for reflection.

In a layout, the Devil card describes someone who regards almost anything new or different with suspicion. This resistance to change prevents a person from trying something unfamiliar, which perpetuates the current situation. Personal habits and routines are the invisible chains that hold an individual in bondage. Sometimes, this oppression is debt. It's harder to leave a well-paid job when there are ongoing financial obligations.

The Devil can indicate a Capricorn person, as this card describes the spiritual lesson for that sign of the zodiac. This path involves remembering that we are visitors here on earth and although it is practical to make ourselves comfortable for the journey, comfort isn't happiness. Capricorn is an earth sign and these individuals are content with stability, security and routine. Capricorn people usually have a well-developed work ethic, believing that if you want a job done properly, do it yourself. (The other card that often appears in layouts for Capricorns is the Ten of Wands. This shows someone doing everything himself and struggling under the burden of responsibilities and obligations.)

The Devil card can describe someone who has worked tirelessly for a stable life. This can mean the financial ease of a steady income and physical luxury with a big home and car. However, comfort doesn't address personal life purpose. Financial stability can remove stress and increase choice (about where you live, your education, lifestyle, etc.) but it does not guarantee increased happiness.

It's beneficial for the individual to carefully examine their options and notice any resistance to change. This person usually limits their choices to the current path or a disastrous alternative of hardship, poverty and constant struggle. A third viable choice needs to be found before there can be any real possibility of change. For any option to be considered, it needs to look familiar or closely resemble the current path. If it appears foreign or untested, it's likely to be dismissed.

When this card appears upright in a layout, the person is unlikely to be open to new possibilities. There may be a preoccupation with discovering ways to become more comfortable with a current path. New options are quickly discounted but the thought of continuing in the existing direction gives rise to complaints and frustration. This individual is stuck. Nothing will change until the person is ready for a transformation.

The Devil card represents habit, routine and believing only what can be seen, measured and proven. An unspoken rule for earth signs is this: if you are here on earth for seventy or eighty years, the first goal is to make yourself comfortable. What they don't always realise is that making and keeping oneself contented can take every one of those eighty years. Sometimes, life offers a reminder that coffins don't come with luggage racks and all accumulated possessions are surrendered upon death.

In questions about personal happiness, The Devil appears when an individual wants a fulfilment without relinquishing existing luxuries or routines. Comfort doesn't equal contentment. A level of ease is necessary for a balanced life but the pursuit of meaningful purpose may require risks and change. This can be found with The Devil reversed. This is why this card is more encouraging when reversed.

When Silvio asked about his marriage, The Devil appeared in the answer position. It was a loveless situation but Silvio saw only two options. Leave and abandon his two children or stay and feel powerless. As we explored other possibilities, Silvio discounted each one as too difficult, impossible or unaffordable. These included:

- Waiting until the youngest child is eighteen years of age (a twelve-year wait) and then leaving.

- Moving within the district to ensure he is still close to his children.

- Entering couples counselling to try to resolve longstanding differences.

- Discussing how he feels with his wife so they could find a workable solution, together.

- Securing a job with regular travel so he is away periodically while his children grow up.

- Accepting his current circumstances and making the most of this time with his growing family.

The Devil card represents the illusion that there is no choice. As a counsellor, I've learned to ask myself when meeting a new client, "Does this person believe change is possible?" Many counsellors accept that a client's arrival for a session confirms their belief in transformation and their desire to change and grow. Sometimes, however, individuals are searching for a way to become more comfortable with the devil they know and want to justify continuing with old, unrewarding habits.

In a general reading, The Devil describes someone unable to see current choices. This individual might feel stuck in a situation or obliged to finish what was started. It can be a frustrating position because viable options are often invisible when this card appears. When making significant decisions, several suitable choices must be available, to avoid the no-win options of staying on the current path or starving in a worse situation.

In a career layout, The Devil card represents accomplishment, as the person is likely to devote every waking hour to the success of an endeavour — often to the detriment of hobbies, interests and even relationships. When career achievement is vital, victory becomes the only possibility. This individual is unlikely to be distracted by social events, the desire for long holidays or anything else that weakens career focus. Almost every waking hour is devoted to working, planning or meeting with people who can help progress with career goals. Nothing is left to chance. Success gradually becomes inevitable.

In a relationship question, The Devil card describes a partnership based on financial security. It might be a marriage of convenience. It sometimes represents a relationship based on sex but not shared interests or values. This is a relationship where more emphasis is placed on comfort than on spiritual growth or fulfilment. The Devil card sometimes represents obligations and routines where a person feels stuck but cannot see a viable path ahead. Occasionally, small children or an ageing parent might be additional responsibilities in the situation, restricting options for change.

In a health query, this card can indicate the knees, teeth and the skin. It represents a conservative approach to health and someone who generally prefers medication over meditation to reduce stress. It can also represent exhaustion resulting from working too hard to afford material possessions. The person's job is likely to be a factor in current health issues. From workplace posture in a desk job to health and safety issues on a construction site, there are dozens of ways a work environment can impact a person's health.

The Devil Reversed

The Devil reversed indicates a person who is receptive to exploring alternatives in the pursuit of fulfilment. The need for secure habits and routines subsides when individuals accept that the only constant in life is change. When The Devil appears reversed, it's time to return to the wisdom of the previous upright card, Temperance, to glimpse a path home to Spirit. Temperance offers a clear vision of life's bigger picture. The reversed Devil card indicates an opportunity to look beyond physical comforts towards spiritual nourishment and development.

The chains around the necks of the people in this reversed card are weaker and less restrictive, as old habits and beliefs are discarded in favour of new alternatives. The five-pointed star is upright when The Devil card is reversed, signifying the person's mind is governing their desires. The spiritual aspect of the person influences base desires for food, sex, money, power and control. Realising that there are alternatives to the current path, this person is aware that transformation means surrendering to what life presents. Trust in a greater spiritual force, brings a change of heart and the ability to relinquish control over personal destiny. When reversed, The Devil represents a transition from extreme micromanaging to an increased trust that life will provide viable options to challenges.

Sometimes, an individual seeks to control life due to being overwhelmed by sudden upheaval or loss. Surrendering to change means risking further loss but this is sometimes necessary for personal growth. It requires trust that life will eventually bring more rewarding choices, people and opportunities for fulfilment.

In a recent question about an impending divorce, Tina was prepared to forgo some of her entitlement to shared assets so she could move on and end a loveless marriage. Her husband had offered her forty percent of their assets. Her lawyer had negotiated this up to forty-five percent, before suggesting that a lengthy court battle might cost her tens of thousands of dollars and possibly years of her life. Tina realised that her settlement was unfair but she wanted to end that chapter of her life and explore new possibilities for love and happiness. She was effectively breaking the chains that bound her to her husband, as shown in this card and she considered the peace of mind worth the financial compromise.

In a general reading, The Devil reversed can indicate a Capricorn person, especially if the Knight of Pentacles also appears in the layout. It also signals becoming more aware of options, opportunities and choices after a period of rigid thinking. Taking a new path can require a person to dismantle existing life structures. Pursuing an unfamiliar direction can mean leaving a job, a home or a group of friends, so it's necessary to be aware of the costs when making a change. It's also vital to focus on what will be gained by taking the new path. By returning to the previous upright card, Temperance, it's possible to glimpse some of the long-term rewards for making current changes. Remembering these potential advantages can motivate an individual when the going gets tough. It's like reflecting on sunny days in the middle of winter as a reminder that another summer will follow.

In a career layout, the reversed Devil card suggests the person is ready and willing to explore other jobs, locations for work or career avenues. Having choices isn't always easy but it's usually more rewarding than not having options. Some careers don't seem to suit those who train for them. More than sixty percent of my clients who have studied law do not practice legal work in their current jobs. These individuals have moved on to other more suitable careers, ranging from banking to web design.

In a relationship question, the reversed Devil card may describe a sexual relationship without much emotional commitment. It might be a convenient 'friends with benefits' arrangement that isn't leading anywhere. It also indicates an awareness of choices in love relationships. Perhaps the person isn't interested in a conservative, traditional relationship but instead is searching for something unique. This might be a same-gender relationship or a partnership with someone from an unfamiliar culture, religious background or different generation. The reversed Devil doesn't necessarily confirm a new relationship but an awareness of possibilities.

In a health reading, the reversed Devil card indicates an openness to exploring alternative therapies or changes in lifestyle to manage health and increase well-being. It signifies an acceptance that current habits are not working and new behaviour patterns are needed to achieve desired health outcomes.

Physically, this card is associated with the skin, the knees or the teeth. It sometimes indicates an awareness that life cannot be all work with no play. This individual is searching for a more balanced existence and is ready to embrace the changes necessary to make it happen.

The Tower

The Tower is a reminder that attachment can bring disappointment. It represents sudden upheaval, such as separating from a person or an object that is greatly valued. This transformation occurs rapidly and unexpectedly, unlike the Death card where events are more gradual and usually expected. The Tower indicates an immediate change is quickly approaching and will be difficult to avoid. This sudden upheaval might involve a fall from a ladder or winning an enormous sum of money. The person's life alters direction immediately.

The Tower represents a swift change that is often surprising and out of the person's control. Be aware that this disruption is leading to The Star card, that brings an insightful sense of fulfilment. The Star represents restored faith that life or the universe will support personal endeavours.

The people in The Tower card are leaping from a tall building after it has been struck by lightning. The structure that once held them safe now threatens their existence and they must change direction immediately. There is a strong sense of urgency and inevitability about this new course.

The Tower appeared in Jason's career question and I sensed his company was about to be declared insolvent before being bought by a competitor. His plans for progression within the organisation were redundant, as the purchaser was unlikely to want any of the current staff. He was in shock at this unexpected news. I urged him to update his resume and seek new employment immediately. I stressed that he had days, not weeks, to get out ahead of the tsunami of change about to engulf his workplace.

"Take the day off tomorrow and talk to recruiters. Look for contract work if full-time employment might take weeks to arrange," I said. To his credit, Jason updated his resume that afternoon and found several job recruiters the following morning. Within the week, the company was in talks with receivers and office morale had plummeted. Jason secured a new job several days later. Making a sudden career change without having time to thoroughly consider his options must have been stressful and unnerving for Jason. It was probably not as gruelling as for his co-workers, who were forced out of their jobs a few weeks later.

In a general reading, The Tower describes sudden change. Usually unexpected, it can shock a person out of complacency and force them to perceive life differently. It's a reminder of the impermanence of life which can range from an electric shock when touching a live electrical appliance to a close encounter or health scare.

In Carrie's general reading, The Tower in the past position represented a different type of shock. Carrie was spring cleaning one weekend while her husband was away on business. She rearranged some boxes in her garage and discovered a large carton filled with banknotes. Wads of freshly minted notes ran ten deep in stacks, shrink-wrapped in clear plastic. She said she stopped breathing when she saw them. After a rush of excitement, her blood ran cold. Whose money was this? If it was her husband's, how did he come to have this much cash without her knowledge?

"Exactly what is your husband's business?" I asked her.

"I don't really know," she replied, with a worried expression. Her husband returned after three weeks abroad to face some very confronting questions.

In a career layout, this card highlights a quick job change or a sudden upheaval in the workplace. This could be the unexpected departure of a supervisor, followed by an offer of promotion. It might also describe retrenchment or other change in the work environment, including liquidation of the employer or being merged with another company. Tower changes can occur in a heartbeat and don't usually allow time for assessment or consideration.

In a relationship question, The Tower card indicates a sudden beginning or collapse of a relationship. This change is usually unplanned. Sometimes, it signals a new perspective after a revelation about a partner. Occasionally, it can be a reality check after an unexpected event, such as an out-of-character gambling binge or a health scare. It can also forewarn of an accident happening to a partner or maybe a close friend is losing a job or witnessing a shocking incident.

In a recent reading, The Tower appeared after a partner discovered something significant about her spouse's past. He had served five years in prison for armed robbery and neglected to tell her before they were married. Hearing this unexpected news out of the blue forced a reassessment of the relationship.

In a health query, The Tower heralds an abrupt health issue. If this card appears in the outcome position of a health layout, it's best to add another card to determine what follows this 'emergency'. Check surrounding cards to identify areas of concern. The Tower may indicate sudden incidents, such as a heart attack, a stroke or a car accident. However, it more often describes the shock at receiving unexpected news from a medical professional.

The Tower Reversed

The Tower reversed indicates being warned ahead of impending change. The person manages to avoid a change but remains stuck in the same position. Actions to prevent upheaval are reminiscent of The Devil card: someone desperately clinging to familiar people or routine situations that have been a source of security in the past.

This card warns about impending change but when reversed, there is an opportunity to resolve the issues before or as they arise. However, if the warning is ignored, the change will approach again. For instance, after a cancer scare, the person needs to be vigilant with regular health checks.

Averting one issue is not a guarantee that all problems are resolved.

William survived the horrors of World War II as a prisoner of war in Europe for three years. Afterwards, he developed the habit of hoarding junk. He carefully stored away egg cartons, newspapers and old bottles for over twenty years, and his house was cluttered to the ceiling. One morning as William was cooking breakfast, a stack of egg cartons stored above the stove caught fire and his home was soon ablaze. He managed to control the fire but it didn't alter his hoarding habits.

Soon, William's health deteriorated and he was moved into a serviced retirement home, where he could not take anything but his clothes and a few personal items. Within two days of his departure, the entire contents of his house had been cleaned out. William's pattern of hoarding, undiminished after a clear warning of impending change, caused him to be heartbroken over losing his belongings.

In the previous upright card, The Devil, one is brought to the realisation that sometimes possessions can become unnecessary burdens. Physical belongings can distract a person from a spiritual journey, which is an integral part of each physical life.

Sometimes, the reversed Tower indicates surviving sudden changes. This person may not be made redundant, yet still feels the shock and loss of work colleagues during a workplace redundancy. It can be the hurricane that approaches but misses the individual. Someone's home may be one of only a few still standing after a bushfire sweeps through a neighbourhood. Although they have avoided the brunt of the change, this individual is still impacted by the upheaval in the environment.

In a general reading, the reversed Tower indicates an abrupt change that is avoided or affects others. This could describe witnessing a car accident or keeping your job when several close colleagues are retrenched. Personal upheaval is averted but this individual needs to return to the previous upright card, The Devil. Although the person has sidestepped change, stifling routines or obligations remain.

In a career layout, this card describes upheaval in the workplace that does not directly affect the person's job. This isn't always a beneficial outcome, especially after retrenchments, because remaining employees are left to do the extra work of those who are leaving. Sometimes the reversed Tower describes a person who is offered a new job in another organisation days before sweeping changes occur in the current workplace.

In Tao's career reading, the reversed Tower card provided a warning about workplace security. Three offices in the building were targeted by thieves one weekend, costing the company dozens of laptop computers, expensive colour printers and other assorted items. His manager asked staff to be vigilant and Tao took care to ensure his safety. He set up three miniature video cameras around the office and monitored them from his mobile phone. Two weeks later, Tao alerted police when thieves entered the office on a Saturday afternoon, while he was at home. His video footage was used in court proceedings and Tao was glad he had placed the HD cameras in the office.

In a relationship question, the reversed Tower card can indicate the individual's partner is experiencing sudden change or personal upheaval that is affecting the relationship. When unexpected turmoil occurs to someone close, that individual is likely to become hyperalert to threats to their stability.

In a health query, this card describes a near miss with health. This can be the discovery of a benign tumour, a minor heart concern that alerts the person to a more serious issue or the process of catching and resolving a health problem in its infancy. Sometimes these wake-up calls sharpen a person's priorities.

The Star

THE STAR.

The Star represents a time when a person is feeling centred in life, not requiring exterior structures and routines to provide a sense of security or purpose. This is a card for the sign of Aquarius. Part of the lesson for people of this sign is to release structures and routines that bind, while developing mental strength and imagination. When free from conventional thinking and conservative constraints, it's possible to be inventive and unique in one's perceptions.

This card represents a holiday or a period of mental and emotional freedom that results in fresh ideas and creative projects. It indicates ingenuity, re-invention, hopefulness and faith in life's possibilities. The Star represents a time of optimism and fun.

The person in this card is fascinated by the pool of water (representing the subconscious mind) and the source of creativity it represents. She pours water from two jugs, one onto land and the other into the pool, to demonstrate taking inspiration from the imagination and making it tangible in the physical world. The water poured onto the land emphasises ideas becoming real, while the water poured back into the pool represents the way new concepts often stimulate fresh thinking.

There are eight stars in the sky, each with eight points. These eight points represent the eight main chakras or energy centres of the human body (seven in the body and one above the head) aligned to allow the natural flow of creative and spiritual energy into the physical world.

The Star card highlights possibilities such as when inspiration becomes a concept that, with effort, can become a book, a film, a design or a product. It also suggests physical, emotional, mental and spiritual balance.

If The Star appears in the answer to a question, it highlights success that comes from a confident attitude and creative solutions. A person may have tried to cling to possessions in The Devil but now realises how much freedom is available without the unnecessary physical and mental constraints of personal ownership.

The ibis resting on the bush in the background represents Thoth, the Egyptian god of wisdom, knowledge and writing. In questions about creativity, this card sometimes highlights fiction and nonfiction writing. This is especially so if The Moon card appears in the same layout, as it also represents creative writing.

The Star also suggests studying (the act of acquiring wisdom and knowledge) and of instinctively knowing where the path is leading in life. In ancient Egypt, the ibis was a sacred bird, and villagers used them to clear fish ponds and waterways of snails that contained dangerous liver parasites. In The Star, this person is in harmony with her surroundings, including the birds and animals. The ibis and the person share a symbiotic relationship, mutually benefitting both parties.

In a general reading, this is a card for rest and recreation. It can describe a short trip or a holiday, especially if the Ace of Wands, Eight of Wands or Temperance cards are present in the same layout. It is a time of restored faith in life's possibilities and of creative inspiration that can result in writing a book or a blog. Sometimes, even a short break from routines can be a refreshing change.

In a career layout, The Star indicates a career that offers plenty of freedom to think independently. It also allows some latitude in decision-making, plus a sense of autonomy amidst the constraints of corporate hierarchy. This card can describe careers as an outsider, including as a consultant, an independent supplier to companies or in self-employment.

The Star suggests faith in career possibilities, plus the mental self-determination to chart an individual course in life. It sometimes describes an occupation that involves unusual working hours, such as a musician, writer, photographer or trekking guide.

In a relationship question, it can suggest an Aquarian person in or influencing a partnership, especially if the King or Queen of Swords also appear in the layout. Sometimes, it highlights an individual's faith that a rewarding relationship is possible. It describes a liaison which is free from the usual roles, expectations and limitations, allowing each participant to explore new ways to be together.

In a health query, this card represents balanced health, with the expectation of continued well-being. It can also point to possible health issues in the ankles, the nervous system or the retinas of the eyes.

The Star Reversed

The Star reversed suggests a lack of faith in life. A person might feel unable to see a viable alternative to current circumstances. It is time to return to the previous upright card, The Tower, and get jolted awake. At times, it is only through a shock that we recognise life's potential. When The Tower threatens to annihilate someone or something from your life, it's possible to see the real value of that person or object. Returning to the lesson of The Tower is an opportunity to reconnect with life and spiritual purpose in a real way. The Star reversed indicates that an abrupt upheaval might be beneficial at this time.

The reversed Star suggests a holiday is overdue. However, a break at this time may not be rejuvenating, as it may be spent obsessively thinking about work or daily problems, instead of resting and having fun.

The reversed Star card can indicate work travel with deadlines, meetings and targets. This is not a journey for leisure, as every hour is accounted for. Now, the pool of water is above the woman's head, indicating someone feels overwhelmed by emotion and is overdue for a rest.

When The Star appears reversed, it's time to take short breaks in busy days for personal nourishment and recreation. In a travel question, this card suggests a trip that results in exhaustion rather than rest and rejuvenation. This occurs when mothers travel with young children. They often work harder to meet the demands of a partner and children during a holiday than at home, returning frazzled and in need of relaxation.

In a general reading, the reversed Star indicates a lack of faith or confidence in the future. A holiday or a short break might rekindle optimistic expectations. A return to the previous upright card, The Tower, offers direct, sudden change and upheaval that can help the individual release people, habits and situations that are unnecessary for the journey ahead.

In a career layout, this card can describe business travel. Instead of relaxing on a beach, this person is rushing from a conference to a meeting and then back to the airport for the flight home. It can also illustrate someone taking personal work on their holiday or a work issue that interrupts a vacation and prevents the person from relaxing.

In a relationship question, the Star reversed suggests a lack of faith in a relationship or partnership opportunities generally. It may indicate a strong desire for freedom and resistance to the confines of a daily relationship. As The Star represents the sign of Aquarius, it can indicate an Aquarian person in a relationship or significantly influencing a partnership. If The World, the Ace of Wands, the Eight of Wands or the Temperance cards also appear in the same layout, it can indicate a relationship commenced while travelling. It sometimes describes a holiday romance.

In a health query, the reversed Star card describes the process of losing confidence in continued health or reduced faith that current symptoms can be remedied. It can indicate issues with the ankles, the nervous system or the retinas of the eyes. It sometimes suggests a return to the previous upright card, The Tower, where a sudden health shock might inspire the person to focus on maintaining long-term health. Sometimes it describes a trip to care for an elderly relative or a friend who is unwell. As a result, a holiday or a brief rest is required upon return.

The Moon

The Moon symbolises a retreat from life into dreams, rather than realistically dealing with situations. A person may fantasise about a different, easier life, rather than working diligently towards achieving goals. The Moon card can also suggest someone is having compelling dreams at night that provide insight into current struggles as well as the spiritual journey through life. It's time to acknowledge these dreams and heed any underlying messages they offer.

THE MOON.

The face in The Moon has its eyes closed, suggesting going within to seek answers to life's questions. The towers beneath the moon stand far apart, emphasising isolation from the earth (because of their height) and each other. The dog and the wolf are both howling and represent the demands of the subconscious mind, other people and life itself.

The pool symbolises the subconscious mind and the path taken in dreams at night, through astral travel. Although the places and dimensions visited in dreams are a welcome escape from the pressures of life, they cannot replace the direct learning available in the physical world.

When a person remains in The Moon energy for extended periods, they can become unreachable and isolated from the physical body and from others, as shown by the two towers. In these circumstances, imagination is likely to move from being creative to delusional as the individual gradually loses connection to the physical world. One antidote to this is physical exercise. However, if the person is confined to bed with an illness, physical exertion might not be appropriate. Sitting in nature or a garden can suffice.

In a layout, The Moon suggests it is necessary to look closely at what is happening beneath the surface. Some details hidden in the moonlight can be clearly visible in daylight. Sometimes, a person or a situation is much more complicated than first appearances suggest.

Looking beyond exteriors was exactly what Donna needed. I read for her three times over thirty months and each time I questioned her about her relationship with her partner, Tom. The Moon card appeared in each relationship layout and I suggested there were some problems with Tom that she needed to face. However, Donna denied that any difficulties existed and insisted she and Tom were very happy together. People usually hear what is said when they are ready to receive it and not before. However, the fact that she returned to see me three times suggested she wanted me to remind her of what she refused to see. She needed a tarot reader to be her witness and to notice the details she could no longer recognise with her own eyes and heart.

During her fourth visit, she collapsed into tears, admitting she had strong reasons to suspect Tom was having an affair. I wondered if I had been unfair in showing Donna what I glimpsed about Tom, especially after realising how much she had invested in their dream life together. I sensed the coming weeks and months would be difficult, so I asked Donna to focus on the eventual happiness ahead, after the discussions with Tom had taken place and relationship decisions were made.

Facing the truth after a period of self-deception is always painful. The Moon card represents the process of making peace with the creatures of the depths, in and around the pool of water. That is the only way to re-enter the pool comfortably so one may replenish one's soul. The animals represent instincts. In dreams at night, unfathomable instincts surface while the conscious mind is resting. Powerful subconscious imagery encountered during sleep may provide insight into life, as well as into one's unseen spiritual purpose.

Tania asked how she might find a solution to her ongoing issues with her young child. Boris had a short attention span and easily became frustrated and aggressive. I explained she would find the answer in her night-time dreams and urged her to start a dream journal. Ten months later, Tania phoned to say she had been keeping a dream diary and it resulted in her dreaming about a mineral deficiency in her boy. After Boris underwent tests with several medical and alternative practitioners who confirmed what she had recorded in her diary, Tania was able to give her son a mineral supplement that resolved his problems.

Although some dreams represent attempts by the subconscious mind to reorganise events of the day into memory, others address concealed issues which can be obscured by the demands of daily life. The Moon card highlights a powerful night-time connection with the subconscious mind, that can tackle inscrutable personal issues or foretell significant events. Sometimes, the subconscious mind can relay meaningful information to the conscious mind.

The Moon can also suggest a period of disturbed sleep. This might be due to a new baby in the house or sleep issues triggered by allergies, anxiety or breathing difficulties. The Moon also accentuates hidden motives, such as when companies plan sweeping redundancies but don't tell staff until the last minute. In relationship questions, The Moon can highlight unaddressed issues or underlying conflict that needs resolution. Deceit is another possible meaning for the Moon card, especially if the Seven of Swords or the Three of Cups cards also appears in the layout.

In a general reading, The Moon indicates a period of intense and often intuitive dreams at night. Disturbed sleep can result in the individual waking up feeling exhausted. It's not always dreams that interrupt someone's sleep, however, as loud neighbours, construction noise at 6:00 a.m. or a new baby in the house can also shatter tranquillity.

In a career layout, the Moon card sometimes indicates working at night. This can describe nightshift or working in a home office in the evenings. It's a card for writing and creativity, where the public see the finished works but not necessarily the creator. This applies to artists such as writers, painters, designers, composers, photographers or radio presenters.

In a relationship question, The Moon card indicates unspoken issues not being addressed in a relationship. It might be one partner's undeclared fears that subtly influence the direction of a partnership. It can also suggest dreams of past relationship issues are resurfacing so they can be resolved. Sometimes this card describes a Cancerian person, especially if The Chariot card also appears in the layout.

In a health query, The Moon indicates unresolved fears surfacing at night in dreams. It can indicate the breasts (in women) or the stomach. It also highlights poor sleeping patterns affecting health and energy levels such as daily stress interrupting sleep patterns, asthma issues from sleeping in a dusty bedroom, or sleep apnoea.

The Moon Reversed

The Moon reversed suggests there is less deception now than previously. This includes both self-deception and duplicity from others. The pool of water is at the top of the reversed card, indicating that fears and emotions may be dominating thinking, particularly at night. It is time to return to the tranquillity of The Star to restore faith in life and renew valuable connections with spiritual energy sources.

Issues that have previously caused fear and isolation can be resolved now. The Moon reversed represents a need to face life honestly, without hiding from intense, imaginary fears. The Star symbolises that, from the darkness of night, stars provide hope and perspective. Measuring problems against the backdrop of the night sky is often enough to remind someone of the rank of personal issues in the greater scheme. Sometimes the reversed Moon card describes intuitive dreams at night that offer details about approaching opportunities or events.

The Moon reversed indicates intense dreams and interrupted sleep. Powerful personal fears may be surfacing so they can be addressed. It can represent a Cancerian person, especially if The Chariot card appears in the same layout. The Moon card represents the second part of the spiritual lesson for the sign of Cancer. The Chariot is the first part: the process of keeping the mind in charge of emotions. This final part involves using the rich Cancerian imagination in creative ways such as for writing, photography, design (clothing, furniture, fashion or web design), drawing or painting.

In a general reading, this is a card for strong fears surfacing in dreams, interrupting sleep and reducing concentration. It can also suggest hidden agendas, strong undercurrents and avoidance of direct communication. Sometimes, these night dreams provide intuitive glimpses of life ahead or solutions to current problems.

In a career layout, The Moon reversed appears when the person is preparing to leave a job but hasn't yet told colleagues. It can also represent a company that plans to downsize its workforce but has not yet announced these plans. It sometimes suggests night jobs or working from a home office into the evenings. It's also a card for an occupation that requires creative inspiration.

It's not unusual for this reversed card to indicate that workplace stress is adversely affecting sleep. Sometimes, the reversed Moon card can describe fears around job security or competence in a chosen profession. It may indicate working at night or in creative careers such as writing, film, radio or design.

In a relationship question, the reversed Moon can indicate deceit or unspoken fears. It can suggest that one partner is unsure about the direction of the relationship but is unable to express this anxiety aloud. It's time to return to the previous upright card, The Star, to restore faith and confidence in life's possibilities. The simple act of discussing one's apprehensions with a partner may help resolve niggling doubts. However, when the reversed Moon appears in a relationship question, it sometimes requires considerable courage to discuss worries. Perhaps the person doesn't feel the partnership is strong enough to support the intimacy needed for such a conversation.

In a health query, this card indicates interrupted sleep, unspoken fears around health and sometimes vivid dreams about forthcoming health issues. It can also signify possible issues with the stomach, the breasts or the lymphatic system. Sometimes it simply describes the daytime exhaustion that results from poor sleeping patterns. Almost any mother with a newborn knows this feeling and a short daytime nap is usually insufficient to restore vitality. As the baby grows and develops, he or she begins to sleep through the night, allowing the mother's sleep to gradually improve.

The Sun

The Sun represents a time of joy expressed with the exuberance that children exhibit openly. This is not specifically a card for victory but rather for the pleasure that comes from knowing life is good when it is good. It is easy to understand that life was bountiful in hindsight but few people are aware at the time that life is perfect.

Children often live in the moment and are ready for happiness when life provides sunshine and opportunities for joy. The use of orange and yellow in this card highlights a combination of passion and enthusiasm (orange) and ideas with planning (yellow). The orange banner attached to the pole in the child's left hand represents the passion and enthusiasm that were tempered in the Strength card. The eager liveliness represented by the colour orange features in both cards but Strength's has become a banner in The Sun.

Believing in life's possibilities and joyously sharing one's energy requires a reliable source of spiritual nourishment. Playful children have this enthusiasm naturally. Sometimes, adults retain a connection to their spiritual self and inner child. This enables them to access this vivacious energy and creativity more easily.

The Sun is the second card that represents the sign of Leo. It highlights the joy and enthusiasm Leo people can evoke through playfulness. After discovering inner power and self-confidence in Strength (the other Leo card), this person enjoys life. The Sun describes approaching life with optimism, eager for the rewards connected to personal effort. It can highlight a summer to remember, with carefree days spent in a holiday cottage by the sea with friends or trekking through mountains without time constraints. If this card appears as an answer to a question, the outcome is likely to be successful and fun.

THE SUN.

In a general reading, The Sun describes a personal summer in an individual's life. Having faced underlying fears in The Moon, it's time to enjoy the present moment. It can indicate a Leo person, especially if the Queen of Wands or Strength cards also appear in the layout. In answer to a question, The Sun represents a creatively successful outcome.

In a career layout, The Sun card indicates a creative occupation that places an individual in the gaze of the public, such as an actor, singer, performer, vlogger or television presenter. It describes recognition for past effort in the form of an award, a promotion or a feature story in a newspaper or the company magazine. The Sun can describe an occupation with plentiful opportunities for personal creative input, which can be essential for some people to thrive.

In a relationship question, The Sun describes a romantic, creative relationship that encourages childlike playfulness. It suggests an optimistic, inspired partnership with romantic overtones and plentiful opportunities for shared joy. It sometimes indicates a Leo person in the relationship or influencing the partnership, especially if the Strength card also appears in the layout.

In a health query, this card usually indicates robust health with a harmonious work/ life balance. This person is nourished by a well-rounded life with enough time and energy for play, creativity, hobbies, interests and regular recreation. There is a sense of gratitude and appreciation for such bounty. Regarding physical health, The Sun indicates possible issues with the heart or the spine.

The Sun Reversed

The Sun reversed depicts a situation that lacks joy or fulfilment. It also represents feeling overwhelmed by rivalry. It's possible the person is working diligently towards a creative goal amidst robust competition. This reversed card could describe a talented artist whose first public exhibition is shared with another artist who generates all the publicity and demands the lion's share of the attention during the showcase. The shadow side of Leo emerges when rivalry is too fierce or there are too many people vying for limited opportunities. When reversed, The Sun card suggests unhealthy competitiveness, where the urge to win can override creative self-expression.

I witnessed a situation of The Sun reversed in an introductory tarot class many years ago. A student named Michael exuded energy and enthusiasm when he arrived on the first day of the course. His extroverted personality suggested he was a Knight of Wands. However, his behaviour soon changed to reveal the nature of a competitive, spoilt child. He complained that he was unable to ask questions in class and that the other students were talking over him and excluding him. After careful observation, I realised he had regressed into childlike behaviour, demanding all the attention in a room of fifteen people.

During a demonstration reading, Michael revealed he had previously been an actor but had abruptly abandoned his career after a bad review. A pattern emerged of him discarding any activity that did not deliver rapid success. As this tarot course continued, Michael realised that learning the tarot was not as easy as he first imagined, so he began looking for reasons not to participate. He was searching for a way to quit the course, to storm out and blame fellow students for his inability to continue. It was a way to avoid facing the reality that he might only ever be a mediocre reader unless he tried much harder.

This epitomises the circumstances represented by The Sun reversed. Fearing imperfection, Michael sought a face-saving way of leaving the class because he was unable to say, "I don't like this," or "This is too difficult for me right now." If he had devoted the energy he spent on his classroom antics to studying, he probably would have become an excellent reader. Instead, his overly competitive instinct aroused the opposition of all those students who could have supported him in his quest to master the tarot.

The Sun reversed suggests a need to return to the lesson of the previous card, the upright Moon, to face personal fears honestly. Michael might have benefitted more from examining his doubts and inadequacies around reading the tarot. Every other student felt this same pressure for brief moments throughout the course but they persisted. By confronting his concerns, he could have realised they were unfounded or merely a negative learning pattern from the past. However, he squandered his opportunity and focused his creative energy on competing with others in the class. It required the same amount of energy as mastering the tarot but without a rewarding result.

Returning to The Moon card allows people to cry and dissolve the anger that has accumulated. After the tears, it becomes easier to see personal problems in perspective. When fears eventually subside and The Sun returns, an individual can again be happy in the moment and enjoy simple pleasures.

The reversed Sun can also suggest that a person feels pressured to achieve or perform. It often indicates success but the rewards are not enjoyed as much as they were previously. If a singer had another hit song, the reversed Sun card would suggest they are more focused on sales figures, attendance numbers and generating publicity to increase success, instead of enjoying how people feel when they listen to the music. If the performer is exhausted from a relentless tour, it's sometimes difficult to experience the joy of success due to sheer fatigue. The reversed Sun can describe someone who is currently unable to appreciate life's rewards, focusing instead on scarcity, competition or potential threats.

In a general reading, The Sun reversed describes a creative but demanding lifestyle. To outsiders, it seems this person has every success. However, this individual is usually under constant pressure to deliver creative results to maintain their current lifestyle. It is time to quietly return to the previous upright card, The Moon, and reflect. By facing personal fears in The Moon, it's possible to relax and allow life to support current creative endeavours.

In a career layout, the reversed Sun card shows an occupation where performance is key, such as in sales, marketing or as a writer or musician under pressure to deliver new products regularly. These occupations can be steeped in rivalry, both within and outside the team or organisation. Sometimes, competitive colleagues can help an individual refine skills and improve performance. Fighting for market share for a product or a service can be as exhausting as a gym workout, demanding clear focus, energy and persistence. 'Work hard; play hard' is the attitude here.

Sometimes there is a profound fear that if a new song, painting, film or book isn't produced soon, the spotlight will move away and shine on someone else. This reversed card describes a career where past successes soon fade and the person needs to deliver ever-stronger performance to maintain career momentum. This can create relentless pressure that saps the joy out of entertainment and dampens inspiration.

In a relationship question, The Sun reversed indicates a creative but competitive relationship. One partner might motivate the other to aim higher with career or creative goals through subtle rivalry. The competitiveness works effectively, until the spouse or partner achieves sudden success, leaving the formerly supportive partner feeling invisible. Then it's time to revisit the upright previous card, The Moon, to face fears that being loved requires success and achievement.

In a health query, The Sun reversed can indicate career pressure is affecting health. The need to perform, achieve and succeed takes its toll, depleting the individual's energy reserves. This card is associated with the heart and the spine. Sometimes creative endeavours are contributing to health issues. A designer who spends too much time staring at a computer screen, or a musician whose band travels fifteen hours each weekend to play at venues before a busy working week, are likely to exercise less and feel depleted by their creative careers.

Judgement

The Judgement card represents needing to listen to one's inner voice and consider the repercussions of personal actions. Sometimes this card merely indicates clear judgement when making a decision. Suitable choices usually stem from self-awareness and the ability to accurately assess situations and people. These attributes combine to increase the chances of lasting success. Occasionally, short-term sacrifices are necessary for long-term fulfilment.

When Shane released his first novel, friends told him he was lucky. They repeatedly suggested he was fortunate to have written and produced a successful book. However, Shane realised his success was due partly to the evenings and weekends he devoted to writing and re-writing the book while friends were out socialising or relaxing in front of the television. He worked diligently through spring, summer and autumn to push ahead with his creative project. His focus, persistence and sound judgement paid off when the final product was printed and sales were steady.

The rich red cross on the flag on this card shows the meeting of linear time (where Tuesday follows Monday) and universal time (where all different periods exist simultaneously). The Judgement card indicates that success has been earned. This person has exercised clear judgement in the right circumstances and is likely to reap the harvest of seeds planted earlier when learning the lesson of The High Priestess (working hard to turn inspirations and ideas into reality).

An example of this clear judgement and its long-term rewards occurred with Helen, who decided on a career in natural therapies. She studied for six years and despite offers to travel overseas with her friends, kept her focus firmly on this goal. At the age of twenty-six, she started her own business. Now, at thirty-five, she has a thriving enterprise and enjoys an overseas holiday for a month every year.

It can be hard to appreciate the accomplishments and possessions of someone who is achieving more than you, while still valuing your way of life. However, having clear judgement involves realising that your path is unique to you, while another's direction is also distinctive. The lesson of this card is understanding what is right for long-term personal spiritual growth and development. It also includes accepting that we each have different starting and finishing points in life, that make any comparisons useless.

As an answer to whether it is wise to change jobs in the coming year, Judgement confirms that it is prudent. In a general reading, it describes a call within to find profound meaning for one's existence. It's time to explore meditation, prayer, a more rewarding career or to use personal skills and talents to help others thrive.

This card appeared in Sol's general reading. He confirmed that after the loss of his 25-year marriage, he realised working long hours had taken its toll. In striving so hard to support his wife and family, Sol had been absent while his partner Emily, felt lonely inside the big house he had provided. He finally understood she had wanted them to be together, instead of enduring long days alone in a huge home.

In a general reading, Judgement indicates an awareness of life's concealed purpose. It's the ability to live in the physical world while attending to personal spiritual needs. As an answer to a question, it confirms clear judgement. This is a card for awakening to a spiritual purpose that gives life a rich depth of meaning. In short, Judgement indicates an awareness of the long-term consequences of decisions or actions. Being spiritually nourished usually allows more breadth and vision. In turn, this can lead to increased job satisfaction from sharing skills and insights with others to help a team towards success.

In a career layout, Judgement describes an occupation where the person feels that the work makes a difference to others. When a person has a sense of profound motivation, it is easier to provide selfless service. It makes no difference whether it's surgery, dog walking, teaching yoga or waiting on tables. Serving others selflessly adds an element of grace and satisfaction to the everyday process. When Judgement appears upright in a career question, the person requires or already has an occupation that makes a difference to the lives of others. A substantial income is usually not sufficient compensation if daily activities are meaningless.

In a relationship question, this card describes a meaningful spiritual purpose to the bond. If the person is single, it indicates an awareness of what will meet their needs physically, emotionally, intellectually and spiritually in a long-term partnership. Sometimes it describes personal reflection on why past relationships have failed and what type of partnership might offer lasting fulfilment in future.

In a health query, the upright Judgement card indicates that current health issues have spiritual causes. By taking time to consider underlying origins for present ailments, it's possible to return to well-being more rapidly. This card also emphasises the need for spiritual nourishment to maintain balanced health. Regular meditation, yoga, helping others or connecting with nature could ensure robust reserves of spiritual energy. In a question about whether impending surgery is worthwhile, it usually indicates sound judgement.

Judgement Reversed

Judgement reversed suggests a lack of clear vision of the implications of one's actions. 'Act in haste; repent at leisure' summarises this card. Poor judgement has consequences. This card also describes the emptiness that accompanies a lack of awareness of life's bigger picture. Life holds only fleeting interest when spiritual purpose is ignored.

Spiritual fulfilment is a fundamental part of a life lived with conscious awareness and intention, yet almost everything in Western life is geared towards consuming more to be happier. Happiness is not fulfilment. Happiness is fleeting, whereas, with practice, a meaningful sense of personal stillness can become a constant state of being. We are taught to look outside ourselves for completion, instead of within. This makes us more vulnerable to becoming perpetual consumers and making big business thrive.

Often, people seek short-term fulfilment without considering their basic spiritual needs. Bob had a business employing fifteen people. Over the previous eleven years, he had built up this company carefully and steadily. He was comfortable with his efforts and he enjoyed a stable income from the business. Over a long lunch at his golf club one afternoon, Bob was introduced to Reece, a high flier who had accumulated an enormous amount of wealth in under five years. Bob was envious of Reece's lifestyle. Soon, Reece offered Bob a piece of the action. Bob's greed was triggered as Reece filled his head with thoughts of a bigger house, a large yacht and a holiday home in the south of France. What Reece failed to emphasise was that high returns can be very risky.

Despite having arrived at the club satisfied with himself and his life, Bob left the restaurant with a burning hunger for more than he had; Reece had passed on some of his own inner yearning and Bob secured the financing necessary to invest in Reece's new deal. Fourteen months later, the receivers were called in to dismantle Bob's existing business when Reece's exciting deal soured.

This Judgement reversed situation happened because Bob didn't use his sound judgement. He was afraid he'd miss out on a tremendous chance to be seriously wealthy. He became uncentred in his decision-making, due to Reece's internal hunger, plus his own ambitions. After losing his business, the result of all his hard work, Bob realised cutting corners usually doesn't work.

When the Judgement card appears reversed, this is not a suitable time to make financial or relationship decisions because personal judgement is likely to be skewed. Take some time to contemplate your spiritual purpose. Ask yourself what will still be important seventy-five years from now. Consider what you'd miss most if you died today.

When reversed, the angel in this card is now below the humans, suggesting their animal desires are taking precedence over spiritual needs. It is time to return to the previous upright card, The Sun, to play. In recreation, we can discover our creative selves.

Edward explained how his young son had reminded him about spiritual nourishment and the importance of play. He arrived home late one evening after a gruelling day of meetings and negotiations regarding the lease of new business premises. Four-year-old Kyle looked up from his pile of toys on the floor and invited his father to come and play with him.

"Why do you always ask me to play with you as soon as I arrive home?" Edward asked his son.

The boy looked directly at his father and said, "Dad, there's only play."

Edward was stunned. In four short words, Kyle had reminded Edward that he played at being a successful businessman all day. It was simply a different game from what Kyle offered him on the floor. Despite wearing his most expensive suit, Edward immediately sat with his son and they played happily until bathtime.

In a general reading, Judgement reversed indicates clouded thinking around decision-making. As an answer to a question about pursuing a job, relationship or another goal, it suggests it is not wise to do so at this time. Basically, it highlights spiritual emptiness or recurring bouts of yearning, plus a lack of purpose. It's time to return to the previous upright card, The Sun, to discover the joys of play, creativity and inspiration. It's time to rediscover what motivates you towards a more meaningful life.

In a career layout, this card suggests a lack of fulfilment with a current job or its direction. A present occupation lacks lasting personal meaning and is likely to leave the individual feeling emotionally empty. Sometimes, the person has lost connection with a vocation and feels emotionally and spiritually empty. This may be addressed by focusing on the central purpose of personal effort, while engaged in workday responsibilities. When aware of the bigger picture, it's easier to face daily routines without a sense of boredom or lethargy. Instead of telling yourself that you file insurance reports so assessors can gauge whether payouts are required, it might be more motivating to say, "I help people piece their lives back together after accidents and upheavals."

In a relationship question, Judgement reversed describes an inner emptiness or disconnection with a partner. This liaison is unable to nourish the person spiritually. When reversed, Judgement can indicate a partner or the structure of a relationship is depleting the individual. It's time to reconnect with personal sources of emotional and spiritual nourishment before deciding on a course of action. Avenues for replenishment can include making new friends, hobbies, creative pursuits or daily spiritual practices. At times, they might extend to meditation, prayer, yoga, walking the dog, gardening, learning to play an instrument or to sing. It's necessary to pause occasionally, to reflect on what brings you joy.

In a health query, Judgement reversed can indicate non-physical causes to current physical ailments. It also emphasises that profound spiritual emptiness is an underlying cause of a pervasive hollowness the individual is currently experiencing. Occasionally, it shows addictive behaviours used to counteract unacknowledged yearning within the person's daily life. This can include dependency on drugs, alcohol, sex, work, overeating or gambling. Treating these symptoms is unlikely to provide lasting changes without also addressing the accompanying unseen inner needs. Addictions feed the animal part but not the spirit.

The World

The World card suggests long-term success as the result of inner balance and harmony. As an answer to a specific question, it represents a very positive outcome. The World card can also represent travel around the world. Sometimes, it suggests the existence of a partner from another part of the world or someone met while overseas.

The person on the card highlights accomplishment due to an optimistic outlook. She carries her wands lightly, conscious that success is a state of mind. Results are achieved with minimum effort due to an awareness of the importance of appropriate timing. By waiting for the best circumstances and right moment, it's possible to proceed unimpeded towards desired goals and plans.

The World card was the answer to Edward's question about a movie he had directed and entered in a film festival competition. He asked if it would win a prize. I explained it would do better than he imagined. His short movie won a top prize and secured him a deal with a studio for two more productions. He was also given a budget of five times the amount he'd spent on the original project for each of his subsequent films.

In a spiritual direction layout, The World card highlights balance between the four elements of fire, water, air and earth, leading to inner harmony. Maintaining this equilibrium requires effort and concentration. However, it is worthwhile because achievement can sometimes be disappointing, whereas maintaining inner balance provides a sense of purpose and success beyond a desired goal.

Success is the process of enjoying life's journey without postponing happiness until specific goals are reached. Fulfilment is not dependent upon achieving objectives or reaching targets, because this person instinctively understands individual strengths, talents and personal worth, as well as the value of shared goals.

In a general reading, The World is a card for lasting success. It can indicate travel overseas or achievement that is recognised on the world stage. As a culmination of the previous major arcana cards, The World combines wisdom, courage, planning and compassion, plus awareness of spiritual causes and effects, to produce seemingly effortless results from ideas and intentions. As an answer to a question, The World indicates success. It can also suggest moving to another part of the world. Sometimes, it describes discovering a lasting life path with a profound sense of spiritual purpose.

In a career layout, this card highlights overseas travel with employment or relocation to another country for professional success. As an answer to a question about career direction, it heralds continuous achievements. This upright card points to a rewarding, lasting vocation. Sometimes it can signify that a product or a service will be more successful in another part of the world than locally.

In a relationship question, The World card can confirm a long-term, harmonious love relationship. It can also suggest a partner from another part of the world or someone met overseas. There is no need to add another card to this one in the answer position as it's the highest card in the pack. This is the kind of relationship people read about, dream about and aspire to achieve.

In a health query, this card indicates good health or a speedy return to strength after an illness or a surgical procedure. Physical, emotional, mental and spiritual energies are in harmony, resulting in balance, well-being and fitness. In rare health layouts, The World, in combination with three of any of the following cards, Death, The Tower, the Three of Swords, Six of Swords, Ten of Swords or Judgement, may suggest the ending of a life. However, fewer than four cards in combination from this list usually only indicates some health upheavals.

The World Reversed

The World reversed is a constructive card that suggests a person has climbed the highest mountain visible, only to see its summit had obscured an even taller peak. As each challenge is mastered, it is followed by an even greater opportunity.

For continued success, it's necessary to return to the previous upright card, Judgement, to make an appropriate decision regarding the next challenge, aware that it cannot be a goal that distracts from underlying spiritual purpose. If surrounding summits are layered in mist, it's not possible to gauge which is the tallest (the most rewarding life direction). In a situation where the path ahead is obscured, it is necessary to determine one's personal direction with inner vision or intuition.

This occurred with Carla, who built a successful business for over twelve years and then sold it to pursue new horizons. For the first time in her life, Carla had plenty of money in her bank account and no debts. She was free to pursue her next goal but realised that without the pressure of supporting herself financially, she could take her time deciding on a new direction. The freedom to choose turned out to be more difficult than expected, as she explored a range of options, eliminating each of them in turn.

During her reading, Carla explained that at age fifty she was too young to retire but didn't know what to do next. I asked her to describe her greatest challenge in life so far and how she conquered it. She told me immediately that her biggest obstacle was being taken seriously as a woman in business. I enquired if she might have benefited by having a female business coach or a mentor in the early years and she nodded. I then asked if she was prepared to guide other female entrepreneurs who have clear business goals but limited skills.

"It doesn't need to be a full-time pursuit," I explained. "You've started an enterprise alone and then hired staff, while learning how to manage a team as it grew to thirty people. You've built a successful company with an annual turnover of millions of dollars each year and adapted to changing market conditions, despite not being taken seriously as a woman in business. You can't be the only woman taking a career path up the mountain."

She thought about this for a moment and smiled. "It's a possibility," she stated.

"A possibility?" I followed. "As word spreads that you're offering this service, you'll have a line of focused, ambitious candidates around the block. When they ask questions, you can write them down. These queries then form the book you write that leads to your TED talk and the national workshops for women in business. Am I going too fast?" I asked. She laughed.

We agreed to ask the cards if it was a worthwhile pursuit for Carla and the answer was unequivocally yes. The cards also suggested this path might lead Carla to a fresh business idea and a new path up a different personal mountain.

Sometimes, The World reversed suggests the person has travelled from another part of the world to be where they are now and will soon return to their place of origin. It represents the completion of the journey around the world.

In a general reading, The World reversed describes past success but there are opportunities ahead for more significant accomplishments. It's not a permanent success, because the card is reversed. As an answer to a question about the outcome of a new venture, it indicates that although the current endeavour is likely to be rewarding, it's not an enduring venture. It might be a necessary and worthwhile step in the pursuit of longer-term goals.

The World reversed indicates successful accomplishments on a path or rungs on the ladder of success. Sometimes the skills acquired in pursuit of a goal are necessary to achieve the objective. This is not a negative outcome, as the individual might easily move on to other successes beyond this one. It's a card for overseas travel and often indicates returning to a place the person has lived in the past. It's the second half of an around-the-world journey. It's a worthwhile success or achievement but not likely to be the person's final accomplishment.

In a career layout, the reversed World card can suggest overseas travel for a new position, regular trips with a job or relocating to another country to pursue an occupation. It points to success in an occupation but not necessarily for the long-term. Eventually, this individual is likely to progress beyond this achievement to pursue other career goals.

In a relationship question, this card can describe a partner from a different part of the world or meeting a spouse while in a foreign country. Sometimes, the reversed World card indicates a beneficial relationship but not this person's final partnership. It is worthwhile pursuing this option. Although many people want love to last forever, what happens when a person outlives a spouse by twenty years? Is it necessary to refuse all other opportunities for relationships? Perhaps love isn't everlasting because humans are growing, changing, evolving and impermanent.

In a health query, even reversed, this is a card for confidence in ongoing well-being. Sometimes, it indicates physical reserves of energy are not as robust as they once were but this hasn't impacted general health. It is worthwhile returning to the wisdom of the previous upright card, Judgement, to ensure sufficient nourishment. Spiritual imbalances often manifest as mental, emotional or physical conditions, so maintaining harmony on these higher planes can help avert physical symptoms or illness. The reversed World card can describe a temporary health setback that is soon resolved.

Paths to Becoming a Tarot Reader

There are many paths to becoming a reader and many unique tarot readers who bring wide-ranging skills and experiences to their sessions. Some people become readers after receiving a life-changing prediction, some use tarot as a supplementary tool in counselling sessions and others are merely curious and enjoy learning.

I became a tarot reader by chance. I was in a jobcentre looking for work in 1984 when I saw a hand-written card on the wall that read: Palmist Wanted. Experience necessary.

With six years of hand-reading experience, I figured I would be the only person in the room eligible for this position. I took the card to the front desk (well before offices were digital) and handed it to the assistant. Her eyes narrowed and she turned to her co-worker, saying, "Ted, is this a joke?"

She was about to tear the card to pieces when Ted stopped her. "Hold it. I've only put that up this morning," he explained. "It's genuine."

It turned out that I was the second person to enquire about this particular job that day. There were two positions and the first applicant took the day job. I was offered the evening shift, 4:00 pm until 2:00 am, six days a week.

It was a small shop, the size of a key-cutting kiosk and I worked beside a tarot reader. Eduardo and I became friends and during quiet periods each of us had a chance to tell our life stories. By the third week, I had offered to teach him how to read hands in exchange for tarot lessons. I was sceptical at first, reasoning that if I selected five cards each day for a week that I'd pick entirely different cards, thus reducing the accuracy of predictions. How could someone have five unique futures? The odds against selecting the identical five cards in the same order from a 78-card deck were astronomical. Eduardo explained that although I wouldn't select the same five cards, I'd select similar cards that would fundamentally describe the same future.

Eduardo was patient with me, presenting each card as an opportunity to tell a short story. I love stories, so I settled back and focused on each image as his tales unfolded. When customers arrived for tarot readings, Eduardo pulled the curtain across for privacy as the sessions commenced. Although I couldn't see any of the cards, I clearly heard entire readings, so I began trying to gauge what cards might be on the table during each layout.

I'd ask Eduardo after each person left and to keep it more interesting, we made a wager on my accuracy. If I was correct with the seven cards in a layout, he'd buy me a slice of sweet baklava from the small Greek café up the lane. If I was wrong, I'd buy him a slice. Over the next few months, Eduardo's waistline ballooned on a diet of sweets, while I kept fit by walking to buy his snacks several times each day. Gradually, I understood how he phrased his sentences and recognised each card from his descriptions. I improved until I won a few desserts each week.

One day, Eduardo shuffled the deck and laid out seven cards, asking me to tell him a story of his life, using what I remembered about the cards laying face up on the table. I did this, and then he placed those cards back into the deck and selected another seven cards.

"Now tell me a travel story using these cards," he said. I did so and he repeated the process, asking me to tell him a relationship story. When I completed my story, he smiled and said, "You've just given your first reading."

"Oh, no. I'm not a tarot reader, I'm a palmist," I said. He shook his head slowly, smiling.

"Perhaps you're a tarot reader too now." The next morning, I mentioned this to my partner and she immediately produced a tarot deck from her bookshelf.

"Try it with me, just for practice," she said, reaching for a note pad to record it as we went. Later that afternoon her best friend arrived on my doorstep wanting a practice reading and that's when I discovered that a person who reads tarot cards has many friends.

Soon, I was trading readings for haircuts, lunches and other assorted services, building experience as I learned from Eduardo. We worked together for almost six months, sixty hours each week. As summer approached, we became busy and I also read the tarot in the shop when customers arrived together and one didn't want to wait for Eduardo while the other had a reading. As summer faded, Eduardo decided to move on and explore the rest of Australia before returning to Chile. I also left the job and began reading at a market each Saturday, averaging a dozen short sessions each day.

Reading for strangers is the best practice for a tarot novice because there isn't the pressure experienced when reading for friends who might end the relationship if the news isn't positive. The drawbacks of consulting for strangers include not having any concept of their expectations, the pressure to be accurate plus people who insist on telling you what previous readers have told them, effectively influencing your perceptions before or during a reading.

I began teaching in 1985 and my tarot students have included Reiki and massage therapists who wanted to add new skills plus retirees looking to work part-time. Some astute students learned the tarot because they wanted better results from tarot reading sessions as clients. They sought an understanding of how to word questions and be open to valuable unexpected information during the reading process.

Most problems can be addressed by asking clear questions of the tarot. Step by step, option by option, it's possible to distil complex issues into their components. Then choices become clear. Those alternatives usually require decisions, followed by actions. Sometimes it's easier to make a series of smaller resolutions than one monumental choice. Handled efficiently, the tarot can be the difference between confusion and clarity.

The tarot is a powerful, practical tool in the hands of an experienced reader, especially someone who guides clients towards questions that clarify personal issues and viable options ahead. Tomorrow's outcomes depend on the decisions we make today. The tarot is a tool for exploring and illuminating options. If a person is completely confused, the most effective question to ask the cards is simply, "What do I most need to know right now?"

The Meanings of Cards in Combination

Death	The Tower, Three of Swords, Four of Swords, Six of Swords (a peaceful passing), Ten of Swords (death after an illness), Judgement, The World.
	Predicting death is a risky direction to take a reading, especially when free will is considered. Clients have told me remarkable stories of how relatives, given hours to live, suddenly regained vitality and returned to life with renewed vigour. When the Death card appears in a layout with at least three of the cards listed above, the meaning of physical death is more likely.
	At least four of these cards need to appear in a single layout to suggest a physical death. Fewer than four cards usually indicate a profound change. Be cautious in predicting death as it can be devastating news to receive and it's very easy to be wrong with this.
Karmic situations or lessons	Justice, The Hanged Man, The Star or Judgement.
Legalities forthcoming	Justice, Five of Swords, Queen or King of Swords.
Meditation	The High Priestess, The Hanged Man, Four of Cups or Four of Swords.
Money earned	Six, Eight or Nine of Pentacles.
Money spent	Reversed Ace or Four of Pentacles or Six of Pentacles (upright or reversed).
Lack of money	Ace, Two, Six, Nine or Ten of Pentacles, all reversed, or Five of Pentacles upright.
Borrowed money	Six and Ten of Pentacles.
Saved money	Ace, Four, Seven, King or Queen of Pentacles.
Moving house	Three, Four or Knight of Wands.
Pregnancy	The Empress or Nine of Pentacles, with any of the four pages.
Relationship commitment	Four or Six of Wands, Six of Cups or Eight of Pentacles.
Marriage	Six or Ten of Cups with Three of Cups (the celebration), The Empress (domestic stability).

Study	Temperance (learning), Ace of Swords (a clear plan), Three of Pentacles (study) or Eight of Pentacles (graduate studies or commitment to improving yourself).
Psychic or spiritual study	The High Priestess (psychic or spiritual development, meditation), Temperance or Three of Pentacles (study).
Religious/philosophic studies	The Hierophant (knowledge shared), Three of Pentacles (study), Eight of Pentacles (commitment to advanced studies).
Study of law	The Emperor (a judge), The Hierophant (diplomas required for acceptance), Justice (law) or Three of Pentacles (study).
Self-exploration	The reversed Hierophant (taking responsibility for personal spiritual development), The Hermit (reading, personal reflection), Four of Cups (meditation) or Four of Swords (contemplation).
Study for career or financial benefits	The Hierophant (diplomas required for acceptance and advancement), The Devil (focus on material advantages offered), Four of Pentacles (desire for wealth) or Eight of Pentacles (graduate studies to specialise).
Travel	Temperance, Ace, Three, Eight or Knight of Wands or Six of Swords.
Travel by air	Eight of Wands, Page of Swords.
Travel by road or rail	The Chariot, Ace or Three of Wands.
Travel overseas	The Star, The World, Eight of Wands or Six of Swords.
Vivid dreams	The Moon, Nine of Swords.

It's the reader's responsibility to decide what meaning to attribute to each card in a layout, especially when it comes to clarifying a theme or story for clients.

When The Moon and the Nine of Swords appeared in Olivia's general reading, it was immediately apparent she was experiencing interrupted sleep. This was either due to vivid dreams each night or perhaps to a physical interruption.

"You seem to be experiencing some sleep disturbance at the moment," I said.

She nodded her confirmation. "My husband has sleep apnoea and refuses to use his machine. Some nights, he snores so loudly I have to sleep in the spare room. I use earplugs but they're not effective. It's more the roar of a train than a gentle wheeze."

In Astrid's reading, the meaning of cards in combination wasn't immediately clear. The Temperance card in the general reading suggested study, teaching, balancing spiritual needs with physical desires or possible travel. The presence of the Three of Wands strengthened the travel meaning for Temperance, while The Hierophant supported the study option. The Four of Cups also indicated study related to meditation or inner development. I decided to enlist Astrid's help in clarifying the meaning on this occasion.

"I'm a bit confused here," I began. "The cards suggest travelling overseas but there is also a possible course of study or process of self-development involving reflection or meditation."

She smiled and nodded before explaining. "In three weeks, I'm going overseas for a twelve-day meditation retreat run by a monk. Afterwards, I plan to explore Thailand for a week before coming home." In this instance, each card held almost every meaning possible for that card. This is rare but sometimes it does happen.

Card Charts

Minor Arcana Cards Chart

	WANDS	CUPS	SWORDS	PENTACLES
	 ACE of WANDS.	 ACE of CUPS.	 ACE of SWORDS.	 ACE of PENTACLES.
Ace Beginning something new.	Enthusiasm for action. Rising to a challenge.	Inspiration to begin a new venture. A promise of happiness ahead.	Planning a new venture. A clear concept and awareness of how to move forward.	A new financial direction or source of income. Sufficient funds to finance a new project.
Two Decisions.	A locational decision. Planning a change of home or work environment.	An emotional decision to pursue a relationship, friendship or creative partnership.	Examining options and viable choices. Retreating to settle emotions and plan ahead.	Weighing up financial options. Deciding on the best sequence for investing in plans.
Three Growth and progress.	Progress with plans. Travel. The joy of watching plans unfold successfully.	Shared success. The joy of a social gathering or celebration.	Processing a painful realisation. Grieving a loss. Acceptance of a dream abandoned.	Laying foundations for career or financial success. Progress with study on workplace learning.
Four Practical application of plans.	Settling into a new home or work environment. Stability and commitment.	Strengthening sources of emotional nourishment. Meditation and inner peace.	Retreating to reflect on past events. Making practical plans towards future goals.	Saving towards a goal. Pacing yourself to complete an objective.

Five Change and upheaval.	Scattered energy or poor focus. Effort without purpose or structure.	Reflection on lost opportunities. Retreating to grieve and accept the impermanence of life.	Mental chaos. Arguments and strife without immediate resolution. Limited awareness of the consequences of voiced criticisms.	Financial restrictions or loss. Limited income streams making you an outsider. Poor attitudes to money limiting opportunities.
Six Stability and peace after change.	After planning and action, a goal is achieved. A promotion or a new job.	Social and emotional stability after a period of change. Enjoying a safe and comfortable pace of life.	Integrating new beliefs after change and upheaval. Life become stable after a loss.	Stable income streams providing financial stability. Living within your means. Securing funds for a large purchase.
Seven Increased responsibilities and opportunities.	Successfully juggling a range of projects. Rising to the challenge of greater responsibilities.	Reflecting on what constitutes a personally rewarding life. Noticing your sources of happiness.	Being mentally agile when life requires it. Keeping personal plans private until they are in progress.	Reflecting on new income streams from investments. Adapting to new financial possibilities.
Eight Strength to purse greater goals.	The realisation of past dreams. Enjoying the downhill ski slope while it lasts.	Having confidence to walk away from people and circumstances that do not nourish or support you.	Discovering choices within current restrictions. Using the mind to explore previously unseen options.	Focus and commitment to career and financial goals. Past success lends strength and confidence to pursue long-term plans.
Nine Reflection on plans and achievements.	Realising what past actions can teach us about planning future goals. Reflecting on past efforts.	Valuing what you bring to friendships, relationships and circumstances. Having strong foundations of self-worth and self-confidence.	Worry and anxiety about current circumstances. Interrupted sleep at night due to daily stress.	Quiet confidence resulting from effective planning, commitment and consistent effort. Self-generated financial stability.
Ten Completion of plans. Ideas made into tangible achievements.	Time to delegate some of the responsibilities. Trust the value of team efforts.	Enjoying shared happiness with like-minded people. You've found your family or your spiritual group.	Surrender to change and allow life to dissolve past pain. Learn from the past and release it. The future offers new possibilities.	Financial success stemming from large organisations. Less effort is required now to maintain personal sources of wealth.

Minor Arcana Reversed Cards Chart

	WANDS	CUPS	SWORDS	PENTACLES
		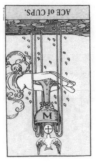		
Ace Delayed starts.	Delays in beginning new projects. Too much on your plate.	Intermittent emotional and spiritual nourishment. Time to strengthen spiritual connections.	Need to clarify plans before beginning. Narrow down your personal options.	Limited financial support for plans. More financial control needed now.
Two Indecision.	Reluctance to accept the need for change. Make a decision.	Issues with intimacy in a relationship. Strengthen personal options for joy.	Retreating from life due to overwhelming emotions. Clarify how life will be when you step forward.	Decisions restricted by personal finances. Make a budget you can live with.
Three Delayed progress.	Delays with travel and life plans. Decide what to focus on for progress.	Personal needs not met by current social groups. Strengthen connection with one friend or a partner.	Burdened by unacknowledged or unresolved grief. Ask yourself what you need to do to release this now.	Limited career or financial foundations for success. Consider study as a fundamental step for career progress.
Four Lack of consolidation.	Temporary opportunities. Not time to settle down. Enjoy living in the moment before it passes.	Seeking emotional nourishment from others through like-minded inclusive groups.	Processing loss. Time to think afresh and move forward. Make room for grief but understand that it will eventually pass.	Spending more than you're saving. Generosity. Invest wisely on study, tools and viable friendships.

Five Improved focus.	Finding cooperation after chaos. Refocusing after struggle. Listen to other's viewpoints and negotiate.	Emotional loss and grief subsiding. Time to venture out into new surroundings and opportunities.	Personal reflection after an intense disagreement. Be aware that repeated disagreements can result in abandonment.	Releasing unsupportive people or circumstances. Realise that the person or situation left behind did not support you properly.
Six Change.	Limited success due to poor focus. Abandoning a personal goal. Focus on one goal and plan a path to reach it.	Change after a period of routine and stability. Remember that change is necessary for emotional growth.	Challenging old beliefs results in overdue change. Sometimes it is necessary to forcefully cut ties to be free to pursue new opportunities.	Spending money. Leaving a job. Lack of financial stability. Hasty decisions or actions can have financial consequences.
Seven Don't hold on.	Overwhelmed by life's demands. Let some go. Focus on important goals.	Current demands overriding spiritual and emotional needs. Take time to remember what nourishes you.	New strategies and approaches are required to resolve current issues. Concealing your personal needs now can make it difficult to allow others to meet them.	Time to strengthen income sources to ensure long term stability. Less work and better strategies can increase wealth.
Eight Strength tested.	Slight delays provide a chance to tweak plans. Additional goals require more attention now.	Indecision with staying or leaving. Identify sources of personal nourishment to clarify choices.	An opportunity to explore new ways to resolve current restrictions. Clearer thinking after a period of confusion.	Lack of commitment to career or personal financial plans. Focus on what motivates you to move forward.
Nine A need for reflection.	Feeling overwhelmed by past or current obligations. Marathons include breaks so take time to rest and recharge.	Reassess sources of emotional nourishment and value what you contribute to relationships. Fulfilment begins within.	Intuitive dreams at night. Interrupted sleep due to stress or personal worries. Be aware of intuitive dreams highlighting solutions to pressing issues.	Working hard without reward. Time to improve skills to increase income and build wealth. Working while studying now will pay dividends later.
Ten Unintended consequences.	Burdened by too many work and life commitments. Learn to delegate and avoid unnecessary obligations.	Not being surrounded by like-minded people. Find friends who value you.	A difficult period is ending. New opportunities will follow. Meditate to still your mind and release personal beliefs that do not support you.	Financial contraction in workplace, industry or the wider economy. Reduce spending and pay down debt.

About The Author

Clairvoyant, writer and regular media guest, Paul Fenton-Smith is the author of eleven books. With simple language and entertaining examples, Paul takes a practical approach to the esoteric. Whether reading for clients, teaching or conveying his knowledge through books, Paul's realistic approach brings clear benefits to people's everyday lives. His engaging, anecdotal approach has won him a worldwide readership and invitations to share his entertaining insights on television, radio and in magazines and newspapers.

Paul began his studies with a course in palmistry in 1978. Moving from Adelaide to Sydney in 1980, he studied the tarot in 1984 and completed a Diploma in Clinical Hypnotherapy (1986) before leaving for London for further study. He also attended a counselling course in 1992 and completed a Grad. Dip. in Counselling in 2015. In 1985, Paul established the Academy of Psychic Sciences in Sydney, aiming to set a standard in the industry. All students who seek certification through the Academy must complete written and practical examinations and abide by a set of ethics.

Aside from his teaching commitments at the Academy, Paul runs a busy private practice in Sydney as a clairvoyant, counsellor and hypnotherapist and conducts courses around Australia. Paul has been practising and teaching the psychic sciences for more than 40 years, and encourages his clients and students to believe only what they can see or experience for themselves.

www.paulfentonsmith.com

For more information on this
or any Blue Angel Publishing release,
please visit our website at:

WWW.BLUEANGELONLINE.COM